SCRIPTURAL TRACES:
CRITICAL PERSPECTIVES ON THE RECEPTION
AND INFLUENCE OF THE BIBLE

22

Editors
Claudia V. Camp, Texas Christian University
Matthew A. Collins, University of Chester
Andrew Mein, University of Durham

Editorial board
Michael J. Gilmour, David Gunn, James Harding, Jorunn Økland

Published under
Library of New Testament Studies

620

formerly the Journal for the Study of the New Testament Supplement series

Editor
Chris Keith

Editorial Board
Dale C. Allison, John M.G. Barclay, Lynn H. Cohick, R. Alan Culpepper,
Craig A. Evans, Robert Fowler, Simon J. Gathercole, Juan Hernandez Jr.,
John S. Kloppenborg, Michael Labahn, Love L. Sechrest, Robert Wall,
Catrin H. Williams, Brittany Wilson

Rediscovering the Marys

Maria, Mariamne, Miriam

Edited by
Mary Ann Beavis
and Ally Kateusz

t&tclark
LONDON • NEW YORK • OXFORD • NEW DELHI • SYDNEY

T&T CLARK
Bloomsbury Publishing Plc
50 Bedford Square, London, WC1B 3DP, UK
1385 Broadway, New York, NY 10018, USA
29 Earlsfort Terrace, Dublin 2, Ireland

BLOOMSBURY, T&T CLARK and the T&T Clark logo are trademarks
of Bloomsbury Publishing Plc

First published in Great Britain 2020
This paperback edition published in 2021

Copyright © Mary Ann Beavis, Ally Kateusz, and contributors, 2020

Mary Ann Beavis and Ally Kateusz have asserted their right under the Copyright,
Designs and Patents Act, 1988, to be identified as Editors of this work.

All rights reserved. No part of this publication may be reproduced or transmitted
in any form or by any means, electronic or mechanical, including photocopying,
recording, or any information storage or retrieval system, without prior permission
in writing from the publishers.

Bloomsbury Publishing Plc does not have any control over, or responsibility for, any
third-party websites referred to or in this book. All internet addresses given in this
book were correct at the time of going to press. The author and publisher regret any
inconvenience caused if addresses have changed or sites have ceased to exist, but can
accept no responsibility for any such changes.

A catalogue record for this book is available from the British Library.

A catalog record for this book is available from the Library of Congress.

ISBN: HB: 978-0-5676-8345-8
PB: 978-0-5677-0212-8
ePDF: 978-0-5676-8346-5
ePUB: 978-0-5676-8349-6

Series: Library of New Testament Studies, volume 620
ISSN 2513-8790

Typeset by Newgen KnowledgeWorks Pvt. Ltd., Chennai, India

To find out more about our authors and books visit www.bloomsbury.com
and sign up for our newsletters.

Contents

List of Figures	vii
List of Abbreviations	x
Introduction *Ally Kateusz and Mary Ann Beavis*	1
Section 1 Revisiting Which Mary: Does Which Mary Matter?	5
1 The Magdalene Effect: Reading and Misreading the Composite Mary in Early Christian Works *Mark Goodacre*	7
2 Which Mary, and Why It Matters *Mary Ann Beavis*	25
3 Why Mary?: The *Gospel of Mary* and Its Heroine *Judith Hartenstein*	39
4 What Is Mary Doing in Acts?: Confessional Narratives and the Synoptic Tradition *Jo-Ann Badley*	47
5 Magdalene, Mother, Martha's Sister, or None of the Above?: The Mary in the *Dialogue of the Savior* *Anna Cwikla*	59
6 Two Mary Magdalenes: Eusebius of Caesarea and the Questionable Reliability of the Gospels' Female Witnesses *Kara J. Lyons-Pardue*	69
7 Two Women Leaders: "Mary and the Other Mary Magdalene" *Ally Kateusz*	79
Section 2 Rediscovering the Marys in Mission and Leadership	97
8 The Power of Leadership through Mediation, or How Mary Exercises Overlapping Authority *Cornelia Horn*	99
9 The Constriction of Female Leadership: Tracing a Trend in the Early Reception of Miriam and Mary Magdalene *Erez DeGolan and Miriam-Simma Walfish*	113
10 Virgin Mary Co-Priest or Not: The Continuing Trend of Redaction and Revision in the Medieval Era *Judith M. Davis*	131

11	The Memory of Mary's Mission According to "Guadalupan Sermons" of the Seventeenth and Eighteenth Centuries *J. L. Manzo*	145

Section 3 Recovering Receptions of the Marys in Literature,
Art, and Archaeology   153

12	Mary of Nazareth and Nazareth Archaeological Excavations 1997–2015 *Richard Freund*	155
13	The Dormition of Miriam in Rabbinic Literature *Michael Rosenberg*	173
14	Dormition Urtext?: Oldest Dormition Wall Painting Combines the Great Angel and Women with Censers *Ally Kateusz*	185
15	Mary in the Qur'an and Extracanonical Christian Texts *Deborah Niederer Saxon*	203
16	The Origin and Manifestations of the Smiling Virgin Mary *Jin H. Han*	215
17	From *Holy Grail* to *The Lost Gospel*: Margaret Starbird and the Mary Magdalene Romance *Mary Ann Beavis*	227

Afterword: The Future of Mariamic Studies *Mary Ann Beavis and Ally Kateusz*   235

References	239
List of Contributors	263
Index	265
Index of Biblical References	267

Figures

Cover Three arms-raised women in liturgical procession. Ivory pyx dated 500s. Metropolitan Museum of Art, New York City. Gift of J. Pierpont Morgan, 1917. Accession no. 17.190.57a, b (CC0).

2.1 *Chairete:* Christ appearing to the Holy Women, Sinai Icon Collection, seventh century. Used with permission of Transfer from UM History of Art Visual Resources Collections History of Art, University of Michigan. 32

2.2 Raising of Lazarus, Grado Ivory, eighth century. British Museum. Source: O. M. Dalton, *Catalogue of the Ivory Carvings of the Christian Era with Examples of Mohammedan Art and Carvings in Bone* (London: Longmans, 1909), plate 12, fig. 27. 33

2.3 *Noli Me Tangere.* Mary Magdalene with Christ, ivory carved in Spain, ca. 1120. Metropolitan Museum of Art, Gift of J. Pierpont Morgan, 1917. Accession no. 17.190.47 (CC0). 35

2.4 Jesus, Mary and Martha Window, Holy Trinity Church, West Sussex, 1860s. Source: By Antiquary—Own work, CC BY 4.0, https://commons.wikimedia.org/w/index.php?curid=58087146. 37

2.5 *Noli me tangere,* sketch, Lilian Broca, 2017 (printed with permission of the artist). 38

7.1 Five scenes on an early sixth-century reliquary box painted in or near Jerusalem. Source: Hartmann Grisar, *Die römische Kapelle Sancta Santorum und ihr Schatz: Meine Entdeckungen und Studien in der Palastkapelle der mittelalterlichen Päpste* (Rome: Laterano, 1908), plate 59. 83

7.2 Redaction analysis: Mary exorcizes demons. Chart comparison of three manuscripts. © Ally Kateusz. 87

7.3 Liturgical scene with Mary, Jesus' mother. Excerpt of one frame of five on early sixth-century reliquary box painted in Jerusalem. Vatican Museum, Rome. Photo courtesy of Ally Kateusz. 90

10.1 Maria Virgo Minester de Tempulo Gerosale. Stone plaque dated 375–500 CE, Sainte-Marie-Madeleine basilica in Saint-Maximin La-Sainte-Baume in Provence, France. Source: Edmond Le Blant, *Les sarcophages chrétiens de la Gaule* (Paris: Imprimerie Nationale, 1886), plate 57, fig. 1. 134

10.2	Mary (MARIA) portrayed arms raised on fourth-century gold glass from the catacombs of Rome. Source: Louis Perret, *Catacombes de Rome*, 5 vols. (Paris: Gide et J. Baudry, 1851), vol. 4, plate 21, fig. 1.	135
12.1	The area of Nazareth and the Greek Orthodox Church of the Annunciation (GOCOA) (#1–7 numbered with the boundaries of the main work identified. The parts from public Mary's Well, the church, crypt, burials, and the excavations marked) a top view of the entire modern city. Courtesy of Professor Philip Reeder, Duquesne University, on behalf of the Scribante Family Nazareth Excavations Project at the University of Hartford.	156
12.2	The map of Mary's Well, the Bathhouse, and the GOCOA. Courtesy of Professor Philip Reeder, Duquesne University, on behalf of the Scribante Family Nazareth Excavations Project at the University of Hartford.	163
12.3	GPR work by Harry Jol, University of Wisconsin-Eau Claire, in the bathhouse adjacent to Mary's Well. Notice on the wall the arch (to the left of the GPR operator's shoulder) indicating where an earlier building ceiling would have been located. The bottom of the arch is over 15 feet below the present street level above. Courtesy of the Scribante Family Nazareth Excavations project at the University of Hartford.	164
12.4	ERT array on the floor of the GOCOA. Courtesy of the Scribante Family Nazareth Excavations Project at the University of Hartford.	165
12.5	The ancient mosaic floor of the GOCOA by Mary's Well, Nazareth. Courtesy of the Scribante Family Nazareth Excavations Project at the University of Hartford.	168
12.6	The map of our excavations, showing the excavated areas, the present back of the church, and the possible ancient church inset. Courtesy of Professor Philip Reeder, Duquesne University, on behalf of the Scribante Family Nazareth Excavations Project at the University of Hartford.	169
14.1	Women swing censers at Mary's deathbed. Wall painting. Dated before 925. Deir al-Surian, Egypt. Photo courtesy of Karel Innemée.	186
14.2	Twelve men surround Mary on her deathbed. Peter swings a censer. Tenth- to eleventh-century ivory. Image: The Walters Art Museum, Baltimore. Acquired by Henry Walters, 1926. Accession no. 71.135 (CC0).	188

14.3	Redaction analysis: Mary with a censer and incense. Chart comparison of three manuscripts. © Ally Kateusz.	192
14.4	Redaction analysis: Women with censers and incense. Chart comparison of three manuscripts. © Ally Kateusz.	194
14.5a	Women with censers at the Anastasis altar. Ivory pyx dated 500s. Metropolitan Museum of Art, New York City. Gift of J. Pierpont Morgan, 1917. Accession no. 17.190.57a, b (CC0).	197
14.5b	Women in liturgical procession to the Anastasis altar (back of pyx).	197
14.6	Pola ivory reliquary box carved with a liturgical scene depicting the sanctuary of Old Saint Peter's Basilica in Rome, ca. 430s. Men and women flank the mensa in parallel. Museo Archeologico, Venice. © Alinari Archives-Alinari Archive, Florence.	200
14.7	Sarcophagus front with liturgical scene in the second Hagia Sophia, Constantinople, ca. 430s. Man and woman on opposite sides of the altar. Photo courtesy of Ally Kateusz and the Archeological Museum of Istanbul.	200
15.1	Mary (MARA) portrayed arms-raised between date palms. Fourth-century gold glass from the Christian catacombs of Rome. Source: Louis Perret, *Catacombes de Rome*, 5 vols. (Paris: Gide et J. Baudry, 1851), vol. 4, plate 21, fig. 7.	209
16.1	Smiling Madonna and Child in elephant ivory, Musée de Cluny. Photo courtesy of Jungyoon Han.	219
16.2	Smiling Virgin Mary, statue of walnut wood, ca. 1325–50. Photo Ann Bredol Lepper; courtesy of Suermondt-Ludwig-Museum, Aachen.	221
16.3	Smiling Virgin and Child, statue of fruitwood carved in Austria ca. 1410. Metropolitan Museum of Art, The Cloisters Collection, 1985. Accession no. 1985.214 (CC0).	222

Abbreviations

1 Apol.	Justin, *First Apology*
AAS	*Acta Apostolicae Sedis*
AB	Anchor Bible
Acts Phil.	*Acts of Philip*
ad Mar.	Eusebius, *Ad Marinum*
AJ	*Antiquaries Journal*
AJS	*Review – Association for Jewish Studies Review*
AnBoll	*Analecta Bollandiana*
ANF	Ante-Nicene Fathers
ANTC	Abingdon New Testament Commentaries
Atiqoh	*'Atiqot*
Aug	*Augustinianum*
b.Sotah	Babylonian Talmud, Tractate *Sotah*
BAIAS	*Bulletin of the Anglo–Israel Archaeological Society*
BJRL	*Bulletin of the John Rylands Library*
BRev	*Bible Review*
BSAC	*Bulletin de la Société d'archéologie copte*
CBET	Contributions to Biblical Exegesis and Theology
CBQ	*Catholic Biblical Quarterly*
CHJ	Cambridge History of Judaism
Col	column
CSCO	Corpus Scriptorum Christianorum Orientalium
CT	Codex Tchacos
CurTM	*Currents in Theology and Mission*
Dial. Sav.	*Dialogue of the Savior*
ERT	Electrical Resistivity Tomography
GOCOA	Greek Orthodox Church of the Annunciation
Gos. Mary	*Gospel of Mary*
Gos. Phil.	*Gospel of Philip*
Gos. Thom.	*Gospel of Thomas*
GPR	Ground-Penetrating Radar
Hist.	Herodotus, *History*
HThS	Harvard Theological Studies
HTR	*Harvard Theological Review*
ICMR	*Islam and Christian–Muslim Relations*
Int	*Interpretation*
JAC	*Journal of Ancient Christianity*
JBL	*Journal of Biblical Literature*
JECS	*Journal of Early Christian Studies*

JES	*Journal of Ecumenical Studies*
JFSR	*Journal of Feminist Studies in Religion*
JJS	*Journal of Jewish Studies*
JR	*Journal of Religion*
JRPC	*Journal of Religion and Popular Culture*
JSNT	*Journal for the Study of the New Testament*
JSNTSS	Journal for the Study of the New Testament Supplement Series
JSS	*Journal of Semitic Studies*
JTS	*Journal of Theological Studies*
MS	Manuscript
MW	*Muslim World*
NAB	New American Bible
NHS	Nag Hammadi Studies
NICNT	New International Commentary on the New Testament
NovT	*Novum Testamentum*
NRSV	New Revised Standard Version
NT	New Testament
NTOA	Novum Testamentum et Orbis Antiquus
NTS	*New Testament Studies*
OECS	Oxford Early Christian Studies
PAAJR	*Proceedings of the American Academy of Jewish Research*
PEQ	*Palestine Exploration Quarterly*
PRSt	*Perspectives in Religious Studies*
POxy	Papyrus Oxyrhynchus
PRyl	Rylands Papyrus
PTS	Patristische Texte und Studien
RBL	*Review of Biblical Literature*
SBL	Society of Biblical Literature
SBLSS	Society of Biblical Literature Symposium Series
SC	Sources chrétiennes
SNTSMS	Society of New Testament Studies Monograph Series
SP	Sacra Pagina
StPatr	*Studia Patristica*
Strom.	Clement, *Stromateis*
StSin	Studia Sinaitica XI.
SVTQ	*St. Vladimir's Theological Quarterly*
ThH	Théologie Historique
TynBul	*Tyndale Bulletin*
VC	Vigiliae Christianae
Vulg.	*Vulgate*
WGRWSup	Writings from the Greco–Roman World Supplement Series
WUNT	Wissenschaftliche Untersuchung zum Neuen
ZAC	*Zeitschrift für Antikes Christentum*
ZKT	*Zeitschrift für katholische Theologie*
ZNW	*Zeitschrift für die neutestamentliche Wissenschaft und die Kunde der älteren Kirche*

Introduction

Ally Kateusz and Mary Ann Beavis

As is often the case with respect to a new field of scholarship, sometimes opening one door reveals more doors. This is especially true with respect to the field of Mariamic studies because it is relatively young. While Jesus, Paul, Moses, Muhammad, and other men have been the focus of centuries of androcentric scholarship, female founding figures remained relatively unexamined except through the infrequent lens of a specifically male gaze. In the last few decades, however, especially with the rise of feminist scholarship, the origin and reception of the various Marys has received increasing focus—Mary the Magdalene, Miriam the sister of Moses, Mary the mother of Jesus (Maryam in Islam), and Mary of Bethany. This interdisciplinary volume both offers new insights into the Marys and also reveals new doors to open.

Two prior volumes underlie this anthology. The first is the 2002 *Which Mary? The Marys of Early Christian Tradition*, edited by F. Stanley Jones. This volume of essays focused largely on the debate around Stephen J. Shoemaker's contention that the Mary in early Christian texts that did not clearly identify which Mary *could* have referred to Mary of Nazareth instead of Mary Magdalene.[1] The present volume's first section, *Revisiting Which Mary—Does Which Mary Matter?*, expands the previous debate, adding both granularity and complexity to the question of *Which Mary*, as well as peeling away some of the historiography obscuring our view of these women in the early Christian past. Deirdre Good, editor of the second related volume, the 2005 *Mariam, the Magdalen, and the Mother*, coined the phrase *Miriamic tradition* with respect to scholarship on the reception of the Marys in Christianity, Judaism, and Islam.[2] Here again, with an acute recognition of the ways Miriamic traditions are interrelated, the current volume expands on previous work.

Mariamic traditions are interconnected with the historiography of women, as seen in the portrayal of these women variously as founders, prophets, apostles, community leaders, and ministers—but also as whores, virgins, and silent sisters. The

---

[1] Stephen J. Shoemaker, "A Case of Mistaken Identity? Naming the Gnostic Mary," in *Which Mary? The Marys of Early Christian Tradition*, ed. F. Stanley Jones (SBLSS 19; Atlanta, GA: Society of Biblical Literature, 2002), 5–30; see also the responses by Antii Marjanen, Karen L. King, Ann Graham Brock, and François Bovon.

[2] Dierdre Good, ed., *Mariam, the Magdalene, and the Mother* (Bloomington: Indiana University Press, 2005).

Marys themselves are sometimes conflated, often implicated in later reception, and always part of the larger cultural milieu in which real women lived. The traditions are interreligious, echoing back to the Hebrew Bible, forward to the Qur'an, and into the modern era. As this volume demonstrates, questions regarding who the Marys were, as soon as answered, often multiply. As we dig, we discover precious artifacts that tell part of their story, yet at the same time expose more layers to excavate.

Revisiting Which Mary: Does Which Mary Matter?

Mary Magdalene continues her hold on Christian imagination. Our first section addresses questions about her identity as understood among the first three centuries of the Jesus movement, essentially up to the Council of Nicaea. These questions include whether the Magdalene was a composite figure—comprising also Mary of Bethany, or alternatively, Mary of Nazareth—as well as whether there was more than one Mary called the Magdalene.

In recent decades, feminist scholarship associated with the Magdalene has focused more on jettisoning Pope Gregory the Great's hypersexualized portrait of Mary Magdalene as a composite of Mary of Bethany and the sinful woman, and restoring her New Testament reputation as the first witness to the resurrection and Jesus' first apostle. In "The Magdalene Effect: Misreading the Composite Mary in Early Christian Works," Mark Goodacre argues that both the canonical gospels and extracanonical texts such as the *Gospel of Philip* validate the early conflation of Mary of Bethany as the Magdalene. Mary Ann Beavis reviews previous scholarship and employs art, both ancient and modern, to answer "Which Mary, and Why It Matters." In "Why Mary? The Gospel of Mary and Its Heroine," Judith Hartenstein asks why the author of the *Gospel of Mary* made Mary the principal protagonist, the recipient of Jesus' teachings, and the one who taught the other disciples.

Since Shoemaker's influential assertion in *Which Mary* that the unspecified Mary of early Christian tradition could have represented Mary of Nazareth, Jesus' mother has hovered in the foreground of many questions related to Mary Magdalene's identity. In "What is Mary Doing in Acts? Reception History within the Synoptic Tradition," Jo-Ann Badley focuses upon why Jesus' mother was the only woman identified by name at Pentecost, an elevation that seemingly should have gone to the Magdalene. Next, Anna Cwikla addresses the identity of an unspecified Mary who is prominent among the disciples in a Nag Hammadi text, and asks, "Magdalene, Mother, Martha's Sister, or None of the Above? The Mary in the Dialogue of the Savior." Kara J. Lyons-Pardue investigates a curious tract wherein Eusebius identified two Mary Magdalenes in her essay, "Two Mary Magdalenes: Eusebius of Caesarea and the Questionable Reliability of the Gospels' Female Witnesses." Finally, in "Two Women Leaders: 'Mary and the Other Mary Magdalene,'" Ally Kateusz demonstrates that Jesus' followers appear to have remembered his mother as a leader among the disciples, and hypothesizes that this helps explain why so many authors in Ancient Syria imagined Jesus' mother in the garden with her risen son.

Rediscovering the Marys in Mission and Leadership

Expanding on the portrayal of Jesus' mother as a leader in Ancient Syria, Cornelia Horn investigates texts that remembered her as an intercessor. In "The Power of Leadership through Mediation, or How Mary Exercises Overlapping Authority," Horn concludes that literary artifacts of Mary's mediation preserve a powerful early form of her leadership.

The next two chapters continue the theme, begun in Kateusz's "Two Leaders," regarding the trajectory of scribal redaction with respect to markers of female authority in texts. In "The Constriction of Female Leadership: Tracing a Trend in the Early Reception of Miriam and Mary Magdalene," Erez DeGolan and Miriam-Simma Walfish demonstrate that the later narrative traditions of both Miriam and the Magdalene preserve evidence of a cultural constriction of women's leadership roles. With "Virgin Mary Co-Priest or Not: The Continuing Trend of Redaction and Revision in the Medieval Era," Judith M. Davis investigates censorship, in both the medieval and modern eras, of depictions of the priesthood of Mary.

J. L. Manzo presents the complex and powerful role of Mary of Guadalupe in the Catholic colonization of Latin America. In "Mary's Mission According to 'Guadalupan Sermons' of the Seventeenth and Eighteenth Centuries," Manzo demonstrates how Mary simultaneously was *Mediatrix*, apostle to the Americas, and benefactor of the downtrodden.

Recovering Receptions of the Marys in Literature, Art, and Archaeology

Research into the reception of the Marys can reveal past lives as well as new uses for old symbols. In "Mary of Nazareth and Nazareth Archaeological Excavations 1997–2015," Richard Freund details the intersection of literary sources and archaeology in analyzing sites associated with Mary in Nazareth, including Mary's Well and Mary's Cave, two places identified in Marian apocrypha, especially in the second-century *Protevangelium of James*.

Continuing down the track of Marian apocrypha, in "The Dormition of Miriam in Rabbinic Literature," Michael Rosenberg argues that the Dormition narrative about the death of Mary, Jesus' mother, influenced rabbinic reception of the death of Miriam, the sister of Moses. Ally Kateusz also digs into the Dormition narrative in "Dormition Urtext? Earliest Dormition Wall Painting Combines the Great Angel and Women with Censers," and argues that the oldest Dormition iconography witnesses both an ancient source text behind the three main Dormition text traditions and a kernel of historicity regarding the practice of women using censers liturgically. Also evincing the influence of extracanonical texts in the reception of Jesus' mother, Deborah Niederer Saxon investigates Quranic artifacts of apocryphal narratives and Mary's leadership in "Mary and Her Son in the Qur'an and Extracanonical Christian Texts."

Sallying into the Middle Ages, in "The Origin and Manifestations of the Smiling Virgin Mary," Jin H. Han asks why Marian iconography changed to the extent that artists began to portray Mary smiling. Mary Ann Beavis completes the circle by placing into cultural context in our own era Margaret Starbird's highly influential body of work regarding the Magdalene. In "From *Holy Grail* to *The Lost Gospel*: Margaret Starbird and the Mary Magdalene Romance," Beavis advocates more scholarly attention to Starbird's arguments, in part because of their resonance in the wider culture, but also because to ignore them is to bypass legitimate avenues of inquiry related to sexuality, the female divine, the role of women in church leadership, and church censorship of the same. Finally, we place into larger context the connective threads running through these chapters.

Book Cover

The front cover illustration is a sixth-century ivory pyx today in the Metropolitan Museum of Art. The carving represents a procession of women, often thought of as the Marys, to the altar in Jerusalem, the holy city of three great Mariamic traditions. The other sides of the pyx are in Figures 14.5 and 14.5A.

Section One

Revisiting Which Mary: Does Which Mary Matter?

1

The Magdalene Effect

Reading and Misreading the Composite Mary in Early Christian Works

Mark Goodacre

Introduction

It is rare for biblical scholars to make an impact on popular culture, but there is one area where they have achieved something remarkable. After centuries of confusion over the character and reputation of Mary Magdalene, scholars of early Christianity have achieved a coup. They have successfully persuaded novelists, documentary makers, and even film producers that Mary Magdalene was not a sex worker[1] and, moreover, that she was one of the most important figures in the emerging Christian movement, the first witness of the resurrection, the apostle to the apostles. The success of the coup has a lot to do with popular culture's love of revisionist history, alongside the gratifying anti-ecclesial sentiment that the church has done a key character a grave injustice.[2] But the roots and energy for the coup are found in the pioneering work done over the last generation by scholars like Elaine Pagels, Elizabeth Schüssler Fiorenza,

---

[1] I am grateful to several people for helpful feedback on earlier versions of this paper, including the Christianity in Antiquity reading group at UNC Chapel Hill and the Department of Theology at Uppsala Universitet; I would also like to thank Sarah Parkhouse and Elizabeth Schrader for helpful comments.
The term "prostitute" is almost always used by NT scholars, almost always without any critical reflection and often with more than a hint of condescension to those involved in sex work both in antiquity and the contemporary world. Although the term "sex worker" is arguably anachronistic when discussing the ancient world, I use it here in order to encourage critical reflection on complacent attitudes to "prostitution" in scholarship on Christian origins. For a historical exploration of the terminological and other issues, see Melissa Hope Ditmore, *Prostitution and Sex Work* (Historical Guides to Controversial Issues in America; Santa Barbara, CA: Greenwood, 2011).

[2] The dramatic change in perspective is also a result of the popularity of Dan Brown's *The Da Vinci Code* (New York: Doubleday, 2003). For the influence of this book on popular culture, and on the reception of the *Gospel of Jesus' Wife*, see Mark Goodacre, "Jesus' Wife, the Media and *The Da Vinci Code*," in *Fakes, Forgeries, and Fictions: Writing Ancient and Modern Christian Apocrypha: Proceedings from the 2015 York Christian Apocrypha Symposium*, ed. Tony Burke (Eugene, OR: Cascade, 2017), 341–8.

Karen King, Ann Graham Brock, Jane Schaberg, and Esther De Boer, all of whom have established beyond reasonable doubt that Mary Magdalene is a key character worthy of careful study not only in the synoptic gospels and John but also in other early Christian gospels.[3]

The primary stimulus for the rehabilitation and celebration of Mary has been the discovery of her own gospel, the *Gospel of Mary*, interest in which coincided with the development of feminist hermeneutics.[4] Here was a gospel that bore the name of a woman, which had been lost for centuries and which may well have been suppressed by male authorities. In spite of its apparent popularity, attested in three separate witnesses, two from the third century,[5] it is not even dignified with a mention by any patristic author.

If the publication and study of the *Gospel of Mary* has provided a major motivation for the reassessment of Mary's reputation, interest in her character has been further stimulated by the exploration of other early Christian gospels in which she appears, not only those discovered at Nag Hammadi in 1945, the *Gospel of Thomas*, the *Dialogue of the Saviour*, and the *Gospel of Philip*,[6] but also *Pistis Sophia*, first published in 1776 but only now beginning to get the attention it deserves.[7] What has emerged in the scholarship on Mary in these works is a fascinating portrait of a leading woman in early Christianity, a spokesperson for the disciples, a visionary who is Jesus' confidante, a leader who holds her own in debate and whom Jesus loves more than anyone else.

There is, however, an important question about this woman that is seldom asked. It is usually simply assumed that the woman in question is Mary Magdalene. The *Gospel of Mary* is often christened *The Gospel of Mary Magdalene* and scholars characterize the woman found in early Christian gospels as "the Magdalene." But is this description accurate? Is it clear that the woman witnessed in these works is Mary Magdalene, or is she in fact a composite character who has traits drawn not only from Mary Magdalene

---

[3] Elaine Pagels, *The Gnostic Gospels* (New York: Random House, 1979), 5–6, 11–13, 64–7; Elisabeth Schüssler Fiorenza, *In Memory of Her: A Feminist Theological Reconstruction of Christian Origins* (Tenth anniversary edition; New York: Crossroad, 1983); Karen King, *The Gospel of Mary of Magdala: Jesus and the First Woman Apostle* (Santa Rosa, CA: Polebridge, 2003); Ann Graham Brock, *Mary Magdalene, The First Apostle: The Struggle for Authority* (HThS 51; Cambridge, MA: Harvard University Press, 2003); Jane Schaberg, *The Resurrection of Mary Magdalene: Legends, Apocrypha, and the Christian Testament* (New York: Continuum, 2002); Esther A. De Boer, *The Gospel of Mary: Beyond a Gnostic and a Biblical Mary Magdalene* (JSNTS 260; London: T&T Clark, 2004).

[4] Esther A. De Boer writes, "When I was a student in 1982, I came upon the Gospel of Mary by chance while reading Elaine Pagels' book *The Gnostic Gospels*. I vividly remember the shock when I saw the words 'the Gospel of Mary' in print before me. A Gospel named after a *woman*?" (De Boer, *Gospel of Mary*, vii; italics original).

[5] The two Greek papyrus fragments, P.Ryl 463 and P.Oxy 3525, both appear to date from the third century. The Coptic text, Papyrus Berolinensis, dates from the late fourth or early fifth century. See further Christopher M. Tuckett, *The Gospel of Mary* (Oxford: Oxford University Press, 2007), 3–10.

[6] For English translations, see James M. Robinson, ed., *The Nag Hammadi Library in English*, 4th rev. ed. (Leiden: Brill, 1996). For Coptic texts, see James M. Robinson et al., eds., *The Facsimile Edition of the Nag Hammadi Codices* (Leiden: E. J. Brill, 1972–84) as well as the relevant volumes in the Nag Hammadi Studies series.

[7] For introduction, text, and English translation, see Carl Schmidt and Violet MacDermot, Pistis Sophia (NHS 9; Leiden: Brill, 1978). For a useful discussion of the text, see Deirdre Good, "Pistis Sophia," in *Searching the Scriptures: Volume 2: A Feminist Commentary*, ed. Elisabeth Schüssler Fiorenza (New York: Crossroad, 1994), 678–707.

but also from Mary of Bethany? I would like to argue that the Mary of early Christian gospels is not Mary Magdalene. Or, more precisely, the point is that she is not solely Mary Magdalene. As a literary character, she is drawn with elements that derive not only from Mary Magdalene but also from Luke's and John's portraits of Mary of Bethany—she has a sister called Martha, she prostrates herself at Jesus' feet, she weeps, she listens, and she loves Jesus very much.[8]

The Gospel of Mary of Magdala?

Karen King's important and influential book on *The Gospel of Mary* characterizes the work as *The Gospel of Mary of Magdala*. It is the new title of the work. The identity of its lead character is clear—this is Mary Magdalene.[9] Jane Schaberg is so certain about the identity of Mary, both here and in other early Christian gospels, that she repeatedly simply calls her "the Magdalene."[10] Esther de Boer and Marvin Meyer, on their first mention of "the Gospel of Mary," clarify immediately: "— that is, the Gospel of Mary Magdalene."[11] Likewise, Bruce Chilton explains, as he introduces the gospel, that "The *Mary* in the title refers to the Magdalene."[12] Others make the identification as a simple aside, as when Hal Taussig introduces her as "the figure of Mary (most likely Magdalene)."[13] Indeed, the identification goes back

---

[8] After presenting a first draft of this paper, I was delighted to come across Mary Ann Beavis, "Reconsidering Mary of Bethany," *CBQ* 74 (2012): 281–97, which makes the point of Mary of Bethany's marginalization with clarity and force.

[9] King, *Gospel of Mary*; see similarly Karen L. King, "The Gospel of Mary Magdalene," in *Searching the Scriptures: Volume 2: A Feminist Commentary*, ed. Elisabeth Schüssler Fiorenza (New York: Crossroad, 1994), 601–34. King is less forthright over the identification of the heroine in Karen L. King, "The Gospel of Mary with the Greek Gospel of Mary," in *The Nag Hammadi Scriptures*, ed. Marvin W. Meyer and Wolf-Peter Funk (New York: HarperOne, 2007), 741–7, esp. 739, "Most likely Mary of Magdala."

[10] Jane Schaberg, "How Mary Magdalene Became a Whore," *BRev* 8 (1992): 30–7, 50–2. She says, for example,

> Another tradition about the Magdalene is preserved in several Gnostic works of the second to fourth centuries, including the Gospel of Thomas, the Gospel of Philip, the Sophia of Jesus Christ, Dialogue of the Savior, Pistis Sophia and the Gospel of Mary (Magdalene). These Gnostic works preserve a tradition about a rivalry, or conflict, between the Magdalene and Peter or other male disciples ... But unlike the Magdalene of later Western art and legend, the Gnostic Magdalene had not been a prostitute or sinner.

On the "whore" and "prostitute" language, see further n. 62 below.

[11] Marvin Meyer with Esther A. De Boer, *The Gospels of Mary: The Secret Tradition of Mary Magdalene, The Companion of Jesus* (New York: HarperOne, 2006), vii.

[12] BruceChilton, *Mary Magdalene: A Biography* (New York: Doubleday, 2005), 123. However, by identifying the anonymous woman in Bethany as Mary Magdalene (49–53), Chilton echoes early Christian interpreters who harmonized Mary Magdalene with Mary of Bethany.

[13] Hal Taussig, *A New New Testament: A Bible for the 21st Century Combining Traditional and Newly Discovered Texts* (Boston, MA: Houghton Mifflin Harcourt, 2013), 217; cf. xvii, "the Gospel of Mary (Magdalene)" and "the newly discovered Gospel of Mary, in which Mary Magdalene courageously comforts all of the disciples." See also Bart Ehrman and Zlatko Pleše, *The Apocryphal Gospels: Texts and Translations* (Oxford: Oxford University Press, 2011), 587, "We have no record of a Gospel according to Mary (Magdalene) from the early church" and "presumably Mary Magdalene" (589).

to the first publication of the gospel by Carl Schmidt at the end of the nineteenth century.[14]

It is, in other words, a matter largely established in scholarship on early Christianity that the *Gospel of Mary* is rightly re-titled *the Gospel of Mary of Magdala* and that its heroine is Mary Magdalene. If there were any doubt about Mary's identity in this work, it is thought to be further established by other early Christian gospels. The *Gospel of Thomas*, the *Gospel of Philip*, the *Dialogue of the Saviour*, and *Pistis Sophia* are all regarded as works that feature Mary *Magdalene* as a character.

In the light of this kind of certainty, a reminder about the title of the *Gospel of Mary* is in order. In the Codex Berolinensis Gnosticus (BG 8502), the work is called ⲡ[ⲉ]ⲩⲁⲅⲅⲉⲗⲓⲟⲛ ⲕⲁⲧⲁ ⲙⲁⲣⲓϩⲁⲙⲙ, "the gospel according to Mary." The character is called ⲙⲁⲣⲓϩⲁⲙⲙ ("Mariham") throughout. The gospel is not called "the Gospel of Mary Magdalene," the character is never called "Mary Magdalene," and the town "Magdala" is never mentioned.[15] Similarly, in the two Greek fragments, P.Oxy 3525 and P.Ryl 463, she is called Μαριάμμη ("Mariammē") and not Mary Magdalene. The same is true of the *Gospel of Thomas*, the *Dialogue of the Saviour*, and the *Sophia of Jesus Christ*.[16] In each of these works, the character's name is simply Mary.[17]

Mary of Bethany in Early Christian Gospels

Given the rarity of the epithet "Magdalene" in these works, it is worth asking whether the character should be read as Mary Magdalene. It is certainly the case that the character called Mary often has traits derived from the depiction of Mary Magdalene in the Synoptics and John.[18] The post-resurrection dialogue format of the *Gospel of Mary* and the *Dialogue of the Saviour* provides a context that coheres with Mary Magdalene's presence, given her prominence in the resurrection narratives in the Synoptics (Matt 28:1–10; Mark 16:1–8; Luke 24:1–11) and especially John (John 20:1–18). There is also a possible echo of John's resurrection narrative in the *Gospel of Mary*:

---

[14] Carl Schmidt, *Gnostische Schriften in koptischer Sprache aus dem Codex Brucianus* (TU 8/1; Leipzig: Hinrichs, 1892), 453–4.
[15] The name "Mary of Magdala" is a modern scholarly convention. See Joan Taylor, "Missing Magdala and the Name of Mary 'Magdalene,'" *PEQ* 146.3 (2014): 205–23, for a skeptical exploration of the relationship between "Magdala" and Mary Magdalene's name, but see further Richard Bauckham and Stefano De Luca, "Magdala as We Now Know It," *Early Christianity* 6 (2015): 91–118.
[16] Cf. Beavis, "Reconsidering," 290–1.
[17] So too *The Greater Questions of Mary* (see Frank Williams, *The Panarion of Epiphanius of Salamis. Book I (Sects 1–46)* [Leiden: Brill, 2009], 88). On the *Gospel of Philip* and *Pistis Sophia*, see below.
[18] I assume in this chapter that the *Gospel of Mary*, *Pistis Sophia*, *Dialogue of the Saviour*, the *Acts of Philip*, and so on, are familiar with the Synoptics and John. This is uncontroversial in relation to most of these texts. For a cautious case that the *Gospel of Mary* may show some knowledge of the Synoptics and John, see Tuckett, *Gospel of Mary*, 55–74 (Mark 16.10 on 57 should read Mark 16.15, correct on 61).

John 20:18	Mary 7.1-2 (Greek)	Mary 7.1-2 (Coptic)
ἔρχεται Μαριὰμ ἡ Μαγδαληνὴ ἀγγέλλουσα τοῖς μαθηταῖς ὅτι ἑώρακα τὸν κύριον, καὶ ταῦτα εἶπεν αὐτῇ.	[καὶ ἦρχεν αὐτοῖς τού]των τῶν λόγ(ων), ἐμ[οῦ] ποτε ἐν ὁράματι ἰδ[ούσης] τὸν κύριον εἶπον], κύριε σήμερον …	ⲁⲩⲱ ⲁⲥⲁⲣⲭⲉⲓ ⲛ̄ϫⲱ ⲛⲁⲩ ⲛ̄ⲛⲉⲓϣⲁϫⲉ ϫⲉ ⲁ{ⲓ̈}ⲛⲟⲕ ⲡⲉϫⲁⲥ ⲁⲓⲛⲁⲩ ⲉⲡⲭ̄ⲥ̄ ϩⲛ ⲟⲩϩⲟⲣⲟⲙⲁ ⲁⲩⲱ ⲁⲉⲓϫⲟⲟⲥ ⲛⲁϥ ϫⲉ ⲡⲭ̄ⲥ̄ ⲁⲓ̈ⲛⲁⲩ ⲉⲣⲟⲕ ⲙ̄ⲡⲟⲟⲩ ϩⲛ ⲟⲩϩⲟⲣⲟⲙⲁ ⲁϥⲟⲩⲱϣⲃ ⲡⲉϫⲁϥ ⲛⲁⲓ̈ ϫⲉ …

John 20:18	Mary 7:1-2
Mary Magdalene went and announced to the disciples, "I have seen the Lord"; and she told them that he had said these things to her.	She said, "I saw the Lord in a vision and I said to him, 'Lord, I saw you today in a vision.'"

Although the agreement is not close, the parallel is suggestive. In John's gospel, Mary Magdalene announces to the disciples that she has seen the Lord while in the *Gospel of Mary*, Mary announces that she has seen the Lord "in a vision." The *Gospel of Mary* may be evoking Mary Magdalene's words from John's gospel,[19] but the parallel is not close enough for the reader to be sure.[20]

However, other motifs that might be linked to Mary Magdalene are at least equally characteristic of Mary of Bethany. Thus, Mary is often characterized by weeping (*Gos. Mary* 9.5; *Dial. Sav.* 126.13-14; *Pistis Sophia* 5.138), and this has an obvious parallel in John 20:11-18, when Mary Magdalene weeps at the tomb, but the motif of Mary's weeping is something that is also found in relation to Mary of Bethany.[21] Her weeping at Lazarus's tomb in John 11:33 leads directly to one of the most famous and memorable moments of John's gospel, when Jesus wept (John 11:35).[22]

---

[19] Cf. Judith Hartenstein, *Die zweite Lehre: Erscheinungen des Auferstandenen als Rahmenerzählungen frühchristlicher Dialoge* (Berlin: Akademie, 2000), 130, "Ausserdem bestehen beim Bericht von ihrer Vision (p.10,10-13) Anklänge an Joh 20,18. Der weitgehende Konsens in der Forschung, Maria als Maria Magdalena zu verstehen, ist also gerechtfertigt, obwohl weder im EvMar noch in anderen Schriften Interesse an de historischen Person und ihrer Unterscheidung von anderen Jüngerinnen dieses Namens deutlich wird."
[20] It is not counted among Tuckett's "clear echoes and allusions" (*Gospel of Mary*, 56-67), nor even his "less clear parallels" (67-71), but he does add in his section on "Other Parallels" that "Mary appears here as one who has had a vision in which she has 'seen' the Lord; this may well have grown out of the report that Mary gives to the disciples after seeing the risen Jesus in the garden on the first Easter Day in John 20:18 ('I have seen the Lord')" (71).
[21] Cf. Tuckett, *Gospel of Mary*, 72.
[22] Moreover, the parallels in John between the two Marys invite this comparison—Mary (of Bethany) weeps at the tomb in John 11 and Mary (Magdalene) weeps at the tomb in John 20.

Similarly, one of the most characteristic actions of Mary in *Pistis Sophia*, her prostration at Jesus' feet, is not peculiar to Mary Magdalene in the Synoptics or John; it is characteristic of Mary of Bethany. In *Pistis Sophia*, the motif is repeated over and over again (italics used to draw attention to the prostration-at-the-feet motif):[23]

> 1.19: But when Maria heard the Saviour saying these words, she rejoiced greatly and she came before Jesus, she prostrated herself in his presence, *she worshipped at his feet*, she said to him …[24]
> 1.24: It happened now when Jesus finished speaking these words to his disciples, Maria, the beautiful in her speech, came forward. *The blessed one prostrated herself at the feet of Jesus* and said: "My Lord, suffer me that I speak in thy presence …"
> 2.83: It came to pass then again, after all this, that Mary came forward, adored the feet of Jesus and said: "My Lord, be not wroth with me, if I question thee …"
> 2.94: Then Mary Magdalene came forward, *threw herself at the feet of Jesus, kissed them and wept aloud* and said: "Have mercy upon me, my Lord …"
> 2.98: It came to pass, when Jesus had finished speaking these words unto his disciples, that Mary Magdalene came forward, *kissed the feet of Jesus* and said unto him: "My Lord, bear with me and be not wroth with me, if I question thee …"
> 3.108: It came to pass, when Jesus had finished saying these words unto his disciples, that *Mary adored the feet of Jesus and kissed them*. Mary said: "My Lord, bear with me, if I question thee, and be not wroth with me …"
> 3.110: When then Jesus had said this, Mary continued, *threw herself at Jesus' feet, kissed them* and said: "My Lord, still will I question thee. Reveal [it] unto us and hide [it] not from us …"
> 4.128: And when the Saviour had said this unto Mary, she smote her breast, she cried out and wept, she and all the disciples together, and said: "Woe unto sinners, for their chastisements are exceedingly numerous!" Mary came forward, *she fell down at the feet of Jesus, kissed them and said*: "My Lord, bear with me if I question thee …"
> 5.138: And Mary drew nigh unto him, *fell down, adored his feet* and kissed his hands and said: "Yea, my Lord, reveal unto us …"

Although this has a possible analogue in Matt 28:9, where "the women," previously identified as "Mary Magdalene and the other Mary" (Matt 28:1), clasp Jesus' feet and worship him (αἱ δὲ προσελθοῦσαι ἐκράτησαν αὐτοῦ τοὺς πόδας καὶ προσεκύνησαν αὐτῷ), it is more clearly characteristic of Mary of Bethany, who sits at Jesus' feet while Martha busies herself in Luke 10:39 (ἣ καὶ παρακαθεσθεῖσα πρὸς τοὺς πόδας τοῦ Ἰησοῦ ἤκουεν τὸν λόγον αὐτοῦ), who falls at Jesus' feet in John 11:32 (ἡ οὖν Μαριὰμ ὡς ἦλθεν ὅπου ἦν Ἰησοῦς ἰδοῦσα αὐτὸν ἔπεσεν αὐτοῦ πρὸς τοὺς πόδας), and who pours

---

[23] In two of these examples, Mary is called "Mary Magdalene." See further on this below.
[24] It is unclear whether this "Maria" is the mother of Jesus. However, at this point in *Pistis Sophia*, Jesus' mother has not been introduced. On the case that *Pistis Sophia* and other works incorporate motifs from Mary the mother of Jesus, see further below. This action is characteristic of Mary but not exclusive to her—Philip (1.22), Martha (1.38), Jesus' mother Mary (1.62), and the disciples (2.100; 5.138) all also worship at Jesus' feet.

perfume on Jesus' feet and wipes them with her hair in John 12:3 (ἤλειψεν τοὺς πόδας τοῦ Ἰησοῦ καὶ ἐξέμαξεν ταῖς θριξὶν αὐτῆς τοὺς πόδας αὐτοῦ; see also John 11:2).[25]

Moreover, Mary's character in the *Gospel of Mary*, as one who listens to Jesus and who has special revelations from him, may be influenced by Luke's depiction of Mary as one who receives special instruction, listening alone at Jesus' feet while Martha busies herself with work (Luke 10:38–42).[26] It is also possible that the origin of the notice that Jesus loved Mary "more than the rest of women" (*Gospel of Mary* 9.2) and "more than us" (*Gospel of Mary* 18.14–15) is found in the note in John 11:5 that Jesus loved Mary and Martha.[27] There is no parallel note anywhere in the Synoptics or John that mentions Jesus' love for Mary Magdalene, a fact that places a question mark over the insistence on the identification with Mary Magdalene.[28]

Mary and Martha

The difficulty with identifying Mary of Bethany is that where she appears in Luke and John, her name is simply "Mary."[29] The term "Mary of Bethany" is a scholarly convention, used to distinguish her from other women of the same name. Indeed, "Bethany" is itself derived only from John (11:1; 11:18; 12:1)[30] and is not found in Luke's story of Martha and Mary (10:38, κώμη, "a village").[31] The term "Bethany" largely drops out of use in other early gospels, which tend to be far less specific about geographical markers than the Synoptics and John, and it is correspondingly easy to

---

[25] It is also characteristic of the anonymous "sinner" in Luke 7:36–50 (see Luke 7:38, 44–46). See further on this character below.

[26] Cf. Beavis, "Reconsidering," 293.

[27] Cf. Beavis, "Reconsidering," 293, and Tuckett, *Gospel of Mary*, 72. See further *Gos. Phil.* 63.32–64.6 and the discussion below. Again, see further the anonymous "sinner's" love for Jesus in Luke 7:36–50 (7:47).

[28] The motif is, of course, reminiscent of John's depiction of the disciple Jesus loved (John 13:23–25; 19:26–27; 19:35; 21:20–24). For the identification of the beloved disciple with Mary Magdalene, see De Boer, *Gospel of Mary*, 178–90. She mentions Jesus' love for Lazarus, Martha, and Mary in John 11:5 but suggests on the basis of John 20:16–18 that Mary Magdalene is "implicitly one of the disciples Jesus loved" (182).

[29] Variation in the spellings of the names of the Marys in the texts does not help a great deal with the identification of the different Marys. The spellings of the same Mary vary not only between the different works but also often in the textual witnesses to the single works. Cf. François Bovon, "Mary Magdalene in the *Acts of Philip*," in *Which Mary? The Marys of Early Christian Tradition*, ed. F. Stanley Jones (SBLSS 19; Atlanta, GA: Society of Biblical Literature, 2002): 75–89 (80),

> There is evidence that the same person may have received each of the three forms of the name. The mother of Jesus is called Μαριάμ or Μαρία in the New Testament, Μαριάμμη in three passages of the *Protevangelium of James* ... The assignment of names to Mary Magdalene is identical. She is called Μαρία ἡ Μαγδαληνή in Matt 27:56, Μαριὰμ ἡ Μαγδαληνή a few verses later in Matt 27:61; and Μαριάμμη in the *Gospel of Mary*, Hippolytus *Haer.* 5.1.7, Origen *Cels.* 5.62, and, in a Latin form, Priscillian's *Apologeticum* 1.

See also the full discussion in Stephen J. Shoemaker, "A Case of Mistaken Identity? Naming the Gnostic Mary," in *Which Mary? The Marys of Early Christian Tradition*, ed. F. Stanley Jones (SBLSS 19; Atlanta, GA: Society of Biblical Literature, 2002), 5–30, esp. 9–17.

[30] Mark and Matthew's parallel anointing by an anonymous woman also occurs at Bethany (Mark 14:3; Matt 26:6). See further on this below.

[31] Cf. Beavis, "Reconsidering," 283.

miss references to Mary of Bethany in these works. However, there is a clear way of identifying her, and that is to notice places where she is found alongside her sister Martha.

In several early Christian works, Mary is depicted alongside Martha. Given Martha's presence, it is remarkable that so many scholars continue to identify Mary unequivocally as "Mary Magdalene" or even "the Magdalene."[32] In *Pistis Sophia*, Mary is one of only a handful of female characters in the entire, lengthy work, and one of the others is Martha,[33] who on one occasion appears alongside Mary (*Pistis Sophia* 2.73), where they are both commended in the same way, "Well said, finely, Mary, blessed one ... Well said, and finely, Martha." To any reader familiar with Luke and John, the pairing of Mary with Martha will clearly evoke those texts.[34] It might be different if Martha were a character who is found independently in early Christian works, but she is not. If Martha is present, Mary is always present too.

The same is true of the *Acts of Philip*, where Mary[35] and Martha appear alongside one another and where their attributes reflect those found in Luke and John:

> But when Philip heard the name of the region and the city that had been allotted to him, it seemed harsh to him, and grumbling he wept. Now when he wept, the Savior turned to him with John and Mariamne, his sister (for she was the one who held the register of the regions, and it was she who prepared the bread and the salt, and the breaking of the bread. Martha was the one who served the crowds and worked very much). Mariamne spoke with the Savior about Philip, since he was distressed because of the city to which he was being sent. And she was saying: "My Lord Jesus Christ, it is not pleasing for my brother Philip." (*Acts of Philip* VIII.94)[36]

Martha is characterized as the woman who "served the crowds and worked very much" (ἡ δὲ Μάρθα ἐστὶν ἡ διακονοῦσα τοῖς πλήθεσιν καὶ κοπιῶσα σφόδρα), while Mary is Jesus' right-hand woman who has chosen the better part, traits obviously reminiscent of Luke 10:38–42, where Martha similarly busies herself with serving (ἡ δὲ Μάρθα περιεσπᾶτο περὶ πολλὴν διακονίαν, 10:40), and John 12:2, where she is again serving

---

[32] Antti Marjanen, *The Woman Jesus Loved: Mary Magdalene in the Nag Hammadi Library and Related Documents* (Leiden: E.J. Brill, 1996), concedes that the presence of Martha in the *Acts of Philip* 94 may evoke the character of Mary of Bethany, but the idea that the character is Mary Magdalene controls the way he frames the discussion: "The prominent role which Mariamne assumes within the circle of disciples makes it probable that she is to be identified with Mary Magdalene, although she has gained new legendary features and possibly also Mary of Bethany has been integrated into her person" (49). Marjanen's "possibly" is weak given Mary's presence alongside Martha.

[33] The others are Salome and Mary, mother of Jesus.

[34] With respect to John, see now Elizabeth Schrader, "Was Martha of Bethany added to the Fourth Gospel in the Second Century?" *HTR* 110 (2017): 360–92.

[35] She is here called Mariamne, which may also be the reading in Hippolytus, *Haer.* 5.7 and 9.13, but see Miroslav Marcovich, ed., *Hippolytus: Refutatio omnium haeresium* (PTS 25; Berlin: de Gruyter, 1986), 142 and 384. He reads μαριαμμη in *Haer.* 5.7 and μαριαμνη in 9.13.

[36] This translation is from François Bovon and Christopher R. Matthews, eds. and trans., *Acts of Philip: A New Translation* (Waco, TX: Baylor University Press, 2012), 74. For the Greek text, see François Bovon, Bertrand Bouvier, and Frédéric Amsler, eds. and trans., *Acta Philippi: Textus* (Corpus Christianorum, Series Apocryphorum 11; Turnhout: Brepols, 1999).

(ἡ Μάρθα διηκόνει). It seems clear that the Lukan and Johannine portraits of Mary and Martha are influencing the depiction of Mary in works like these.

Given that Mary sometimes appears alongside Martha, a key point becomes clear. These works are harmonizing Mary Magdalene and Mary of Bethany. They imagine that Mary Magdalene and Mary of Bethany are the same person.[37] Thus, in early Christian works outside of the Synoptics and John, they rarely appear together. Mary is sometimes called Magdalene and she is sometimes seen alongside Martha, but the two Marys seldom appear together—they have become one.[38] One of the clearest examples of this is Hippolytus's Commentary on Song of Songs in which Mary and Martha are witnesses of Jesus' resurrection (*In. Cant.* 25.6).[39]

The invitation to harmonize these two women was probably straightforward and obvious. Mary the sister of Martha appears once in Luke (10:38–42) and once in an extended connected story in John (11–12), while Mary Magdalene's presence is almost entirely located in the Synoptic and Johannine Passion Narratives, the only exception being the early mention in Luke 8:1–3. Unlike other Marys, Mary Magdalene and Mary of Bethany are never seen in the same room at the same time, and they share similar traits like weeping at the tomb before a resurrection (John 11:33–4; John 20:11, 13, 15).[40] Although Mary "of Magdala" has become a scholarly commonplace, it is worth remembering that she is never described this way in the Synoptics or John, where she is always "Mary Magdalene" or just "Mary." The invitation to treat these two characters as the same person was an invitation the harmonizer would be unlikely to resist.

Misdirection and the Mother of Jesus

The notion that the unspecified Mary of early Christian gospels is the Magdalene has faced a major and important challenge from Stephen Shoemaker,[41] who argues that

---

[37] Cf. Bovon, "Mary Magdalene in the *Acts of Philip*," 82 n. 33, "The text presupposes that Mary Magdalene and Mary of Bethany are the same person." Cf. Beavis, "Reconsidering," 289–90.

[38] Cf. Richard Bauckham, *Gospel Women: Studies of the Named Women in the Gospels* (Grand Rapids, MI: Eerdmans, 2002), 237, "Throughout the whole of Gnostic literature no more than six women disciples of Jesus are ever named (Mary [Magdalene], Martha, Salome, Arsenoe, Mary the mother of Jesus, Mary the sister of Jesus) and no more than four in any work." Bauckham lists several references to "Mary Magdalene" as one of these six (237–8, n. 54), but most of his references speak only of Mary and do not clearly designate her as Mary Magdalene (cf. 238, n. 57).

[39] See now Yancy Smith, *The Mystery of Anointing: Hippolytus' Commentary on the Song of Songs in Social and Critical Contexts: Texts, Translations, and Comprehensive Study* (Piscataway, NJ: Gorgias, 2015). See also *Epistula Apostolorum* in which Mary, Martha, and Sarah appear together at the cross, though there are differences between the Ethiopic and Coptic recensions. For a thorough investigation of the Martha traditions, see Allie M. Ernst, *Martha from the Margins: The Authority of Martha in Early Christian Tradition* (VC Supplements 98; Leiden: Brill, 2009).

[40] Cf. Beavis, "Reconsidering," 286, "Whether the Johannine reader/audience would have recognized the name and made a distinction between μαρία ἡ μαγδαληνή and the μαριάμ of the Bethany stories is questionable."

[41] Stephen Shoemaker, "Rethinking the 'Gnostic Mary': Mary of Nazareth and Mary of Magdala in Early Christian Tradition," *JECS* 9 (2001): 555–95; Shoemaker, "A Case of Mistaken Identity?"; Shoemaker, "Jesus' Gnostic Mom: Mary of Nazareth and the Gnostic Mary Traditions," in *Mariam, the Magdalen, and the Mother*, ed. Deirdre Good (Bloomington: Indiana University Press, 2005), 153–82; and Shoemaker, *Mary in Early Christian Faith and Devotion* (New Haven, CT: Yale University Press, 2016), 75–87. *Which Mary?* provides a helpful discussion of Shoemaker's case

Mary the mother of Jesus needs to be brought into play in the discussion of these works. Shoemaker's articles provide a helpful corrective to the assumption that these works must be talking about Mary Magdalene, and he has also been successful in illustrating that key motifs can evoke Mary the mother of Jesus, not least the tendency of lines from Luke's Birth Narrative (especially Luke 1:28, 42, 45, 48) to appear in the way that Mary is described. In the *Acts of Philip*, for example, Mary is "chosen among women" (*Acts of Philip* VIII.95),[42] and in *Pistis Sophia*, she is "blessed among all the women of the earth" and "called blessed by all generations" (*Pistis Sophia* 28.21–22; 56.11–13).[43]

This discussion, though, has effectively provided misdirection over the issue of Mary's identity. By framing the debate as one of Mary Magdalene versus Mary the mother of Jesus, scholars tend to forget Mary of Bethany altogether.[44] It is like rivals passionately arguing over whether Chelsea or Manchester United is the best football team in England without mentioning Manchester City. As soon as the discussion is framed as one in which the choices are Mary Magdalene and the mother of Jesus, it is inevitable that the clues pointing to Mary of Bethany are missed.[45]

The reactions to Shoemaker's work are disappointing in missing what is in fact his key contribution to the debate. By arguing that works like the *Gospel of Mary* and *Pistis Sophia* are actually focused on Mary Magdalene, they fail to appreciate that Shoemaker's argument is not about replacing Mary Magdalene with Mary the mother of Jesus but about underlining her nature as a composite literary figure, what Shoemaker calls "the composite 'apocryphal' Mary."[46] Although he may have overplayed the significance of Mary the mother of Jesus in the construction of this character, and largely ignored Mary of Bethany, his essential insight about "the apocryphal Mary's markedly 'intertextual' character"[47] should not be gainsaid.

(among other things), but there is little discussion of Mary of Bethany. Shoemaker was to some extent anticipated by Enzo Lucchesi, "Évangile selon Marie ou Évangile selon Marie–Madeleine?," *AnBoll* 103 (1985): 366–92.

[42] Shoemaker, "A Case of Mistaken Identity?," 14.

[43] For a critique of Shoemaker on this point, see Antti Marjanen, "The Mother of Jesus or the Magdalene? The Identity of Mary in the So-Called Gnostic Christian Texts," in *Which Mary? The Marys of Early Christian Tradition*, ed. F. Stanley Jones (SBLSS 19; Atlanta, GA: Society of Biblical Literature, 2002), 31–41 (36–7); and Ann Graham Brock, "Setting the Record Straight—The Politics of Identification: Mary Magdalene and Mary the Mother in Pistis Sophia," in *Which Mary? The Marys of Early Christian Tradition*, ed. F. Stanley Jones (SBLSS 19; Atlanta, GA: Society of Biblical Literature, 2002), 43–52.

[44] See, e.g., Ann Graham Brock, "The Identity of the Blessed Mary, Representative of Wisdom in Pistis Sophia," in *Walk in the Ways of Wisdom: Essays in Honor of Elisabeth Schüssler Fiorenza*, ed. Shelly Matthews, Cynthia Briggs Kittredge, and Melanie Johnson-Debaufre (Harrisburg, PA: Trinity Press International, 2003), 122–35, which sets up the discussion as one of "the strong apostolic role or the generally more acquiescent figure of Mary, Mother of Jesus" (124).

[45] Brock, in fact, raises the key question only to drop it again:

> One has to acknowledge the possibility of a third Mary in Pistis Sophia 1–3. The presence of an unspecified Martha in the text, for example, at least raises the possibility of the presence of Mary of Bethany. However, based on the absence of any further designation or concrete indication of a third Mary, we will proceed with Mary Magdalene as the most logical choice for the "other Mary."

Brock, "Identity," 128, n. 11.

[46] See especially Shoemaker, "Jesus' Gnostic Mom," 157–61.

[47] Shoemaker, "Jesus' Gnostic Mom," 161.

How Strong Is the Identification with Mary Magdalene?

In the light of these reflections on the evidence in early Christian gospels, it is worth looking again at the case for the identification of Mary Magdalene. Although the term "Magdalene" is absent from the *Gospel of Mary*, the *Dialogue of the Saviour*, the *Gospel of Thomas*, and other early Christian texts, there are two works from the early centuries where she is explicitly named, the *Gospel of Philip* and *Pistis Sophia*.[48] In the *Gos. Phil.* 59.6–11, Mary Magdalene is famously distinguished from others called Mary:

ⲚⲈⲞⲨⲚ̄ ϢⲞⲘⲦⲈ ⲘⲞⲞϢⲈ ⲘⲚ̄ ⲠⲬⲞⲈⲒⲤ ⲞⲨⲞⲈⲒϢ ⲚⲒⲘ ⲘⲀⲢⲒⲀ ⲦⲈϤⲘⲀⲀⲨ ⲀⲨⲰ ⲦⲈⲤⲤⲰⲚⲈ ⲀⲨⲰ <u>ⲘⲀⲄⲆⲀⲖⲎⲚⲎ</u> ⲦⲀ ⲈⲒ ⲈⲦⲞⲨⲘⲞⲨⲦⲈ ⲈⲢⲞⲤ ϪⲈ ⲦⲈϤⲔⲞⲒⲚⲰⲚ ⲞⲤ ⲘⲀⲢⲒⲀ ⲄⲀⲢ ⲦⲈ ⲦⲈϤⲤⲰⲚⲈ ⲀⲨⲰ ⲦⲈϤⲘⲀⲀⲨ ⲦⲈ ⲀⲨⲰ ⲦⲈϤϨⲰⲦⲢⲈ ⲦⲈ

There were three who always walked with the Lord: Mary, his mother, and her sister, and <u>Magdalene</u>, the one who was called his companion. For his sister and his mother and his companion were each a Mary.[49]

The connection is made again in a second passage (*Gos. Phil.* 63.32–64.6):

ⲀⲨⲰ [Ⲧ]ⲔⲞⲒⲚⲰⲚⲞⲤ Ⲙ̄ⲠⲤ[... ⲘⲀ]ⲢⲒⲀ Ⲧ<u>ⲘⲀⲄ[ⲆⲀ]ⲖⲎⲚⲎ</u> ⲚⲈⲢⲈ Ⲡ[... ... ⲘⲈ]Ⲙ̄ⲘⲞ[Ⲥ Ⲛ̄] ϨⲞⲨⲞ ⲀⲘ̄ⲘⲀⲐⲎⲦ[ⲎⲤ ⲦⲎⲢⲞⲨ ⲀⲨⲰ ⲚⲈϤ]ⲀⲤⲠⲀⲌⲈⲘ̄ⲘⲞⲤ ⲀⲦⲈⲤ[... . Ⲛ̄ϨⲀϨ] Ⲛ̄ⲤⲞⲠ ⲀⲠⲔⲈⲤⲈⲈⲠⲈ Ⲙ̄[ⲘⲀⲐⲎⲦⲎⲤ. .] . ⲈⲢⲞ . [.] . [. .]ⲘⲀ ⲠⲈϪⲀⲨ ⲚⲀϤ ϪⲈ ⲈⲦⲂⲈ ⲞⲨ ⲔⲘⲈⲘ Ⲙ̄ⲘⲞⲤ ⲠⲀⲢⲀⲢⲞⲚ ⲦⲎⲢⲚ̄ ⲀϤ ⲞⲨⲰϢⲂ̄ Ⲛ̄ϬⲒ ⲠⲤⲰⲦⲎⲢ ⲠⲈϪⲀϤ ⲚⲀⲨ ϪⲈ ⲈⲦⲂⲈ ⲞⲨ ϮⲘⲈ Ⲙ̄ⲘⲰⲦⲚ̄ ⲀⲚ Ⲛ̄ⲦⲈⲤϨⲈ

And the companion of the ... Mary <u>Magdalene</u> ... loved her more than all the disciples, and used to kiss her often on her []. The rest of the disciples ... They said to him "Why do you love her more than all of us?" The Savior answered and said to them, "Why do I not love you like her?"

The *Gospel of Philip* therefore provides one of the strongest indicators that Mary can be more than simply a composite, harmonized Mary based on the Synoptics and John, and that she remains Mary "Magdalene" with a specific identity that can be distinguished from other NT Marys. Nevertheless, it is worth noticing what it is that is apparently piquing the interest of the author of *Philip*. The passage distinguishing the different Marys appears to be based on John 19.25:

John 19:25: Εἱστήκεισαν δὲ παρὰ τῷ σταυρῷ τοῦ Ἰησοῦ ἡ μήτηρ αὐτοῦ καὶ ἡ ἀδελφὴ τῆς μητρὸς αὐτοῦ, Μαρία ἡ τοῦ Κλωπᾶ καὶ Μαρία ἡ Μαγδαληνή.

Meanwhile, standing near the cross of Jesus were his mother, and his mother's sister, Mary the wife of Clopas, and Mary Magdalene.

---

[48] Cf. Shoemaker, "A Case of Mistaken Identity?," 7, who correctly notes that "in all but two instances, those being the *Gospel of Philip* and the *Pistis Sophia*, this woman is known only by the name 'Mary,' without any further clarification."

[49] Translation adapted from Wesley Isenberg, "The Gospel of Philip," in *Nag Hammadi Library*, 139–60 (adding "for" for ⲄⲀⲢ, which is left untranslated in Isenberg).

This is the only occasion in the Synoptics or John where three characters named Mary are all found together,[50] and the three are in the same order in John and *Philip*, an order that is unique to these two passages, with Jesus' mother at the head of the list and Mary Magdalene, unusually, at the foot of it. On every other occasion, Mary Magdalene appears first.[51] The author of the *Gospel of Philip* appears to have been fascinated by the coalescing of these three Marys all in the one place.[52]

It is worth noting here that *Philip* does not draw in Mary of Bethany as an additional character in a place where different Marys are being distinguished and in a context where John's gospel is in view. Although one can only guess, it may well be that *Philip*, like other early Christian gospels, identified Mary Magdalene with Mary of Bethany.[53] This is certainly what appears to be presupposed in *Pistis Sophia*, where the character is repeatedly identified as Mary Magdalene but in a text that situates her alongside another character named Martha.

Outside of the *Gospel of Philip* and *Pistis Sophia*, the character is always called Mary and not "Mary Magdalene." Since the name "Mary Magdalene" or "Mary of Magdala" is repeatedly read into these works, it is worth looking at the explicit arguments given for identifying the unspecified Mary as Mary Magdalene, especially in the *Gospel of Mary*. Esther De Boer offers three reasons for identifying Mary in the *Gospel of Mary* as the Magdalene:[54]

1. The rivalry between Peter and Mary (*Gos. Mary* 17.15–18.21) is paralleled in the *Gospel of Thomas* (114) and *Pistis Sophia* (59 and 83). In *Pistis Sophia*, the woman in question is explicitly identified as Mary Magdalene.[55]
2. Levi says that the Savior loved Mary "more than us" in the *Gospel of Mary* (18.14-15) and the disciples make a similar claim in the *Gospel of Philip* (63–64).[56]
3. Mary "is supposed to know more about the Savior than the rest of her brothers and sisters" in the *Gospel of Mary*. This parallels the NT gospels where "it is Mary Magdalene who knows more than the others."[57]

[50] John does not name Jesus' mother as Mary (cf. John 2:1–11), but it would be easy for early Christian readers of John to provide the name from elsewhere.
[51] The only curiosity is the second figure in the list, the sister. She is initially ⲧⲉⲥⲥⲱⲛⲉ ("her sister") and then ⲧⲉϥⲥⲱⲛⲉ ("his sister"), one of which must be an error. Bauckham, *Gospel Women*, 233-4, suggests that this is a sister of Jesus named Mary, so that "her sister" is the mistake. However, there is no sister of Jesus named Mary in the Synoptics or John, whereas there is a sister of Jesus' mother, Mary of Clopas, in John 19:25, where she appears in the same order. On balance, it is more likely that *Philip* is referring to this known Mary, all the more so as the text stresses that they "always walked with the Lord," a note that echoes Mark 15:41 and Matt 27:55.
[52] For speculation on why the *Gospel of Philip* is fascinated by these three characters called Mary, see Marjanen, *The Woman Jesus Loved*, 161–2.
[53] The focus on how Mary loved Jesus more than others suggests that this is the same composite Mary that we see in *Gospel of Mary*, *Dialogue of the Saviour*, and *Pistis Sophia*. See further below.
[54] De Boer, *Gospel of Mary*, 18. See similarly the useful extended footnote in King, *Gospel of Mary of Magdala*, 205, n. 58, though she plays off Mary Magdalene and Mary the mother of Jesus.
[55] She suggests that the rivalry begins in the NT over who saw the risen Christ first, citing Mark 16:9, Matt 28:9 and John 20:1–18 against Luke 24:34.
[56] Cf. Marjanen, *The Woman Jesus Loved*, 95, "The similarity of the statements [in *Philip* and *Mary*] suggest that the author of the *Gospel of Mary* is familiar with a tradition, utilized also in the *Gospel of Philip*, according to which Mary Magdalene was known to be a special favorite of Jesus."
[57] De Boer, *Gospel of Mary*, 18.

These points are not strong. The first point relies on parallels between the *Gospel of Mary*, *Gospel of Thomas*, and *Pistis Sophia*, but in the *Gospel of Thomas*, the woman is simply "Mary" (ⲘⲀⲢⲒϨⲀⲘⲘ). She is not Mary Magdalene. And in *Pistis Sophia*, Mary Magdalene appears in a work that also regularly features Martha (see above). Peter can hardly be determinative of Mary's identity in *Pistis Sophia* when Martha is alongside her too. It is problematic to identify Mary in one work by appealing to the evidence of a later work in which the identity is also ambiguous.

De Boer's second point is similar. It is true that the *Gospel of Philip* and the *Gospel of Mary* both celebrate Mary as one whom Jesus loved, but the motif does not have any basis in the characterization of Mary Magdalene in the Synoptics or John. Unlike Mary Magdalene, Mary of Bethany is said to have been loved by Jesus (John 11:5; see above), and in any case, the motif is one that is developing along its own trajectory in these early Christian gospels, in which the harmonization between Mary Magdalene, Mary of Bethany, and the anonymous synoptic woman who anoints Jesus (Mark 14:3–9, Matt 26:6–13, Luke 7:36–50) is underway.

De Boer's third point, about Mary's knowledge, is also not distinctive of Mary Magdalene. Given the portrait of Mary of Bethany as one who listens and learns at Jesus' feet (Luke 10:39), the idea of Mary's superior knowledge is as likely to be influenced by her character as it is by Mary Magdalene's. After all, Mary Magdalene does not receive any teaching in the Synoptic and Johannine Passion narratives. Rather, her status is connected with her witness to the empty tomb and to the resurrected Jesus.

Harmonization and Pedagogy

Given the evidence that many early Christians were harmonizing Mary Magdalene and Mary of Bethany, it is worth asking why it is that we have tended to miss something so straightforward. The problem may be due to the habits of the modern biblical scholar. One of the key elements in our introductory courses on the NT is to stress the importance of reading each gospel in its own right and to avoid harmonizing. We invest a great deal in training our students to see Matthew as Matthew, Mark as Mark, and so on.[58] Given the amalgamation of gospel stories, characters, and theological perspectives in popular culture, the church, and film, we are at pains to encourage our students to disentangle one gospel from another, to learn to use a Synopsis, to work out how John differs from the Synoptics, and so on.[59] Perhaps, after a while,

---

[58] This is not intended as any kind of criticism of this perspective, which I regard as foundational in NT introduction. Indeed, I began my introductory textbook to the Synoptic Problem with several pages stressing the difference between harmonies and synopses, Mark Goodacre, *The Synoptic Problem: A Way Through the Maze* (London: Continuum, 2001), 13–15. The point is rather the transference of a mindset from one area of study to another.

[59] The scholarly reaction to *The Passion of the Christ* (dir. Mel Gibson, 2003) provides a good illustration of the difficulty. Scholars were repeatedly at pains to point out to their popular audiences that Gibson's film was a harmony of the gospels, as if this were something surprising or unwelcome. See Mark Goodacre, "The Power of *The Passion of the Christ*: Reactions and Overreactions to Gibson's Artistic Vision," in *Jesus and Mel Gibson's The Passion of the Christ: The Film, the Gospels and the Claims of History*, ed. Robert Webb and Kathleen Corley (London: Continuum, 2004), 28–44, esp. 29–34.

this becomes such a habit of mind that we forget that Christians of the early centuries had not taken one of our introductory NT classes. They had not received the memo about harmonizing. For them, as for most Christians across the centuries, biblical texts invited and encouraged the interpreter to harmonize.

In other words, it is a peculiar perspective of the contemporary biblical scholar that insists on choosing between one character and another, as if Mary in the *Gospel of Mary* has to be either Mary Magdalene or Mary of Bethany, as if Mary in the *Dialogue of the Saviour* corresponds to only one character. It is a mindset that leads to the kind of confirmation bias that only sees evidence for the presence of Mary Magdalene and that brushes aside any evidence that disconfirms it, most strikingly the presence of Martha alongside Mary in several of these works.

There is a further, related issue. One of the great advances of recent years in scholarship on Christian origins is the consciousness of canonical bias and the resulting attempts to avoid it.[60] In the context of scholarship on Mary, it has led to the attempt to take seriously the full range of early Christian works that mention her, many of which are still relatively recent discoveries, and to avoid focusing solely on the canonical gospels. This laudable aim, however, runs the risk of confusing a confessional perspective, which stresses canon, with a historical perspective, which stresses the earliest works. Although we might hope to find the historical Mary Magdalene in works like the *Gospel of Mary*, what we actually find is a composite character that postdates and presupposes the Synoptics and John. Indeed, the vagueness with which these works characterize their protagonists, with place names and relationships absent, may itself be a sign of their familiarity with the Synoptics and John.[61] In this context, then, it is important to distinguish between earlier works in which Mary Magdalene and Mary of Bethany are two distinct characters (Luke and John) and later works in which Mary is a composite character (*Gospel of Mary*, *Pistis Sophia*, etc.).

Harmonizing and the Route to the Sex Worker

The resistance to noticing the harmonization of Mary Magdalene with Mary of Bethany may also be related to the coup with which the discussion began—the scholarly stress that Mary Magdalene was not a sex worker. The sense that Christian tradition has done Mary Magdalene a grave injustice runs through much of the scholarship on Mary, and this leads to the attempt to explain how the injustice came about—through harmonizing Mary Magdalene with other characters, specifically the "Sinner" of Luke 7:36–50. Where harmonizing is the demon that destroyed Mary Magdalene's reputation, scholars are naturally wary to see it in action several centuries before Pope Gregory's notorious sermon.

But Pope Gregory's pronouncement was not a piece of new, manipulative genius at the end of the sixth century. It was, rather, the result of a process that had been underway

---

[60] See in particular Helmut Koester, "Apocryphal and Canonical Gospels," *HTR* 73 (1980): 105–130.
[61] No one takes the idea that *Pistis Sophia* contains historical Mary material seriously, and most are pretty guarded also about the *Gospel of Mary*.

since the second century. The process of harmonization is straightforward for the eager interpreter looking for clues in the text. Already Mary Magdalene and Mary of Bethany have similar traits like weeping at a tomb (John 11:33; 20:13; 20:15), and, as we have seen, they are never present in Luke or John together. Both wish to anoint Jesus, Mary in Bethany before the Passover (John 12:1–11) and Mary Magdalene at the tomb (Mark 16:1; Luke 23:56–24:1). Mary of Bethany's anointing of Jesus before the Passover inevitably invites harmonization with the anonymous woman who anoints Jesus in Mark 14:3–9 and Matt. 26:6–13, also just before Passover (Mark 14:1; Matt 26:2), and also in Bethany. That anointing woman, in Simon the Leper's house, similarly invites harmonization with the similar account in Luke 7:36–50, in Simon the Pharisee's house, where another anonymous woman anoints Jesus, a woman who—like Mary of Bethany in John—also wipes Jesus' feet with her hair.[62] It is not an especially circuitous route that takes one from Mary Magdalene and Mary of Bethany to the anonymous woman of Luke 7:36–50, and if one takes that journey, there are elements that might appear to corroborate the identification of all these women, elements that emerge in the early Christian gospels. Like Mary Magdalene and Mary of Bethany, the woman weeps (Luke 7:38, 44), and like Mary of Bethany, she places herself at Jesus' feet (Luke 7:38, 44–46). The stress on her great love for Jesus (Luke 7:47) may have influenced the stress in the *Gospel of Mary* and the *Gospel of Philip* on Jesus' love for her. Further, there is an almost universally ignored link between the story of the "Sinner" and Mary Magdalene in that Mary Magdalene is the first character mentioned by Luke after the story of the "Sinner" (Luke 8:2).[63]

Although we are in the habit of explaining that Pope Gregory made Mary Magdalene into a sex worker, this is not quite right. What Pope Gregory did, like so many before and after him, was to gather several women altogether into one, composite identity. This repentant sex worker is not Mary Magdalene. She is a woman of multiple identities, Mary of Bethany, the sinner of Luke 7, the anointing woman of Mark 14, and, yes, Mary Magdalene too. But to choose to be offended on Mary Magdalene's behalf is to marginalize Mary of Bethany and, for that matter, the anointing woman—or women— at Simon's house.[64]

---

[62] The invitation to harmonize is, of course, different from the question of the sources and influences and interrelationships, orally and textually, of these different stories. Although a good case can be made that Mark 14:3–9, Matt 26:6–13, Luke 7:36–50, and John 12:1–11 all tell essentially the same story, a conclusion on this issue is not necessary to the appreciation of the way that they may have appeared to Christian readers in the early centuries.

[63] For an exception, see Edith Humphrey, Review of Ann Graham Brock, *Mary Magdalene: The First Apostle and the Struggle for Authority*, RBL [http://www.bookreviews.org] (2004),

> However, she is named in first place with the women who heard the news from the mysterious heavenly visitors, and we encounter her early in the Gospel. There she is introduced as one whom Jesus has healed of demon possession and placed at the head of Luke's patron-women (8:1–3). Luke's reference to the ministering women, following the story of the woman with the alabaster jar, implies that Magdalene, along with the other women, were those who "loved much" because they had been healed. In the context of Luke's pairing technique, they become a parallel cohort to the twelve (8:1) and are integral to the story; in the other Gospels, they are named only toward the end.

[64] An unintended but nevertheless problematic result of the insistence that Mary Magdalene was not a sex worker has been an implicit denigration of sex workers in the ancient world as well as in the

The Magdalene Effect

One of the reasons, of course, for our interest in Mary Magdalene is the desire to find a figure who stands as a pioneer of women's leadership in the pages of the NT and, even better, to see evidence of the same representation in other early Christian works.[65] In many respects, Mary Magdalene has proved to be the ideal figure, the first apostle who meets Jesus at the tomb and goes out to preach the gospel. Though the archetypal narrative is in John, Mary Magdalene clearly satisfies even the stringent Lukan criteria for apostles—a witness from Galilee who has seen the risen Jesus and who is commissioned to preach the gospel (Acts 1:21–22). It is this figure who has proved so strong a character in discussions about women's ordination. Furthermore, unlike Junia (Rom 16:7), she has an extended narrative, from Galilee to Jerusalem and beyond. And although the key narrative is in John, she participates in what has become the academic's favorite gospel, Mark, in which she stands at the head of a group of successful women who follow Jesus to the cross, his burial, and his resurrection (Mark 15:40–1, 47; 16:1), in stark contrast to the failing male disciples so beloved of contemporary NT scholarship.

And yet, the ascendancy of Mary of Magdalene in NT scholarship has had the strange effect of marginalizing other women in the gospel story. Her namesake, Mary of Bethany, is chief among them, but the anonymous woman who anoints Jesus in Mark 14:3–9 is another who is now getting much less attention than her named counterpart. Perhaps, in the end, we have become complicit in the kind of marginalization that robbed her of her name, the woman who also bears the right to be called an apostle, as the first to connect Jesus' identity with his mission, anointing Jesus for his burial, whom we are supposed to remember whenever the gospel is preached in the whole world.[66] We

---

contemporary world (as well as condescension toward the anonymous woman of Luke 7.36–50). Feminist attitudes to sex work are famously conflicted, but for a useful exploration of the issues, see Maggie O'Neill, *Prostitution and Feminism: Towards a Politics of Feeling* (Cambridge: Polity, 2001). The issue has gone without comment in studies of Mary Magdalene, which almost always condemn sex work and sex workers without further discussion, though see A. J. Levine, Review of Jane Schaberg with Melanie Johnson-Debaufre, *Mary Magdalene Understood* in *Bible History Daily*, http://www.biblicalarchaeology.org/reviews/mary-magdalene-understood/ (2011), "Also missing in this treatment are the contemporary voices of women from the numerous 'Magdalene' programs that provide rehabilitation and job training. Many of the women in these programs find the image of 'penitent sinner' and redeemed lover not simply meaningful, but life-saving."

[65] This is not a hidden agenda but an open one; cf. Brock, "Setting the Record Straight," 52, repeated in "The identity," 135:

> It is important to acknowledge that current debates concerning the identification of early Christian female leadership, especially the unspecified Marys, are more than merely scholarly exercises. They have implications for reconstructing women's role in early Christianity and female leadership within the early church. This is especially relevant with respect to Mary Magdalene, whose apostolic example has proven pivotal in the debate concerning women's ordination in many Christian congregations today.

[66] This is not to deny that Mark 14:3–9 is a key text in feminist reconstructions of Christian origins (see especially Fiorenza, *In Memory of Her*) but to draw attention to the increasing role of Mary Magdalene as the named standard bearer.

needed a named woman, and for those purposes, Mary Magdalene is the one we have chosen.⁶⁷

The ascendancy of Mary Magdalene in scholarship on early Christianity is a little like the "Matthew effect" whereby prominent figures become ever more prominent and others are increasingly marginalized.⁶⁸ The term is derived from Matt 13:12, "For to those who have, more will be given, and they will have an abundance; but from those who have nothing, even what they have will be taken away."⁶⁹ One might coin a similar term, "the Magdalene effect," according to which Mary Magdalene becomes ever more prominent in our discussions of early Christianity, and Mary of Bethany becomes increasingly marginalized.

The Magdalene effect, however, has not only resulted in a failure to see the traits of Mary of Bethany in the early Christian Mary, but it has also caused us to overlook the apostolic characteristics of this other Mary. In the *First Apocalypse of James*, for example, there is just one mention of Mary in the extant text, and her presence alongside Martha aligns her more closely with Mary of Bethany than with Mary Magdalene. Mary, along with Martha, Salome, and Arsinoe, are singled out by the Lord for James's encouragement (40.22–26). And in the *Acts of Philip* 8.2, Mary prepares the bread and salt for communion while Martha serves the crowds.⁷⁰ Although this is the composite Mary, the reader familiar with the gospels of Luke and John is here reminded of Mary and Martha of Bethany.⁷¹

It might be argued that the stress on Mary Magdalene in recent scholarship runs the risk of making her a kind of special case, *the* apostle to the apostles, a counterpart to the one and only mother of Jesus, revered by tradition as a unique character whose identity and function cannot be imitated by other women.⁷² Of course, this is not the intention

---

⁶⁷ It is worth adding that Mary Magdalene's ascendancy is something mirrored also in popular culture. See, e.g., Mary Ann Beavis, "The Deification of Mary Magdalene," *Feminist Theology* 21 (2012): 145–54, for a discussion of Mary Magdalene as goddess or embodiment of the female divine, exemplified in the work of Margaret Starbird.

⁶⁸ Daniel Rigney, *The Matthew Effect: How Advantage Begets Further Advantage* (New York: Columbia University Press, 2010), 4,

> The term Matthew effect was coined by the Columbia University sociologist Robert K. Merton (1968a) to refer to the commonly observed tendency, noted above, for initial advantages to accumulate through time … In his pioneering studies of prestige systems in scientific communities, Merton demonstrated that prestigious scientists and institutions tend to attract inordinate attention and resources, leading to the further accumulation of prestige, which in turn attracts further resources.

⁶⁹ The term itself ironically illustrates the phenomenon given that the verse in question occurs first in Mark (4:25; see also Luke 8:18; Matt 25:29; and Luke 19:26). The more famous, prominent gospel, Matthew, lends its name to the feature that is thereby illustrated. I am grateful to Stephen Carlson for drawing my attention to "the Matthew effect."

⁷⁰ See above.

⁷¹ See similarly Bovon, "Mary Magdalene in the *Acts of Philip*," 82–3, "At the very beginning of the Christian movement, at the time of the sending of the apostles, her actions evoke the Last Supper, and to have participated in the preparation of the Last Supper confers authority and prestige to Mariamne, of course." Although he notes the motifs of Mary of Bethany in the characterization of the Acts of Philip's Mariamne, Bovon still calls the character "Mary Magdalene."

⁷² Cf. Ardyth L. Bass, "Composition and Redaction in the Coptic Gospel of Mary" (PhD dissertation, Marquette University, 2007), who argues that "feminist scholars have idealized Mary Magdalene as the model disciple, visionary and prophet" (3).

of feminist approaches to Christian origins, which seek, quite rightly, to underline Mary Magdalene's importance in the face of patriarchal distortions of history and tradition. Nevertheless, it is worth remembering that the very patriarchal approaches in question have always acknowledged Mary Magdalene's importance at the tomb but have often used her exceptional status as a subtle means of reinforcing stereotypes of male leadership. Recognizing that Mary Magdalene is not, in fact, unique and that she is one among many female apostles may do more to underscore the scandal of the male-only leadership that far too many interpreters have claimed to find in the text.

2

Which Mary, and Why It Matters

Mary Ann Beavis

Introduction

The title of this chapter echoes that of the book *Which Mary?*;[1] it reflects my interest in the neglected figure of Mary of Bethany.[2] In fact, two previous anthologies have been dedicated to the "which Mary" question; the other is *Mariam, the Magdalene, and the Mother*.[3] However, of the seven or so Marys named in the NT,[4] the only two to receive much attention in these books are Mary Magdalene and Mary of Nazareth, especially the former. Mary of Bethany is mentioned only four times in *Which Mary*, quickly to be dismissed as one of the Marys fused into the composite figure of Mary Magdalene in the early church.[5] Contributor Ann Graham Brock is typical of Mary Magdalene scholars when she admits the possibility that Mary of Bethany may be a "third Mary" in *Pistis Sophia* 1–3, since Martha is also present in the text, but she quickly concludes that "based on the absence of any further designations or concrete indications of a third Mary, we will proceed with Mary Magdalene as the most logical choice of the 'other Mary.'"[6] Similarly, in *Mariam, the Magdalene and the Mother*, Mary of Bethany is mentioned six times, in similar contexts.[7] Notably, in his discussion of the Marys of Manichaeism, J. Kevin Coyle quotes Peter Nagel's opinion that "the link Manichaeans made (and not only they) of Mary Magdalene with Mary of Bethany does not alter the fact that Mary Magdalene is meant."[8]

---

[1] F. Stanley Jones, ed., *Which Mary? The Marys of Early Christian Tradition* (SBLSS 19; Atlanta, GA: Society of Biblical Literature, 2002).
[2] Mary Ann Beavis, "Reconsidering of Bethany," *CBQ* 74 (2012): 281–97; Beavis, "Mary Magdalene and the Hermeneutics of Remembrance," *CBQ* 75 (2013): 739–55.
[3] Deirdre Good, ed., *Mariam, the Magdalene, and the Mother* (Bloomington: Indiana University Press, 2005).
[4] Mary of Nazareth, Mary Magdalene, Mary the mother of James and Joseph (possibly "the "other Mary"), Mary of Bethany, Mary Clopas, Mary of Jerusalem, Mary of Rome (Rom 16:6).
[5] Jones, *Which Mary?*, 8, 41, 43, 48 (see also 124).
[6] Ann Graham Brock, "Setting the Record Straight—The Politics of Identification: Mary Magdalene and Mary the Mother in *Pistis Sophia*," in *Which Mary? The Marys of Early Christian Tradition* (SBLSS 19; Atlanta, GA: Society of Biblical Literature, 2002), 48, n. 10.
[7] Good, *Mariam*, viii, 91, 117, 201, 204, 206.
[8] J. KevinCoyle, "Twelve Years Later: Revisiting the Marys of Manichaeism," in *Mariam, the Magdalene, and the Mother*, ed. Deirdre Good (Bloomington: Indiana University Press, 2005), 206, n. 18, quoting Peter Nagel, "Mariammê—Netzwerferin und Geist der Weisheit," in *Divitiae*

The marked interest in Mary Magdalene reflects the efflorescence of scholarship on that figure undertaken by feminist and nonfeminist researchers (including myself[9]) over the past thirty years, intensified by the vivid popular interest in the Magdalene sparked by the publication of *The Da Vinci Code*.[10] However, the scholarly and cultural fascination with Mary Magdalene has promoted something of a bandwagon mentality, where every Mary mentioned in postbiblical Christian literature is, with little argument, identified as Mary Magdalene based on the circular reasoning that the Magdalene figure was so prominent in the early churches that any *Maria*, *Mariam*, or *Mariamne* mentioned in early Christian literature is probably her, unless otherwise overwhelmingly clearly specified. In view of the often-cited fact that the Western conflation of Mary Magdalene and Mary of Bethany never happened in Eastern Christianity, I became curious as to why there seem to be so few early traditions about Mary of Bethany, in contrast with the many about Mary Magdalene, and whether there were Eastern (or early Western) traditions about Mary of Bethany comparable to the Magdalene traditions. Two monograph-length studies of ancient Martha traditions have been published in recent years,[11] so it would be odd if her sister Mary had been forgotten.

This chapter summarizes some Mary of Bethany traditions uncovered in my previous work, with particular attention to her status as "apostle to the apostles" and holy myrrhbearer. This will be followed by some reflections on why the question of "which Mary" matters and a tentative suggestion about the implications of Mary of Bethany's apostolic persona for the interpretation of Christian art, particularly the ancient *Chairete* scene and the later *Noli me tangere*.

Apostle to the Apostles

In both academic and popular literature, it is common to read the claim that Mary Magdalene was regarded as the "apostle to the apostles" in the early church, a title ascribed to her by Augustine.[12] Prominent scholars who have attributed Mary Magdalene with this supposedly ancient title include, for example, Elisabeth Schüssler Fiorenza, Jane D. Schaberg, Karen King, Bruce Chilton, Ann Graham Brock, Bart Ehrman, and Esther A. De Boer.[13] This scholarship usually traces the earliest usage of the title not

---

Aegypti: Koptologische und verwandte Studien zu Ehren Martin Krause, ed. G. Fluck, Lucia Langener, and Siegfried Richter (Wiesbaden: L. Reichert, 1995), 224, n. 113.

[9] Mary Ann Beavis, "The Deification of Mary Magdalene," *Feminist Theology* 21 (2012): 145–54; Beavis, "The Cathar Mary Magdalene and the Sacred Feminine: Pop Culture Legend vs. Medieval Doctrine," *JRPC* 24 (2012): 419–31; Beavis, "Who is Mary Magdalene?," in *Christian Reflection: A Series in Faith and Ethics. Women in the Bible*, ed. Robert B. Kruschwitz (Waco, TX: Baylor University Press, 2013), 23–9.

[10] Dan Brown, *The Da Vinci Code* (New York: Doubleday, 2003).

[11] Diane E. Peters, *The Many Faces of Martha of Bethany* (Ottawa: St. Paul University, 2008); Allie M. Ernst, *Martha from the Margins: The Authority of Martha in Early Christian Tradition* (Leiden: Brill, 2009).

[12] E.g., http://en.wikipedia.org/wiki/Mary_Magdalene; http://en.wikipedia.org/wiki/Apostle_%28Christian%29.

[13] Elisabeth Schüssler Fiorenza, "Mary Magdalene, Apostle to the Apostles," *Union Theological Seminary Journal* (April 1975): 22–4; Jane D. Schaberg, *The Resurrection of Mary Magdalene: Legends,*

to Augustine but to Hippolytus's *Commentary on the Song of Songs* 25.6, 7 (early third century), where the women who meet with the resurrected Christ "were made apostles to the apostles, having been sent by Christ."[14] However, on closer inspection, it's not so clear that Hippolytus was thinking of Mary *Magdalene* when he wrote these words, for the women he names are Martha and Mary (24.2; 25.3), whom he interprets as fulfilling Song 3:1: "By night I was searching for the one whom my soul loved. ... See this fulfilled in *Martha and Mary*" (italics added).[15] In fact, as Yancy Warren Smith notes, Hippolytus actually shows a preference for Martha over Mary: "According to Hippolytus, Martha both anoints Christ (*In Cant*. 2.29) and is primary witness of the resurrection to the apostles, personally vouchsafed by the resurrected Christ (*In Cant.* 25)."[16] More germane to my topic, the women lauded by Hippolytus as apostles are the so-called Bethany sisters (Luke 10:38–41; John 11:1–45; 12:1–8), not Mary Magdalene, almost four centuries *before* Gregory the Great's authoritative pronouncement in 591 that Mary Magdalene, Mary of Bethany, and the sinful woman who anointed Jesus' feet were one and the same.

The association of Martha and Mary with the empty tomb/resurrection is not unique to Hippolytus, but it is found quite often in early Christian literature: for example, in a fragment of Hippolytus's commentary on Exodus, and in both the Coptic and Ethiopic versions of the *Epistle of the Apostles* (9.1).[17] The Georgian, Armenian, and Paleo-Slavonic translations of the Hippolytus commentary all attest to the presence of the Bethany sisters at the empty tomb.[18] In her study of ancient Martha traditions, Allie M. Ernst found that an early tradition of Mary and Martha at the empty tomb was geographically and temporally widespread;[19] John A. Cerrato observes that "a tradition did flourish in the second century which placed Martha and Mary (perhaps with Mary Magdalene already identified as Mary of Bethany) at the tomb and made much of their presence."[20]

Thus, the commonplace assertion that Mary Magdalene was called the apostle to the apostles in the early church is unfounded—the only early writer to use this phrase, Hippolytus, used the title with reference to Mary the sister of Martha, and to Martha herself. It's impossible to know whether Mary of Bethany and Mary Magdalene had

---

Apocrypha, and the Christian Testament (New York: Continuum, 2002), 1, 86, 89, 91, 99; Karen L. King, *The Gospel of Mary of Magdala: Jesus and the First Woman Apostle* (Santa Rosa, CA: Polebridge, 2003), 142; Ann Graham Brock, *Mary Magdalene, The First Apostle: The Struggle for Authority* (HThS 51; Cambridge, MA: Harvard University Press, 2003), 161; Bruce Chilton, *Mary Magdalene: A Biography* (New York: Doubleday, 2005), 114; Bart D. Ehrman, *Peter, Paul, and Mary Magdalene: The Followers of Jesus in History and Legend* (Oxford: Oxford University Press, 2011), 253; Esther A. De Boer, *The Mary Magdalene Cover-up: Sources behind the Myth* (London: T&T Clark, 2015), 113.

[14] Translation by Yancy Warren Smith, "Hippolytus' Commentary on the Song of Songs in Social and Critical Context" (PhD dissertation, Brite Divinity School, 2009), 356–7.
[15] Ibid., 356.
[16] Ibid., 343, n.b.
[17] For other examples, see Beavis, "Reconsidering," 289; "Mary of Bethany," 741.
[18] See Smith, "Hippolytus," 351. A Greek paraphrase simply refers to the women at the tomb without naming them.
[19] Ernst, *Martha*, xiv, 7, 16, 163, 175.
[20] John A. Cerrato, *Hippolytus between East and West: The Commentaries and the Provenance of the Corpus* (Oxford: Oxford University Press, 2002), 15.

been blended into a single figure by Hippolytus's time, or whether Hippolytus was relying on an extra-biblical tradition where the Bethany sisters, not Mary Magdalene and various other women, were identified as the women at the tomb. Certainly there were differences of opinion as to whether the Marys were one or many in the third and fourth centuries, but prior to the famous dictum of Gregory the Great, there was no consensus.[21] So, contrary to the assertions cited above, the "original" apostle to the apostles was Mary of Bethany, along with Martha, not Mary Magdalene. Augustine never used the title with reference to any of them, although he did describe Mary Magdalene's visit to the tomb as "ocular proof" of the resurrection (*Commentary on John* 35, col. 1955–9), and Jerome called her "the first before the apostles" to see the risen Christ (Jerome, E. CXXVII *ad Principiam virginem*, 22, col. 1090). In fact, the medievalist Katherine Ludwig Jansen was unable to find any reference to Mary Magdalene as *apostolorum apostola* prior to the twelfth century, although she notes that by that time, the title had passed into common currency.[22]

There are many other possible (or probable) references in early Christian literature to Mary of Bethany that have been overhastily assumed by scholars to be references to Mary Magdalene. Among writings where both Mary and Martha (or Mary "Magdalene" and Martha) figure in various roles are *Pistis Sophia*, the Manichaean Psalms, a Greek version of the *Gospel of Nicodemus*, and the *Acts of Philip*.[23] In addition, several of the documents that scholars have offered as evidence of Mary Magdalene's importance in early (especially sectarian) Christianity do not specifically identify the woman as "Mary Magdalene" but simply refer to a Mary (*Mariam, Mariamne*) who shares many of the attributes of the biblical Mary of *Bethany*:[24] she is especially loved by Jesus (John 11:5; cf. 12:1–8); Jesus converses with her (John 11:28–33; Luke 10:38–42); she is rebuked by a disciple and defended by Jesus (Luke 10:40–42; John 12:7–8); Jesus commends Mary (Luke 10:42; John 12:7–8); Martha is present (Luke 10:38–42; John 12:1–18). If the extra-biblical references are interpreted as references to Mary of *Bethany*, as opposed to Mary Magdalene, then she appears in a stellar array of roles:

> disciple, apostle to the apostles, symbol of the church, new Eve, participant at the Last Supper, myrrh-bearing witness to the empty tomb and resurrection, administrator, deacon, miracle-worker, baptiser, eucharistic minister, missionary, preacher, Gnostic illuminata, and martyr.[25]

Commenting on a Greek hymn dated prior to the sixth century that portrays the myrrhbearing Martha and Mary weeping by the tomb of Christ and being comforted by an angel, Ernst remarks that "insofar as there has been a fusion of Mary Magdalene

---

[21] See Magdalen LaRow, "The Iconography of Mary Magdalene: The Evolution of a Western Tradition Until 1300" (PhD dissertation, New York University, 1982), 4–10.

[22] Katherine Ludwig Jansen, *The Making of the Magdalen: Preaching and Popular Devotion in the Later Middle Ages* (Princeton, NJ: Princeton University Press, 2000), 62. Jansen excludes the Hippolytus reference because "the Latin version is modern, made from a Georgian text" (67, n. 47). As argued above, it should also be excluded because the Mary in question is not the Magdalene.

[23] For specific references, see Beavis, "Reconsidering," 290–1.

[24] For specific references, see ibid., 291–3.

[25] Beavis, "Mary of Bethany," 755.

with Mary of Bethany, this fusion has resulted in the absorption of the Magdalene into Mary of Bethany, rather than the reverse."[26] That is, in the Eastern tradition, Mary the sister of Martha was usually identified as the Mary at the empty tomb and resurrection. I suggest that this observation applies to many of the ancient texts interpreted as evidence of Mary Magdalene's significance to early Christians; the Mary they revered as "apostle to the apostles" was the sister of Martha. Even if the Mary of these documents is a "composite figure" who fuses the two Marys, the significant role of Mary of Bethany in the construction of this figure has not been adequately recognized by scholars; indeed, it has been suppressed so as to highlight the preeminence of Mary Magdalene.

Mary and Martha as Myrrhophores

How did some early Christians come to identify the myrrhbearing women at the empty tomb as Mary and Martha, as opposed to the several female characters, notably Mary Magdalene, explicitly mentioned in the Gospels? The answer seems to lie in the way that the female characters in Jesus' circle are presented in the Gospel of John. Unlike the Synoptics,[27] John does not introduce Mary Magdalene as one of Jesus' female followers from Galilee. The first "Mary" (*Mariam*) mentioned is Mary the sister of Martha and Lazarus, whom Jesus "loved" (John 11:5). When Jesus approaches Bethany and is informed by Martha that her brother has died, Jesus calls for her sister Mary, who is at home in mourning; when she meets him, she falls at his feet, and Jesus is so moved by her tears that he begins weeping himself (11:23–33). Subsequently, he raises Lazarus from the tomb (11:38–44). The raising of Lazarus induces "many of the Jews" who had been with Mary to believe in him (11:45). The next Johannine incident with Mary and Martha, in the house of Lazarus, is the scene where Mary anoints Jesus' feet with nard; she is challenged by Judas and commended by Jesus for buying the ointment to keep for the day of his burial (12:7). These stories associate the sisters with resurrection (11:25) and, especially Mary, with the burial of Jesus (12:7).

Mary Magdalene is first mentioned by John, without any introduction, as one of the women at the foot of the cross, along with Jesus' mother, his mother's sister, and Mary Clopas (19:25). Next, she is mentioned as the first to find the empty tomb (20:1–2), after which she tells Peter and the beloved disciple that the body is gone. Most famously, the weeping Mary Magdalene meets the risen Jesus in John 20:11–18, and she is commissioned to announce the resurrection to the disciples, which she does (20:17–18). Here, both NT spellings of Mary are used to refer to the Magdalene, *Maria* (20:1) and *Mariam* (20:16, 18), the latter of which, Mariam, always refers to the sister of Martha and Lazarus in the NT.

It is easy to see how an ancient reader of John might identify the Mary (*Mariam*) associated with the raising of Lazarus, signifying that Jesus is the "resurrection and the

---

[26] Ernst, *Martha*, 130.
[27] Mark 15:40–51; Matt 27:55–56; Luke 8:1–3.

life" (11:25), and with the anointing scene, where the ointment for Jesus' burial is used instead to honor him for raising Mary's brother (12:7),[28] with the *Maria/Mariam* of the empty tomb and resurrection accounts.[29] Notably, John's Mary Magdalene, unlike the women witnesses of the Synoptics, does *not* visit the tomb to anoint the body; she goes there to weep (20:11, 13, 15; cf. the lachrymose Mary of Bethany in 11:31, 33). When she finds the empty tomb, she tells not only Peter but also the disciple Jesus loved about it, echoing the notice in John 11:5 that Jesus *loved* Martha and her sister and Lazarus. It would be easy to surmise that the Mary at the empty tomb was the same one introduced in John 11:1 and that this Mary informed the "beloved disciple" because he was her brother, Lazarus. In view of the proximity of Bethany to Jerusalem (11:18), and the association of the anointing at Bethany with the burial of Jesus (John 12:8; Mark 14:8; Matt 26:12), it would a short step to conclude that Mary "Magdalene" must have been accompanied by her sister when she met with Jesus—a surmise encouraged by the varying names and numbers of women in the Synoptic empty tomb/resurrection narratives (Mark 16:8;[30] Matt 28:1;[31] cf. Mark 16:9[32]), especially Luke 24:10, which mentions that it was "Mary Magdalene, Joanna, Mary mother of James, and *the other women with them*" who told the apostles about the empty tomb. In the early Christian imagination, the "other women" likely included the Bethany sisters, especially the Mary who had anointed him.

Why It Matters

Why does it matter which Mary was the "apostle to the apostles" of early Christian tradition? Certainly, in canonical terms, in the sense that Mary Magdalene is the foremost of the women commissioned to "go and tell his disciples" that Jesus is risen in the Gospels (Mark 16:7; Matt 28:7; John 20:17–18; cf. Luke 24:8), she functions as such. However, the frequent assertion that the Magdalene is the apostle to the apostles referred to by Hippolytus is highly tendentious and makes me wonder if some of the scholars who make it have simply relied on secondary references. Those who have consulted Hippolytus tend to conveniently disregard the preeminence of *Martha* in Hippolytus's exposition, not to mention the absence of the title "Magdalene." This seems to me to be a massaging of the evidence to assert the presence of Mary Magdalene that is not only inaccurate but also misleading to other scholars and to the many nonacademic readers who have enthusiastically taken up the "apostle to the apostles" factoid. Moreover, the rush to see Mary Magdalene in as many early Christian texts as possible to bolster her apostolic significance is not only academically questionable, but from the standpoint of feminist biblical scholarship, it has also led

---

[28] Cf. John 19:38–39, where Joseph of Arimathea and Nicodemus anoint the body.
[29] As Raymond E. Brown notes, the spelling of the name translated in English as Mary "fluctuates wildly" between *Maria* and *Mariam* in the Johannine textual tradition (*The Gospel according to John XIII-XXI* [AB 29A; Garden City, NY: Doubleday, 1970], 990).
[30] Mary Magdalene; Mary, the mother of James and Jose; and Salome.
[31] Mary Magdalene and the other Mary.
[32] Mary Magdalene.

to the downplaying of another significant biblical woman, Mary of Bethany, and, to a lesser extent, of Martha as well.[33]

Mary of Bethany, the *Chairete* and the *Noli Me Tangere*

Whether or not the kind of scriptural imagination concerning the Johannine Marys suggested above is behind the ancient tradition of Mary and Martha at the tomb, this motif is ancient, as witnessed by iconographic evidence collected by Allie Ernst: a Syrian Gospel illumination; an Egyptian amulet; three Ethiopian Gospel books; and an image of "Martha and Mary bearing spices" in a Mozarabic manuscript, all dated between the fifth and seventh centuries.[34] Ernst suggests that the tradition of the Bethany sisters as myrrhbearers originated in the Easter celebrations of the ancient churches, especially in the East.[35] The art historian Diane Apostolos-Cappadona notes that in early Christian and Byzantine art from the fifth to the seventh centuries, the women at the tomb were often shown as two in number, sometimes with one standing, head bowed, and one kneeling at the feet of the angel, or of the risen Christ, as seen in Figure 2.1.[36] Similarly, according to Gertrud Schiller, in the iconography of the other prominent Gospel resurrection story, the raising of Lazarus, from the fourth century onward, "one of Lazarus' sisters often kneels at Christ's feet ... —from the fifth century onwards both may do so."[37] This composition is seen in Figure 2.2.[38] Further,

> by the seventh century, the icon identified as the *Chairete* is confirmed as the visualization of the apostolic charge to Mary Magdalene ... This is the scriptural first encounter between the risen Christ and the two Marys, following the arrival at and discovery of the empty tomb, the announcement of the Resurrection by the angel, and the dispersal of the male apostles at the empty tomb. In this icon, the risen Christ holds a scroll in his left hand pressed against his abdomen, perhaps to highlight his side wound, as he raises his hand in a gesture of greeting to the two

---

[33] There are several recent studies that highlight the canonical Mary and Martha: Satoko Yamaguchi, *Mary & Martha: Women in the World of Jesus* (Maryknoll, NY: Orbis, 2002); Mary Stromer Hanson, *The New Perspective on Mary and Martha* (Eugene, OR: Wipf & Stock, 2013); see also Philip F. Esler and Ronald Piper, *Lazarus, Mary and Martha: Social-Scientific Approaches to the Gospel of John* (Minneapolis, MN: Fortress, 2006); Adele Reinhartz, "From Narrative to History: The Resurrection of Mary and Martha," in *"Women Like This": New Perspectives on Jewish Women in the Greco-Roman World*, ed. Amy-Jill Levine (Atlanta, GA: Scholars, 1991), 161–84.

[34] Ernst, *Martha from the Margins*, 139–76. For further discussion, see Beavis, "Mary of Bethany," 748. Cf. LaRow, "Iconography," 25.

[35] Ernst, *Martha*, 139.

[36] Diane Apostolos-Cappadona, "On the Visual and the Vision: The Magdalene in Early Christian and Byzantine Art and Culture," in *Mariam, the Magdalene and the Mother*, ed. Deirdre Good (Bloomington: Indiana University Press, 2005), 139–40. See also LaRow, "Iconography," 29.

[37] Gertrud Schiller, *Iconography of Early Christian Art*, vol. 1, trans. Janet Seligman (Greenwich, CT: New York Graphic Society, 1966), 282. See also Robin M. Jensen, "The Raising of Lazarus," *BRev* 11 (1995): 20–28, 45; Esler and Piper, *Lazarus*, 75–103.

[38] Image is from O. M. Dalton, *Catalogue of the Ivory Carvings of the Christian Era with Examples of Mohammedan Art and Carvings in Bone* (London: Longmans, 1909), plate 12, fig. 27. On the Grado Ivories, see Kurt Weitzmann, "The Ivories of the Grado Chair," *Dumbarton Oaks* 26 (1972): 43–91.

Figure 2.1 *Chairete:* Christ appearing to the Holy Women, Sinai Icon Collection, seventh century. Used with permission of Transfer from UM History of Art Visual Resources Collections History of Art, University of Michigan.

Figure 2.2 Raising of Lazarus, Grado Ivory, eighth century. British Museum. Source: O. M. Dalton, *Catalogue of the Ivory Carvings of the Christian Era with Examples of Mohammedan Art and Carvings in Bone* (London: Longmans, 1909), plate 12, fig. 27.

women that the Byzantine tradition identifies as his mother, the *Theotokos*, or the God-bearer, and Mary Magdalene.[39]

The *Chairete* scene sometimes straightforwardly illustrates Matt 28:9, where the two women take hold of Jesus' feet,[40] but others, like the famous Sinai icon (Figure 2.1), show two women, one standing, one kneeling.[41] If there is a biblical scene that the *Chairete* represents, perhaps it is not simply an illustration of the Matthean story. Rather, it is conceivable that the earliest viewers of such images imagined them as Mary and *Martha*, or two Marys, one of whom was Mary of Bethany, in her characteristic pose at the feet of Jesus (John 11:32; 12:3; cf. Luke 10:39).[42] By the seventh century, as in the Sinai icon, Martha is replaced by the Theotokos,[43] and the other Mary is fully identified with Mary Magdalene. However, the ancient tradition of Mary and Martha as witnesses to the empty tomb and resurrection, "apostles to the apostles," is preserved in the Byzantine tradition of the Holy Myrrhophores, who, as Ernst has shown, continued to be identified as Martha and Mary post-Constantine.[44] This ancient identification of the women at the tomb continues to be acknowledged in the Orthodox tradition, which includes four (or five) Marys, including Mary Magdalene and Mary of Bethany, as well as Martha, among the myrrhbearing women.[45]

In Western art, the characteristic kneeling posture of Mary of Bethany is echoed in the many portrayals of the *Noli Me Tangere* scene, which purports to be an illustration of John 20:11–18, Mary Magdalene's meeting with the risen Jesus at the garden tomb. Barbara Baert notes that the scene has been "an important convention

---

[39] Apostolos-Cappadona, "On the Visual and the Vision," 139–40.
[40] As, e.g., in the Rabbula Gospels (http://www.thebyzantinelegacy.com/rabbula-gospels).
[41] See, e.g., https://www.thebyzantinelegacy.com/diptych-milan. For variations on the *Chairete* scene, see Erik Thunø, *Image and Relic: Mediating the Sacred in Early Medieval Rome* (Roma: «L'Erma» di Brettschneider, 2002), 98–101; P. Konis, "The Post-Resurrection Appearances of Christ. The Case of the Chairete or 'All Hail,'" *Rosetta* 1 (2006): 31–40.
[42] A Byzantine ivory panel (twelfth century) features three scenes: the Transfiguration (top), the raising of Lazarus (center), and the *Chairete* (bottom), with two women, one keeling and one standing in the latter two. The image, held at the Victoria and Albert Museum, is not viewable online (http://collections.vam.ac.uk/item/O72850/scenes-from-the-life-of-panel-unknown/).
[43] See Beavis, "Mary of Bethany," 748. M. R. James noted the tendency of ancient Egyptian Christianity to identify the Virgin Mary with all the other Marys of the Gospels: "In the Book of Bartholomew the appearance of Christ to Magdalene after the resurrection is turned into an appearance to his mother: and so too in another Coptic fragment on the Passion" (*The Apocryphal New Testament* [Oxford: Clarendon, 1953], 88). A notable example is from the twentieth discourse of Cyril of Jerusalem:

> I was a child promised to God, and my parents dedicated me to Him before I came into the world. My parents ... were of the tribe of Judah and house of David. My father was Joakim, which is being interpreted Kleopa. My mother was Anna ... who was usually called Mariham. I am Mary Magdalen because the name of the village wherein I was born was Magdalia. My name is Mary of Cleopa. I am Mary of James the son of Joseph the carpenter. (ibid., 87)

[44] Ernst, *Martha*, 167.
[45] Mary Magdalene, Mary of James, Mary Clopas, Mary and Martha of Bethany, Joanna, Salome, and Susanna. Sometimes the Theotokos is included among the Myrrhophores.

Figure 2.3 *Noli Me Tangere*. Mary Magdalene with Christ, ivory carved in Spain, ca. 1120. Metropolitan Museum of Art, Gift of J. Pierpont Morgan, 1917. Accession no. 17.190.47 (CC0).

since the early Middle Ages."[46] Innumerable iterations depict the Magdalene kneeling or prostrate before Jesus.[47] However, John does not portray the meeting between the risen Jesus and Mary this way: when Jesus calls her by name (as *Mariam*, not the usual *Maria* for Mary Magdalene), she does *not* fall down before him but turns to him and greets him as *rabboni*, after which he instructs her not to hold on to

---

[46] Barbara Baert, "Touching with the Gaze: A Visual Analysis of the *Noli me tangere*," in *Noli me tangere— Mary Magdalene: One Person, Many Images*, ed. Barbara Baert et al. (Leuven: Peeters, 2006), 44.
[47] See Barbara Baert, Reimund Bieringer, Karlijn Demasure, and Sabine Van Den Eynde, eds., *Noli me tangere—Mary Magdalene: One Person, Many Images* (Leuven: Peeters, 2006), 55–118.

him (as in Figure 2.3)—in Latin, *noli me tangere* (John 20:17).[48] This artistic motif is so entrenched that the art historian Magdalen LaRow mistakenly assumed that John 20:11-18 portrays Mary falling at Jesus' feet, which it manifestly does not.[49] It's impossible to determine definitively when and where the convention of painting this scene with Mary kneeling originated; possibly, artists simply considered it fitting or natural for her to bow down before the risen Christ. Likely, there is some influence from the older *Chairete* scene. A third and final influence, as suggested above, is the kneeling Mary of Bethany (John 11:32; 12:3; Luke 10:39), in a pose reminiscent of her stance in the raising of Lazarus (Figure 2.2),[50] and Luke's portrayal of Mary sitting at the feet of Jesus (Figure 2.4).[51]

The question of "which Mary," then, has implications beyond questioning the academic and popular overemphasis on the singular figure of Mary Magdalene and the restoration of the memory of Mary of Bethany as an apostle to the apostles, who functioned in many other roles besides, notably, holy myrrhbearer. Barbara Baert describes the dynamic of the *Noli me tangere* as "*Mary Magdalene hankers and Christ recoils* … The iconographic history … is situated within the *contraposto* of feminine desire and masculine prohibition."[52] The artistic insertion of the kneeling pose from the Bethany stories introduces an element of female abjection and male rejection that is not found in any of the Gospel scenes of Mary at Jesus' feet (Luke 10:38; John 11:32; 12:3), where she is praised for her insight and devotion.[53] The *Noli me tangere* chooses not to portray, or even suggest, the immediate sequel, the risen Christ's apostolic commission to Mary to proclaim the resurrection to the disciples, which she faithfully carries out (John 20:17b-18). From a feminist standpoint, the question here is not whether the Mary intended was the Magdalene or the sister of Martha, but "which Mary" the iconographic tradition reifies: the abject supplicant or the commissioned apostle?[54] The answer is overwhelmingly the former. However, the impact of feminist theology on even this entrenched tradition is beginning to be seen, for example, in the works of contemporary artists such as Katharina Kraus (1980), Jan Vanriet (1993-4), Claire vanden Abbeele (1999), Lucy D'Souza-Krone (2005), Malou Swinnen (2005), Brody Neuenschwander (2006),[55] and Lilian Broca, whose forthcoming Mary

---

[48] See also LaRow, "Iconography," 45-7.
[49] Ibid., 32.
[50] On the typological correspondence between the raising of Lazarus and the resurrection in early Christian art, see J. Spencer Northcote and W. R. Brownlow, *Roma Sotterranea: An Account of the Roman Catacombs, Especially of the Cemetery of St. Callixtus*, vol. 2 (London: Longmans, Green, 1897), 99-100.
[51] This is a pose that, like the *Noli me tangere*, has frequently been the subject of Western art, e.g., Velásquez, Vermeer, Aertsen, Overbeck, Jouvenet, Steen, Campi, Adrianssen, Moser, and many others.
[52] Baert, "Touching with the Gaze," 44. Baert's essay does not discuss the implications of the kneeling pose in these artworks.
[53] Even the scene of the anonymous "sinful woman" who anoints Jesus' feet (Luke 7:36-50) is commended for her piety.
[54] On the relationship between feminist theology and art, see Mary Ann Beavis, "The Influence of Feminist Theology on Canadian Women Artists," in *Feminist Theology with a Canadian Accent: Canadian Perspectives on Feminist Contextual Theology*, ed. Mary Ann Beavis, with Elaine Guillemin and Barbara Pell (Ottawa: Novalis, 2008), 291-306.
[55] Baert et al., *Noli me tangere*, 88-104.

Which Mary, and Why It Matters 37

Figure 2.4 Jesus, Mary and Martha Window, Holy Trinity Church, West Sussex, 1860s. Source: By Antiquary—Own work, CC BY 4.0, https://commons.wikimedia.org/w/index.php?curid=58087146.

Magdalene series features a *Noli me tangere* with an ecstatic Mary running toward the risen Jesus (see Figure 2.5) and culminates with a messianic Mary enthroned next to an empty space for the absent Christ.

Figure 2.5 *Noli me tangere,* sketch, Lilian Broca, 2017 (printed with permission of the artist).

3

Why Mary?
The Gospel of Mary *and Its Heroine*

Judith Hartenstein

The *Gospel of Mary* is one of the very few gospels from ancient Christianity named after a woman and—as far as I know—the only one that is at least partly preserved.[1] It therefore attracts attention in a broader public as well as in scholarly circles. Those who take the trouble to read the text tend to be disappointed, though. Most of the *Gospel of Mary* is not what modern readers (especially feminist women) expect or hope from the title. The *Gospel of Mary* discusses the dissolution of matter, the sin of the world, the existence of the son of man, and the ascent of the soul. Only the end of the gospel, which depicts the conflict between Peter and Mary, seems to meet the expectations of modern readers.

However, the *Gospel of Mary* is not a modern text; it is a writing from antiquity, probably composed in the second century.[2] Why was it called the *Gospel of Mary*? How is Mary presented in the text? What implications did the name[3] have for early Christian readers? What does the choice of the name and the presentation of Mary tell us about the place of the *Gospel of Mary* in early Christianity?

---

[1] The *Gospel of Mary* is the first writing of the Coptic codex BG 8502 from the fourth or fifth century and covers pp. 7–10 and 15–19,5. Probably ten pages of the text are missing (pp. 1–6 und 11–14). In addition to the Coptic version, two Greek fragments from the third century have survived (P.Oxy 3525 and P.Ryl 463) but do not add to the known text. Cf. Karen L. King, *The Gospel of Mary of Magdala: Jesus and the First Woman Apostle* (Santa Rosa, CA: Polebridge, 2003), 7–12; Christopher Tuckett, *The Gospel of Mary* (Oxford Early Christian Gospel Texts; Oxford: Oxford University Press, 2007), 3–10.
[2] In my opinion, it should be dated in the second half of the second century, Tuckett, *Gospel*, 12, and King, *Gospel*, 184, suggest an earlier date.
[3] I am presuming that Mary is Mary Magdalene. She is only called Mary (ⲘⲀⲢⲒϨⲀⲘⲘ) as no other Mary present makes a further identification necessary. The interactions between the disciples and their respective address as brother and sister show clearly that she is not the mother of Jesus. Cf. Esther A. de Boer, *The Gospel of Mary: Beyond a Gnostic and a Biblical Mary Magdalene*, JSNTSS 260 (London: T&T Clark, 2004), 17–18; Tuckett, *Gospel*, 15–18. The use of John 20:17–18 points to Mary Magdalene while specific attributes of Mary of Bethany are missing: Martha is not present and neither ointment nor tomb are mentioned. Cf. Chapter 2 by Mary Ann Beavis. Only Peter's statement that Jesus loved her more than he loved the other women (*Gos. Mary* BG p. 10,1-3) could be considered as a reference to Mary of Bethany (John 11:5). However, the comparison to the other women seems to imply a special status like the leading position of Mary Magdalene in the lists names in Mark 15:40 and parallels.

The Title: Gospel according to Mary

In the Coptic manuscript of the *Gospel of Mary*, the title ⲠⲈⲨⲀⲄⲄⲈⲖⲒⲞⲚ ⲔⲀⲦⲀ ⲘⲀⲢⲒϨⲀⲘⲘ is found at the usual place at the end of the manuscript (BG p. 19,3-5).[4] Apart from a Coptic article at the beginning (Ⲡ-ⲈⲨⲀⲄⲄⲈⲖⲒⲞⲚ), the wording of the title is Greek; it is the same manner in which the canonical (Mark, John) and other apocryphal gospels (*Gospel of Thomas*) are titled. As the grammatical construction with the preposition κατά is specific and unlikely to be used independently by different authors, a first conclusion is possible: Whoever gave the *Gospel of Mary* its title knew the titles of other gospels and saw the *Gospel of Mary* as part of this group of texts and as somehow similar to them.[5]

Although the grammatical construction of the title is the same, the roles of the persons named in the titles differ in the gospels. He or she is the one who guarantees the content of the gospel, has a position as witness, writer, or author. In the Gospel of Mark, the name might be a recollection of a real author—but the name does not appear at all in the text of the gospel. Matthew is a character in the gospel named after him, but there is no indication in the text that he has something to do with the writing of the gospel. In the Gospel of Luke, the author addresses the reader explicitly in the prologue (Luke 1:1–4) but without giving his or her name—the name Luke is not mentioned in the text. The Gospel of John, on the other hand, tells us that the "beloved disciple," who is not named throughout the gospel, wrote the gospel (John 21:24). The name "John" in the title might be an early Christian interpretation of this figure, an attempt to identify him with a known disciple. Even though the gospels of Luke and John give some information on the author (quite different in character), none of the canonical gospels show a clear connection between the name in the title and the text of the gospel.

The case is different in the *Gospel of Thomas*. At the beginning, Thomas is introduced as the writer of the sayings of Jesus, a position more like a scribe than like an author, although he probably comments on his work (*Gos. Thom.* 1: "Whoever discovers the interpretation of these sayings will not taste death"). In *Gos. Thom.* 13, Thomas appears for a second (and last) time in the gospel. His ability to understand Jesus much better than Peter and Matthew shows his qualification for his position.[6] Moreover, Jesus tells him some words the others do not hear and are not told—thus the *Gospel of Thomas* might actually contain secret words as is stated at the beginning.

The position of Mary in the *Gospel of Mary* is in several ways similar to the position of Thomas in the *Gospel of Thomas*. She is mentioned in the text and has an important role in it as she delivers significant words of Jesus to the other disciples. Nearly half of the *Gospel of Mary* is direct speech of Mary! Like Thomas, Mary is a disciple with great understanding and closeness to Jesus: She comforts the disciples after Jesus has left, she does not waver at the vision of Jesus, and she is known and loved by Jesus.

---

[4] For the Greek fragment P.Ryl 463, this title can be reconstructed.
[5] Cf. Tuckett, *Gospel*, 33–4.
[6] Cf. Ann Graham Brock, *Mary Magdalene, the First Apostle: The Struggle for Authority*, HThS 51 (Cambridge, MA: Harvard University Press, 2003), 76–7.

Like Thomas, Mary is acquainted with words of Jesus unknown to the others. In the extant text of the *Gospel of Mary*, Mary is not commissioned to write the words of Jesus, although something like that could have been written on the first now lost pages. It is more likely in my opinion, though, that Mary is not seen as the writer but as the preacher of Jesus' words as this is actually narrated in the gospel itself.

There are other gospels from the second century in which the person named in the title has a special position in the text. The *Gospel of Peter* is—as far as we know from the few fragments we have—a text written in the first person with Peter as the speaker. He might have been requested to write the gospel in the now lost parts of the text. In the *Apocryphon of John*, the *First Apocalypse of James*, and the *Apocryphon of James*, John and James respectively receive a revelation of Jesus and are told how and to whom they should transmit it. In the *Gospel of Judas*, Judas is the most important dialogue partner of Jesus although Jesus talks to the Twelve as well. It seems to be typical for second-century gospels[7] to refer in the text itself to an authority well qualified to witness the content of the gospel and to use the name in the title.[8]

Nevertheless, the comparison shows some differences between Mary, Thomas, and the others as well.[9] While Mary willingly shares her knowledge of the words of Jesus (*Gos. Mary* BG p. 10,7-9), Thomas does not. He is certain the other disciples are unable to understand them and anticipates violence against himself in consequence (*Gos. Thom.* 13). In the *Gospel of Mary*, Peter and Andrew attack Mary verbally and do not understand what she is saying, but Levi defends her and the discussions among the group continue (BG p. 17,10-18,15). Both Thomas and Mary have a special position and exclusive knowledge, but they act in a different manner. Thomas draws a clear line between himself and the other disciples, and shares his secrets only with the readers of the gospel, thereby exalting their position as a special and separate group, too. Mary, on the other hand, tries to convince Peter and the whole group (*Gos. Mary* BG p. 9,14-20; 10,7-9; 18,1-5). Throughout the *Gospel of Mary*, the disciples address each other as brother and sister (BG p. 9,14; 10,1-2; 17,11; 18,2) Although it remains open whether Mary and Levi are successful in their strategy to win Peter and Andrew, there is no separation. The writings ascribed to James show an even stricter separation between James and the Twelve than the *Gospel of Thomas*. Both of them seem to start a tradition not available to everyone. Their special relationship to Jesus—as brother and twin— has an excluding effect.[10]

To sum up: The *Gospel of Mary* has a patroness in its title who is presented in the gospel as well qualified for her task. She has understanding, insights, and a special position with Jesus, which leads to exclusive knowledge. At the same time, she tries to include the whole group. As a woman well known as the most important female

---

[7] The Gospel of John might be included here.
[8] Cf. Judith Hartenstein, "Autoritätskonstellation in apokryphen und kanonischen Evangelien," in *Jesus in apokryphen Evangelienüberlieferungen: Beiträge zu außerkanonischen Jesusüberlieferungen aus verschiedenen Sprach- und Kulturtraditionen*, ed. Jörg Frey and Jens Schröter, WUNT 254 (Tübingen: Mohr Siebeck, 2010), 423-44, 438.
[9] Cf. ibid., 429.
[10] Cf. ibid., 430.

follower of Jesus, she can fill this position very well.[11] In contrast to Thomas and James, she does not stand for a separate branch of early Christianity.

Traditions in the *Gospel of Mary*: The Ascent of the Soul

So far, I have tried to show that Mary as a widely known and acceptable disciple might be a suitable choice for a gospel appealing to a broader public. The *Gospel of Mary* does not present itself as aiming at a small separate group. However, Mary has an exclusive message as well; she is telling words of Jesus nobody else has heard. Was she already connected to the ideas she is expressing in the *Gospel of Mary*? Are there "Mary-traditions" to be found in the gospel?[12] Or are there other possible reasons why she is connected to the content of the gospel?

The most important part of Mary's speech (*Gos. Mary* BG p. 10,10-17,7) is concerned with the ascent of the soul. As there are some pages missing in the middle of the gospel, we do not know how the report about the ascent of the soul was introduced and whose soul is being talked about. Probably Mary repeats words of Jesus, who narrates adventures of the soul overcoming hostile powers on its way up. The idea of a heavenly journey of the soul, often after death, can be found in many religious contexts. Hostile powers trying to stop it are included in some of them.

The closest parallel to the text of the *Gospel of Mary* can be found in the *Book of Allogenes* from Codex Tchacos (CT pp. 59-66).[13] Allogenes hears a voice from a cloud of light promising him his future ascent that evil powers cannot prevent. This text contains close parallels to the first six of the seven names of the fourth of the evil powers in the *Gospel of Mary* (BG p. 16,4-13) and then a lacuna; so maybe the last name was mentioned too. The *Book of Allogenes* was probably composed later than the *Gospel of Mary*. The figure of Allogenes is well known from another writing in Nag Hammadi Codex XI and other sources. I cannot see any connection to Mary. Possibly both the *Gospel of Mary* and the *Book of Allogenes* used a source including the names of the powers, but the *Gospel of Mary* might have revised this source more extensively.

In the *Book of Allogenes*, Allogenes is given instructions about his future ascent: after the dissolution of his body, he will encounter the powers but will be able to overcome them by giving specific answers to their questions. A similar setting is found in the *First Apocalypse of James*; here, James is addressed.[14] *Gospel of Thomas* 50 is a shorter dialogue about the same topics that might concern the ascent of the disciples, though not necessarily a postmortal ascent. There are more examples from later writings like the *First Book of Jeû* and *Pistis Sophia*.

---

[11] Peter himself observes that Jesus loved Mary more than the other women (*Gos. Mary* BG p. 10,1-3).

[12] De Boer (cf. *Gospel*, 207-8) considers the possibility that first-century traditions about Mary Magdalene survived in the *Gospel of Mary* independently from the NT.

[13] Most editions and translations of CT do not yet include the interesting passage. Only recently placed fragments allow us to read the text on CT pp. 63-6. Cf. Gregor Wurst, "Weitere neue Fragmente aus Codex Tchacos. Zum 'Buch des Allogenes' und zu Corpus Hermenticum XIII, in *Judasevangelium und Codex Tchacos*, ed. Enno Edzard Popkes and Gregor Wurst, WUNT 297 (Tübingen: Mohr Siebeck, 2012), 1-12.

[14] Cf. *First Apocalypse of James* NHC V pp. 33-6.

The *Gospel of Mary*, on the other hand, does not speak about a future ascent of, for example, Mary's soul. It narrates an already completed ascent from an outside perspective. Although the recipients of the words might learn from this, the text does not give direct instructions to help them on the way up. The answers of the soul are not simply formulae that are to be learned but more like real individual dialogues. So the *Gospel of Mary* is an exception among a number of similar texts.

A vision and report about the struggles of a soul on its way up can be found in *Apocalypse of Paul* 14 and 16.[15] Similar to the *Gospel of Mary*, hostile powers try to prevent the ascent and are overcome in a dialogue that is linked to the individuality of the soul; it does not consist of formula. A very short reference to a vision of an ascending (?) soul is given in the *Dialogue of the Saviour* (NHC III pp. 136–7). Here, Judas (Thomas) is probably the main witness although Mary might be included as well.

Even these few examples show that there is no specific association between Mary and traditions about the ascent of the soul. There are distinct versions connected to a number of different witnesses; the *Gospel of Mary* seems to be a special mixture using elements (like the names of the powers and the outside perspective on the struggles of the soul) that are not joined anywhere else as far as I know.

But why, then, is Mary the one who talks about the ascent of the soul? There might be an exegetical reason. At the beginning of her speech, Mary says to the disciples, "I saw the Lord in a vision" (ⲁⲓⲛⲁⲩ ⲉⲡⲭ̅ⲥ̅ ϨⲚ ⲞⲨϨⲞⲢⲞⲘⲀ *Gos. Mary* BG p. 10,10-11) and then reports what he told her. In John 20:18, she says to them, "I have seen the Lord" (Ἑώρακα τὸν κύριον), just after an encounter with the risen Jesus who told her about his ascent to the father. Many people have recognized that the *Gospel of Mary* probably uses the Gospel of John and elaborates the story of Mary Magdalene in John 20.[16] It fits very well with the topic of ascent and with the idea that Mary has special knowledge of Jesus. If this is the case, most parts of the picture of Mary are derived from a generally known literary source, the Gospel of John. There is not some specific or even esoteric Mary-tradition behind the *Gospel of Mary* but exegetical skill in combining already existing elements to a new story with a new message. Again, the name of Mary connects her gospel to generally accepted parts of early Christianity, not to a special branch.

Traditions in the *Gospel of Mary*: Sayings of Jesus

The idea that the *Gospel of Mary* works exegetically using already known literary texts to express its opinion is supported by other parts of the gospel. At the beginning of Mary's report of Jesus' words, Jesus praises her for her ability to see him in a vision without wavering. And he explains this ability by saying, "For where the mind (ⲚⲞⲨⲤ) is, there is the treasure" (ⲠⲘⲀ ⲄⲀⲢ ⲈⲦⲈⲢⲈⲠⲚⲞⲨⲤ ⲘⲘⲀⲨ ⲈϤⲘⲘⲀⲨ ⲚϬⲒ ⲠⲈϨⲞ *Gos. Mary* BG p. 10,15-16). A similar saying is known from Matt 6:21 (par. Luke 12:34): "For

---

[15] The generally known *Apocalypse of Paul* preserved in Greek, Latin, and other languages, not the one from Nag Hammadi Codex V. It describes in detail the visions of Paul about heaven and hell, and the fate of the righteous and sinners.

[16] Cf. King, *Gospel*, 130–1; Tuckett, *Gospel*, 17–18, 71–2.

where your treasure is, there your heart will be also" (ὅπου γάρ ἐστιν ὁ θησαυρός σου, ἐκεῖ ἔσται καὶ ἡ καρδία σου.) That is not a verbal quotation; instead of heart (καρδία), the *Gospel of Mary* uses mind (νοῦς)—both words are nearly interchangeable and νοῦς fits better in a more philosophical context. More important for the interpretation is the change of the order of the elements and of the time. In the synoptic version, the heart will follow the treasure, so it is important to collect a treasure in heaven, not on earth. In the *Gospel of Mary*, the treasure follows the mind, it is where the mind is—both are nearly identical; the mind can be regarded as a treasure.

The *Gospel of Mary* is not the only early Christian text to use a variant of the saying.[17] It can be found in Justin, Clement of Alexandria, and Macarius, in all cases with νοῦς instead of καρδία and in the present tense. In Justin (*1 Apol.* 15.16), the order of the elements is the same as in the synoptic version. Clement and Macarius, like the *Gospel of Mary*, have the reversed order. Thus, the *Gospel of Mary* seems to pick up a saying widely used in different forms; there is no indication of a special tradition. Nevertheless, by placing the saying in its new context, the *Gospel of Mary* gives it a new and specific meaning. In its synoptic context, the saying is part of a discussion on the use of worldly possessions—they are devalued; "possessions" in heaven are more important. In Clement (ὅπου γὰρ ὁ νοῦς τινος ... ἐκεῖ καὶ ὁ θησαυρὸς αὐτοῦ; *Strom.* 7.12.77.6), the wording is very close to the *Gospel of Mary*, but treasure still means worldly possessions: they should be used to help the brother who needs them. The focus is still on treasure, on the question of what should be done with money and goods. In the *Gospel of Mary*, the focus is shifted onto νοῦς; the saying seems to exalt its importance. In order to work as an explanation of Mary's ability, a material sense of treasure is not helpful; it is rather used as a praise of Mary's mind (νοῦς).

However, the fact that Jesus' words start with a widely known saying might be important, even if it is used in a different sense. The *Gospel of Mary* shows that Jesus' teaching is not completely different from what is known from other sources. After Mary's speech, Andrew attacks her because her report gives "different ideas" and Andrew does not believe that Jesus really said this (*Gos. Mary* BG p. 17,10-15). He is, of course, quite right about the ascent of the soul, but at the beginning, the words of Jesus resemble what is already known. Again, the *Gospel of Mary* connects itself to a general, not a special, tradition.

Earlier in the *Gospel of Mary*, more well-known words of Jesus are quoted. At the end of the dialogue with the disciples, Jesus kisses them and gives them some final instructions (*Gos. Mary* BG p. 8,14-9,4) before he departs.[18] This farewell speech is quite different in character than the more philosophical explanations to the questions of the disciples. It is composed of short separate sayings, most of which are known

---

[17] Cf. Tuckett, *Gospel*, 65–7.
[18] *Gos. Mary* BG p. 8,14-9,4 (translation Tuckett, *Gospel*, 88–91):

> When the blessed one had said this things, he greeted them all, saying "Peace be with you. My peace receive for yourselves. Beware that no one leads you astray saying, 'See here!', or 'See there!', for the Son of Man is within you. Follow him. Those who seek him will find him. Go then and preach the gospel of the kingdom. Do not lay down any rules beyond what I have appointed for you, and do not give a law like the law-giver lest you be constrained by it."

from the NT. Although the sayings can be found in different contexts, they form a unified speech in the *Gospel of Mary* that expresses a new meaning.

This can be exemplified in the passage about the Son of Man: "Jesus says: Beware that no one leads you astray saying, 'See here!' or 'See there!', for the Son of Man is within you. Follow him. Those who seek him will find him" (*Gos. Mary* BG p. 8,15-21).[19] In Luke 17:23-24, Jesus warns his disciples not to believe those who pretend to know that the son of man is "here" or "there" (Ἰδοὺ ἐκεῖ Ἰδοὺ ὧδε). His real coming will be quite different and a cosmic event. Just before this saying about the son of man, Jesus talks about the kingdom of God that cannot be seen "here" or "there" (Ἰδοὺ ὧδε ἢ Ἐκεῖ) but is within (ἐντός) the disciples (Luke 17:21).[20] In my opinion, the *Gospel of Mary* uses the fact that both the kingdom of God and the son of man cannot be seen "here" or "there" in the Gospel of Luke to shift the statement about the kingdom of God (which is within the disciples) to the son of man. The result is a completely new idea about the son of man: In the *Gospel of Mary*, he is neither identified with Jesus nor an apocalyptic figure but rather an inner reality of the disciples, their true human potential.[21] Added is a request to follow him—the common idea that Jesus should be followed in this context suddenly leads into the disciples themselves. If the son of man is within them, they have to concentrate on their inner reality to follow him. The passage ends with the promise that those who seek him will find him—the general statement about seeking and finding[22] is adapted to the specific context of the inner son of man.

In my opinion, this passage demonstrates how cleverly the *Gospel of Mary* uses phrases from an already known text and reshapes them to express its own theology. There is no evidence for a separate, independent tradition, although the *Gospel of Mary* shows creative, sometimes unique, theological ideas. In the case of the Jesus-tradition, the *Gospel of Mary* takes advantage of what is widely known and accepted, and I think the figure of Mary is part of this. Its specificity is in what it does with these traditions.

In Conclusion

Why was the *Gospel of Mary* named after Mary? What implications does the title have? If my observations are correct, we do not learn anything new about Mary (Magdalene) as a historical figure or about traditions connected with her. On the contrary, Mary might have been chosen as the heroine of the gospel exactly because she was generally known and accepted, and because what was known about her could be used to link her to the topics the *Gospel of Mary* wanted to discuss, especially to the topic of the

---

[19] Coptic text: ⲀⲢⲈϨ ⲘⲠⲦⲢⲈⲖⲀⲀⲨ Ⲣ̄ ⲠⲖⲀⲚⲀ ⲘⲘⲰⲦⲚ̄ ⲈϤϪⲰ ⲘⲘⲞⲤ ϪⲈ ⲈⲒⲤ ϨⲎⲠⲈ ⲘⲠⲈⲒⲤⲀ Ⲏ ⲈⲒⲤ ϨⲎⲠⲈ ⲘⲠⲈⲈⲒⲘⲀ ⲚϢⲎⲢⲈ ⲄⲀⲢ ⲘⲠⲢⲰⲘⲈ ⲈϤϢⲞⲠ ⲘⲠⲈⲦⲚ̄ϨⲞⲨⲚ ⲞⲨⲈϨⲦⲎⲨⲦⲚ̄ Ⲛ̄ⲤⲰϤ ⲚⲈⲦϢⲒⲚⲈ Ⲛ̄ⲤⲰϤ ⲤⲈⲚⲀϬⲚ̄ⲦϤ̄.

[20] Ἰδοὺ γὰρ ἡ βασιλεία τοῦ θεοῦ ἐντὸς ὑμῶν ἐστιν. The Greek ἐντός can be translated as "among" you or "within" you.

[21] Cf. Jens Schröter, "Zur Menschensohnvorstellung im Evangelium nach Maria," in *Ägypten und Nubien in spätantiker und christlicher Zeit*, Band 2: *Schrifttum, Sprache und Gedankenwelt*, ed. Stephen Emmel, Sprachen und Kulturen des christlichen Orients 6, 2 (Wiesbaden: Reichert, 1999), 178-88.

[22] Cf. Mt. 7:7 par and *Gos. Thom.* 92, 94.

ascent of the soul. By doing so, the *Gospel of Mary* presents itself as a text connected to and based on generally accepted gospels. There is nothing special or secret about the traditions used. The interactions among the disciples in the gospel give the same impression: Mary's perspective is part of and discussed in the whole group.[23] However, the theological ideas expressed are sometimes quite new, though they seem to grow from what is already known. This might be another reason for choosing Mary: Although a well-known character from the gospels, she is not connected to a specific theology like, for example, Peter, who might be seen as representing the general opinion of the developing church.

One last question: Was Mary chosen just because she was an accepted and useful disciple? The choice of a woman seems to imply that the *Gospel of Mary* advocates the right of women to lead and to teach. Surely, Peter rejects Mary's message because she is a woman. It is possible that this discussion is one of the topics the *Gospel of Mary* wants to address.[24] However, the confrontation might just serve the purpose to give Mary an advantage over Peter and to deflect attention from the much more dangerous questions posed by Andrew, who suggests that the words of Mary are incompatible with the known teaching of Jesus (*Gos. Mary* BG p. 17,10-15). What Mary says is—in its main part—really new compared to other Jesus-traditions. Mary is easily defended against Peter's attack, but there is no reaction to Andrew. Moreover, the text does not indicate that the position of Mary should be generalized to include other women like in *Gos. Thom.* 114. Yet, women in antiquity as well as modern women could have read and continue to read the gospel as an encouragement for women to teach and to preach.[25]

---

[23] The text portrays itself in this way—it is not necessarily the social reality of the author and readers of the *Gospel of Mary*.

[24] Cf. King, *Gospel*, 88–90; Brock, *Mary Magdalene*, 84.

[25] The *Gospel of Mary* portrays Mary as teaching—more than half of the text is direct speech of her. In the Coptic version, she is probably included in the group starting to preach at the end (BG p. 19,1-2). The Greek version depicts only Levi as preaching, though (P.Ryl 463 p. 22,14-16).

4

What Is Mary Doing in Acts?

Confessional Narratives and the Synoptic Tradition

Jo-Ann Badley

This essay begins with a straightforward question: What is Mary doing in Acts? She is mentioned only once—when Jesus' followers are gathered in the upper room praying, after Jesus' ascension and before the experience of Pentecost (Acts 1:14). Luke identifies those present as the eleven apostles who had returned to Jerusalem after seeing the ascension of Jesus, and then he adds that some women, including Mary the mother of Jesus, as well as Jesus' brothers, were also present.[1] Mary is identified both by name and by title; we cannot miss her.[2] But some commentators do overlook her.[3] Perhaps they conflate gospel stories and assume her presence here is unremarkable.[4] Before

---

[1] The list of apostles in Acts 1:13 is the same as in Luke 6:14, although ordered differently. I assume that "Luke" wrote both Luke and Acts and that we do not know who that person is.

[2] Uncial D includes children with the women, suggesting these women are wives of apostles; for discussion see Richard I. Pervo, *Acts: A Commentary*, ed. Harold W. Attridge, Hermeneia (Minneapolis, MN: Fortress, 2009), 40; Luke Timothy Johnson, *The Acts of the Apostles*, ed. D. J. Harrington, SJ, SP (Collegeville, MN: Liturgical, 1992), 34. The spelling of Mary's name also varies: Mary or Miriam (fourth century uncials are divided).

[3] C. K. Barrett says, "It is clear that Luke either has no information, or is not concerned to provide information, about Mary in the post-resurrection period," *A Critical and Exegetical Commentary on the Acts of the Apostles*, 2 vols. (Edinburgh: T & T Clark, 1994–98), I: 89. Cf. Hans Conzelmann, *Acts of the Apostles: A Commentary on the Acts of the Apostles*, trans. A. Thomas Kraabel James Limburg and Donald H. Juel, Hermeneia (Philadelphia, PA: Fortress, 1987) (German 1972), 9; F. F. Bruce, *The Acts of the Apostles: The Greek Text with Introduction and Commentary*, 3rd ed. (Grand Rapids, MI: Eerdmans, 1990), 74. Exceptions are Pervo, *Acts: A Commentary*, 47; Joseph A. Fitzmyer, *The Acts of the Apostles: A New Translation with Introduction and Commentary*, AB 31 (New York: Doubleday, 1998), 216; Craig Keener, *Acts: An Exegetical Commentary, vol. 1, Introduction and 1:1–2:47* (Grand Rapids, MI: Baker Academic, 2012), 1: 746; Johnson, *The Acts of the Apostles*, 34.

[4] There are various Mary's present at Jesus' death in the synoptic tradition, but none are clearly identified with Mary, the mother of Jesus. For a full discussion see Richard Bauckham, *Jude and the Relatives of Jesus in the Early Church* (Edinburgh: T&T Clark, 1990), 9–15; Bauckham says, "We must conclude that no relatives of Jesus appear among the women disciples named by the Synoptic evangelists." A. J. Levine noted that various fragments of women's stories from the NT are often conflated by readers, with the result that the significance of any one woman's story is lost, "Gender and Faith," in School of Theology and Ministry, Great Theologians Lecture Series (Seattle University, 2008); this is even more true of a Mary story.

making a positive proposal about the significance of Luke's inclusion of Mary in his story, I need to describe why the question is worth investigating.

What is the Problem? Mary in the Gospel of Luke and the Acts of the Apostles

If Mary had a continuing role in the Acts account, the question would not arise, but she literally does not appear again in the story of Acts, and the incarnation, Mary giving birth to Jesus, does not seem to matter to Luke's understanding of the gospel message as it is presented in the speeches of Peter and Paul.[5] In the clear words of Richard Pervo, the "Christology of Acts is based on the resurrection, without reference to the events and empowerment of Luke 1–2."[6] As Luke summarizes the contents of the gospel in the opening verses of Acts, what matters is what Jesus did and taught from the beginning until he was taken up (1:1–2). When the eleven, under Peter's leadership, look for a replacement for Judas, the criterion is "one of the men who have accompanied us during all the time that the Lord Jesus went in and out among us, beginning from the baptism of John until the day he was taken up from us" (1:21–22). I agree with Pervo that the focus of Luke's narrative in Acts is Jesus' resurrection—being taken up.[7] While I might nuance "taken up" to include the ascension as well as the resurrection, Peter's statement indicates that Jesus' baptism by John and his resurrection and ascension bookend the important events of Jesus' life.[8] Mary's cooperation with God's request, her prophetic words in the Magnificat, and the birth and nurturing of her child are all outside these bookends. And yet Luke includes the infancy narratives in the gospel and he reintroduces Mary in the introductory pericopes in Acts. My question about her presence is rooted in this anomaly.

Mary's presence in the upper room interests me for a second reason. If Luke had not mentioned Mary in Acts, Mary's story in Luke's gospel would be open-ended.[9] In

---

[5] For a discussion of the parallel lack of connection between the infancy narratives and Luke's Gospel, see Raymond E. Brown, *The Birth of the Messiah: A Commentary on the Infancy Narratives in Matthew and Luke*, rev. ed. (Garden City, NY: Doubleday, 1993), 239–50.

[6] Pervo, *Acts: A Commentary*, note 116, 19.

[7] ἀναλαμβάνω in Acts 1:2, 1:11, 1:22 with respect to the ascension; in Luke 9:51 the noun is used. The significance of the resurrection is indicated elsewhere in Acts: when Peter explains the experience of Pentecost, he links it to the resurrection of which many are witnesses (2:32); when Peter bears witness to God's actions through his and Cornelius's dreams, he includes the resurrection (10:40) and, as this witness is given, the Spirit comes upon the Gentiles; when Paul defends himself before the Jewish council, he focuses on his belief in the resurrection (23:6), and similarly in his explanation of his actions before the Roman governor (24:15, 21). Daniel Marguerat speaks of the "unprecedented role" of "the paschal turning point," *The First Christian Historian: Writing the 'Acts of the Apostles'*, STNSMS (Cambridge: Cambridge University Press, 2002), 27.

[8] I assume that the speeches in Acts reflect Luke's theology in that he gives the characters the appropriate words for the situation, which was typical practice in ancient Greco-Roman historiography; Marion L. Soards, *The Speeches in Acts, Their Content, Context, and Concerns* (Louisville, KY: Westminster/John Knox, 1994), 160–1.

[9] Fitzmyer notes the transformation of Mary from mother to believer but does not develop the idea other than to say it is a "development beyond what has said of her in the beatitude pronounced over her by Elizabeth" (in Luke 1:45; Fitzmyer, *Acts*, 216). In the words of Raymond E. Brown et al., *Mary in the New Testament: A Collaborative Assessment by Protestant and Roman Catholic Scholars*

the infancy narratives in the gospel, she has a significant role. Obviously, she bears the child. But Luke also puts the great song of praise for God's deliverance into her mouth—what we commonly call the Magnificat (Luke 1:46–55). This song announces important prophetic motifs that Jesus, citing the prophet Isaiah, reiterates in his inaugural address in Nazareth (Luke 4:18–19) and embodies in his earthly ministry.[10] These values are echoed in Luke's summarizing comments when he describes the first community of Jesus followers in Acts (2:43–45 and 4:32–35). Peter and Paul continue to carry out the agenda of Mary's song in their ministries. As Joel Green says, "the Song brings to expression themes that are integral to the Lukan narrative as a whole."[11] However, as is well known, Mary is hardly mentioned outside the infancy narratives in the gospel, and her name is never used again. She comes with Jesus' brothers and wants to see him, but is not received because Jesus redefines kinship relationships (Luke 8:19–21). Without the brief mention of Mary in the introductory material of Acts, the story of the woman who responded to the initiative of God with faith and obedience at the time of Jesus' birth would be inconclusive.[12] But why did Luke bother to close her story when Mary has no further role in his story of the church?

A Proposal: Mary in Acts Considering the Synoptic Tradition

The anomalous character of Mary's presence in Luke's narratives is moderated somewhat if we assume, with the majority of New Testament scholars, that Luke used Mark's gospel as a source. In Luke's version of the gospel, he moderates Mark's harsh depiction of Mary.[13] Mark speaks of Mary twice in his gospel, both during Jesus' ministry in Galilee. In the first instance, Mary comes with Jesus' siblings to restrain Jesus because he is gaining a bad reputation. According to Mark, some people think that Jesus is out of his mind (Mark 3:21) and the religious leaders think that he is possessed by Beelzebul (Mark 3:22). In Mark's gospel, this is the context for Jesus' saying that whoever does the will of God is Jesus' relation (Mark 3:35), with the clear implication that such a person is not anyone in Jesus' family of origin. This is incongruous with a birth story like the one Luke tells, and Luke reorders the elements of this event: the family still visit Jesus and Jesus still revises the definition of family, but the motivation for the family visit is not stated (Luke 8:19–21), and the accusation that Jesus is possessed by Beelzebul appears in a very different context (Luke 11:15).

(Philadelphia, PA: Fortress and Paulist, 1978), "the real import of Acts 1:14 is to remind the reader that she had not changed her mind," 177.

[10] Barbara Reid, "An Overture to the Gospel of Luke," *Cur TM* 39 (2012): 429.
[11] Joel B. Green, *The Gospel of Luke*, NICNT (Grand Rapids, MI: Eerdmans, 1997), 99.
[12] This is consistent with Jesus' teachings elsewhere: the woman in the crowd proclaims Mary blessed: "Blessed is the womb that bore you and the breasts that nursed you" to which Jesus replies, "Blessed rather are those who hear the word of God and obey it" (Luke 11:27–28); cf. Luke 14:26 and 18:28–30 on families.
[13] A classic description of the dissonance is Brown et al., *Mary in the New Testament*, where, in their conclusons, the authors speak of a "negative portrait" of Mary in the Gospel of Mark, 286.

The implication is that Jesus' family of origin could be included among those who hear and do the word of God.

The second instance where Mark refers to Mary may best be understood as a slur on Jesus' character.[14] When Jesus preaches in Nazareth, Mark reports that his detractors ask if he is not Mary's son, perhaps implying that he does not have a father (Mark 6:3). Luke tells the story slightly differently: the people of Nazareth ask in amazement if Jesus is Joseph's son (Luke 4:22); there is no slur on Mary's good name. Luke's reworking of these two stories, while they do nothing to bring Mary's story to a positive conclusion, leave open the characterization of Mary as faithful disciple in a way that Mark's narrative does not.

Mary's presence in the upper room, while giving some closure to her story overall, and in accord with Luke's mitigation of Mark's negative depiction of her, still presents a fissure in the narrative, a narrative hole.[15] My proposal is that Mary's presence in these early pericopes of Acts invites the reader to think about the broader contours of Luke's orderly account of events. Her presence works in two different ways. Both in the birth narratives and here in the upper room, her presence destabilizes Luke's primary narrative framework—between Jesus' baptism and being taken up—and encourages readers to locate this witness to Jesus' life and death in a broader context of the actions of God. But, simultaneously, Mary also restabilizes Luke's narrative by providing a paradigm by which to interpret God's presence in the profane events of human life.[16] Attention to her narrative role—both as link to a wider frame and as paradigm—provides insight into the ways that two dimensions of being, the sacred and the profane, are to be understood. Through Mary's story, Luke narratively develops a Christian grammar of the resurrection, making Mary's participation in the incarnation exemplary for resurrection life. Mary, as a character in Luke's story, is not the only mechanism by which he signals these connotations of the resurrection, but she is a significant one.[17] My argument is both a literary one, proceeding by way of observations on the Acts text, and a hermeneutical or theological one, moving to a reevaluation of Mary's role in the Acts narrative as a vantage point from which to assess and clarify her ubiquitous presence in the Christian tradition.[18]

---

[14] Joel Marcus, *Mark 1-8: A New Translation with Introduction and Commentary*, AB (New York: Doubleday, 2000), 375.

[15] H. Porter Abbott, *The Cambridge Introduction to Narrative*, 2nd ed., Cambridge Introduction to Literature (Cambridge: Cambridge University Press, 2008), 90.

[16] Mircea Eliade speaks of "manifestations of sacred realities," *The Sacred and the Profane: The Nature of Religion* (San Diego, CA: Harcourt, Brace, Jovanovich, 1959), 11. More recently, see the work of John J. Pilch describing "sky journeys"; in particular, his discussion of the place of Jerusalem as an ancient place of entry to the abode of God and the question of whether such descriptions represent "veridical or imaginal events," "The Ascension of Jesus: A Social Scientific Perspective," in *Flights of the Soul: Visions, Heavenly Journeys, and Peak Experiences in the Biblical World* (Grand Rapids, MI: Eerdmans, 2011), 168 (on Jerusalem); 171 concluding the ascension was a veridical event: "a group trance experience." Originally published in *Kontexte der Schrift: Wolfgang Stegemann zum 60*, ed. Christian Strecker (Stuttgart: W. Kohlhammer, 2005).

[17] Thus, attending to Mary's role in Acts may also develop a more substantial biblical foundation for the Marian tradition which may contribute to the recovery of her significance for theology and practice of Protestant faith.

[18] In this way, this work serves ecumenical conversations.

Observations from Acts: Mary in the Upper Room

The story of waiting in the upper room (Acts 1:12-14) is the first of Luke's minor summaries in Acts. The minor summaries are considered primary redactional elements in Acts, indicators of Luke's interests and purposes.[19] Luke tells us in this first summary that Mary is among people gathered in what will be the nucleus of the believing community in Jerusalem. These people are depicted as ideal followers of Jesus: they are obedient to Jesus' instruction—they wait in Jerusalem; they are cognizant of Jewish law—Olivet is a Sabbath's day journey away from the city; they are unified and at prayer.[20] Two observations can be made. First, including Mary in this first of the summaries suggests that her presence is not incidental to this account; Luke chose to include her in this story. Second, her presence in the early Christian community reminds the reader of the community into which Jesus was born.[21] Luke portrayed Elizabeth and Zechariah, Anna and Simeon as loyal to the temple, obedient to the initiatives of God, prayerful, and unified.

This narrative summary follows Luke's second narration of Jesus' ascension and precedes the account of the replacement of Judas and the events of Pentecost. We might speak of the upper-room account as a narrative bridge between the accounts of the ascension and the empowering of the community. A consideration of both sides of the bridge is instructive for our reconsideration of Mary's presence on it.

Luke first tells the story of Jesus' ascent into heaven as the conclusion to the gospel. In the gospel, after Jesus' death, women from Galilee meet two dazzling men at Jesus' empty tomb who tell them of Jesus' resurrection (Luke 24:1-12). Then, two travelers meet an incognito Jesus on the way to Emmaus and he reveals his identity to them as they eat together (Luke 24:13-35). In a third appearance, Jesus comes to a wider group of disciples in Jerusalem and eats fish with them (Luke 24:36-49). Mary is not present in any of the stories,[22] but each account draws attention to Jesus' prior teaching: the heavenly messengers remind the women of Jesus' teaching that resurrection would follow crucifixion (Luke 24:6-7); Jesus interprets himself in light of the teaching of Moses and the prophets (Luke 24:26-27); Jesus reminds the disciples that he had told them that the law of Moses, the Prophets, and the Psalms must be fulfilled (Luke 24:44-46).[23] Then, at the end of this very long day, Jesus instructs them to wait in Jerusalem

---

[19] "Luke effected a transition from the narrative of the Ascension to the next stage in his story and now he gives a summary which prepares the way for the next event. Like his other summaries it contains little that could not have been generalized out of details supplied by narrative tradition. Luke's own hand is at work," Barrett, *Acts*, I: 86. Cf. Fitzmyer, *Acts*, 212; Pervo, *Acts: A Commentary*, 88-9.

[20] Elsewhere in Acts, followers act with one accord: 2:46, 4:24, 5:12, 8:6, 15:25 (although in 7:57, 12:20, 18:12 and 19:29 enemies also act with one accord), and prayer is a significant practice in all the Lukan materials: cf. Fitzmyer, *Acts*, 215. Helmut Koester, although he does not include Acts 1:12-14 in his list of summary accounts, says that such accounts are "Lukan compositions" that give "information about the ideal life of the Christian community in Jerusalem," *Introduction to the New Testament*, Vol. 2: History and Literature of Early Christianity (Philadelphia, PA: Fortress, 1982), 318.

[21] So also Pervo, *Acts: A Commentary*, 47.

[22] The women are named in Luke 24:10; Mary, the mother of Jesus, is not included.

[23] Joshua W. Jipp suggests the Davidic Psalms are particularly important, "Luke's Scriptural Suffering Messiah: A Search for Precedent, a Search for Identity," *CBQ* 72 (2010): 257.

until they receive power to be effective witnesses (Luke 24:49). Finally, he leads his followers outside Jerusalem to Bethany, blesses them, and is carried into heaven. The audience at the ascension is the eleven and their companions (τοὺς ἕνδεκα καὶ τοὺς σὺν αὐτοῖς, Luke 24:33). These followers return to Jerusalem and the temple, blessing God (24:50–51).

In the beginning of Acts, Luke re-narrates these events.[24] As is well known, the re-narration in Acts is not entirely consistent with the gospel account.[25] There are inconsistencies of time, space, and audience. One long day in the gospel account becomes forty days in Acts (1:3). The place of ascension is named as Olivet, not Bethany (1:12), although both are proximate to Jerusalem. In the gospel, the disciples can go to and return from the place of ascension at the end of the long day (24:50 and 52). In Acts, there is no evidence that they are outside Jerusalem until they return (1:4 and 1:12). The audience to the ascension is also different: the eleven are specifically named in Acts as those who return to the upper room after seeing Jesus ascend and receiving the reproach of the heavenly messengers (1:11–13).[26] Any companions, as in the gospel, are not mentioned.

The narrative discrepancies between these two accounts of the ascension can be assessed as inadvertent, as Luke's clumsy use of sources, effectively a narrative blank to use Sternberg's terminology. Or they may be narrative gaps; that is, they may signal issues that are noteworthy if we are to understand more deeply what Luke is saying.[27] To use the language of James Dunn, the narration of the ascension is a test case for hermeneutics because it calls for a conception of "the interface between heaven and earth" which we do not know how to re-conceptualize.[28] The tendency in modern critical readings has been to attempt to resolve the discrepancies—as recently as 2013, Henk Jan de Jonge made another proposal.[29] However, if we focus on resolving the

---

[24] For Pervo, this re-narration is "one in excess of the maximum," *Acts: A Commentary*, 45. However, re-narration is a widely recognized Lucan technique: Carol Stockhausen, "Luke's Stories of the Ascension: The Background and Function of a Dual Narrative," *Proceedings—Eastern Great Lakes and Midwest Biblical Societies* 10 (1990): 251–63; cf. Marguerat's treatment of the duplicated accounts of Paul's experience on the Damascus Road, *The First Christian Historian*, chap. 9.

[25] There are text-critical issues in the ascension narratives indicating the difficulty of the differences for readers historically. The classic redactional study of the narratives is Mikeal C. Parsons, *The Departure of Jesus in Luke-Acts: The Ascension Narratives in Context*, vol. 21 (JSNTSS; Sheffield: Sheffield Academic, 1987). For more recent discussions, see A.W. Zwiep, "The Text of the Ascension Narratives (Luke 24.50–3; Acts 1.1–2, 9–11)," *NTS* 42 (1996): 219–44. Some scholars dispute that Luke is re-narrating the same story, recently H. J. de Jonge, "The Chronology of the Ascension Stories in Luke and Acts," *NTS* 59 (2013): 151–71. For discussion of the anomalies of the two narratives, and various solutions, see John F. Maile, "The Ascension in Luke-Acts," *TynBul* 37 (1986): 29–59.

[26] Fitzmyer, *Acts*, 213. This lack of precision is typical of Luke who clearly identifies the twelve as apostles but is not always clear about their relation to the wider group of disciples. Cf. Quentin Quesnell, "The Women at Luke's Supper," in *Political Issues in Luke-Acts*, ed. R. J. Cassidy and P.J. Scharpen (Maryknoll, NY: Orbis, 1983), 59–79.

[27] As Koester notes, "It is unlikely that this work [the Gospel of Luke and the Acts of the Apostles] ever existed as a single book that was later divided," *Introduction to the New Testament*, 310. The narrative redundancy and discrepancies thus need to be considered for their potential impact on meaning.

[28] J. D. G. Dunn, "The Ascension of Jesus: A Test Case for Hermeneutics," in *Auferstehung—Resurrection: The Fourth Durham-Tübingen Research Symposium: Resurrection, Transfiguration and Exaltation in Old Testament, Ancient Judaism and Early Christianity*, ed. F. Avemarie and H. Lichtenberger, WUNT (Tübingen: Mohr Siebeck, 2001), 302 and 313.

[29] de Jonge, "Chronology."

inconsistencies in Luke's description of the events, we miss indicators of the difficulty of articulating the nature of the resurrection and ascension for their significance for Christian faith.[30] It may be that Jesus' resurrection was as difficult a concept to unpack in the ancient world as it is in the modern one. Considered this way, the narrative discrepancies of time, space, and audience signal that, while events of history are revelatory of the activity of God, recounting those events in their significance may not rehearse the events in the same sequence or with the same details.[31] If so, Mary's story in the gospel provides a road map, writ large, for interpreting human life in divine categories. Her story in the infancy accounts of the gospel becomes paradigmatic for other disciples who would also respond to God in faithful ways.[32] Mary's presence in the upper room after the re-narration of the ascension reminds readers of the continuity of the character of God's actions for Israel and the world, and thereby provides a foundational framework for bearing witness to God's continuing work in Jesus. Thus, counter to those who assume a radical discontinuity between God's story with Israel and the new community post-Pentecost, Mary's presence in the upper room affirms Luke's understanding of the continuity of community and God's purposes. As Mary's song of praise in Luke draws on the traditions of Israel, so Mary's new community can follow suit. And this is what we immediately see in the pericopes following the upper room account.

The narrative bridge on which Mary stands joins the story of the ascension to the story of the reconfiguration of the new community. First, Peter superintends Judas' replacement and then he interprets the Spirit's arrival (1:15–2:36).[33] Peter is clear that the twelfth apostle must be a witness to the whole life of Jesus, beginning with the baptism of John until Jesus was taken up (1:21–22).[34] This emphasis on John as the beginning of the significant events of Jesus' life might seem to undermine an argument for Mary's story as paradigmatic for the life of the new community. However, I note that Peter interprets Judas' betrayal and death by citing several Psalms and the community looks to God for a sign to select Judas' successor. This is like Mary who asks God for a sign (Luke 1:34) and whose song uses common phrases from scripture (Luke 1:46–55).[35] Certainly Mary bore her child before John's ministry but by her prophetic participation in the initiatives of God, she provides a paradigm of human

---

[30] This question exists whether Luke's writings have primarily an apologetic purpose or were written for the edification of the church.

[31] See, e.g., James L. Kugel's explanation of biblical "seconding" in poetry and prose that calls for reading that takes into account the similarities and differences between two, *The Idea of Biblical Poetry, Parallelism and its History* (New Haven, CT: Yale University Press, 1981). Matthew Sleeman articulates such a geographical reconfiguration, *Geography and the Ascension Narrative in Acts*, SNTSMS (Cambridge: Cambridge University Press, 2009).

[32] Drawing similar conclusions by comparing Mary with Elizabeth, see Greg W. Forbes and Scott D. Harrower, *Raised from Obscurity: A Narratival and Theological Study of the Characterization of Women in Luke-Acts*, trans. with Foreword by Lynn H. Cohick (Eugene, OR: Pickwick, 2015), 47.

[33] There is no indication of a change of setting between Acts 1:12 and 2:36, so presumably these three scenes happen in the same location, certainly in Jerusalem, but perhaps even in the same room. This is complicated by how one imagines a room big enough for 120 persons (1:15) or even the 3,000 who heard the tongues (2:41).

[34] This time frame is consistent between the gospel and Acts: Luke 7:28 (no parallel in Mark; cf. Matt 11:7–19); Luke 16:16 (no parallel in Mark); Acts 10:37–41 (Peter's speech to Cornelius).

[35] Forbes and Harrower, *Raised from Obscurity*, 51–2.

participation in divine work. By clearly including her in the community, alongside the focus on the public events of Jesus' life, Luke reconfigures the temporal parameters of the Christian community; any discussions that distinguish God's recent actions in Jesus (from baptism to being taken up) from God's prior actions in Israel must be ruled out.

The event of Pentecost also reiterates Mary's paradigmatic role in the narrative. As the Spirit came to Mary, the Spirit comes to the fledgling community of Jesus' followers. Mary's participation in the work of God was not possible without the Spirit—a virgin became pregnant because the Holy Spirit came upon her and the power of the Most High overshadowed her (Luke 1:35)—and the Spirit is necessary for the community's participation in the work of God—they would receive power for witness when the Holy Spirit had come upon them (Acts 1:8). And as Mary interpreted God's intervention in language that relied on the language of the Hebrew Scriptures, so also Peter interprets the events of the Spirit in light of the Hebrew Scriptures. This is to say that Luke, while affirming that the crucifixion, resurrection, and ascension are pivotal events, also portrays them as consistent with what God has done previously. These new actions of God must be understood in light of the witness to God's actions in the Hebrew Scriptures. Mary, present in the upper room, reminds us of the constancy of Luke's God.

After the accounts of Matthias' appointment and the coming of the Spirit, Luke provides a second summary description (Acts 2:41–47). Like the summary that named Mary, this one provides a bridge between the stories of the founding of the community and the accounts of the actions and struggles of that community to bear unified, prayerful, powerful witness. This second summary also includes seeing signs and wonders and sharing material goods. The overall picture is of a community that embodies Mary's prophetic words of reversal from the Magnificat.

I suggest that the first two chapters of Acts are best understood as preparation narratives.[36] The subsequent public witness of the community parallels, in many ways, the public witness of Jesus that follows the infancy narratives in the gospel. The great things that the Mighty One did for Mary have been replicated in a new generation that fears God (Luke 1:49–50). Mary is paradigmatic for individual believers and, in some way, paradigmatic for the community as a whole. You might say, Mary's way is blessed—which was Elizabeth's opinion (Luke 1:42). Her presence in the upper room is part of Luke's rhetorical strategy for creating a theological framework that reimagines the people of God within the continuing purposes of God.

Reading Acts as a Confessional Narrative

This attention to Mary's role in Acts has implications on several levels. There is potential for these observations to contribute to several larger critical questions in the study of

---

[36] So also Beverly Roberts Gaventa, *Acts*, ATNC (Nashville, TN: Abingdon, 2003), Table of Contents; Forbes and Harrower, *Raised from Obscurity*, 11.

Luke–Acts such as the unity and genre of the two books,[37] the structure of Acts,[38] the relationship of the infancy narratives to Luke's gospel, and the importance of narrative for Lukan Christology. I also think this analysis creates an obvious parallel with the depiction of Mary in John's Gospel, which is worth exploring; in both gospels, Mary bookends Jesus' public ministry. But these are not the primary implications that I want to draw out. Rather, I want to attend to the ways in which careful attention to Mary in the story of Acts contributes to understanding how we read the gospels, in this case, using the differences between Mark's and Luke's Gospels to provide a point of leverage for the conversation about synoptic differences. This is a hermeneutical argument, and Paul Ricoeur provides a helpful category for analysis.

Ricoeur describes a type of narrative that he calls "interpretative narratives" or "confessional narratives."[39] By this he means narratives "in which the ideological interpretation these narratives wish to convey is not superimposed on the narrative by the narrator but is, instead, incorporated into the very strategy of the narrative."[40] That is, the narrative simultaneously describes the event itself and makes an ideological or theological statement, a confession, about it. To unpack the way the components of the narrative work—time, space, characters—is to unpack the confession that those components encourage with respect to the events. Petri Merenlahti uses terminology from Meir Sternberg to explore this kind of gospel poetics. He argues that the gospel narratives have *a truth*, which is what readers will understand by reading the story, but narratives also speak *a whole truth*, which are ways that primary meaning can be explored by other clues in the text.[41] In the case of Luke–Acts, we can perhaps speak of its truth as the narrative witness to Jesus' resurrection and ascension, and its whole truth as the exploration of the meaning of those events in terms of the identity of Jesus and paradigms of faithful following, both explored in relation to God's prior relationship with Israel. To turn to the language of Hans Frei, Luke creates a world for his readers to live in, both by the ostensive reference of the narrative and by the connotations that become visible if we follow particular details of the text.[42] To read

---

[37] I suggest my work indicates that, rather than making claims for single authorship, we need to claim that Luke–Acts is best read in a unified way; as well, it is best read as history (rather than biography); Andrew Pitts argued similarly in "The Genre of the Third Gospel and Greco-Roman Historiography: A Reconsideration" (Paul J. Achtemeier Award, SBL Annual Meeting, Atlanta, GA, November 21–24, 2015).

[38] Recognizing that Acts is notoriously difficult to outline—important interpreters like Pervo structure their commentary without major divisions (*Acts: A Commentary*, Table of Contents, vii–ix). Gaventa recognizes these chapters as preparatory narratives, as found in the gospel, *Acts*, 62.

[39] Paul Ricoeur, "Interpretative Narrative," in *The Book and the Text: The Bible and Literary Theory*, ed. Regina Schwartz (Cambridge, MA: Basil Blackwell, 1990), 237 and 247. M. Eugene Boring makes a similar kind of argument for narrative Christology in Mark's gospel, "Markan Christology: God-Language for Jesus?," *NTS* 45 (1999): 451–71.

[40] Ricoeur, "Interpretative Narrative," 237 and 245.

[41] Petri Merenlahti, *Poetics for the Gospels? Rethinking Narrative Criticism*, Studies of the New Testament and its World (London: T&T Clark, 2002), 62–3.

[42] Hans W. Frei, *The Eclipse of Biblical Narrative: A Study in Eighteenth and Nineteenth Century Hermeneutics* (New Haven, CT: Yale University Press, 1974), 2–3 and 30. As Frei suggests when critiquing mythological readings, "In a sense, every narrative of the sort in which story and meaning are closely related may have its own special hermeneutics" … "the meaning [exists] only to the extent that it is instantiated and hence narrated; and this meaning through instantiation is not

well is to read within the world established by the text. Including Mary in the upper room is a significant narrative strategy by which Luke makes his connotations clear. By noting her name and title, Luke makes it clear that the reader is to consider her presence.[43]

Conclusion

Overall, then, we can say that Mary's presence in the upper room reminds Luke's readers of her earlier participation in the initiatives of God. The recalled infancy narrative provides a paradigm by which readers are invited to make additional sense of the new actions of God. Mary points to Luke's understanding of the continuity of God's purposes in Israel, in Jesus her son, and now in the nascent followers gathered with her in Jerusalem. We could say that Mary's presence frames the events between Jesus' baptism by John and his ascension, providing continuity with the larger story of Luke's God through her prophetic ability to interpret God's actions and her confident participation in God's initiatives. Her narrative presence in Acts recalls her proleptic role in the gospel story.

In this way, it is also possible to make some sense of the dissonance between Mark and Luke. Both gospels bear witness to the centrality of the resurrection (and ascension) for making sense of Jesus' life and death, but they do it in very different ways. Markan irony, that even those closest to Jesus did not know him before his death, is a very different narrative strategy from Luke's prophetic Mary who provides a paradigm for interpreting how God is at work in human events.[44] If readers are only reading for the redescription of the events, if they are not concerned to articulate the relation of the sacred and the profane, the accounts of the two gospels will be at odds.[45] A story works within space and time whether it is imaginary space and time, or historical space and time, or idealized space and time. The difficulty comes when readers do not differentiate between kinds of space and time of a story. Historical criticism of Acts

---

illustrated ... but *constituted* through the mutual, specific determination of agents, social context, and circumstances that form the indispensable narrative web," *Eclipse*, 273 and 280.

[43] This is not dissimilar to the ways Luke's geography in Acts has been understood: E.g., Loveday Alexander, "Narrative Maps: Reflections on the Toponymy of Acts," in *Bible in Human Society: Essays in Honour of John Rogerson*, ed. R. M. D. Carroll, D.J.A. Clines, and P. R. Davies, JSNTSS (Sheffield Academic, 1995), 17–57; Loveday Alexander, "Mapping Early Christianity: Acts and the Shape of Early Church History," *Int* 57 (2003): 163–73. Or the geography in Luke: Frank J. Matera, "Jesus' Journey to Jerusalem (Luke 9:51–19:46): A Conflict with Israel," *JSNT* 51 (1993): 57–77; Mikeal C. Parsons, "The Place of Jerusalem on the Lukan Landscape: An Exercise in Symbolic Cartography," in *Literary Studies in Luke–Acts: Essays in Honor of Joseph B. Tyson*, ed. Richard P. Thompson and Thomas E. Phillips (Macon, GA: Mercer University, 1998), 155–71; Joseph A. Fitzmyer, *The Gospel According to Luke: Introduction, Translation, and Notes*, AB 28, 28a (Garden City, NY: Doubleday, 1981–85), 28:56.

[44] Irony is well documented as a narrative strategy in Mark; e.g. Jerry Camery-Hoggatt, *Irony in Mark's Gospel: Text and Subtext*, SNTMS (Cambridge: Cambridge University Press, 1992).

[45] A parallel argument is made with respect to gospel presentations of the law by Forbes and Harrower, *Raised from Obscurity*, 37. This also recasts the conversation about the genre of the infancy accounts as in Andrew T. Lincoln, *Born of a Virgin? Reconceiving Jesus in the Bible, Tradition, and Theology* (Grand Rapids, MI: Eerdmans, 2013).

assumes a historical frame and interprets Mary in that way—either assessing Luke's use of sources, or ignoring her. However, exploring the narrative implications of Mary's presence in Acts suggests that this is probably not the only way that time, space, and characters work for this narrative.[46] Mary teaches us to read Jesus' story from John's baptism to his ascension as an origins narrative rather than as a history of salvation. And, I would argue, given the significant figure Mary has become in literature, art, and liturgy in the Christian tradition, many Christian readers of Luke's gospel have read her in precisely this way. We could say that Mary in Mark's gospel and in Luke's gospel does the same job of work but in two very different ways. The question is whether readers are willing to learn to read in such a way that she can indicate wider connotations to the story.

---

[46] Cf. Loveday Alexander, "Fact, Fiction and the Genre of Acts," *NTS* 44 (1998): 380–99.

5

Magdalene, Mother, Martha's Sister, or None of the Above?

The Mary in the Dialogue of the Savior

Anna Cwikla

The unspecified Mary in noncanonical texts, including the Nag Hammadi codices, has traditionally been associated with Mary Magdalene.[1] In recent years, however, some scholars have challenged this presumption, suggesting that this Mary could be referring to the mother of Jesus, or to Mary of Bethany, or an amalgamation of at least two of the Marys. Yet another possibility that has not been fully considered is that Mary may not be referring to a specific woman from the canonical gospels at all.[2] Mary was the most common name in ancient Palestine[3] and was also popular in parts of Egypt beginning in the fourth century.[4] This essay argues that given the commonality of the name Mary in antiquity, the unspecified Mary need not be referring to any of the canonical Marys at all. Instead, I argue that this name was merely included in these various noncanonical texts when the narrative or discussion required a female disciple. In order to test this hypothesis, I will focus on the characteristics attributed to Mary in the *Dialogue of the Savior* and compare them to the Marys of the canonical gospels.[5]

With the exception of a few noncanonical texts such as the *Gospel of Philip* and portions of *Pistis Sophia*, the character Mary is never explicitly identified with any of the canonical Marys.[6] Most scholars, however, have tended to identify the unspecified

---

[1] This paper is based on portions of my MA thesis, "'Pray in the Place Where There Is No Woman': Mary in the Dialogue of the Saviour" (University of Alberta, 2013).
[2] In his discussion of the unspecified Mary in the *Gospel of Thomas*, Marvin Meyer suggests that perhaps "'a universal Mary' is in mind, and that specific historical Marys are no longer clearly distinguished, just as other historical personages may be blended into a 'universal James' or 'universal Philip' in later Christian literature." "Making Mary Male: The Categories 'Male' and 'Female' in the Gospel of Thomas," *NTS* 31 (1985): 560.
[3] Tal Ilan, *Lexicon of Jewish Names in Late Antiquity: Part I Palestine 330 BCE–200 CE*, vol. 1, 4 vols. Texts and Studies in Ancient Judaism 91 (Tübingen: Mohr Siebeck, 2002), 57.
[4] Lincoln H. Blumell, *Lettered Christians: Christians, Letters, and Late Antique Oxyrhynchus* (Leiden: Brill, 2012), 269, n. 156.
[5] Unless otherwise specified, all translations of the *Dialogue of the Savior* are from Stephen Emmel, ed., *Nag Hammadi Codex III, 5: The Dialogue of the Savior* (Leiden: Brill, 1984).
[6] For a comprehensive list of these texts, see Mary Ann Beavis, "Reconsidering Mary of Bethany," *CBQ* 74 (2012): 290–3.

Mary with Mary Magdalene, usually on account of the prominence placed on her in certain scenes such as at the crucifixion and resurrection in the canonical gospels. Some scholars have even constructed a "Gnostic Mary," arguing that Mary is so common in these so-called Gnostic texts that the communities who read them likely held Mary Magdalene in higher esteem than the other traditional disciples such as Peter.[7] One of the first scholars to make a strong case in favor of a different identification of Mary was Stephen Shoemaker, who argued that it is just as likely that this Mary refers to Jesus' mother.[8] Though some scholars mentioned this possibility in passing, such as Enzo Lucchesi,[9] Shoemaker has repeatedly made the case that Jesus' mother should at the very least be considered as part of the "Composite Mary" who appears in noncanonical texts.[10] In particular, he points to a number of later traditions including the writings of Ephrem the Syrian that indicate that roles traditionally ascribed to the Magdalene in the canon were also ascribed to Jesus' mother.[11] Additionally, he convincingly argues against those who posit that one can distinguish whether a given text refers to the Magdalene or the mother depending on a variation in the spelling of the name Mary.[12]

More recently, another Mary, Martha's sister in the gospels of Luke and John, labeled by scholars as Mary of Bethany, has also been added to the "Which Mary?" debate. Mary Ann Beavis notes that in the Gospel of John, Mary along with her siblings Martha and Lazarus are described as beloved by Jesus (John 11:5).[13] She also observes that Mary Magdalene is not introduced prior to her first appearance at the crucifixion in ch. 19.[14] This leads her to suggest that regardless of the intent of the author, the readers might have conflated these two Marys.[15] Ultimately, Beavis is careful not to create a Mary of Bethany versus Mary Magdalene dichotomy in her discussion of the unspecified Mary. Instead, she concludes that it is necessary "for the purposes of exegetical accuracy" to identify the unspecified Mary as Mary of Bethany when she is in close proximity to Martha and is not identified as the Magdalene or the mother.[16]

---

[7] See, e.g., April D. DeConick, *Holy Misogyny: Why the Sex and Gender Conflicts in the Early Church Still Matter* (New York: Continuum, 2011), 141; Jane Schaberg, *The Resurrection of Mary Magdalene: Legends, Apocrypha, and the Christian Testament* (New York: Continuum, 2002), 121; Robert M. Royalty, *The Origin of Heresy: A History of Discourse in Second Temple Judaism and Early Christianity* (New York: Routledge, 2013), 129–30; Elaine H. Pagels, *The Gnostic Gospels* (New York: Random House, 1979), 77–8.

[8] Stephen J. Shoemaker, "Rethinking the 'Gnostic Mary': Mary of Nazareth and Mary of Magdala in Early Christian Tradition," *JECS* 9 (2001): 555–95; Shoemaker, "A Case of Mistaken Identity? Naming the Gnostic Mary," in *Which Mary? The Marys of Early Christian Tradition*, ed. F. Stanley Jones (SBLSS 19; Atlanta, GA: Society of Biblical Literature, 2002), 5–30; Shoemaker, "Jesus' Gnostic Mom: Mary of Nazareth and the 'Gnostic Mary' Traditions," in *Mariam, the Magdalen, and the Mother*, ed. Deirdre Good (Bloomington: Indiana University Press, 2005), 153–82. More recently, see Shoemaker, *Mary in Early Christian Faith and Devotion* (New Haven, CT: Yale University Press, 2016), 74–99.

[9] Enzo Lucchesi, "Évangile selon Marie ou Évangile selon Marie-Madeleine?," *AnBoll* 103 (1985): 366.

[10] Shoemaker, "Rethinking the 'Gnostic Mary' "; Shoemaker, "Jesus' Gnostic Mom."

[11] Shoemaker, "Rethinking the 'Gnostic Mary,' " 562–7.

[12] Shoemaker, "Jesus' Gnostic Mom," 158–9; for a critique of Shoemaker's conclusions, see Antti Marjanen, "The Mother of Jesus or the Magdalene? The Identity of Mary in the so-Called Gnostic Christian Texts," in *Which Mary? The Marys of Early Christian Tradition*, ed. F. Stanley Jones (SBLSS 19; Atlanta, GA: Society of Biblical Literature, 2002), 31–42.

[13] Mary Ann Beavis, "Mary of Bethany and the Hermeneutics of Remembrance," *CBQ* 75 (2013): 745.

[14] Mary Ann Beavis, "Reconsidering Mary of Bethany," *CBQ* 74 (2012): 281–97.

[15] Ibid., 287.

[16] Beavis, "Mary of Bethany and the Hermeneutics of Remembrance," 755.

The identification of Mary with the mother or sister of Martha has spurred defenses of the identification with Magdalene for other scholars. These strategies of defense vary. They include holding Mary Magdalene's encounter with the resurrected Jesus in the Gospel of John as one of the most significant characteristics;[17] using the various spellings of the name Mary to determine if a text is referring either to the Magdalene or the mother;[18] and using conflict between Mary and other disciples, namely Peter, as a means of determining that Mary in a given context should refer to the Magdalene.[19] There are two presuppositions that underlie these approaches to the unnamed Marys of noncanonical texts. First, these theories seem to imply that the noncanonical texts were familiar with the stories and characters of the New Testament gospels. Not only this, but they also imply that the authors or final redactors attentively adhered to the characterizations of the disciples in the canonical texts. Secondly, there seems to be a tendency to lump all the unnamed Marys together, whether intentional or not. This leads to the unarticulated assumption that if one is able to determine the identity of one Mary, then this identity also fits the Mary of the rest of the texts.[20] Regardless of which specific Mary one argues for, this "one-Mary-fits-all" approach runs the risk of robbing the individual narratives of the differences and variety with which they might utilize this female character. To be sure, Shoemaker warns us, "we must proceed in our study of this curious, apocryphal woman with a caution that is nuanced by ambiguities present in what is in fact a composite figure, who draws both the Nazarene and the Magdalene into her identity."[21]

Although I do not wish to grant a priori status to the canonical gospels in my analysis of Mary in the *Dialogue of the Savior*, one cannot engage with previous scholarship in the "Which Mary?" debate without doing so. Since previous scholarship has used the canonical gospels as its baseline Mary comparison, this study engages in a similar approach. Dispelling the notion that the *Dialogue of the Savior*'s Mary refers to any of the canonical Marys is significant for two reasons. First, the *Dialogue of the Savior*'s Mary is most frequently assumed to be Mary Magdalene and subsequently grouped together with the unspecified Mary of the *Gospel of Thomas*, the *Gospel of Mary*, *Sophia of Jesus Christ*, and so on, in order to suggest that Mary Magdalene had a prominent role in noncanonical or "Gnostic" texts. As such, by demonstrating that the *Dialogue*

---

[17] Karen L. King, "Why All the Controversy? Mary in the Gospel of Mary," in *Which Mary?: The Marys of Early Christian Tradition*, ed. F. Stanley Jones (SBLSS 19; Atlanta, GA: Society of Biblical Literature, 2002), 63–70.

[18] Marjanen, "Mother of Jesus or the Magdalene?," 33–4.

[19] Ibid., 37–9; King, "Why All the Controversy?"

[20] See, e.g., Marjanen, "Mother of Jesus or the Magdalene?" Although he evaluates each of the "so-called gnostic texts" on an individual basis, some of Marjanen's analysis is precluded on the identification with Mary Magdalene in other unspecified texts. This is especially the case in his analysis of the *Dialogue of the Savior* where he reasons, "The conjecture that Mary in the two remaining revelation dialogues, the Sophia of Jesus Christ and the Dialogue of the Savior, is also the Magdalene basically depends on the similarity of the genre to those Mary texts in which the identification is more obvious" (39–40). To be fair, Marjanen himself admits that this evidence "is not very strong" (40). Nevertheless, such an approach speaks to the prevalent tendency to associate all unspecified Marys of non-canonical texts with the Magdalene. See also Jane Schaberg, *The Resurrection of Mary Magdalene: Legends, Apocrypha, and the Christian Testament* (New York: Continuum, 2002), 121–203, esp. 129–35.

[21] Shoemaker, "A Case of Mistaken Identity?," 30.

of the Savior's Mary is not the Magdalene forces us to withdraw this Mary from the corpus of noncanonical Mary Magdalene traditions, which in turn calls into question how popular Mary Magdalene actually was.

Secondly, if we cannot definitively link the Mary of the *Dialogue of the Savior* to any canonical Mary, this recognition ought to disrupt our reliance on canonical texts as a framework of interpreting texts that feature these familiar characters. Rather than assuming a dependence on canonical sources, it is equally possible that texts such as the *Dialogue of the Savior* have little interest in adhering so strictly to traditions depicted in the canonical texts that they reflect anything more than general similarities, such as the name of a character or just their mere presence in the life of Jesus.[22] Nevertheless, each noncanonical Mary should be investigated on an individual case-by-case basis. In terms of the current discussion, I argue that the commonality of the name Mary might indicate that no specific (canonical) Mary is to be identified in the *Dialogue of the Savior*.

As previously mentioned, most studies have been preoccupied with associating a particular canonical or combination of Mary to the unspecified Marys, but few, if any, have seriously considered relevant onomastic data in their studies. A lexicon of Jewish names from 330 BCE to 200 CE by Tal Ilan suggests that "Mary," or its related forms, would have been an extremely common name in Palestine during this period.[23] The names in this lexicon are taken from sources such as ossuaries, Judean desert finds, Josephus, rabbinic literature, and early Christian writings.[24] The name "Mariam," and its variants, which I will refer to as "Mary" for convenience, was the most common name with eighty different women having that name, followed by the name Salome with sixty-three, Shelmazion with twenty-five, and, in fourth place, Martha with twenty.[25] Overall, the statistics suggest that one out of every four women was named Mary.[26] It is not surprising, then, that in one single gospel such as Luke, there is Mary the mother of Jesus, Mary Magdalene, Mary the mother of James, and Martha's sister who all have the same name yet refer to different women. As such, it was necessary for the gospel authors to distinguish between these Marys in their own narratives in order to avoid confusion. But how common was the name Mary in Egypt at the time when the Nag Hammadi codices were composed?

In his book *Lettered Christians: Christians, Letters, and Late Antique Oxyrhynchus*, Lincoln Blumell analyzes names of Christians in various papyri written in Greek, including letters, from the third to the seventh century CE found in the town of Oxyrhynchus, Egypt. He suggests that although initially Mary was a very common Jewish name, it was later adopted by Christians as well.[27] Blumell reports that Mary

---

[22] The other disciples mentioned in the *Dialogue of the Savior*, Matthew and Judas, also lack explicit biographical details in the text. A more in-depth investigation concerning why these three—Matthew, Judas, and Mary—were chosen as the disciples to have this discussion with the Savior is very much warranted but beyond the scope of this study.

[23] Ilan, *Lexicon of Jewish Names*, 1:57.

[24] Ilan, *Lexicon of Jewish Names*, 1:39–45.

[25] Ilan, *Lexicon of Jewish Names*, 1:57.

[26] See also Tal Ilan, "Notes on the Distribution of Jewish Women's Names in Palestine in the Second Temple and Mishnaic Periods," *JJS* 40 (1989): 186–200.

[27] Blumell, *Lettered Christians*, 269.

is not found in any of the documents at Oxyrhynchus prior to the end of the third century but subsequently becomes a common name in Christian circles.[28] Blumell also cautions about drawing conclusions concerning the trend of women's names given the relatively small sample size of data. Nevertheless, at the very least it can be said that the name "Mary" did not disappear but remained common in Christian communities in Egypt. Therefore, it is not surprising that we have Marys in various Nag Hammadi documents including the *Gospel of Thomas*, *Dialogue of the Savior*, and *Sophia of Jesus Christ*. But is the name Mary in these noncanonical texts meant to correspond to any of the Marys in the NT gospels? Or was the name simply an obvious choice for an author requiring a female disciple?

The *Dialogue of the Savior*, found in codex 3, tractate 5 of the Nag Hammadi codices, will serve as my test text for this proposition. It should be noted that regardless of the conclusion, it does not necessarily mean that the same should be concluded about the unnamed Marys in the other noncanonical texts. Rather, each text should consider the role and identity of its Mary independently. Although there are other Marys mentioned in the canonical gospels, such as Mary the mother of James (Mark 16:1; Luke 24:10) and Mary the wife of Clopas (John 19:25), my analysis focuses on only three: Mary Magdalene, the mother of Jesus, and Mary of Bethany. The reason for this approach is twofold. First, these three Marys occur most frequently in the "Which Mary?" debate. Second, the other Marys do not appear in contexts other than those in which at least one of the three appears, such as the crucifixion or resurrection scenes. In other words, because these other Marys only appear in contexts where at least one of the main three Marys appear, the characteristics they have are not in any way unique but rather only overlap with others. For example, Mary Magdalene is mentioned alongside Mary the mother of James and Joseph in the Gospel of Mark (15:40, 47; 16:1). Mary the mother of James and Joseph appears nowhere else in this gospel on her own. Thus, her characteristics—her presence at the crucifixion (Mark 15:40, 47) and tomb (Mark 16:1)—are shared in common with Mary Magdalene. As a result, Mary Magdalene encompasses these features on her own, and so if there is no mention of the crucifixion or tomb visit in relation to the Mary of the *Dialogue of the Savior*, then it follows that this Mary cannot be Mary the mother of James either because these are the only cases where she appears in the canonical gospel narrative.

However, among the three main Marys, there are several defining characteristics that are attributed to the each. Mary Magdalene is his follower, who had seven demons cast out (Luke 8:2), was present at his crucifixion (Mark 15:47; John 19:25; Matt 27:56), went to the tomb (Matt 28:1; Luke 24:10; John 20:1), weeps when she finds the tomb empty (John 20:11), and receives a resurrection appearance and commission to tell the disciples about the resurrection (John 20:2–18). Mary of Bethany is beloved by Jesus (John 11:5), commended by him (Luke 10:42), is defended by him when she is criticized by another disciple (Luke 10:41–42; John 12:7–8), listens to him teach (Luke 10:39), is described as weeping (John 11:33), and anoints his feet with perfume (John 12:3). The mother of Jesus gives birth to him (Matthew 1–2; Luke 1–2), is referred to in passing as his mother (Matt 13:55; Mark 6:3), and is mentioned as being present at

---

[28] Ibid.

the crucifixion, though not by name (John 19:25–26). If one or more of these Marys is to be identified with the Mary of the *Dialogue of the Savior*, at least one of these characteristics ought to be present to make a convincing case for this argument. In order to determine the attributes associated with Mary in the *Dialogue of the Savior*, I will look at what is said about her, either by the narrator or the other characters, and highlight the discussions and situations in which she is prominent to see if she has any implicit traits.

The Mary of the *Dialogue of the Savior* is not explicitly identified as the Magdalene, the mother, or the sister of Martha. And while this Mary has traditionally been identified as Mary Magdalene, Shoemaker rightly observes that "the evidence for this is simply lacking."[29] In fact, there is no description attached to Mary concerning her geographical origin, familial connections, or specific role in the Jesus community. The only other named disciples in the text, Matthew and Judas, also do not have any sort of specific description that would tie them to any canonical characters. For example, one might expect Judas to be called Judas Thomas, as he is in the *Gospel of Thomas* and the *Book of Thomas the Contender*,[30] but he is simply called Judas, just as Matthew is simply called Matthew. It is also worth noting that the Jesus figure is never called "Jesus" but only "the Savior" or "the Lord." It could be argued that further descriptive details about Mary, Matthew, and Judas are mentioned in the now lost portions of the *Dialogue of the Savior*, but given the lack of dependence on other characteristics throughout the rest of the text, it seems rather that the author had no need or interest in reinforcing the canonical portraits of any of these disciples. The only possible exception to this is when the disciples address each other as "brother" (135.8) and likewise Mary is addressed as "sister" by Jesus (131.2). However, this type of sibling language is commonplace in early Christian writings, especially in the letters of Paul, and more than likely does not refer to actual biological relationships.[31]

One determinative characteristic of the Marys of the canon is their presence at the crucifixion or tomb. There is no crucifixion scene or resurrection scene in the *Dialogue of the Savior*, though it is usually assumed that the discussion takes place with a risen Jesus.[32] Even if one is to view this discourse as taking place in a post-resurrection setting, it does not seem to reflect any of the canonical episodes of the resurrection where any of the Marys encounter the risen Jesus either alone (John 20:11–18) or as part as a group of women (Mark 16:1–8; Matt 28:1–10). In the *Dialogue of the Savior*, Mary along with Matthew and Judas appear to be engaging with Jesus at the same time, and no other women are mentioned. Moreover, none of the three are singled out as

---

[29] Shoemaker, *Mary in Early Christian Faith*, 88.
[30] In addition to Judas Thomas, Marvin Meyer suggests that an identification with Judas Iscariot is just as likely *Judas: The Definitive Collection of Gospels and Legends about the Infamous Apostle of Jesus* (New York: HarperOne, 2007), 69–70.
[31] See, e.g., Abera Mitiku Mengestu, *God as Father in Paul: Kinship Language and Identity Formation in Early Christianity* (Eugene, OR: Pickwick, 2013), 20–2.
[32] Beate Blatz, "The Dialogue of the Saviour," in *New Testament Apocrypha*, ed. Wilhelm Schneemelcher and Robert McLachlan Wilson (Louisville, KY: Westminster John Knox, 2005), 300–3; Ann Graham Brock, *Mary Magdalene, the First Apostle: The Struggle for Authority* (Cambridge, MA: Harvard Divinity School, 2003), 99; Madeleine Scopello, "The Dialogue of the Savior," in *The Nag Hammadi Scriptures*, ed. Marvin W. Meyer (New York: HarperOne, 2007), 298.

receiving any special appearance or teachings over and above the others as is the case with Mary Magdalene in John 20:11–18 and the secondary ending of Mark (16:9–10).

Mary of Bethany in the Gospel of John is depicted as weeping, which also moves Jesus to tears (John 11:33–35). Another Mary, likely the Magdalene, weeps when she finds the tomb empty later in the same gospel (John 20:11). There is a brief discussion concerning weeping in the *Dialogue of the Savior*. Mary asks Jesus, "Lord, behold! Whence do I bear the body while I weep, and whence while I [laugh]?" Jesus responds, "… weeps on account of its works … remain and the mind laughs …" (126.17–23). Although this portion of the text is fragmentary, there is no indication that the discussion of weeping ought to be related to the Johannine narrative, but rather it appears to be a general discussion concerning the opposing concepts of weeping and laughing. Moreover, the fact that Mary is only presented as discussing weeping and not actually weeping herself makes it difficult to link this Mary to the canonical Marys' weeping.

Another canonical feature of the Marys that scholars link to the noncanonical Mary in the *Dialogue of the Savior* is that Jesus converses with Mary.[33] In the case of the *Dialogue of the Savior* and even other noncanonical writings that consist mostly of dialogue, I argue that Jesus speaking to Mary is a rather general, and unremarkable, characteristic. Most of the *Dialogue of the Savior* is in the form of a discussion. Therefore, if Mary, or any disciple for that matter, appears in a given sayings genre text, then they will almost be guaranteed to be speaking to Jesus. Otherwise, why would the author include them? For the canonical gospels, which have larger narrative episodes and perhaps include fewer dialogue scenes between Jesus and his disciples, it might be worth noting which disciples engage in conversation with Jesus. But in the case of the *Dialogue of the Savior*, and the *Gospel of Thomas*, for example, practically everyone who is explicitly named asks Jesus a question or talks to him.

In a similar vein, some scholars point to the fact that Jesus commends Mary of Bethany in the canonical gospels, just as he does in the *Dialogue of the Savior*.[34] Here too I would argue that if Mary is one of three named disciples in the text, she is likely to be commended by Jesus at some point during the discussion to reaffirm her interpretations or comments concerning his teachings. To be sure, while Mary is described as "the woman who had understood everything" (139.12–13) and Jesus tells her, "You make clear the abundance of the revealer!" (140.17–19), he tells all the disciples that they will rule over the governors (138.14–15), and after Matthew asks a question, Jesus tells him that he has never been asked about this saying except from him (139.20–140.4). Therefore, praising the disciples for their insights or questions seems relatively common and by no means unique to Mary. The other characteristics that are unique to Mary of Bethany, being described as beloved by Jesus or washing his feet with perfume, are absent from the Mary of the *Dialogue of the Savior*. Thus, there is nothing distinctive of Mary of the *Dialogue of the Savior* up until this point to link her either with Mary of Bethany or the Magdalene.

---

[33] Beavis, "Reconsidering Mary of Bethany," 294–6.
[34] Ibid., 296–7.

As mentioned earlier, Jesus in the *Dialogue of the Savior* at one point addresses her as "sister" (131.22). This does not automatically eliminate the possibility that she could be his biological mother, so it is necessary to see if there is any evidence to suggest that this Mary could be referring to Jesus' mother. Later in the text, Mary engages in a conversation with Matthew, Judas, and Jesus concerning the destruction of the "works of womanhood," that is, reproduction and birth (144.12–145.7).[35] I argued in my master's thesis that what could be implicit in Mary's response, "They will never be destroyed," is first-hand knowledge of her own experience as a mother, namely the mother of Jesus, perhaps alluded to by his response, "You know that they will not be destroyed."[36] This hypothesis on my part, however, was influenced by the notion that this Mary *had* to reflect one or more of the canonical Marys.

While there are no conclusive traits to link the *Dialogue of the Savior*'s Mary with any of those in the canonical gospels themselves, there is, however, one passage in the book of Acts that requires consideration. Acts 1:13–14 comes as close as we can get to compelling evidence to link any of the canonical Marys to the unspecified Mary of the *Dialogue of the Savior*. Acts states that after seeing Jesus ascend, the disciples return to Jerusalem. In v. 13, all eleven remaining disciples are named, including "Matthew" and "Judas son of James." The following verse explains that they "were constantly devoting themselves to prayer, together with certain women, including Mary the mother of Jesus, as well as his brothers" (Acts 1:14, NRSV). Although Shoemaker mentions Acts 1:13–14 in advocating the association with Jesus' mother to the unspecified Mary in general,[37] this account in Acts is rarely, if ever, considered in conversation with *Dial. Sav.* 144.12–145.2, where Judas, Matthew, and Mary participate in a discussion with Jesus about prayer. The reference in Acts to these three names in and of itself might not be convincing enough to suggest even a loose parallel to the pericope in the *Dialogue of the Savior*. However, given that they engage in a discussion about prayer, an activity to which all three "were constantly devoting themselves" warrants a closer analysis.

The post-ascension/resurrection context of Acts draws yet another potential connection to the *Dialogue of the Savior*. As previously mentioned, the majority of scholars assume that the dialogue takes place with a risen Jesus,[38] and while Mary, Judas, and Matthew are the only named disciples, on eight occasions, the text refers to "disciples" in general[39] and once specifically mentions "his [disciples], numbering twelve, asked him …" (*Dial. Sav.* 142.24–25), which could imply a post-ascension context like Acts. Are these individually minor details, when cobbled together, indicative of a conclusive association with the mother of Jesus from Acts? Given that many of these details relate not to Mary herself, but to incidental details, I am quite hesitant to answer in the affirmative. Rather, based on the *Dialogue of the Savior*'s seemingly lack of interest or effort in associating any overtly specific canonical details

---

[35] E.g., April D. DeConick, *Voices of the Mystics: Early Christian Discourse in the Gospels of John and Thomas and Other Ancient Christian Literature* (Sheffield: Sheffield Academic, 2001), 160.
[36] Cwikla, "'Pray in the Place,'" 54–7.
[37] Shoemaker, "A Case of Mistaken Identity?," 21. See also Shoemaker, *Mary in Early Christian Faith*, 39, 81–2.
[38] See n. 30 above.
[39] *Dial. Sav.* 120.2, 126.6, 136.1, 136.6, 136.10, 137.2, 139.13, 141.20.

to any of its named characters, coupled with the commonality of the name Mary, I am inclined to conclude that the unspecified Mary in this text fulfills her narrative function as an interlocutor without being associated with the Magdalene, Martha's sister, the mother, or even another.

The so-called Gnostic or Apocryphal Mary continues to intrigue scholars of early Christianity. She went from being identified almost unanimously as Mary Magdalene to potentially incorporating the portraits of other canonical Marys including Jesus' mother and Mary of Bethany. Previous studies have largely refrained from suggesting the possibility that the unspecified Mary need not refer to any of the canonical Marys. Onomastic data from antiquity suggest that Mary was a common name both in ancient Palestine and later in fourth-century Egypt. Using the Mary of the *Dialogue of the Savior*, I demonstrated that none of the distinguishing features of the canonical Marys are definitively evoked with this particular Mary. While this professedly in determinate conclusion may not entirely satisfy the "Which Mary?" debate, perhaps reframing the question to "Why does it matter which Mary?" can yield even more fruitful answers not only about the texts but also ourselves in future discussions.

6

Two Mary Magdalenes

Eusebius of Caesarea and the Questionable Reliability of the Gospels' Female Witnesses

Kara J. Lyons-Pardue

Many interpreters and historians have established that Christian tradition has melded into one figure, Mary Magdalene, the identities and descriptions of several women.[1] It is less commonly known that the reverse scenario can be found in the writings of Eusebius. Instead of conflating several female figures into one, Eusebius suggests that there may have been two Mary Magdalenes.[2] This is only one of the several solutions he identifies for resolving discrepancies between the evangelists' descriptions of the resurrection appearances—particularly apparent differences in expressing the timing of the resurrection and whether or not Mary Magdalene was permitted to touch Jesus—but it is arguably the one Eusebius expressly prefers. The better reading, he says, is that there *were* two women called Mary Magdalene referenced in the Gospels (*Ad Marinum* II.9; Matt 28:1; John 20:1–2, 11–18).

In what follows, I describe the "questions and solutions" document in which Eusebius's suggestion occurs. Then I summarize the questions of the interlocutor, one Marinus, pertaining to resurrection narratives. In more detail, I trace the range of proposed answers Eusebius provides to the literary conflicts with which he is presented. Two of his suggested solutions provide unique insight into his interpretations of Mary Magdalene's behavior in the canonical resurrection appearance passages. But Eusebius's most unusual proposal, of course, is that there were two women known as Mary Magdalene recorded in the gospel tradition.

Finally, I propose that we can identify some of Eusebius's crucial hermeneutical and historical allegiances on the basis of this narrow example. That is, despite the

---

[1] E.g., Mary Ann Beavis has demonstrated that there is some biblical and the early postbiblical Christian tradition precedent, which makes these two figures "amenable to blurring" ("Reconsidering Mary of Bethany," *CBQ* 74 [2012]: 282); See also on a similar theme, but focused on noncanonical texts, primarily F. Stanley Jones, ed., *Which Mary? The Marys of Early Christian Tradition* (SBLSS 19; Atlanta, GA: Society of Biblical Literature, 2002).

[2] Eusebius suggests that there are two disciples of Jesus called Mary Magdalene or "the Magdalene" (*Ad Marinum*, II.9; III.4), as he sometimes phrases it.

complications of doing so, Eusebius represents a steadfast commitment to the centrality and reliability of the female witnesses to Jesus' empty tomb and resurrection. This commitment arises from and undergirds his conviction that the Gospels speak in harmony. Eusebius's interlocutors raise a large number of concerns, homing in on discrepancies in the birth and resurrection narratives—passages with a greater concentration of women than the rest of the Gospels. The gender balance of these texts, I argue, may be the cause (subconsciously or otherwise) for the skepticism, whether actual or invented. Remarkably, Eusebius is ready to argue to *increase* the number of women upon whom this testimony relies rather than dismiss or ignore any of them.

Eusebius's *Ad Marinum* and Other *Erotapokriseis* Treatments of Gospels

The unusual proposition that the canonical Gospels reference *two* women named Mary Magdalene is found among a set of questions and answers on gospel topics. The questions were posed by a (real or imagined) interlocutor, Marinus, and the answers were penned by Eusebius of Caesarea. The document, entitled in Latin *Quaestiones ad Stephanum et Marinum*, includes another set of questions and answers addressed to Stephanus. These date to the early fourth century and seem to have only survived in an abbreviated form as well as in excerpted selections in ancient commentaries.[3]

This ancient genre, *Erotapokriseis*, represents a type of apologetics aimed, most likely, toward an audience of educated believers rather than skeptics.[4] In the sequence of questions, an interlocutor raises questions about the conflicts he or she has noticed in his or her reading of the Gospels. The author provides answers to the queries, taking the position of a knowledgeable authority. In this instance, Eusebius addresses each question and offers an answer or, sometimes, several potential solutions to the questioner.[5]

---

[3] Throughout this chapter, I refer to Eusebius's *ad Stephanum* and *ad Marinum* (*ad Mar.*) independently, as is customary. There is only a partial critical edition of the text available presently, undertaken with translation and commentary in French by Claudio Zamagni (*Eusèbe de Césarée, Questions Évangéliques: Introduction, texte critique, traduction et notes* [SC 523; Paris: Cerf, 2008]). I follow Zamagni's numbering where available. In 2010, Roger Pearse produced the first full English translation of the main texts, along with additional fragments in Syriac, Coptic, and Arabic (*Eusebius of Caesarea, Gospel Problems and Solutions; Quaestiones ad Stephanum et Marinum*, trans. David J. D. Miller, Adam C. McCollum, Carol Downer et al. [Ancient Texts in Translation 1; Ipswich: Chieftain, 2010]). I refer to Pearse's numbering and text for the fragments not found in the critical text. Zamagni notes that several scholars date Eusebius's composition of the *ad Marinum* around 320 CE and estimates that its present, epitomized form may have developed between the fourth and fifth centuries (*Questions Évangéliques*, 45–46). See also James A. Kelhoffer, "The Witness of Eusebius' *ad Marinum* and Other Christian Writings," *ZNW* 92 (2001): 78.

[4] On the "Question-and-Answer" genre—which is also called *erotapokriseis* (from ἐρωτάω, "ask," and ἀποκρίνομαι, "answer") or ζητήματά ("issues"), among other things, by the authors themselves—cf. Annelie Volgers, "Preface," in *Erotapokriseis: Early Christian Question-and-Answer Literature in Context*, eds. Annelie Volgers and Claudio Zamagni (CBET 37; Dudley, MA: Peeters, 2004), 3–4.

[5] In its fourth-century context, Eusebius's *Quaestiones et Responsiones* represents an early answer to a growing need to assuage worries that the Fourfold Gospel included irresolvable discrepancies: cf. Ambrosiaster (*Quaestiones veteris et novi testamenti*), Jerome (esp. *Epistula* CXX [*ad Hedybian*]), and Augustine (*De consensus evangelistarum*). Arguably, once the establishment of the Gospel canon

In the four-question set comprising the *ad Marinum*, each included question concerns an element Marinus finds incompatible with another Gospel's witness on the matter. While the questions seem most consumed with making sense of differences across the four-Gospel canon, this is not always the case. There are other questions that express confusion over an element self-contained within one Gospel in the *ad Stephanum*: for example, one of the Greek fragments addresses the question regarding how Elizabeth and Mary can be related, when Elizabeth is presumed to be from the tribe of Levi, whereas Mary is likely from the tribe of Judah.[6]

If Eusebius's *ad Marinum* has achieved any renown, it is for its testimony to the variety of ways in which the second Gospel concludes. Eusebius's first answer directed to Marinus constitutes the earliest reference by an ancient scholar to the absence of Mark 16:9–20 in known copies of Mark. Because passages concerning the death and resurrection of Jesus were lightning rods for internal disagreement and external critique, it is unsurprising that passages that feature these subjects (e.g., Mark 16:9–20) would be the subject of scrutiny. Eusebius responds to Marinus's question comparing Matthew's and Mark's last chapters. In doing so, Eusebius acknowledges the lack of 16:9–20 in many manuscripts of the second Gospel. In fact, as his argument proceeds, Eusebius's presentation of the manuscript situation becomes more dismal for the Long Ending.[7] Eusebius rephrases from its "not being present in *all*" to its being excluded from "accurate copies [τὰ ... ἀκριβῆ τῶν ἀντιγράφων]" of the "history according to Mark" (*ad Mar.* I.1).[8]

After the rise of modern textual criticism and the debate over the Markan endings, critics have paid attention to this acknowledgement from Eusebius with both praise and blame.[9] James Kelhoffer summarizes Eusebius well: "A discernible pattern is

had reached a formal stage and included Matthew, Mark, Luke, and John, the harmonizing impulse that we find in Tatian—which sought to iron out differences and present a logically and historically coherent narrative of Jesus' life—had to find a different genre for expression; rewriting the Gospel was no longer an acceptable solution. The texts of the Gospels, for the most part, were fixed (although scribal tendencies to harmonize, intentionally or not, remain evident long after the New Testament canon was officially established). Thus, asking a question of an accepted text or, in the present case, the relationship of two authoritative texts that seem to contradict one another requires an answer that demonstrates the harmony of the texts without changing the Gospels themselves.

[6] Fr.St.14; Greek fragment to Stephanus (see Pearse, *Gospel Problems and Solutions*, 157).
[7] Eusebius is perfectly clear that the ending in question is that which extends beyond the words of the young man to the women and their fear and flight, concluding with ἐφοβοῦντο γάρ (*ad Mar.* I.1).
[8] There is some significance, I think, to the fact that Eusebius characterizes Mark's account as ἱστορία. While the term can mean "narrative" or "account," it is sometimes used for systematic and scientific inquiries, or, in Herodotus, "history" (e.g., *Hist.* 1. praef.; 2.99; 7.96). Eusebius's endeavor in the *Quaestiones* is to do technical, historical work in the way of his time, and, thus, he treats the materials at his disposal as historical accounts. Many of these methods do not accord with modern ideas of history-writing, but Eusebius's terminology points to his intention to engage in historical research.
[9] Since its initial publication by Cardinal Angelo Mai in 1825, the *ad Marinum* has figured into the debate over Mark's endings. One staunch defender of the Long Ending, John W. Burgon, was particularly perturbed by Eusebius's witness (*Last Twelve Verses of Mark: Vindicated Against Recent Critical Objectors & Established* [Oxford: James Parker, 1871], 47). William R. Farmer follows Burgon's arguments and evidence closely in the 1974 study of Mark's Longer Ending that reignited the scholarly debate over the Second Gospel's endings. In fact, Farmer begins his investigation of the Long Ending with an image of the *ad Marinum* manuscript, followed by an extended discussion of the text, relying entirely on Burgon's edition and translation of the pertinent portion of the text (*The Last Twelve Verses of Mark*, xii–22).

evident: *an awareness of the text-critical problem concerning Mark 16,9–20 does not necessarily lead to a decision to refrain from making use of this passage.*"[10] That is, while Eusebius presents the possibility that a reader of the Gospels could find Mark 16:9 difficult to reconcile with the timing of the resurrection in Matt 28:1, and—knowing that the most reliable manuscripts lack 16:9–20—one could simply excise the questionable portion of the text. He suggests this as a solution first. Nonetheless, Eusebius goes on to propose that the texts are not actually in conflict and that, in fact, the preferable approach is to retain 16:9–20.

An ancient author's acknowledgement that there was variation between manuscripts of the Gospel according to Mark has had significant repercussions for the debate over Mark's endings.[11] This impact is compounded by the fact that this information in the *ad Marinum* was likely written by no less reputable source than Eusebius.[12] Of course, Eusebius's comments on the endings come in a context, which has often been forgotten or neglected. Kelhoffer's remarks on Eusebius's method are important for remembering his purpose in answering Marinus:

> Its author's main interest lies not, for example, in presenting text-critical observations concerning Mark's Longer Ending. On the contrary, and as the Preface states, his aim here and elsewhere is to offer resolutions to perplexing questions ... stemming from the accounts of the NT Gospels. Accordingly, the writing's primary purpose is *to defend the integrity of scripture*; thus, the author need not insist upon one particular way of responding to the questions.[13]

---

[10] Kelhoffer, "Witness of Eusebius," 111; italics original.

[11] Eusebius testifies that at least two ways of ending Mark were known in ancient times and, second, that the majority of what he perceived to be "accurate" texts known at the time ended at 16:8.

[12] Kelhoffer's study of the *ad Marinum* raises the question of authorship but does not answer it:

> On the basis of rather little evidence, scholars for nearly two centuries have unquestioningly accepted the Eusebian designation. The evidence for this ascription stems primarily from the superscription in the Vatican codex published by Mai. The ascription is also attested in later Syriac fragments of this material and in certain later Christian writings. The attribution to Eusebius, which has never been questioned, needs to be tested, but such an inquiry lies beyond the scope of this investigation. ("Witness of Eusebius," 81)

Claudio Zamagni's full-length French study of the text has been published since Kelhoffer wrote. Zamagni rebuffs the suggestion that the text might be pseudepigraphal: "Il ne s'agit certainement pas d'un texte pseudo-épigraphe, même si des savants ont mis en doute l'attribution eusébienne" (*Questions Évangéliques*, 11 n. 1). Zamagni points to Eusebius's *Demonstratio evangelica* (*Demonstration of the Gospel*) VII.3, which references the *Quaestiones ad Stephanum* (I.1–12). W. J. Ferrar (*Eusebius's The Proof of the Gospel* [Eugene, OR: Wipf and Stock, 2001; repr. 2 vols., London: SPCK, 1920], 2:88) translates the lines as follows:

> But the reason why the holy evangelists give the genealogy of Joseph, although our Saviour was not His son, but the son of the Holy Ghost and the holy Virgin, and how the mother of our Lord herself is proved to be of the race and seed of David, I have treated fully in the First Book of my *Questions and Answers concerning the genealogy of our Saviour*, and must refer those interested to that book, as the present subject is now occupying me.

In light of the internal reference to the first part, *ad Stephanum*, of the *Quaestiones* in another, accepted work of Eusebius's, attributing the question-and-answer text to him seems far less speculative than Kelhoffer depicts.

[13] Kelhoffer, "Witness of Eusebius," 93. The acuity of Kelhoffer's observation on this point cannot be overemphasized.

Eusebius answers Marinus's questions with a series alternatives or possibilities.[14] Nevertheless, each of the solutions he provides to Marinus's questions are possibilities that do not comprise a cohesive approach, cumulatively. If read as a series of alternative solutions, the "answers" make greater sense. Among those solutions he presents, Eusebius demonstrates preferences. He does so in regard to the initial two alternate ways of understanding the Long Ending. He does so also in his solutions that are our primary interest regarding Mary Magdalene.

Questions and Answers Pertaining to the Resurrection Narratives

Whereas Stephanus's questions concern the beginnings of the Gospels—including genealogical and virgin birth concerns—Marinus's questions concern the endings. Eusebius answers four questions from Marinus on apparent conflicts between the Gospels' witnesses to the resurrection appearances of Jesus.[15] The questions are, paraphrased:

I) How can one make sense of the timing of the resurrection, which Matthew says happened "late on the Sabbath," but Mark says was "early in the morning on the first day of the week"?[16]
II) How can Mary Magdalene have both witnessed the resurrection "late on the Sabbath," according to Matthew, and stand at the tomb weeping "on the first day of the week," according to John?[17]
III) How can it be that the same Mary Magdalene, according to Matthew, touched the Savior's feet along with the other Mary late on the Sabbath, who is also told "Do not touch me" early in the morning on Sunday according to John?[18]
IV) How might we understand the varying arrangements and angels or men at the tomb in Matthew (Mary Magdalene and the other Mary who see one angel outside sitting on the stone), in John (Mary Magdalene sees two angels inside the tomb), in Luke (two men appear to the women), and Mark (Mary Magdalene, James's Mary, and Salome see a young man sitting to the right of the tomb)?[19]

---

[14] Because we are lacking the full text, we cannot insist that this was intentional; it could be a result of the structure of the text as it is extant.
[15] In the surviving (likely abbreviated) text of Eusebius's *ad Marinum* there remains part of an answer to a question that is not asked in full and is unlike the other question–answer pairs in several ways. Regarding a partial answer to an unasked question in *ad Mar.* IV.5–6, Zamagni and Pearse each note signals of a different hand or epitomizer (see *Questions Évangéliques*, 222–3, n. 2; *Gospel Problems*, 121, n. 24).
[16] The questions' numbering with Roman numerals corresponds to their location in the text of the *ad Mar.* Although I offer a paraphrase of the gist of each question, I will include page citations corresponding to Pearse's English edition of each (here: *Gospel Problems*, 97).
[17] See ibid., 101.
[18] See ibid., 115.
[19] See ibid., 121.

The first question and answer sequence has occupied the majority of modern scholarly interest in the *ad Marinum*. It is fascinating, indeed, to see Eusebius wend his way through a tangled web of significant differences in manuscript attestation. He suggests the possibility of rejecting Mark 16:9–20 if it is conflict with the other Gospels' witness (*ad Mar.* I.1). But he settles on a broader definition of the time frames in reference (i.e., that there is not much conflict between late on the Sabbath and early on the first day of the week, especially when one may refer to Jesus' resurrection and the other to his appearance to Mary; I.3). Eusebius seems to side with the reader who is "someone who does not dare to reject as spurious anything at all contained in the writing of the gospels, might say that the reading is twofold, as in many other places, and that both are to be accepted; it is not for the faithful and devout to judge either as acceptable in preference to the other" (I.2).[20]

In the questions treating Mary Magdalene, we see consistency in Eusebius's desire to retain each Gospel's witness as valid, even if they seem to conflict, rather than adjudicating between them. In answer to Question II, which, like Question I, concerns the statements on the timing of the resurrection, except addressing the apparent conflict between Matthew and John, Eusebius restates this approach. He writes, "For thus the harmony [ἡ συμφωνία] of the voices of the Evangelists [τῶν εὐαγγελικῶν φωνῶν] would coincide" (*ad Mar.* II.3).

Eusebius's Answer to the Question of Mary Magdalene Clinging and Not Touching

As I have shown, it was not unusual for Eusebius to present several potential solutions to each question Marinus asked. One solution can exclude another; they do not have to operate together seamlessly. And so it is with Question II, concerning how it might make sense for Mary Magdalene to grasp Jesus' feet in worship "late on the Sabbath," but then be found weeping at the tomb "early in the morning" on the first day of the week. If the reader does not accept the solution that these are referencing one and the same instance (II.3), simply using two different ways of expressing that time period—ὀψὲ δὲ σαββάτων (Matt 28:1) and τῇ μιᾷ τῶν σαββάτων (John 20:1)—then Eusebius puts forward another solution. Eusebius himself returns to the episodic arrangement of these passages in future solutions (especially *ad Mar.* III).

Episodic Arrangement Solution

One *might* understand it that "the same Mary Magdalene saw both what is from Matthew and from John" (II.4). In fact, she is present in each Gospel's account not because they are describing the same moment but, instead, because she stays there, stunned, "longing to be found worthy of a second and third divine appearance, as well as the first" (II.4).[21] The other women come and go, recorded variously by the Gospels,

---

[20] Author's translation (throughout, unless otherwise noted).
[21] Translated by David J. D. Miller in Pearse, *Gospel Problems*, 107.

but Mary Magdalene is present for the events recorded by each Evangelist. In reference to the third question, which also seeks to figure out the relationship of Matthew and John, Eusebius says that *if* the Mary Magdalene in reference by both Evangelists is the "one and the same [μία καὶ ἡ αὐτὴ]" Mary across both Gospels (III.1), then she must have returned to the same place several times, drawn by astonishment and joy. He proposes a sequence that places John's events prior to Matthew's, primarily (III.1–3).

According to Eusebius, Matthew records events happening over a wider span of time, the angel rolling back the stone much earlier; after that John's account of Mary and the two male disciples who visit the tomb occurs. Somewhere in that sequence, two Marys visit the tomb and the angel proclaimed the good news to the women *again* [αὖθις εὐαγγελίζεται τὰς γυναῖκας] (II.5). While this sequential rearrangement seems like an all-encompassing solution to the problem—and one to which Eusebius returns (see III.2–3; IV.1)—all Eusebius claims for it is that "this, then, is one solution [Αὕτη μὲν οὖν μία λύσις]" to the difficulties present (II.5).

Eusebius reinforces that the episodic arrangement is merely one of several possibilities by stating immediately, "But the things set forth might be solved otherwise, if one interprets the Marys in Matthew to be different from the one in John" (II.6). Eusebius then distinguishes four different Marys in Matthew and John (II.6) before suggesting that there are two Marys from the same location, designated by τῆς Μαγδαληνῆς. Thus, the solution that comprises the major contribution of this project is to be seen as distinct from, but simultaneously textually intermingled with, the sequential rearrangement of each Evangelist's account. That is, the sequential mode is required for both, but different sequences are necessitated by the different understandings of the configurations of women involved.

Preferred Solution: Two Mary Magdalenes and Eusebius's Description of Each

Eusebius argues first that there are four Marys between Matthew's and John's account. They are, as he orders them: (1) first, the *Theotokos*, "the Savior's own mother"; (2) her sister Mary the wife of Clopas; (3) Mary Magdalene; and (4) the mother of James and Joseph (*ad Mar.* II.6). Despite arguing that there should be no conflict between these Gospels (II.7), Eusebius admits that the name "Magdalene" used in both Matthew and John may confuse the meaning (II.8). He is difficult to read on the matter, because he seems to dispute whether a single name or word in divine Scripture can be rightly considered to "introduce confusion." Nevertheless, Eusebius is ready to blame this on a scribal error: he suggests that maybe an early scribe made an error when listening to dictation. His theory is that the scribe incorrectly attached the designation "Magdalene" to one of the Marys to whom it did not belong (II.8). Eusebius contends that by removing the appellation "Magdalene" from one of the accounts, it would effectively remove any question concerning the passages (II.9).

Blaming the confusion on a scribal error is possible, as far as Eusebius is concerned. As before, however, simply providing a workable solution does not make it his favored solution. "*But*," Eusebius proceeds, "it is better not to assert any fault at all against the passages" (II.9). While scribal error is plausible, a *preferable solution* is to affirm that there were actually two women from a place called Magdala.

Mary Ann Beavis has noted that there is no indication internal to the Gospels themselves that "Magdalene [Μαγδαληνή]" refers to a geographic location.[22] Nevertheless, Eusebius uses the genitive "of Magdala [τῆς Μαγδαληνῆς]" several times (e.g., II.8-9). Without much explanation, Eusebius says that there may have been two woman called Mary "from one city or village of Magdalene [ἐπὶ μιᾶς πόλεως ἢ κώμης τῆς Μαγδαληνῆς]" (II.8). Eusebius defends the idea of two Marys from the same town even more stringently in the next section, calling it "not at all extraordinary/out of place [οὐδὲν ἄτοπον]" (II.9).

Once Eusebius reasons that it is fitting to say that there were two Marys from the same village of Magdala, he puts the theory to exegetical use in order to sort through the difficulties Marinus posed. One of the two is the Magdalene who comes to the tomb late on the Sabbath, like Matthew says (II.9), while the other Mary from the same village comes early in the morning, as in John (II.9). His argumentation takes on an additional nuance of divergent characterizations of each Mary from Magdala. He identifies the Magdalene of John, who is not permitted to touch Jesus (John 20:17), as the same one who is referenced in some copies of Mark as having had seven demons cast out of her (Mark 16:9; cf. Luke 8:2).[23] Eusebius compares John's Mary Magdalene negatively to Matthew's. For, as Eusebius reasons, "divine Scripture [ἡ θεία ... γραφή]" does not denounce Matthew's Mary Magdalene in such a way (*ad Mar.* II.9).

The Two-Magdalenes preference resurfaces again as Eusebius answers the third question, which focuses in on how Mary Magdalene can both grasp Jesus' feet in Matthew and *not* touch Jesus in John. Eusebius must formulate these answers taking into account the options he presented for resolving the previous question. Thus, it is in answer to Question III that we encounter the most elaborate rendition of the ordering of the resurrection appearances. The sequencing of appearances is of particular importance only if there is but one Mary Magdalene who both touches and does not

---

[22] Mary Ann Beavis states, "It is also debatable whether the title μαγδαληνή would have been taken as a gentilic ("Mary of Magdala") ..." ("Reconsidering Mary of Bethany," 286). Beavis's description of the canonical Gospels' references to Mary Magdalene continues to draw attention to the mismatch between many interpreters' assumptions and what the text says. Earlier, speculative Mary Magdalene researcher and popular author Margaret Starbird argued against taking "Magdalen," as she spells it, geographically (*The Woman with the Alabaster Jar: Mary Magdalene and the Holy Grail* [Santa Fe, NM: Bear, 1993], iii–iv, 78-9). Joan E. Taylor wrote an article on the matter ("Missing Magdala and the Name of Mary 'Magdalene,'" *PEQ* 146 [2014]: 205-23). In addition to raising serious archaeologically based objections to the conventional assumption that the Byzantine Magdala existed in the first century, Taylor attends to nicknaming practices Jesus seemed to have used for his closest disciples and includes Mary Magdalene among them (ibid., 207). Without contradicting these text-based arguments, it is vital to note that Eusebius represents a very early instance—perhaps the earliest recorded instance—of an interpreter taking μαγδαληνή to be a reference to a hometown associated with Mary (or two Marys). This serves as a corrective to Taylor's dating of the earliest citation of Magdalene as a place name to the sixth century (ibid., 213, 15).

[23] This is an extremely rare reference to demon possession—or former demon possession—as reflecting poorly on a person's character. Human complicity is never invoked relative to demonic possession in the New Testament. There is no question that being possessed is an undesirable state. However, in the Gospels, there are no indications that being possessed was thought to reflect negatively on the possessed person (cf. John 9:2). For more on this subject, see Loren T. Stuckenbruck, "The Human Being and Demonic Invasion: Therapeutic Models in Ancient Jewish and Christian Texts," in *Spirituality, Theology, and Mental Health: Multidisciplinary Perspectives*, ed. Christopher C.H. Cook (London: SCM, 2013), 94–123.

touch Jesus (III.1-3). In the face of this ostensible contradiction in Jesus' permissions, Eusebius posits a growth in Mary Magdalene's theological understanding of Jesus. She must progress in her conceptualization of Jesus—from teacher (John 20:16) to worshipped as God (Matt 28:9)—in order to make sense of Jesus' change in approach, from refusal to be touched (in John) to later acceptance of touching while worshipping (in Matthew).

But, for those readers who followed Eusebius into his preferred possibility that the Mary Magdalene in reference in Matthew is distinct from—and morally superior to, it seems—the Mary Magdalene in John 20 and Mark 16, Eusebius explains again why one is permitted to touch Jesus but the other is not. In this instance—and this is crucial—the order is opposite: the women come to the tomb late on the Sabbath and are allowed to worship Jesus, clasping his feet (*ad Mar.* III.4). The order of events necessarily shifts, based on what one accepts regarding Mary Magdalene.

In this way of viewing things, the Johannine Mary Magdalene arrives later (early in the morning) and is the same Mary Magdalene who is the former demoniac referenced Mark 16:9. To the disparaged Magdalene of John, Eusebius attributes an "exceeding disturbance" of ψυχή (III.4). Her lack of faith is evidenced by her standing and weeping, assuming the forced removal of her Savior's body (John 20:11-15). Eusebius sees this extreme emotional confusion as accounting for her lack of receptivity to the appearance of two angels and perception that Jesus is the gardener (*ad Mar.* III.4).

Eusebius calls the explanation that there are two Mary Magdalenes "better [κάλλιον]" (II.9) than its alternatives. That is, either that they are the same or that there was a scribal error in surnaming one of the two different Marys. Further, the Two-Magdalenes hypothesis allows him to solve two problems—the timetable *and* Mary Magdalene's varying reception by Jesus—with one explanation. It is clear that Eusebius does not merely allow the possibility that two of Jesus' followers were named Mary and hailed from Magdala but rather that this is his *preferred* explanation for the Evangelists' witness regarding the person or persons identified as Mary Magdalene.[24]

In summary, from Eusebius's perspective, the seeming differences in the Gospels' accounts can be explained as arising from the Evangelists' covering different episodes in the post-resurrection encounters of Jesus. As he rearranges sequencing, Eusebius repeatedly seems to prefer the solutions in which the women's presence and actions are accepted without question, rather than dismissed. Thus, Eusebius privileges the explanation of two Mary Magdalenes within this sequence, rather than the view of one Mary Magdalene who is repeatedly and laudably present at the tomb through several subsequent episodes. Although the latter might demonstrate her exceptional faithfulness, it also places in question her reliability in the accounts, from Eusebius's perspective. Eusebius would prefer two Mary Magdalenes (of varying emotional stability and moral quality) who cast no doubts upon the Evangelists' accounts than

---

[24] An obvious objection to Eusebius's Two-Magdalenes theory is that any identifying information added to a woman's name in the Gospel accounts—whether it is a relationship of marriage, motherhood, geography, or even "other"—is included in order to distinguish one person from another. Tal Ilan has established the extreme commonality of the name "Mary" in this time period and area (*Lexicon of Jewish Names in Late Antiquity: Part I, Palestine 330 BCE-200 CE* [Tübingen: Mohr Siebeck, 2002], 57). It is unclear whether Eusebius was aware of this onomastic phenomenon.

one increasingly faithful Mary Magdalene who throws a few wrinkles into sequencing the narrative episodes.

Insecure, but Indispensable: Implications of Women and Crucial Gospel Narratives

In conclusion, in the *ad Marinum*, Eusebius's testimony to the distribution of Markan endings in the manuscripts of which he was aware is indisputably important. His own text-critical methodology evidences the priorities of his age—seeking harmony in the face of ostensible conflict—that differentiate it from our own. Nevertheless, these issues have dominated what little discussion of the *ad Marinum* has taken place. So far, there has been hardly a passing notice to the fact that the passages under scrutiny are predominantly—and likely not accidentally—contingent on the testimony and activities of female disciples.

Of Marinus's four overarching questions that Eusebius addresses regarding the Gospels' resurrection accounts, *all four* of them come from verses and pericopae featuring women.[25] Although Eusebius lists Jesus' mother "first [πρῶτον]" (*ad Mar.* II.6; cf. Mark 16:9), the attention Eusebius devotes to securing Mary Magdalene, or the two Mary Magdalenes, as it were, evidences that she is his real priority. Only the first inquiry lacks the name "Mary Magdalene" in the question's wording itself; nonetheless, the verses in question involve her explicitly (Matt 28:1; Mark 16:1-2:9), and, thus, the answer mentions her frequently. Likewise, Eusebius does not streamline the list of women by consolidating the various Marys into one. Rather, he multiplies them. It is worth noting that he does *not* do so without disparaging some of the women implicated, disparaging the Johannine/Markan/Lukan Magdalene as a former demoniac.[26] Nevertheless, for Eusebius, the women are a fixed and indispensable element of the resurrection stories. He is determined to make sense of the reliability of their place in the stories rather than eschew their witness.

Thus, a major implication of Eusebius's series of explanations, and especially the highly unusual support for the doubling of Mary Magdalene, is that Eusebius is more inclined to increase the number of women on whose testimony the resurrection accounts rely, rather than subtract them. This stands as a contrary instance to a noticeable trend of erasing or minimizing women in Christian tradition. For Eusebius, securing the reliability of the Gospels requires arguing for the reliability of the women therein, especially the two Mary Magdalenes.

---

[25] In contrast, of the sixteen questions in the *ad Stephanum*, all of which concern some aspect of the genealogy and birth narratives in Matthew and Luke, only five pertain (in question or answer) to women. The difference is, perhaps, unsurprising, for each Gospel's resurrection accounts feature women in at least one episode, but the vast majority of names in the genealogy belong to males. Why Tamar, Uriah's wife, and Ruth appear in the genealogy is the subject of questions 7, 8, and 9, respectively (*Ad Stephanum* 7.1-8; 8.1-4, 9.1-3).

[26] Eusebius connects the Markan reference to Mary Magdalene's former possession by seven demons "according to some copies [κατά τινα τῶν ἀντιγράφων]" (II.9; Mark 16:9) to John's Mary Magdalene who is not to touch Jesus (20:17), without naming the additional connection to Mary Magdalene as a former demoniac in Luke 8:2.

7

Two Women Leaders
"Mary and the Other Mary Magdalene"

Ally Kateusz

Introduction

Where today in John 20 we see Mary the Magdalene in the garden with the risen Christ, authors of extracanonical narratives as well as church fathers and other writers in Ancient Syria instead often identified Jesus' mother as the Mary there. This ancient phenomenon is relatively well known. Robert Murray in his 1975 book on the early Syriac tradition gave numerous witnesses, and Thierry Murcia in his 2017 book on this very topic adds dozens more.[1] In this chapter, I argue that a specific variant in the Diatessaron may have been an important early source of the phenomenon.

Four examples will suffice for those less familiar with the phenomenon. The most famous example is the second-century Diatessaron. William L. Petersen calls the Diatessaron "the first Syriac gospel,"[2] and it was the primary gospel for many churches in Ancient Syria into the early fifth century.[3] Our best source for its text is Ephrem the Syrian's early fourth-century commentary on it, in which Ephrem did not mention the "Magdalene" and instead three times identified Jesus' mother as the Mary with the risen Christ.[4] For example, he wrote, "Why, therefore, did he prevent Mary from

---

[1] Robert Murray, *Symbols of Church and Kingdom: A Study in Early Syriac Tradition* (1975; repr., Cambridge: Cambridge University Press, 1977), 146–8, 329–35; Thierry Murcia, *Marie appelée la Magdaléenne: Entre traditions et histoire (Ier-VIIIe siècle)* (Aix-en-Provence: Presses Universitaires de Provence, 2017), 41–52 (Talmudic writers), 71–83, 297–300, 355–56; and Murcia, "Marie de Magdala et la mère de Jésus," *Revue des Études Tardo-Antiques* RET Supp 6 (2018-19): 47–69, esp. 56–66.
[2] William L. Petersen, *Tatian's Diatessaron: Its Creation, Dissemination, Significance, and History in Scholarship* (Vigiliae Christianae Supplements 25; Leiden: Brill, 1994), 432.
[3] Petersen, *Tatian's Diatessaron*, 432–3; Bruce Metzger, *The Early Versions of the New Testament: Their Origin, Transmission, and Limitations* (Oxford: Clarendon, 1977), 30–2; Carmel McCarthy, trans., *Saint Ephrem's Commentary on Tatian's Diatessaron: An English Translation of Chester Beatty Syriac MS 709 with Introduction and Notes* (JSS Supplement 2; Oxford: Oxford University Press, 1993), 3–9; and Arthur Vööbus, *Early Versions of the New Testament, Manuscript Studies* (Stockholm: Estonian Theological Society in Exile, 1954), 23–6.
[4] Ephrem, *On the Diatessaron* 2.17, 5.5, 21.27 (McCarthy, *Saint Ephrem's Commentary on Tatian's Diatessaron*, 67–8, 96–7, and 330–1).

touching him? Perhaps it was because he had confided her to John in his place, Woman behold your son."[5]

Perhaps the very oldest witness for the phenomenon is Irenaeus, born near Ancient Syria in the early second century. He also may have relied upon the Diatessaron tradition, for he also did not use the term "Magdalene" to distinguish the Mary in the garden from the Mary who was Jesus' mother. Instead, he wrote about "Mary" who gave birth to Jesus, compared "Mary" and Eve, and then described "Mary" as the first witness to the resurrection.[6]

Epiphanius of Salamis (ca. 310–403), who lived a day's sail from Ancient Syria, was more explicit in identifying Jesus' mother as a Magdalene. He listed "Mary the Magdalene" first in the list of women at the cross—conflating mother and Magdalene, since the mother is listed first in John 19:25—but then, like Ephrem, he identified Jesus' mother in the garden, saying, "The Lord enjoined it in the Gospel by illustrating it from one woman and telling his mother, 'Touch me not, for I am not yet ascended to my Father.'"[7]

Finally, the compiler of the third- or fourth-century Syriac *Didascalia apostolorum* apparently believed—like Eusebius of Caesaria, as Kara J. Lyons-Pardue discusses in her chapter—that there were *two* Magdalenes. The Syriac *Didascalia apostolorum* says, "Now in the Gospel of Matthew it is written thus: 'On the evening of the Sabbath as the first day of the week was dawning came Mary *and the other Mary Magdalene* to see the tomb.'"[8]

Murray proposed that confusion was the cause of the phenomenon.[9] A decade or so later, Ann Graham Brock and Jane Schaberg proposed that instead of confusion, perhaps scribes had deliberately substituted Jesus' mother for the Magdalene in order to undermine the Magdalene's female authority.[10] Yet Murray, Murcia, and Brock, as well as Stephen J. Shoemaker, R. H. Connolly, Walter Bauer, Alfred Loisy, and others,

---

[5] Ephrem, *On the Diatessaron* 21.27 (McCarthy, *Saint Ephrem's Commentary on Tatian's Diatessaron*, 330–1).

[6] Irenaeus, *Against Heresies* 3.22.2–7, 5.18.1–2, and 5.31.1 (*ANF* 1:455–56, 547, and 560). See Murcia, *Marie appelée la Magdaléenne*, 77, n. 47; 180, n. 34; 268 n. 40; 339.

[7] Epiphanius, Panarion 78.13.2 and 80.9.4 (Frank Williams, trans., *The Panarion of Epiphanius of Salamis*, 2 vols. [Nag Hammadi and Manichaean Studies 35 and 36; Leiden: Brill, 1994/1997], 2:610, 636); I have omitted Frank's "(sic!)" on 2:636. See also Murcia, *Marie appelée la Magdaléenne*, 132–5, 173–4, 177–83.

[8] Syriac *Didascalia Apostolorum* 21.11 (Alistair Stewart-Sykes, trans. *The Didascalia apostolorum: An English Version with Introduction and Annotation* [Studia Traditionis Theologiae, Explorations in Early and Medieval Theology 1; Turnhout: Brepols, 2009], 214], my emphasis; also note that various translators have attempted to harmonize this passage with our Greek gospels, e.g., translating it as "Mary Magdalene and the other Mary," or as here, adding a comma after the second "Mary," which I have corrected. Connolly rearranged the order to match our modern Matt 27:61; R. H. Connolly, *Didascalia apostolorum: The Syriac Version Translated and accompanied by the Verona Latin Fragments* (Oxford: Clarendon, 1929), 182. Vöörbus points out the consistency of the literal reading with Syrian tradition; Arthur Vööbus, *The Didascalia apostolorum in Syriac (Versio)* (CSCO 402/408; Leuven: Peeters, 1979), 190. Per Brock, Chrysostom had the same reading in his homilies as seen in the Syriac *Didascalia Apostolorum*; see Brock, *Mary Magdalene*, 132.

[9] Murray, *Symbols of Church and Kingdom*, 330.

[10] Ann Graham Brock, "What's in a Name: The Competition for Authority in Early Christian Texts," in *Society of Biblical Literature 1998 seminar papers* (Atlanta, GA: Society of Biblical Literature, 1998), 106–24; Brock, *Mary Magdalene, The First Apostle: The Struggle for Authority* (HThS 51; Cambridge, MA: Harvard University Press, 2003), 123–42; and Jane Schaberg, *The Resurrection of Mary Magdalene: Legends, Apocrypha, and the Christian Testament* (New York: Continuum, 2002), 236–7.

have also suggested that the text of the Diatessaron itself may have been the source of this early tradition.[11] Here, I argue that a specific variant in the Diatessaron may have been the source. In other words, Christians in Ancient Syria were neither confused nor substituting. In identifying the mother in the garden, they were simply following their own gospel.

Magdalene and Mother, Two Women Leaders

In recent decades, feminist scholarship has largely restored the memory of the Magdalene's leadership among the Jesus followers. Comparatively less attention, however, has been dedicated to recovering the memory of Jesus' mother as a leader in the Jesus movement. Yet two, or even more, women named Mary could have been leaders.

Both the author/s of Luke–Acts and the author of John appear to have remembered Jesus' mother in a strong role akin to leadership. Luke–Acts is best known for this. Luke 1:46–55 associates Jesus' mother with prophecy in the *Magnificat*, and Acts 1:14 again associates her with prophecy when the Holy Spirit descended in the upper room at Pentecost, naming only "Mary the mother of Jesus" among all the women there, as Joanne Badley notes in her chapter earlier in this book.

The author of John, more than any other gospel writer, elevated Mary the Magdalene as the first resurrection witness and apostle to the apostles. Yet, this author also elevated Jesus' mother during her son's adult ministry more than any other gospel writer did. Whereas the gospels of Luke, Mark, and Matthew almost entirely ignore Jesus' mother during his ministry[12]—or worse, seem to denigrate her (Mark 3:21, 31–35; Matt 2:46–50)—the Gospel of John depicts her with her son during three different events of his ministry and each time presents her positively. The first time is at the famous wedding at Cana, where she has an active role, instigating her son's miracle of changing water into wine and initiating his ministry (John 2:1–11). The second is directly afterward, in John 2:12, which says that Jesus, his mother, his brothers, and his disciples (in that order) traveled from Cana to Capernaum. The third is on Golgotha at his crucifixion (John 19:25–27), where—unlike in the synoptic Passion narratives—she is clearly identified as the mother of *Jesus*, her most important son and the protagonist of the narrative. The fact that John highlights Jesus' mother during his ministry is even more interesting when we see that John does not identify "Mary the Magdalene" until the very end of

---

[11] Murray, *Symbols of Church and Kingdom*, 332; Murcia, *Marie appellee la Magdaléenne*, 51; Brock, *Mary Magdalene*, 133; Stephen J. Shoemaker, *Mary in Early Christian Faith and Devotion* (New Haven, CT: Yale University Press, 2016), 85–6; R. H. Connolly, "Jacob of Serug and the Diatessaron," *JTS* 8 (1906–7): 581–90, esp. 587–88; Walter Bauer, *Das Leben Jesu im Zeitalter der Neutestamentlichen Apokryphen* (Tübingen: Mohr, 1909), 448; and Alfred Loisy, *Le Quatrième Évangile* (Paris: Alphonse Picard, 1903), 908, n. 1. For other scholars, see Murray, *Symbols of Church and Kingdom*, 332.

[12] Even at the cross and tomb, if Jesus' mother is named, it is not by the name of her most important son, which would seem to diminish her status as the mother of the savior. She is sometimes identified as Mary of James, but according to Richard Bauckham, *Gospel Women: Studies of the Named Women in the Gospels* (Grand Rapids, MI: Eerdmans, 2002), 206, the identification of a woman by the name of her son without also the word "mother"—μήτηρ—is apparently unattested.

the list of women at the cross—a seemingly belated mention that nonetheless does not diminish the Magdalene's subsequent elevation as the first witness in the garden and apostle to the apostles. In John, mother and Magdalene are not seen as competitors. John simply elevates one and then the other.

Additional evidence in John clarifies the author's intent to depict not only the Magdalene but also Jesus' mother as a leader among the disciples. The first person named in a list usually identified the leader. For example, in the lists of twelve disciples (Matt 10:2–4; Mark 3:16–19; Luke 6:14–16), Peter is named first. Likewise, Luke 8:2–3 names "Mary called the Magdalene" first among the women who followed Jesus. Yet in John 19:25, the mother is identified first in the list of women standing at the foot of at the cross. One might argue that she was named first because she was his mother, but the synoptic gospels always name Mary the Magdalene first. Further affirming that the author of John was highlighting Mary the mother's leadership of disciples, male as well as female, in John 2:12, on their trip to Capernaum, Jesus' mother is listed first, before "his brothers" or his "his disciples."

A foundation for the reception of Jesus' mother as a leader of disciples, thus, is in the canonical gospels themselves. Not surprisingly, some later artists and authors portrayed her in the same way. Illustrating this, the painter of a sixth-century painted reliquary box from Jerusalem painted five scenes on it, each of which depicted the same woman with a black *maphorion*. In one scene, she is clearly identified as Jesus' mother, shown resting after she gave birth. In another scene, she is portrayed as the liturgical leader of twelve deferential-looking men—her arms are raised and she stands slightly in front of them.[13] See Figure 7.1.

What is most remarkable here is *not* that that the artist portrayed Jesus' mother as an arms-raised liturgical leader; it is the ease with which the artist identified her in a third scene as the lead Mary of the two witnesses to the resurrection—as if both leadership constructs were consistent. The top left frame on the box depicts a woman dressed in a black *maphorion* carrying a censer and leading a second woman, who is dressed in red, toward the Anastasis rotunda and the shrine that was over the tomb of Christ. The top right frame depicts the same woman in a black *maphorion* as a liturgical leader—she is in the center, twelve men stand behind her, and her arms are raised, a gesture that Alexei Lidov says "is interpreted in iconographic studies as a liturgical one."[14] This scene mirrors passages in the *Gospel (Questions) of Bartholomew* and the Six Books Dormition narrative, both of which describe Jesus' mother raising her arms and then leading the male disciples in prayer.[15] The middle scene shows the same woman at

---

[13] For more information on this box, see Gary Vikan, *Early Byzantine Pilgrimage Art* (Dumbarton Oaks Byzantine Collection Publications 5, rev. ed.; Washington DC: Dumbarton Oaks Research Library and Collection, 2010), 18–20, fig. 6. A color version of this box can be seen online by googling "sancta sanctorum painted reliquary box."

[14] Alexi Lidov, "The Priesthood of the Virgin Mary as an Image–Paradigm of Christian Visual Culture," *IKON* 10 (2017): 9–26, quotation on 10. Filipova points out that in some areas, bishops were depicted with raised arms in art; Alzbeta Filipova, "Santo, Vescovo e Confessore: L'immagine di Apollinare nei mosaici di Classe," in *Lévêque, l'image et la mort: Identité et mémoire au Moyen Âge*, ed. Nicolas Bock, Ivan Folletti, and Michele Tomasi (Rome: Viella, 2014), 431–44, esp. 436.

[15] *Gospel (Questions) of Bartholomew* 2.6–13 (Wilhelm Schneemelcher, ed. *New Testament Apocrypha, Volume One: Gospels and Related Writings*, trans. R. McL. Wilson, rev. ed. [Louisville, KY: Westminster/John Knox, 1990], 1:540–53, esp. 545–6); and Agnes Smith Lewis, ed. and trans.,

Figure 7.1 Five scenes on an early sixth-century reliquary box painted in or near Jerusalem.
Source: Hartmann Grisar, *Die römische Kapelle Sancta Santorum und ihr Schatz: Meine Entdeckungen und Studien in der Palastkapelle der mittelalterlichen Päpste* (Rome: Laterano, 1908), plate 59.

the foot of the cross where Jesus' mother usually stands, and the bottom right scene shows her behind John the Baptist, with one of the two angels apparently holding out her black *maphorion*, as if to dry off Jesus or, perhaps, her.[16] The bottom left frame, however, unmistakably identifies the woman in black as Jesus' mother. It depicts her in an early example of the Nativity, resting after having given birth, an ox and a donkey peering at her infant son swaddled in the manger.[17]

The Mother's Markers of Liturgical Leadership

Authors of various extracanonical texts, such as the *Gospel of Mary* and the *Dialogue of the Savior*, which Judith Hartenstein and Anna Cwikla address in this volume, portrayed a Mary as a leader but do not clearly specify *which Mary* she was. An important text that specifically identifies Jesus' mother Mary as a leader, however, is the Dormition narrative, a text that is without question about Jesus' mother because it is explicitly about her later life and death. Research into Dormition narratives has expanded dramatically in the last fifteen years. Some scholars may privilege one branch or another of the Dormition text as the very oldest, but as my next chapter in this volume argues, all three main branches likely had a common source. Most scholars date the *Gospel of Mary* and the *Protevangelium of James*, a narrative about Mary's birth and early life, to the second century, and a variety of scholars now suggest that the Dormition narrative may have been as early.[18]

"Transitus Mariae," in *Apocrypha Syriaca: The Protevangelium Jacobi and Transitus Mariae* (StSin 11; London: C. J. Clay, 1902), 12–69 (English), 32. For more on this scene, see Ally Kateusz, "Ascension of Christ or Ascension of Mary?: Reconsidering a Popular Early Iconography," *JECS* 23 (2015): 273–303, esp. 273–92.

[16] For more on two ancient witnesses that placed Mary at her son's baptism, see Ally Kateusz, *Mary and Early Christian Women: Hidden Leadership* (New York: Palgrave Macmillan, 2019), 140–4.

[17] For an example of the Nativity scene, see Savvas Agouridis, "The Virgin Mary in the Texts of the Gospels," in *Mother of God: Representations of the Virgin in Byzantine Art*, ed. Maria Vassilaki (Milan: Skira editore, 2000), 58–65, plates 25 and 29. A color version of this box with better detail can be seen online by googling "sancta sanctorum painted reliquary box."

[18] Donato Baldi and Anacleto Mosconi, "L'Assunzione di Maria SS. negli apocrifi" in *Atti del congresso nazionale mariano dei Fratei Minori d'Italia* (Studia Mariana 1; Rome: Commissionis Marialis Franciscanae, 1948), 75–125, esp. 121-5; Bellarmino Bagatti, "La verginità di Maria negli apocrifi del II–III secolo," *Marianum* 33 (1971): 281–92; Frédéric Manns, "La mort de Marie dans le texte de la Dormition de Marie," *Aug* 19 (1979): 507–15; Richard Bauckham, *The Fate of the Dead: Studies on Jewish and Christian Apocalypses* (Leiden: Brill, 1998), 358–60; Stephen J. Shoemaker, *Ancient Traditions of the Virgin Mary's Dormition and Assumption* (Oxford: Oxford University Press, 2002), 238–45; Édouard Cothenet, "Traditions bibliques et apocalyptiques dans les récits anciens de la Dormition," in *Marie dans les récits apocryphes chrétiens*, ed. Édouard Cothenet (Paris: Médiaspaul, 2004), 155–75; Enrico Norelli, "La letteratura apocrifa sul transito di Maria e il problema delle sue origini," in *Il dogma dell'assunzione di Maria: problemi attuali e tentativi di ricomprensione*, ed. Ermanno M. Toniolo (Rome: Edizioni Marianum, 2010), 121–65; Shoemaker, "Jesus' Gnostic Mom: Mary of Nazareth and the Gnostic Mary Traditions" in *Mariam, the Magdalen, and the Mother*, ed. Deirdre Good (Bloomington: Indiana University Press, 2005), 153–82, esp. 162; Hans Förster, *Transitus Mariae: Beiträge zur koptischen Überlieferung mit einer Edition von P. Vindob. K 7589, Cambridge Add 1876 8 und Paris BN Copte 12917 ff. 28 und 29* (Berlin: Walter de Gruyter, 2006), 225–9; Shoemaker, "New Syriac Dormition Fragments from Palimpsests in the Schøyen Collection and the British Library," *Le Muséon* 124 (2011): 259–78, esp. 266; and Ally Kateusz, "Collyridian Déjà Vu: The Trajectory of Redaction of the Markers of Mary's Liturgical Leadership," *JFSR* 29 (2013): 75–92, esp. 77–78, 92.

The very oldest nearly complete Dormition manuscript is fifth century, the under script of an Old Syriac palimpsest.[19] Its narrative is sometimes called the Six Books Dormition narrative because it says the apostles wrote six books about Mary's passing,[20] although it is also sometimes called the "Bethlehem and incensing" tradition because it depicts Mary and other women going to Bethlehem and using censers and incense.[21] In a scene where Jesus descends on his chariot of fire to take his dying mother up to heaven, the palimpsest text appears to preserve the cultural memory of his mother as the Mary who had been with him in the garden. It reads:

> And our Lord Jesus the Christ called to His mother and said to her, "Mary!" And she said to Him, "Here I am, Rabbuli," which is, being interpreted, Teacher.[22]

These are almost the same words that the Magdalene and Jesus exchange in the garden in John 20:16–17, yet here the author wrote them between Jesus and his mother, and did so without any polemic or explanation, as if everyone knew Jesus' mother had been in the garden with her resurrected son.[23]

The text of the fifth-century palimpsest is most striking, however, in the way that it portrays Jesus' mother with many markers of leadership—more than found in the text of any other published Dormition manuscript. It would hardly make sense for a scribe interested in subverting female authority to substitute one woman leader with another woman leader, and the palimpsest's text, which is explicitly about Jesus' mother, describes her raising her arms and leading the male apostles in prayer, "serving in essence as their liturgical leader"[24]—just as she was painted in the top right frame of Figure 7.1. The palimpsest text also portrays Jesus' mother preaching the gospel,[25] setting out the censer of incense to God,[26] healing with her hands,[27] sprinkling, sealing, and exorcising,[28] and teaching.[29] Perhaps the most remarkable scene of her leadership in the palimpsest text, however, describes women coming to Jerusalem to learn from

---

[19] For its discovery, editing, and fifth-century dating, see Agnes Smith Lewis, ed. and trans., *Apocrypha Syriaca: The Protevangelium Jacobi and Transitus Mariae with Texts from the Septuagint, the Corân, the Peshiṭta, and from a Syriac Hymn in a Syro-Arabic Palimpsest of the Fifth and Other Centuries, with an Appendix of Palestinian Syriac Texts from the Taylor-Schechter Collection* (StSin 11; London: C. J. Clay, 1902), ix–x; and for its fifth-century dating today, see Shoemaker, *Ancient Traditions*, 33; and Shoemaker, "New Syriac Dormition Fragments," 264. Only much smaller Old Syriac Dormition fragments composed of a few folios are as early or perhaps a little earlier.
[20] Smith Lewis, "Transitus Mariae," 12–69 (English), esp. 17.
[21] Michel-Jean van Esbroeck, "Les textes littéraires sur l'Assomption avant le Xe siècle," in *Les actes apocryphes des apôtres*, ed. François Bovon (Publications de la faculté de théologie de l'Université de Genève 4; Geneva: Labor et Fides, 1981), 265–85, 273; see also Kateusz, *Mary and Early Christian Women*, 29–42.
[22] Smith Lewis, "Transitus Mariae, 55.
[23] See Murcia, *Marie appelée la Magdaléenne*, 355, who makes the same observation.
[24] Smith Lewis, "Transitus Mariae," 32. Quote is from Stephen J. Shoemaker, "Mary the Apostle: A New Dormition Fragment in Coptic and Its Place in the History of Marian Literature," in *Bibel, Byzanz und Christlicher Orient: Festschrift für Stephen Gerö*, ed. Dmitrij F. Bumazhnov et al. (Leuven: Peeters, 2011), 217, regarding a similar scene in the *Gospel (Questions) of Bartholomew*.
[25] Smith Lewis, "Transitus Mariae," 47–8.
[26] Ibid., 47.
[27] Ibid., 34, 35, and 48.
[28] Ibid., 34.
[29] Ibid., 24, 34, 47–8.

her, after which she gave these women writings[30] to take to their home cities around the Mediterranean so that others might believe[31]—essentially a portrait of Jesus' mother teaching and sending out women evangelists.

Later scribes redacted many of these markers of Mary's liturgical authority.[32] The trajectory of this redaction can be seen by comparing the fifth-century palimpsest text against that of two later manuscripts in the Six Books manuscript tradition. One comparison text is the second-oldest nearly complete Dormition manuscript that has been published, a late sixth-century Old Syriac Dormition manuscript translated by William Wright.[33] The other is an Ethiopic translation in a late medieval manuscript, which Shoemaker translated and considers an early recension.[34] Figure 7.2 illustrates how the two later scribes excised a passage that described Mary exorcising demons from a woman.

As can be seen in Figure 7.2, the two later scribes excised different parts of the older, longer passage. On the one hand, the scribe of the sixth-century Syriac manuscript removed most of the description of Mary exorcising demons—but preserved most of Malchū's name and family lineage.[35] On the other hand, the scribe behind the Ethiopic translation preserved most of the exorcism but anonymized Malchū. This scribe anonymized *all* the women whom Mary healed in the text, apparently following a trend of anonymizing women also seen in Sozomen and Theodoret's fifth-century church histories.[36] This redaction analysis demonstrates that the long text of the fifth-century palimpsest is not only from the oldest manuscript, but it is also the most original. The two later scribes simply made different decisions about what to cut.

Older Is Longer versus *Lectio Brevior Lectio Potior*

The idea that the longest recension of a text is the most original reading contradicts the old NT rule of thumb, *lectio brevior lectio potior*, that is, the shortest reading is the most probable reading. Figure 7.2, thus, demonstrates the validity of well-known caveats with respect to that old rule of thumb. Expert text critics are aware of its limitations. For example, Larry Hurtado says, "At least in the NT papyri from the second and third centuries, contrary to the assumptions of some previous scholars, omission is notably more frequent than addition (calling into question the sometimes rigid use of the 'prefer the shorter reading' canon in assessing

---

[30] The Syriac word used here can mean writings, small books, or letters.
[31] Smith Lewis, "Transitus Mariae," 34.
[32] Kateusz, "Collyridian Déjà vu," 79–86.
[33] William Wright, "The Departure of My Lady Mary from This World," *Journal of Sacred Literature and Biblical Record* 7 (1865): 129–60. For dating, see Shoemaker, *Ancient Traditions*, 47.
[34] Shoemaker, *Ancient Traditions*, 375–96.
[35] William Wright, trans., "The Departure of My Lady Mary from This World," *Journal of Sacred Literature and Biblical Record* 7 (1865): 129–60, esp. 141–2.
[36] Ethiopic Six Books, 35–6 (Shoemaker, *Ancient Traditions*, 384–5. For more on the anonymization of women, see Anne Jensen, *God's Self-Confident Daughters: Early Christianity and the Liberation of Women*, trans. O. C. Dean Jr. (Louisville, KY: Westminster, 1996), 6–8.

5th-c. Syr. palimpsest	6th-c. Syr. ms	Medieval Ethiop. ms
Malchū came also to her,	Came to her Malchū,	Came another woman,
the daughter of Sabinus, the Procurator,	the daughter of Sabinus,	omitted
in whom were two demons;	who had two devils,	who was beset by many demons
one that tormented her by night; and the other that came upon her by day, and buffeted her;	one that tormented her by night; and another that came upon her by day;	omitted
and she entreated the Lady Mary;	omitted	and she cried out to Mary with a great voice, saying, 'Have mercy on me, my master.'
and immediately when she had prayed over her, and had placed her hand upon her, and had spoken thus:	and she prayed over her,	She extended her hand and prayed, saying,
"I adjure thee, in the name of my Master Who is in heaven, at this time concerning this soul, that she may be healed."	omitted	"I adjure you, in the name of the Lord Jesus Christ, come out of this soul, and do not afflict her again."
And straight away these demons came out of her, and they wailed, and cried out, saying,	and she was healed.	And at that moment, the demons went forth from that woman, crying out and saying,
"What is there between us and thee, O Mother of God?"…		"What do you have agains us Mary, the one who bore Christ?"…
Then the Lady Mary		Then Mary
rebuked them in the name of our Lord Jesus the Christ.	omitted	omitted
And straightaway they departed towards the sea.		plunged them into the depths of the sea.

Figure 7.2 Redaction analysis: Mary exorcizes demons. Chart comparison of three manuscripts. © Ally Kateusz.

textual variants)."³⁷ Eldon J. Epp and Gordon D. Fee say *lectio brevior lectio potior* must "be used *with great caution* because scribes sometimes made omissions in the text either for smoothness or to remove what might be objectionable."³⁸ Bruce Metzger similarly says that the *longest* reading can be the best reading in a variety of scenarios, including when what was omitted was considered "offensive to pious ears."³⁹

The scholarly trend away from the old NT rule of thumb is even stronger with respect to texts *outside* the canon, because later scribes even more commonly excised passages from those texts. In a study of Christian and Jewish apocalypses, including the apocalypse at the end of the Six Books Dormition narrative, Richard Bauckham says, "The textual tradition tended to abbreviation rather than expansion."⁴⁰ François Bovon, who worked with the various manuscripts of the *Acts of Philip*, a text that included the female evangelist Mariamne, explains, "Apocryphal texts were sometimes perceived by their readers to be overly redundant or even heretical in places. Consequently these texts were often abbreviated."⁴¹ Shoemaker has also advocated that a long Dormition narrative is more likely to be older than a short one.⁴²

The old NT rule of thumb, thus, should never be considered a rigid rule. It especially should not be considered the most appropriate rule of thumb for narratives about a woman portrayed with leadership authority. That is because, as seen in Figure 7.2, if a later scribe or their master considered the description of a woman leader "objectionable," or "offensive to pious ears," or "even heretical," they might (and often did) excise that description.

Here, I restrict my conclusions about this rule of thumb to *narratives* about women in the early Jesus movement who were depicted with leadership authority, that is, a story about a woman leader *doing* something that portrayed her with authority—especially when she was depicted with authority that later became restricted to men. A narrative format where a woman is portrayed as an active leader is different from a homily or other tract where an author simply lauds the woman with florid descriptions of her purity or submissiveness, such as is often seen in later homilies about Jesus' mother. As seen in Figure 7.2, as well as in the two charts (Figures 14.3 and 14.4), which I provide in my next chapter regarding passages about Mary and the women who were with her using censers and incense, later scribes excised passages that described women with

---

[37] Larry W. Hurtado, "*The Pericope Adulterae: Where from Here?*" in *The Pericope of the Adulteress in Contemporary Research*, ed. David Alan Black and Jacob N. Cerone (London: Bloomsbury T&T Clark, 2016), 147–58, quotation on 152.

[38] Eldon J. Epp and Gordon D. Fee, *Studies in the Theory and Method of New Testament Textual Criticism* (Grand Rapids, MI: Eerdmans, 1993), 14. My emphasis.

[39] Bruce M. Metzger, *The Text of the New Testament: Its Transmission, Corruption, and Restoration* (New York: Oxford University Press, 1968), 120. Emphasis mine.

[40] Bauckham, *Fate of the Dead*, 347.

[41] François Bovon, "An Introduction to the *Acts of Philip*," in *The Acts of Philip: A New Translation*, ed. Bovon and Christopher R. Matthews (Waco, TX: Baylor University Press, 2012), 1–30, quotation on 7–8. Also see Bovon's student, Richard N. Slater, "An Inquiry into the Relationship between Community and Text: The Apocryphal *Acts of Philip* 1 and the Encratites of Asia Minor," in *The Apocryphal Acts of the Apostles*, ed. François Bovon, Ann Graham Brock, and Christopher R. Matthews (Cambridge, MA: Harvard University Press, 1999), 281–306, quotation on 286.

[42] Shoemaker, "Mary the Apostle," 203–29, esp. 212–13.

such authority. Thus, for narratives about women leaders, another rule of thumb—*lectio difficilior potior*—the most difficult *or unusual* reading is probably the original text—is more likely to be correct. That is because as later generations of scribes excised such markers, over time passages with those markers indeed became rarer and more unusual.[43]

The substitution of Peter for Jesus' mother

A later Coptic scribe substituted Peter for Mariamne in the manuscript tradition of the *Acts of Philip*.[44] This is particularly significant because the original *Acts of Philip* calls Mariamne an "apostle"[45] and describes her evangelizing,[46] breaking the communion bread,[47] exorcizing,[48] and baptizing.[49] Brock was correct when she said, "The replacement of Mary by Peter as Philip's companion in the Coptic version of the Acts of Philip eliminates the authoritative position she held in the original Greek text."[50] Brock in particular has influentially argued that Mariamne in the *Acts of Philip* was the Magdalene, while others, including Mary Ann Beavis and myself, have observed that arguments can be made that readers alternatively could have understood Mariamne as Mary of Bethany, because Martha was also present,[51] or as Jesus' mother, because the oldest *Protevangelium* manuscript similarly names her *Mariamne*.[52] What is of key importance here is not which Mary but that a later Coptic scribe replaced Mariamne with Peter—yet this phenomenon of replacement is by no means unique to a Mary identified as the Magdalene. Sometimes later scribes of the Dormition narrative replaced Jesus' *mother* with Peter. One important Dormition passage where some scribes substituted Peter for Mary the mother was the scene that portrayed her leading the male apostles in prayer as their liturgical leader.[53] This scene was popular in early Christian art, and it comprises the top right frame of the early sixth-century reliquary box seen in Figure 7.1, here seen as Figure 7.3.

---

[43] For more discussion see Kateusz, *Mary and Early Christian Women*, 19–65.
[44] Brock, *Mary Magdalen*, 124–8.
[45] *Acts Phil.* 8.21 and 9.1 (François Bovon and Christopher R. Matthews, trans., *The Acts of Philip: A New Translation* [Waco, TX: Baylor University Press, 2012], 74). These specifically reference Mariamne as the apostle, plus the author elsewhere presented her as one of the "apostles."
[46] *Acts Phil.* 8.2–3, 15.3 and 15.9 (Bovon, *Acts of Philip*, 74, 95).
[47] *Acts Phil.* 8.2–3 (Bovon, *Acts of Philip*, 74).
[48] *Acts Phil.* 9.3–4 (Bovon, *Acts of Philip*, 81).
[49] *Acts Phil.* 14.9 (Bovon, *Acts of Philip*, 91).
[50] Brock, *Mary Magdalen*, 128.
[51] Mary Ann Beavis, "Mary of Bethany and the Hermeneutics of Remembrance," *CBQ* 75 (2013): 739–55, esp. 750–52; Allie M. Ernst, *Martha from the Margins: The Authority of Martha in the Early Christian Tradition*, VC Supplements 98 (Leiden: Brill, 2009), 2, 6, 7–8, 116, 130.
[52] Kateusz, "Collyridian Déjà vu," 91; François Bovon, "Mary Magdalene in the *Acts of Philip*," in *Which Mary? The Marys of Early Christian Tradition*, ed. F. Stanley Jones (SBLSS 19; Atlanta, GA: Society of Biblical Literature, 2002), 75–89, esp. 78–9; and Murcia, *Marie appelée la Magdaléenne*, 115–24.
[53] Smith Lewis, "Transitus Mariae," 32. A similar scene is found in the third-century *Gospel (Questions) of Bartholomew*; *Gospel (Questions) of Bartholomew* 2.6–13 (Schneemelcher, *New Testament Apocrypha*, 1:540–53, esp. 545–6, with dating on 540).

Figure 7.3 Liturgical scene with Mary, Jesus' mother. Excerpt of one frame of five on early sixth-century reliquary box painted in Jerusalem. Vatican Museum, Rome. Photo courtesy of Ally Kateusz.

Art historians used to suppose that this iconography was a strange rendering of the Ascension of Jesus, because both Mary and Paul are in the scene, which does not comport with the canonical account. (Here Paul, balding, is portrayed left of Mary.) Recently, however, the origin of this iconography was identified as a scene in the early Dormition narrative, a scene that says Jesus returned to earth to take his dying mother up to Heaven.[54] According to the text of the fifth-century Dormition palimpsest, the male apostles, *including specifically Paul*, came from their missions around the Mediterranean to see Mary before she died. They arrived all at once, and each informed her what he had been doing.[55] Then Mary lifted her hands, praised God, and spoke the prayer.

> And when my Lady Mary heard these things from the Apostles she stretched out her hands to heaven and prayed, saying, "I worship and praise and sing and

---

[54] See Kateusz, "Ascension of Christ or Ascension of Mary?" 273–92.
[55] Smith Lewis, "Transitus Mariae," 27–32.

laud that I am not a mockery to the nations of the Gentiles ... and I will praise His gracious name for ever and ever. And I cannot glorify His grace sufficiently; that He hath sent His holy disciples to me." And after Mary had prayed, the Apostles set forth the censer of incense, and knelt with their faces down and prayed.[56]

The scribes of the two later Dormition manuscripts diminished the impression of Mary's authority over the men, again with different edits. The sixth-century scribe excised that the apostles prostrated after Mary prayed.[57] The scribe behind the Ethiopic translation preserved the men's prostration but excised that Mary raised her hands.[58] Other later recensions likewise omit that Mary lifted her hands to pray, which explains why the iconography of this scene was misunderstood for so long.[59] Perhaps scribes omitted Mary raising her hands to pray in order to bring the text into compliance with 1 Tim 2:8, which instructs *men* to lift their hands to pray.

Another Dormition scribe diminished the liturgical authority of Jesus' mother in this scene by substituting Peter for her as the prayer leader. Perhaps this redaction also was to bring the text into compliance with 1 Timothy, because 2:11–12 instructs that women should be silent and *not* have authority over men. This substitution is found primarily in a wide number of medieval manuscripts of one branch of the Dormition narrative, which is called the Palm Dormition narrative because it typically says Jesus gave Mary a palm branch. This homily is found in medieval manuscripts of the popular homily attributed to John of Thessalonica, a seventh-century bishop.[60] According to this homily, when the men arrived at Mary's house, instead of Mary raising her arms and leading their prayer, Peter raised *his* arms and led the prayer.[61] The text then repetitively describes Peter preaching for hours upon hours until it finally ends with the following: "After Peter had said these things and exhorted the crowd until dawn, the sun rose. And Mary got up and went outside, and raised her hands and prayed to the Lord."[62] For this scribe, Peter was the proper prayer leader, not a woman—and although Mary still could raise her hands to pray, she only could do so when she was alone, outside, away from the men.

Two Gaelic Dormition manuscripts demonstrate a similar substitution. Again Jesus' mother is silenced when she is replaced by Peter. In the original text, both she and Peter ask Jesus questions. In the later recension, Peter asks both his questions

---

[56] Ibid., 32. Shoemaker says that the title "my Lady Mary" is better translated as "my master Mary," in Shoemaker, *Ancient Traditions*, 370, n. 3. The final sentence, that the men knelt with their faces down to pray, is especially curious in light of the *Apostolic Church Order*, which quotes "Kephas" alternatively saying, "Women should not pray upright but seated on the ground," in *Apostolic Church Order* 27 (Alistair Stewart-Sykes, trans., *The Apostolic Church Order: The Greek Text with Introduction, Translation, and Annotation* [Strathfield, NSW: St. Paul's, 2006], 113).
[57] Wright, "Departure of My Lady Mary," 140.
[58] Ethiopic Six Books 33 (Shoemaker, *Ancient Traditions*, 383).
[59] For details, see Kateusz, "Ascension of Christ," 293–4. See also most of the homilies in Brian E. Daley, *On the Dormition of Mary: Early Patristic Homilies* (Popular Patristics Series 18; Crestwood, NY: St. Vladimir's Seminary, 1998).
[60] John of Thessalonica, *On the Dormition* 3 (Daley, *On the Dormition of Mary*, 49).
[61] John of Thessalonica, *On the Dormition* 7 (Daley, *On the Dormition of Mary*, 55–6).
[62] John of Thessalonica, *On the Dormition* 12 (Daley, *On the Dormition of Mary*, 62).

and Mary's questions.⁶³ The scribal practice of using the figure of Peter to remove the authority of a woman leader named Mary thus included scribes who used Peter to replace Jesus' mother Mary.

A Possible Variant

Prior to Constantine, Christianity was strongest in the Eastern Mediterranean, with Ancient Syria probably the most influential area of all. Authors from Justin Martyr to Jerome were either born in Ancient Syria or visited there. Jerusalem, as well as all the major pilgrimage sites associated with Jesus' life, were in Ancient Syria, and the traditions of this land traveled with pilgrims around the Mediterranean.⁶⁴

In the second century, the Diatessaron was compiled in Ancient Syria, in either Old Syriac or Greek, and, subsequently, very early, it was translated into Latin, as well as into other ancient languages. Arthur Vööbus says vestiges of the Diatessaron are found "from Armenia to Abyssinia, and from Persia to the British Isles."⁶⁵ A Greek fragment found at Dura-Europos, which was abandoned by 257 CE, appears to provide a very early witness to its popularity.⁶⁶ In the third century, the Diatessaron was the primary gospel in Ancient Syria and it remained in good standing there until the early fifth century, when all copies were rounded up and replaced by the four canonical gospels.⁶⁷ A variant in the text of the Diatessaron thus potentially could have been influential very early, not only in Ancient Syria, but also around the Mediterranean.

I propose that the reason writers in Ancient Syria described the mother in the garden was not because they were confused, nor because they were trying to subvert women's authority by replacing the Magdalene with the mother, but because of a textual variant. I propose that writers such as Ephrem in his commentary on the Diatessaron placed the mother in the garden with the resurrected Christ because the Diatessaron—and quite likely also the fourth-century Old Syriac Gospel of John—had a critical variant that facilitated reading the text that way. John 19:25 is the *only* place in all four canonical gospels where Jesus' mother and the Magdalene are clearly identified in the same room at the same time: "There stood by the cross of Jesus his mother, and the sister of his mother Mary of Clopas, *and Mary the Magdalene*." I propose that the Diatessaron variant was that "and Mary the Magdalene" was *not* at the end of the list of women at the foot of the cross. This variant could explain the identification of Jesus' mother as the Magdalene, because if a reader never clearly saw mother and Magdalene

---

⁶³ Charles Donahue, *The Testament of Mary: The Gaelic Version of the Dormitio Mariae together with an Irish Latin Version* (New York: Fordham University Press, 1942), 10.

⁶⁴ This tradition continued into the medieval era in both East and West; for a discussion of its retention in the West, see Katharine Ludwig Jansen, *The Making of the Magdalen: Preaching and Popular Devotion in the Later Middle Ages* (Princeton, NJ: Princeton University Press, 2000), 59–62.

⁶⁵ Vööbus, *Early Versions of the New Testament*, 22–3.

⁶⁶ I follow Jan Joosten, "The Dura Parchment and the Diatessaron," *VC* 57 (2003): 157–75.

⁶⁷ McCarthy, *Saint Ephrem's Commentary on Tatian's Diatessaron*, 3–9; Petersen, *Tatian's Diatessaron*, 432; and Vööbus, *Early Versions of the New Testament*, 23–6.

in the same place at the same time, the reader logically could assume that one very important woman named Mary had two roles, two titles—both *mother* and *Magdalene*.

Unfortunately, no copy of the Diatessaron has survived, because in the early fifth century, bishops such as Theodoret of Cyrus collected all the copies of the Diatessaron in their jurisdictions and destroyed them.[68] Making the case even more difficult to prove, both Old Syriac gospel manuscripts have lacunae at John 19:25.[69] Given these lacunae, however, I go next to the Old Latin gospels, because the Old Latin not only had readings that "preserved a large number of readings which are from the Diatessaron," it also went "hand in hand with the Old Syriac."[70] Therefore, the Old Latin might preserve this variant at John 19:25 if either the Diatessaron or the Old Syriac (or both) had it.

The very oldest Old Latin gospel manuscript—which is also the very oldest European gospel manuscript—the fourth-century Codex Vercellensis, also known as Old Latin a, preserves the variant.[71] In Codex Vercellensis, "and Mary the Magdalene" is not at the end of John 19:25. It instead reads: *Stabat autem secus crucem ihū mater eius maria et soror matris eius maria cleophaes*, that is, "Standing also at Jesus's cross was his mother Mary and his mother's sister Mary of Clophas."[72]

So few old manuscripts have survived that just one takes on elevated significance when its variant has the potential to explain a widespread variant reading. John never mentions the Magdalene prior to 19:25, so the omission of "*and Mary the Magdalene*" at the end of this verse would make it quite possible for the reader of Codex Vercellensis to assume that the important Mary at the beginning of the list of women at the foot of the cross was the same important Mary in the garden with the risen Christ, and that mother and Magdalene were simply two important titles for one very important woman.[73]

In Ancient Syria in particular, it would have been easier for a reader to assume that Jesus' mother was the Magdalene than to assume that she was "Mary of James," whom today some exegetes propose could be Jesus' mother. Bauckham says epigraphs in Jewish Palestine identified women by the name of their son, yet none "use this idiom (simply the genitive, without μήτηρ [mother])."[74] Consistent with Bauckham's observation that in this region, "Mary of James" alone would not have identified James's (and Jesus') *mother*, the two Old Syriac gospels specify that Mary of James was "Mary the *daughter* of James." In both manuscripts, in all surviving verses of Matt 27:56; Mark 15:40, 47; 16:1; and Luke 24:10, she is consistently identified as "Mary the *daughter* of

---

[68] McCarthy, *Saint Ephrem's Commentary on Tatian's Diatessaron*, 8; also Theodoret of Cyrus, *Compendium of Heretical Accounts* 1.20 (PG 83, 372A).
[69] Agnes Smith Lewis, trans., *A Translation of the Four Gospels from the Syriac of the Sinaitic Palimpsest* (C. J. Clay, 1896), 106; and William Cureton, *Remains of a Very Antient Recension of the Four Gospels in Syriac* (London: John Murray, 1858), 50.
[70] Vööbus, *Early Versions of the New Testament*, 48.
[71] Dating of codex Vercellensis per Vööbus, *Early Versions of the New Testament*, 38; and Metzger, *Text of the New Testament*, 73.
[72] Aidano Gasquet, *Codex Vercellensis* (Collectanea biblica Latina 3; Rome: Pustet, 1914), 232.
[73] Loisy suggests this would make sense in Loisy, *Quatrième Évangile*, 908, n. 1. Two Marys at the foot of the cross at John 19:25 also could have paralleled the mother and beloved disciple in 19:26–27.
[74] Bauckham, *Gospel Women*, 206.

James."[75] Indicating that this reading was widespread in this region (suggesting it was also in the Diatessaron), the Syriac *Didascalia apostolorum* likewise specifies "Mary the *daughter* of James."[76]

So what did the gospel writers think the name *Magdalene* meant? Almost certainly they did not think it referred to the town today named *Magdala*, because the place name *Magdala* is not in any of the oldest Greek gospel manuscripts. Where today we read *Magdala*, the fourth-century scribes of Vaticanus and Sinaiticus used the place names *Dalmanoutha* at Mark 8:10[77] and *Magadan* at Matt 15:39.[78] *Magdala* appears for the first time in these verses in the fifth century—an appearance that corresponds to when a Palestinian town, which for the previous four centuries had been called "Tarichaea," was renamed "Magdala."[79] Joan E. Taylor suggests that "the *magdalene*" may have been a nickname for a woman named Mary, like *petros*, "the rock," was for Simon Peter.[80] Perhaps second-century Christians thought *magdalene* referred to *migdal*, for tower, because in the Old Syriac gospels, Mary the Magdalene was consistently called "Mariam the Tower-ess."[81] Potentially they might have thought that *migdal* referred to the Temple mount that towered over Jerusalem, where, according to the *Protevangelium*, Mary the mother had resided.[82] Alternatively, the Hebrew for "she magnifies" (*magdeelah*[83]) suggests that some might have supposed *magdalene* referred to Mary magnifying others, such as in Luke 1:46–55, the *Magnificat*, where she says, "My soul magnifies the Lord," or in the *Protevangelium*, where, when Mary was born, her mother said, "My soul is magnified today."[84] Some Christians may have supposed that it referred to the magnification or exaltation implicit in the encounter with the risen Christ; certainly the Syriac *Didascalia apostolorum* would bear out this understanding because its scribe assumed *both* Marys were Magdalenes: "Now in the Gospel of Matthew it is written thus: 'On the evening of the Sabbath as the first day of the week was dawning came Mary *and the other* Mary Magdalene to see the tomb.'"[85]

---

[75] See Matt 27:56; Mark 15:40, 47, and 16:1, and Luke 24:10 in Lewis, *Translation of the Four Gospels*, 30, 48–9, 84; and Luke 24:10 in Cureton, *Remains of a Very Antient Recension*, 85 (all other places have lacunae).

[76] Syriac *Didascalia Apostolorum* 21.14 (Stewart-Sykes, *Didascalia apostolorum*, 215).

[77] Reuben Swanson, ed., *New Testament Greek Manuscripts: Mark* (Sheffield: Sheffield Academic, 1995), 121.

[78] Reuben Swanson, ed., *New Testament Greek Manuscripts: Matthew* (Sheffield: Sheffield Academic, 1995), 152.

[79] See Joan E. Taylor, "Missing Magdala and the Name of Mary 'Magdalene,'" *PEQ* 146 (2014): 205–23, esp. 212–22.

[80] Ibid., 206–7.

[81] Ibid., 207–12, esp. 208.

[82] *Protevangelium* 7.2–9.2 (Schneemelcher, *New Testament Apocrypha*, 1:426–37).

[83] Hayim Baltsan, *Webster's New World Hebrew Dictionary* (Cleveland, OH: Wiley, 1992), 233.

[84] *Protevangelium* 5.2 (Émile de Strycker, trans., *La forme la plus ancienne du Protévangile de Jacques: Recherches sur le papyrus Bodmer 5* [Brussels: Société des Bollandistes, 1961], 88).

[85] Syriac *Didascalia Apostolorum* 21 (Stewart-Sykes, *Didascalia apostolorum*, 214), emphasis mine. Note that various translators have attempted to harmonize this passage with our Greek gospels, e.g., here adding a comma after the second "Mary," which I have corrected; e.g., Connolly rearranged the order to match our modern Matthew 27:61; see Connolly, *Didascalia apostolorum*, 182. Yet Vööbus points out the consistency of the literal reading with Syrian tradition; Vööbus, *Didascalia apostolorum*, 190.

The Diatessaron was the primary gospel in Ancient Syria until the fifth century, but mother and Magdalene likewise are never clearly identified in the same room at the same time in the three synoptic gospels. Communities that read Matthew, for example, could have assumed that one Mary had both roles. Matthew never mentions "the Magdalene" until the Passion scenes. With Jesus' mother having such an auspicious role in Jesus' birth in Matthew, a reader easily might assume that she was the same Mary who had an auspicious role at his death. In any case, given a normal narrative arc, a reader could reasonably expect that.

We cannot know for certain why writers in Ancient Syria so often identified Jesus' mother as the Mary with the resurrected Christ in the garden, but an early reading that did not have "and Mary the Magdalene" at the end of the list of women at the cross provides an economical explanation. Given Ephrem's *Commentary on the Diatessaron*, wherein he nowhere mentioned "the Magdalene" and identified Jesus' mother in the garden, it seems possible that the Syriac Diatessaron had this reading. The sole surviving manuscript witness to this reading is Codex Vercellensis, the oldest manuscript in the Old Latin textual tradition, which was closely related to the Diatessaron as well as to the Old Syriac gospels. Given this reading, Syriac Christians who identified the mother in the garden with her resurrected son were not confused, nor were they trying to subvert women's authority. They were simply reading their own gospel text.

When and where this reading originated is difficult to say, but it seems likely no later than the second century and as early as the first, depending upon the source behind the Diatessaron. Indicating the earlier date, both ancient and modern exegetes have suggested that the Hebrew Gospel may have been behind the Diatessaron[86]—for example, Epiphanius of Salamis said that some people called the Diatessaron "the Gospel According to the Hebrews."[87] The Hebrew Gospel was both early and influential; six second-century writers mentioned it, which is more mentions than any other gospel.[88]

In conclusion, it seems quite likely that, just as seen in the oldest Latin manuscript of John, the equivalent of John 19:25 in the Diatessaron did not end with "and Mary the Magdalene." Is it possible that the author or compiler of the Diatessaron excised "and Mary the Magdalene" from the end of the list of women at the foot of the cross in order to diminish the Magdalene's authority as first witness? On the one hand, yes, it is possible, especially considering the way later scribes often excised passages in order to diminish the authority of a woman leader. On the other hand, however, this conjecture does not at all explain why scribes would have replaced one woman leader with another woman leader. If, however, some Christians identified the Magdalene as Mary of Bethany, as Mary Ann Beavis and Mark Goodacre suggest, this identification itself could explain why some later scribes blotted out the memory

---

[86] For examples, see Petersen, *Tatian's Diatessaron*, 29–33, 39–41, 277–80, and esp. 440–1; Vööbus, *Early Versions of the New Testament*, 19–21; and Pier Franco Beatrice, "The 'Gospel According to the Hebrews' in the Apostolic Fathers," *NovT* 48 (2006): 147–95, esp. 188.

[87] Epiphanius of Salamis, *Panarion* 46.1.9.

[88] For detail on second-century and later witnesses to the Hebrew Gospel, see James R. Edwards, *The Hebrew Gospel and the Development of the Synoptic Tradition* (Grand Rapids, MI: William B. Eerdmans, 2009), 2–41.

of an influential but seemingly sinful woman—perhaps even a woman accused of adultery, perhaps even a woman in a line of prophets' beloved wives thusly accused, from Hosea's to Muhammad's—because no matter how redemptive her story, a seemingly sinful woman as one of the movement's two foremost women leaders could have been a heavy burden for evangelists in the Roman Empire. Or perhaps, as Murcia suggests, John 19:25 is read incorrectly today, instead of as a chiasm within a larger chiasm where Jesus' mother was identified as the historical Magdalene.[89] Finally, however, and again potentially explaining the phenomenon, some Christians apparently believed there were *two* Marys called Magdalene—*Mary and the other Mary Magdalene*.[90]

---

[89] Murcia, *Marie appelée la Magdaléenne*, 229–46.
[90] While Murcia's book drives to the conclusion that the mother was the historical Mary, in his eighth excursus, he nonetheless agrees that two Mary Magdalenes is a possibility; Murcia, *Marie appelée la Magdaléenne*, 331–3.

Section Two

Rediscovering the Marys in Mission and Leadership

Section Two

Rediscovering the Marys in Mission and Leadership

8

The Power of Leadership through Mediation, or How Mary Exercises Overlapping Authority

Cornelia Horn

Setting the Stage and Introducing the Question

Scholarship on Marian traditions continues to push backward and amplify the testimonies to the origins and intensity of an early Christian focus on Jesus' mother Mary, including accompanying practices of turning to her for her intercession.[1] A significant stepping stone for perceptions of Mary as a person empowered to intercede effectively is found in the canonical gospels. The scene of the wedding feast in Cana in the Galilee (John 2:1-12) that presents Mary as alerting Jesus to the lack of wine at the celebrations (John 2:3) and as instructing the attendants to act on all of Jesus' words (John 2:5) lays important foundations for how the NT conceives of Jesus' mother as a figure mediating between those in need and her son.[2] Other relatively early

---

[1] The research and writing of this article occurred during my tenure as Heisenberg Professor of Languages and Cultures of the Christian Orient at the Martin-Luther-University, Halle-Wittenberg (GZ HO 5221/2-1). I wish to express my gratitude to the Deutsche Forschungsgemeinschaft (DFG) for their financial support. Recent years have seen a range of publications that examine diverse aspects of early Christian Mariology. Among them, one may mention here Jaroslav Jan Pelikan, David Flusser, and Justin Lang, *Mary: Images of the Mother of Jesus in Jewish and Christian Perspective* (Minneapolis, MN: Fortress, 2005); the cluster of articles on the *Protoevangelium of James* by Christopher T. Holmes, Meredith Elliott Hollman and the joint article by Michael K. W. Suh and Vernon K.Robbins in *Jesus and Mary Reimagined in Early Christian Literature*, ed. Vernon K. Robbins and Jonathan M. Potter (Writings from the Greco-Roman World Supplement Series 6; Atlanta, GA: Society of Biblical Literature, 2015); or Stephen J. Shoemaker, *Mary in Early Christian Faith and Devotion* (New Haven, CT: Yale University Press, 2017). The proposal that Marian spirituality is a significant factor promoting European unity is advanced with the collection of articles presented by Peter Hofrichter, ed., *Auf der Suche nach der Seele Europas: Marienfrömmigkeit in Ost und West. Studientagung der Pro Oriente-Sektion Salzburg aus Anlass ihres 20jährigen Bestehens, 7. und 8. Oktober 2005* (Pro Oriente 30; Innsbruck: Tyrolia-Verlag, 2007).

[2] Judith Hartenstein, *Charakterisierung im Dialog. Maria Magdalena, Petrus, Thomas und die Mutter Jesu im Johannesevangelium im Kontext frühchristlicher Darstellungen* (NTOA/Studien und Untersuchungen zum Neuen Testament 64; Göttingen: Vandenhoeck & Ruprecht, 2007), 269-73, examines in detail how the author of the Gospel of John portrays Mary in the scene of the wedding at Cana. Further relevant studies include, e.g., Judith M. Lieu, "The Mother of the Son in the Fourth Gospel," *JBL* 117 (1998): 61-77; and Ritva H. Williams, "The Mother of Jesus at Cana. A Social-Science Interpretation of John 2:1-12," *CBQ* 59 (1997): 679-92.

evidence suggests that the developing prayer practices in early Christian churches had the faithful turn directly to this holy woman, Mary, because they were convinced that she possessed sufficient power to protect them.[3] The present study cannot be the place for exploring more fully why Mary was depicted in such roles of exercising influence and leadership, why seemingly only few witnesses to these dimensions of her depiction appear to have been produced and transmitted in the earliest records, and why modern scholars are motivated not only to highlight these roles but also to deepen, widen, and otherwise improve our insights into the rise or fall of such ideas about Mary in Eastern Mediterranean Christian societies. Yet even if this complex set of questions cannot be laid out or illuminated in full here, this chapter strives to contribute a new seed to exploring a new dimension of the study of the characterizations and role(s) early Christian believers were willing to assign to Mary. In pursuit of its goal, this chapter takes as the starting point of its argument a critique of the concept of intercession that is often used to characterize that dimension of Mary's role in the Christian community, which has her act by assisting and helping those in need.

The study of Mary's role as intercessor has received significant and concentrated attention in recent years.[4] Perhaps most prominently this attention is manifested in a new volume on the early history of constructions and perceptions of Mary's role as intercessor in the Eastern Mediterranean world, roughly during the Late Antique, early Byzantine, and Middle Byzantine periods. In 2015, Leena Mari Peltomaa, Andreas Külzer, and Pauline Allen edited thirteen contributions, originally intended for a conference, and published them in the volume, entitled *Presbeia Theotokou: The*

---

[3] See the prayer that is preserved in Greek but is known best under the Latin title *Sub tuum praesidium*. Its oldest witness is Papyrus 470 of the John Rylands Library. For the *editio princeps*, see C. H. Roberts, ed., *Catalogue of the Greek and Latin Papyri in the John Rylands Library Manchester. Volume III. Theological and Literary Texts (Nos. 457–551)* (Manchester: University Press, 1938), 46–7, no. 470 and plate I, which simply describes the text as a Christian prayer and tentatively places it in the fourth century. F. Mercenier, "L'antienne mariale grecque la plus ancienne," *Le Muséon* 52 (1939): 229–33, identified the text by comparing it with later versions used in the Byzantine liturgy. While the origins of the prayer are discussed variously, with attempts at dating it back to the third century, critical reconsiderations of the evidence place the papyrus and prayer at the end of the fourth century. See Otto Stegmüller, "Sub tuum praesidium. Bemerkungen zur ältesten Überlieferung," *ZKT* 74.1 (1952): 76–82; James Shiels, "A Rylands Reminiscence," *BJRL* 76.2 (1994): 181–6; Giovanni Vannucci, "La piu antica preghiera alla Madre di Dio," *Marianum* 3 (1941): 97–101; and Johann Auer, *Unter deinen Schutz und Schirm. Das älteste Mariengebet der Kirche* (Leutesdorf am Rhein: Johannes-Verlag, 1967). Axel Takacs, "Mary and Muhammad: Bearers of the Word—Their Roles in Divine Revelation," *JES* 48.2 (2013): 220–43, discusses the parallel to be observed in how early Christians turned to Mary as intercessor and deliverer of mercy and how Muslims ascribe(d) to Muhammad the same role.

[4] See, e.g., David Beauregard, "Virtue Ethics in Michelangelo's The Last Judgment: Christ as Severity and Mary as Clemency," *Logos: A Journal of Catholic Thought and Culture* 19.2 (2016): 33–52; Gary Marker, "Narrating Mary's Miracles and the Politics of Location in Late 17th-Century East Slavic Orthodoxy," *Kritika: Explorations in Russian and Eurasian History* 15 (2014): 695–727; Michael N. Kane, "Empowerment in the Religious Stories and Art of the Virgin Mary," *Social Work & Christianity* 37 (2010): 45–64; François Rossier and Thomas A. Thompson, "Biblical Perspectives on Maria Mediation: Lessons from a Failure of Mediation," *Marian Studies* 52 (2001): 53–77; and Frederick M. Jelly, "Mary's Intercession: a Contemporary Reappraisal," *Marian Studies* 32 (1981): 76–95; with a reply to this article by F. Klauder, "Observations on Father Jelly's Paper," *Marian Studies* 32 (1981): 96–8.

Intercessory Role of Mary across Times and Places in Byzantium (4th–9th Century).[5] With the title for their volume, the editors chose a distinct theme as a lens through which to look at the history of constructions of Mary's role in early Christianity. The initial Greek phrase in the title, *presbeia theotokou* (πρεσβεία Θεοτόκου), which one could render as "the diplomatic [or ambassadorial] service of the Birthgiver [or Mother] of God," is in keeping with a traditional, liturgical representation of Mary in the orthodox churches and is, of course, strongly programmatic for the volume in question. In the Divine Liturgy of Saint John Chrysostom, for instance, the congregation calls out three times at the end of the Prayer of the First Antiphon: "Through the intercessions of the Theotokos, Savior, save us (Ταῖς πρεσβείαις τῆς Θεοτόκου, Σῶτερ, σῶσον ἡμᾶς)."[6]

I propose to revisit the focus of the interpretive program and articulation of this recent scholarly volume on Marian intercession and argue in this chapter that the idea of considering Mary's activities through the lens of the role of an ambassador or diplomat, which early and medieval Christian traditions in the East were willing to ascribe to Mary, is only partially captured and represented, if and when one considers Mary's role as intercessor. Rather, I argue here that another concept, that of "mediation," comprises the fuller range of her "diplomatic service" on behalf of the interests of humankind as it was envisioned by the minds, and in the hearts, of Christians in earlier centuries and as it is still accessible in the sources, at least in the sources that were not strictly subject to official, ecclesiastical scrutiny. The analysis of more recent studies of medieval and modern theological thoughts concerning Mary's roles in the life of the church that highlight the idea of "mediation" or that speak of her as a "mediator" is a significant and at the same time a challenging and worthwhile undertaking.[7] Yet, in pursuit of the immediate purposes of the present article, the exploration of the possible relevance and implications of such reflections for advancing the understanding of Mary's role as a leader through mediation cannot be undertaken here. For the historical analysis that is at the focus of my argument and discussion, it is decisive that whereas the notion of "intercession" suggests that through her petitioning through words Mary moved her son Jesus to act in favor of Mary's clients, texts from the Eastern Christian tradition, particularly texts I have examined from the Syriac and Arabic milieu that fall into the broader category of hagiographical and apocryphal writings, suggest that Christians were ready to conceive of Mary as a significantly more active and powerful figure than one might associate with the notion of an "intercessor." Christians, whose views and imaginations are captured in these writings, saw Mary

---

[5] Leena Mari Peltomaa, Andreas Külzer, and Pauline Allen, *Presbeia Theotokou: The Intercessory Role of Mary across Times and Places in Byzantium (4th—9th Century)* (Veröffentlichungen zur Byzanzforschung 39; Denkschriften der philosophisch-historischen Klasse 481; Vienna: Verlag der Österreichischen Akademie der Wissenschaften, 2015).

[6] For the text of the liturgy, see, e.g., https://www.goarch.org/-/the-divine-liturgy-of-saint-john-chrysostom (accessed on March 19, 2018).

[7] Such studies include Katharina Mertens Fleury, "Maria mediatrix—*mittellos mittel aller sünder*," *Das Mittelalter* 15 (2010): 33–47; Clare Marie Snow, "Maria Mediatrix: Mediating the Divine in the Devotional Literature of Late Medieval England" (PhD dissertation; Centre for Medieval Studies, University of Toronto, 2012); Egbert Schlootkötter, *Maria, Corredemptrix und Mediatrix: Miterlöserin und Mittlerin aller Gnaden* (Aachen: Shaker, 2013); and Melissa Eitenmiller, "Mary, Mediatrix of All Graces" (MA Theology thesis; Ave Maria University, 2016).

as a woman who was able to exercise leadership on behalf of the Christian faithful through her power of mediation, both through words and through actions, or even through her action accompanied by her word. This form of action, Mary's mediation, I argue, included not only verbal, articulated intercession but also effective deeds, actions of working miracles. It is possible that the latter were felt to be more attractive, because they were more convincing for the faithful, who could perceive themselves as seeing and feeling the results of the miracles Mary mediated more immediately and directly in their lives. Or at least they trusted that the written texts, which they read or to which they listened and which presented themselves as stories about such miracles, did in fact report others' immediate experiences.

The argument of this chapter proceeds along three consecutive steps. First, I present some significant aspects of Mary's role as intercessor that are discernible in the textual record of some of the material in the early Syriac apocryphal tradition. Next, I will examine the relevant apocryphal record in the Semitic-language realm that illustrates that Mary's role as mediator who facilitated the working of miracles through deeds was at least as relevant, if not more, than her mere verbal activities. Finally, in a concluding, third section, the argument draws upon modern political theories of government and administration studies in order to identify and position more precisely how one might best characterize and understand the Oriental Christian tradition, in the Syriac- and Arabic-speaking realm, with regard to its view of Mary's authority in questions of leadership.

Mary's Leadership through Intercession

Throughout the centuries, Christians in the East, in various orthodox and oriental-orthodox churches, have developed aspects of their Christian spirituality by paying attention to, and at times also placing at the center of their focus, the figure and roles of Mary as a guide and aide toward salvation, expressed and understood as a state of wholeness of the human person in union with God.[8] Witnesses from the liturgical tradition amply demonstrate this. Many of the *kontakia* of Romanos the Melodist, for instance, request of Mary that she might intercede for humankind.[9] For Constantinople, the capital of the Byzantine Empire, one can identify the period from the late sixth to the early seventh century as a time when emphasis on Mary as "the most potent intercessor before God" dominated perceptions of her role.[10] Access to this

---

[8] This discussion resumes and develops aspects of the study presented in Cornelia Horn, "Ancient Syriac Sources on Mary's Role as Intercessor," in *Presbeia Theotokou*, ed. Peltomaa, Külzer, and Allen, 153–4.

[9] See, e.g., the examples and discussion in Leena Mari Peltomaa, "'Cease your lamentations, I shall become an advocate for you.' Mary as Intercessor in Romanos' Hymnography," in *Presbeia Theotokou*, ed. Peltomaa, Külzer, and Allen, 131–7. Peltomaa offered further studies of Mary's role as intercessor in "Roles and Functions of Mary in the Hymnography of Romanos Melodos," StPatr 44 (2010): 496, 498; and Peltomaa, "Romanos the Melodist and the Intercessory Role of Mary," in *Byzantina Mediterranea. Festschrift für Johannes Koder zum 65. Geburtstag*, ed. Klaus Belke, Ewald Kislinger, Andreas Külzer, and Maria A. Stassinopoulou (Vienna: Böhlau, 2007), 495–502.

[10] For the quote, see Averil Cameron, "The Theotokos in Sixth-Century Constantinople," JTS 29 (1978): 104.

intercessory power was understood to be granted to the faithful not merely through their prayers and petitions during the liturgies. Employing access to her through visual and material objects likewise was understood to be an effective means one could use. During the crisis of 626 CE, when facing "the moment of the battle," the Avar Khagan, for instance, supposedly said that he "beh[eld] a woman in respectable dress rushing about on the wall, being alone (θεωρῶ γυναῖκα σεμνοφοροῦσαν περιτρέχουσαν εἰς τὸ τεῖχος μόνην οὖσαν)."[11] Whether the Khagan may have seen one of the imperial ladies walking about on the city walls and encouraging the populace to resist, or a vision of the Virgin Mary moving about to mark the city walls with her presence for protection, or images of the Virgin carried about from gate to gate, which the Patriarch was said to have commissioned to have been written for that purpose, is not so easy to determine. According to Theodore Synkellos, the latter was the case.[12] Through the presence of the Virgin, through her image or in some other, even direct form, the imperial city was understood to have been protected efficiently against the siege of the forces of the Avars and the Persians.[13] The question of whether or not an image of the Virgin Mary could stand in as a representation of the person of the Virgin herself is certainly relevant for the interpretation of this data. The accounts concerning this siege of Constantinople do not state that one heard that the image of a woman that some thought they saw was uttering words. The act of protection, then, which may or may not have been worked through an icon, cannot easily be understood or interpreted as an act of intercession in the direct and customary sense of the word. Since the image was said to have been seen moving about, whether on its own or because it was carried about, one might argue

---

[11] *Chronicon Paschale* (Ludwig August Dindorf, ed., *Chronicon Paschale* [Corpus scriptorium historiae Byzantinae 14.15; Bonn: Marcus & Weber, reprinted 1924], 725; Mary and Michael Whitby, trans., *Chronicon Paschale 284–628 AD* [Translated Texts for Historians 7; Liverpool: Liverpool University Press, 1989], 179–80 [modified]). See also Anthony Kaldellis, "'A Union of Opposites': The Moral Logic and Corporeal Presence of the Theotokos on the Field of Battle," in *Pour l'amour de Byzance. Hommage à Paolo Odorico*, eds. Christian Gastgeber et al. (Eastern and Central European Studies III; Frankfurt am Main: Peter Lang, 2012), 141.

[12] Theodore Synkellos 304.4–16 (Leo Sternbach, ed., *Analecta Avarica* [Cracow: Bibliopolam Societatis Librariae Polonicae, 1900]). For interpretations of this event, including some that seem to read more into the scene than what is backed up by the text, see, e.g., Norman H. Baynes, "The Supernatural Defenders of Constantinople," *AnBoll* 67 (1949): 165–77, reprinted in Norman H. Baynes, *Byzantine Studies and Other Essays* (London: Athlone, 1955), 248–60; Cameron, "Theotokos in Sixth-Century Constantinople," 79–108; Avril Cameron, "The Virgin's Robe: An Episode in the History of early-seventh century Constantinople," *Byzantion* 49 (1979): 42–56; Whitby and Whitby, *Chronicon Paschale 284–628 AD*, 180, n. 476; James Howard-Johnston, "The Siege of Constantinople in 626," in *Constantinople and Its Hinterland. Papers from the Twenty-Seventh Spring Symposium on Byzantine Studies, Oxford, April 1993*, ed. Cyril Mango, Gilbert Dagron, and Geoffrey Greatrex (Aldershot, Hampshire: Variorum, 1995), 131–42; and Walter E. Kaegi, *Heraclius, Emperor of Byzantium* (Cambridge: Cambridge University Press, 2003), 136.

[13] Bissera Pentcheva, "The Supernatural Protector of Constantinople: the Virgin and Her Icons in the Tradition of the Avar Siege," *Byzantine and Modern Greek Studies* 26 (2002): 2–41, argued that a firm connection between the usage of Marian icons and the question of the protection of Constantinople against invaders only occurred in the period after Iconoclasm. Yet Paul Speck, "The Virgin's help for Constantinople," *Byzantine and Modern Greek Studies* 27.1 (2003): 266–71, based on a careful review of the relevant historical textual sources that have been preserved, has shown convincingly that Pentcheva's reading of the sources is seriously flawed and that there is no good reason to doubt that already in the seventh century, the image and icon of the Mother of God and her cult played an influential role in Constantinople in connection with the city's protection in times of crisis, based on the historical textual sources that have been preserved.

that the power of the image, and thus of the person behind the image in a literal sense, was made to go as if in between the walls of Constantinople and the enemies' troops. Here, one could say perhaps that by way of a closer approximation to the Latin verb *intercedere*, "going in between," the image was going or made to go "in between," in a spatial sense. Whether or not one can understand the image as moving about on the initiative of the person, whose image was seen, depends on one's interpretation of the evidence. If one assumes that a historical figure was seen moving about, the question of intercession arises only in a more strongly derivative sense. If one presumes that the Avar Khagan could have seen a vision, a rather strong sense of active protection and perhaps less of a sense of intercessory activity on the part of the Virgin may have been suggested to the audience at Byzantium. If one opts for an icon as the fitting interpretation, the patriarch and his assistants carried the icon or icons around. Here, even if one allows for a relatively close identity between the image or icon and the person represented by it, the situation in which power was made to be active and protective in this scene would then be depended on the will and initiative of other human agents involved in the events, not upon those of the Virgin. Despite such limitations, the trajectory of perceptions of Mary's image and rank that was proposed through what was thought to have happened in 626 was set in the direction of not simply regarding the Virgin Mary as an effective intercessor but as the powerful protectress for those who turned to her for help.

The developments in seventh-century Constantinople could build on and transform, as desired, elements that had already emerged during a longer, preceding phase of Christian history, in which notions of Mary as intercessor had begun to circulate and intensify in the regions of the Christian East. In a recent study, I have examined in great detail the witnesses from the patristic and apocryphal record in the Syriac language that speak to variations of an understanding of Mary as an intercessor.[14] Perhaps the most important witness to that development of Mary's intercessory role in the sixth century, and perhaps already in the fifth century, is the apocryphal Syriac text of the *Transitus Mariae*, which came to be an integral part of an apocryphal *Life* or *Book of Mary* that developed over the course of several centuries.[15] A sizeable and crucial witness to the early stages of the *Book of Mary* was edited by Agnes Smith Lewis in 1902 on the basis of a palimpsest manuscript.[16]

---

[14] Horn, "Ancient Syriac Sources." Parts of the material from this publication are reused and developed further in the present chapter.

[15] See Cornelia Horn, "Syriac and Arabic Perspectives on Structural and Motif Parallels regarding Jesus' Childhood in Christian Apocrypha and Early Islamic Literature: The 'Book of Mary,' the *Arabic Apocryphal Gospel of John*, and the Qur'ān," *Apocrypha* 19 (2008): 267–91, for a discussion of important steps in the development of this *Life* or *Book of Mary*.

[16] Agnes Smith Lewis, ed. and trans., *Apocrypha Syriaca. The Protevangelium Jacobi and Transitus Mariae with Texts from the Septuagint, the Corân, the Peshiṭta, and from a Syriac Hymn in a Syro-Arabic Palimpsest of the Fifth and Other Centuries, with an Appendix of Palestinian Syriac Texts from the Taylor-Schechter Collection* (StSin 11; London: C. J. Clay, 1902). Additional evidence for the early shape of the *Transitus Mariae* in Syriac has been published in Stephen J. Shoemaker, "New Syriac Dormition Fragments from Palimpsests in the Schøyen Collection and the British Library," *Le Muséon* 124.3–4 (2011): 259–78. Questions of dating that material, which complicate the record, but which do not invalidate locating the evidence to a relatively early period, can safely be addressed elsewhere.

At the end of the first book of the *Transitus Mariae*, the author (or the scribe) expressed the hope that "by the prayers of the mother of God, Mary, and also of all the saints, may God make to pass away from the earth and from this place where this book is, the sword, captivity, famine, pestilence, and all plagues and rods of anger."[17] Here, the text articulated the expectation that intercessory prayers of the saints, including those of Mary, the Birthgiver of God, could offer relief and protection from various types of evil that might afflict human beings. Such an idea fit well with patristic ideas, for instance, those presented by Jacob of Sarugh, who featured Mary's intercessory capabilities in his *On the Death and Burial of the Virgin Mother of God*.[18] In fact, both the *Transitus Mariae* and Jacob of Sarugh's verse homily serve as solid witnesses that the notions of Mary's intercessory prayer and of her role as intercessor were well developed already in the sixth century among wider circles of Syriac-speaking Christendom. Some characteristic features of this role can be singled out.

As one evaluates the evidence for Mary's role as intercessor in the Syriac *Transitus Mariae*, one notices that a prominent liturgical atmosphere characterizes this work. Quite frequently the text refers to persons who were engaged in prayer. Among them, Mary herself is prominent. Yet the text also addresses problems encountered by those who prayed. In the second book, for example, the Jews are said to have restricted access to the tomb of Christ and the site of Golgotha in order to make it difficult or impossible for Christians, including Mary, to pray there. Book two of the Syriac *Transitus Mariae* describes how Mary used to go "to the tomb of the Christ" daily.[19] She regularly "pray[ed] beside Golgotha and the grave."[20] That behavior is said to have enraged the leaders of the Jews, primarily the priests who suggested she should be stoned for it. Undaunted, Mary continued to pray and offer "sweet spices and fire" and "myrrh ... thrown on the censer."[21] Up to this point in the story, Mary's prayer could have simply been considered as the guided conversation between a human person and God, carried by and grounded in that person's trust and reliance on God. Yet the immediately following sections clarify with precision that Mary's prayer included dimensions of petitionary prayer, or that her prayers at least functioned like a petition in the effect they had. Thus, the text offers details of how one Friday

> while she was praying and had lifted up her eyes and gazed at heaven, suddenly the doors of heaven were opened and a scent of myrrh went up, which the Lady Mary had thrown on the censer, and its odor went about all the regions of heaven. And in that hour Gabriel the angel came to her from heaven and knelt [down] to worship her; and he said to her: "Hail to you, mother of God! Your prayer has been accepted in heaven before your Son, our Lord Jesus the Christ."[22]

---

[17] Smith Lewis, *Apocrypha Syriaca*, ܟܠ (Syriac) and 19 (English).
[18] Jacob of Sarugh, *On the Death and Burial of the Virgin Mother of God* (Paul Bedjan, ed., *S. Martyrii, qui et Sahdona quae supersunt omnia* [Paris: Harrassowitz, 1902], 709–19; Mary Hansbury, trans., *On the Mother of God. Jacob of Serug*, with an introduction by Sebastian Brock [Crestwood, NY: St Vladimir's Seminary, 1998], 89–100).
[19] See Smith Lewis, *Apocrypha Syriaca*, ܝܠ—ܐܠ (Syriac) and 19–20 (English).
[20] Smith Lewis, *Apocrypha Syriaca*, ܝܠ (Syriac) and 20 (English).
[21] Smith Lewis, *Apocrypha Syriaca*, ܝܠ (Syriac) and 20 (English).
[22] Smith Lewis, *Apocrypha Syriaca*, ܝܠ (Syriac) and 20 (English, translation modified).

According to the words of how the text narrated the events, the angel Gabriel told Mary, "At the time when you prayed on earth, at once you were answered in heaven; and whatsoever you seek from the Christ, your Son who is in heaven at the right hand of God, you shall have both on earth and in heaven, and your will is done."[23] These words would have suggested to any of their readers that Mary's prayers, including her prayers on behalf of the interests of others, not only her own, were guaranteed a positive response from heaven. They served as the audible manifestation of her power as an intercessor. Yet even more than that, Mary wielded the power of a rather particular and special intercessor, given that she was the only one whose prayers were able to yield immediate responses.

In the Syriac Christian culture of the ancient Near East, the apocryphal *Transitus Mariae* literature functioned as the most significant witness to the early stage of Mary's role as intercessor. Clearly, later liturgical texts also frequently pictured Mary as intercessor and supplicant. It is possible, as I have argued elsewhere, that the Christological controversies of the fifth century played an important role in raising the profile of Mary as an intercessor.[24] Yet considering Mary's leadership of the people of God through intercession, if that intercession is characterized as occurring through prayer and verbal petitions alone, it is a one-sidedly focused reading of the ancient evidence. I will argue in the following, that Mary's mediation through working miracles shows her, in the ancient record, as having in fact filled a more active role, endowed with greater, more immediate, and direct authority.

Mary's Leadership through Working Miracles

In 1899, Ernest A. Wallis Budge published the *editio princeps* together with an English translation of a Syriac apocryphal text concerning the life of Jesus' mother Mary, to be referred to here as the Syriac *History of the Blessed Virgin Mary*.[25] The text manifestly rewrites material related to the New Testament and several of the figures featured therein. That on its own may serve as justification for classifying the work as an apocryphal text.[26] The Syriac *History of the Blessed Virgin Mary* incorporates material from several of the classic examples of early Christian apocryphal texts, reusing more specifically several apocryphal infancy gospels as well as a version of the Syriac *Transitus Mariae*. In fact, its overall scope of apocryphal, contributing texts is even larger. The Syriac *History of the Blessed Virgin Mary* integrates into its framework, in the following

---

[23] Smith Lewis, *Apocrypha Syriaca*, ܠܐ—ܡܐ (Syriac) and 21 (English).
[24] Horn, "Ancient Syriac Sources," 175.
[25] Ernest A. Wallis Budge, ed. and trans., *The History of the Blessed Virgin Mary and The History of the Likeness of Christ Which the Jews of Tiberias Made to Mock at*, 2 vols. (London: Luzac, 1899).
[26] A discussion of definitions of apocryphal literature with ample references is available, e.g., in Cornelia Horn, "Christian Apocrypha in Georgia and in Literature on Georgians: Some Reflections on the Intersections of Apocrypha, Hagiography, and Liturgy," in *Proceedings of the Conference "Renaissance Humanism" in Honor of the 125th Anniversary of Shalva Nutsubidze*, Institute of Philosophy, Ivane Javakhishvili Tbilisi State University, Tbilisi, Georgia, December 12–13, 2013, published in ფილოსოფიურ-თეოლოგიური მიმომხილველი / *Philosophical-Theological Reviewer* 3 (Tbilsi: Ivane Javakhishvili Tbilisi State University, 2013), 186–93.

order, rewritten versions of the *Protoevangelium of James*, a text that parallels what is perhaps best known as the *Arabic Infancy Gospel*, the *Infancy Gospel of Pseudo-Thomas*, various episodes taken from the canonical gospels, the Syriac *Transitus Mariae*, and finally an account of several miracles that came about through Mary's mediation.

This last set of miracles is immediately relevant for our question. Here we find stories that feature the Virgin Mary working miracles, for instance, of rescuing a child who had fallen into a well, recovering the lost purse of a merchant, or reviving a child who had drowned in the sea. Indeed, the text speaks of these miracles directly as "the wonderful thing, which the blessed women, the Lady Mary, wrought; may her prayer be a rock wall unto us!"[27] We encounter a tradition that ascribes to Mary the power to work miracles and that encourages the faithful to turn to her as a holy woman who is capable of offering protection through her prayers as well. Scholars have not yet sufficiently examined how far back one ought to date these miracle traditions concerning Mary. Given that the manuscripts, upon which Budge relied, are from the modern period, it is at least possible that they come from more recent times and may, as such, not witness to late antique or early Byzantine beliefs. Ongoing research into traditions of the Miracles of Mary in the wider Syriac- and Arabic-speaking realms, however, suggests that this material fits in well with a significantly older tradition of ascribing the working of miracles to the Mother of God, a tradition that reaches back to the sixth century or earlier.[28] In addition, within the Syriac *History of the Blessed Virgin Mary*, another contributing apocryphal set of texts that are associated with the traditions of the *Arabic Infancy Gospel* provides a further opportunity to examine views of Mary's role as a worker of miracles.[29] Much of this material has to do with Mary acting on behalf of children and in support of women, especially mothers.[30] I shall present one example in some detail here.

---

[27] *History of the Blessed Virgin Mary* (Budge, *History*, 146 [Syriac] and 160 [English]).

[28] See, e.g., the discussion in Cornelia Horn, "Traditions on Miracles of Mary in the Syriac Literary and Cultural Realm: Toward the Status Quaestionis," paper delivered at the International Workshop Miracles of the Virgin Mary. Medieval Narratives through Time and Space, organized by Ewa Balicka-Witakowska and Anthony Lappin, Maynooth University, Maynooth, Ireland (March 29 to April 1, 2017).

[29] Individual recensions, editions, and/or translations of the text of the *Arabic Infancy Gospel* are available in several places. See, e.g., Henry Sike, *Evangelium Infantiae; vel, Liber Apocryphus de Infantia Salvatoris; ex manuscripto editit, ac Latina versione et notis illustravit Henricus Sike* (Utrecht: Halman, 1697); Mario E. Provera, *Il Vangelo arabo dell'infanzia secondo il Ms. Laurenziano orientale (n. 387)* (Jerusalem: Franciscan Printing Press, 1973); and Charles Genequand, "Vie de Jésus en Arabe," in *Écrits apocryphes chrétiens*, vol. 1, ed. François Bovon and Pierre Geoltrain (Bibliothèque de la Pléiade 442; Paris: Gallimard, 1997), 207–38. Stephen J. Davis, *Christ Child: Cultural Memories of a Young Jesus* (Synkrisis: Comparative Approaches to Early Christianity in Greco-Roman Culture; New Haven, CT: Yale University Press, 2014), appendix B, offers an English translation of chapters 36–53.

[30] For a discussion of the trajectory of the transformation of apocryphal writings on Mary in a direction that elaborates and addresses directly the relevance of the figure of the Mother of God for women, both married and unmarried, and for their everyday life concerns, see Cornelia Horn, "From Model Virgin to Maternal Intercessor: Mary, Children, and Family Problems in Late Antique Infancy Gospel Traditions," lecture delivered at the session "Late Antique Perspectives on *Apocryphal Acts of Apostles*" at the conference "Christian Apocryphal Texts for the New Millennium: Achievements, Prospects, and Challenges," organized by Pierluigi Piovanelli (University of Ottawa, Canada; Fall, 2006). This research will appear in print in due course.

The struggle of parents when they lose one of their children and, as faithful believers, have to hand her or him over into God's hands, and the desire of such parents, nevertheless, to keep behind for themselves at least some of their offspring is a theme that recurs in the *History of the Blessed Virgin Mary*. A mother of twins had already suffered the loss of one of her two sons due to sickness. Asking for Mary's help at the threat of losing her second son who likewise was sickly, the mother prayed that God might treat her justly by being satisfied with taking only one child. Since God had given her both sons, it would be fair for God to take one back, but in the case of such a deal, the second one should be left to his mother.[31] When Mary had the woman lay the second child into Baby Jesus' bed and when she had wrapped him in the Christ Child's swaddling bands, the second one of the twin boys, Thomas, was restored to life and health. Subsequently, in her words of thanksgiving, the mother acknowledged Mary's motherhood as a parent of the Son of God. She also commented that "children who are like unto Him are made whole by the odor of Him."[32] This remark allows one to catch a glimpse at one of the reasons for why a relatively large number of miracles recounted in the *History of the Blessed Virgin Mary* deal with children or the lack of children and parents', especially mothers', troubles that arose from that lack, or with other troubles mothers or those women who wanted to become mothers experienced. The *History of the Blessed Virgin Mary* comprises as one of its structural components the *Arabic Infancy Gospel* material as a narrative that treated miracles that the Christ Child worked during his youth. This incorporation of a significant amount of infancy gospel material focusing on Jesus' childhood allowed the author to emphasize that as a child, Christ would be closer to the needs of children and their families. Perhaps one saw as the reason for this that Christ had shared the experience of childhood with these children. Yet this text also was a narrative that featured the special relationship that existed between the Christ Child and his mother Mary.

The *Arabic Infancy Gospel*, and in part also the Syriac *History of the Blessed Virgin Mary*, feature a number of scenes that present miracles worked through Baby Jesus' diapers, through his bathwater, or also through direct contact with Baby Jesus' body.[33] In one way, indeed, one may regard these miracles as miracles that Jesus worked. Yet they are not only that. Like any other young child, Baby Jesus also depended on the support and assistance of his mother for many to most of his activities. Already from the logic of the story and the flow of events within it, it was clear to any reader that Baby Jesus simply would not have been able to work any of the miracles through his diapers, unless his mother had, in the first place, made these diapers and wrapping clothes available to those in need.[34] His mother controlled whether Baby Jesus'

---

[31] *History of the Blessed Virgin Mary* (Budge, *History*, 59 [Syriac] and 64 [English]).
[32] *History of the Blessed Virgin Mary* (Budge, *History*, 59 [Syriac] and 65 [English]).
[33] Direct contact with the body of Baby Jesus could occur through kissing the child. See, e.g., *History of the Blessed Virgin Mary* (Budge, *History*, 43-4 [Syriac] and 50-1 [English]); and *Arabic Infancy Gospel* 15, 16 (Provera, *Il Vangelo arabo*, 82 [Arabic] and 81, 83 [Italian]; and 82 [Arabic] and 83 [Italian]). In some cases, a mix of direct contact with the child and with garments he is wearing seems to be envisioned. See, e.g., *Arabic Infancy Gospel* 28 (Provera, *Il Vangelo arabo*, 98, 100 [Arabic] and 99, 101 [Italian]).
[34] *History of the Blessed Virgin Mary* (Budge, *History*, 39-40 [Syriac] and 47 [English]; 43 [Syriac] and 50 [English]; 57 [Syriac] and 62 [English]; 59 [Syriac] and 65 [English]; and 64-5 [Syriac] and 69-70

bathwater would be poured out onto the ground or would be preserved and made available to those in need.[35] At times, Mary decided to provide healing or protection to those in need through making available both the bathwater and the diapers.[36] Any reader could or did understand that Baby Jesus would not on his own initiative have been able to climb on the back of a young man, who had been turned into a mule, and through physical contact dispel the transformative magic and return the young man to his natural form, unless his mother Mary had placed Baby Jesus on the back of that very same mule.[37] In other words, no matter to whom precisely one allocates the power and whom one identifies as the source of that power that finally worked the miracle, not a single one of the miracles occurred while being outside of the realm of Mary's full and sovereign control. It is well justified, then, to conclude this set of observations with the insight and understanding that all of the miracles the text had Baby Jesus work, either through his diapers or his bathwater and so on were ultimately miracles that Mary worked as well. In the Syriac and Arabic apocryphal tradition that is represented through the texts that have been examined here, Mary exercised leadership through enabling and controlling the execution of any and all of the miracles her infant son Jesus worked. Through her role as a mediator, as one who actively connected the relevant sides on all ends with one another, and not merely through her role as an intercessor, as a go-between speaker, Mary was the key person in bringing these miracles about that alleviated the needs of the many who suffered.

How to Classify Mary's Authority

When considering the multifaceted portrayal of Mary's role in the Syriac and Arabic apocryphal records in the context of questions of mission and leadership, the analysis of the material and perspectives at hand can be advanced further and into fields not customarily considered in Oriental Christian Studies. The German sociologist Max Weber, for instance, developed a tripartite classification of authority, which differentiates between traditional authority, charismatic authority, and legal authority. A consideration of charismatic authority as the framework within which to understand ancient, medieval, and Byzantine Christian ways of approaching and dealing with Mary's authority is a promising undertaking that requires a fuller, separate study.[38]

[English]); and *Arabic Infancy Gospel* 5, 6, 11, 27 (Provera, *Il Vangelo arabo*, 70, 72 [Arabic] and 71, 73 [Italian]; 76, 78 [Arabic] and 77, 79 [Italian]; and 96, 98 [Arabic] and 97, 99 [Italian]).

[35] *History of the Blessed Virgin Mary* (Budge, *History*, 48–49 [Syriac] and 54 [English]; 51 [Syriac] and 57 [English]; 55–56 [Syriac] and 61–62 [English]; 60 [Syriac] and 65 [English]; 61–62 [Syriac] and 66–67 [English]; and 62–64 [Syriac] and 67–69 [English]); and *Arabic Infancy Gospel* 17, 18, 25, 26, 29, 30 (Provera, *Il Vangelo arabo*, 82 [Arabic] and 83 [Italian]; 82, 84, 86 [Arabic] and 85, 87 [Italian]; 94 [Arabic] and 95 [Italian]; 94, 96 [Arabic] and 95, 97 [Italian]; 100 [Arabic] and 101 [Italian]; and 102, 104 [Arabic] and 101, 103, 105 [Italian]).

[36] *Arabic Infancy Gospel* 31–2 (Provera, *Il Vangelo arabo*, 104, 106, 108 [Arabic] and 105, 107 [Italian]).

[37] *History of the Blessed Virgin Mary* (Budge, *History*, 49–53 [Syriac] and 55–9 [English]); and *Arabic Infancy Gospel* 20–1 (Provera, *Il Vangelo arabo*, 86, 88, 90 [Arabic] and 87, 89, 91 [Italian]).

[38] Max Weber's tripartite classification of authority included a concept of leadership, in which the necessary authority that is operative in an organization has its foundation in the charisma of the leader. The idea of charisma that was in Weber's view here had its roots in the meaning of the Greek word *charisma* as a gift, granted by God. In Weber's understanding and reuse of the term,

In the present chapter, the focus will be on examining and evaluating what one might gain by applying theories from political science and public administration in an attempt to come closer to an understanding of ways in which Mary's authority was perceived and functioned. Especially helpful here is the question of how authority is organized and effective. This might be considered to fall under Weber's category of legal or rational authority. In 1988, the American political scientist and scholar of public administration, Deil Spencer Wright (1930–2009), published the third edition of his description and discussion of the interrelated organization of three basic types or models of intergovernmental relationships, that is, the relationships between the national, the state, and the local governmental levels and relevant entities.[39] In this study, he presented two theretofore well-known models of intergovernmental relationships, one to be labeled "coordinate authority" and one "inclusive authority," and one innovative, new model, that of "overlapping authority."[40] In the first model, which he called "coordinate authority," the responsibility of the different, higher-level governmental entities are clearly separated from one another. Each level operates autonomously and independent from the other two.[41] At the opposite end of the spectrum, Wright placed what he referred to as the "inclusive authority" model. Here, the lower levels of government depend explicitly upon the formal and hierarchical authority of the respective upper level(s), up to the very top. One of the consequences and implications of this model is that the lower levels hardly ever, if at all, have any impact on the decision-making processes. Yet Wright also conceived of an in-between model. This third model, now known as the overlapping authority model, functions in such a way that the lower levels of government implement their own programs and decisions, while at the same time following through with executing regulations that come down to them from the higher level(s). In this model, negotiation and bargaining as part of situational authority play a significant role. Top-down regulations do not have to be executed as initially conceived, while at the same time decisions and expectations

---

especially in its derivation from usage in early Christian settings, charisma was the gift, with the possession of which, as a gift from God, Christians recognized or acknowledge their leaders to be endowed. Thus, charisma also came to be dependent upon the followers' attribution of a divinely granted gift to their respective leaders. Charismatic authority therefore had its origins both in a transcendent or otherworldly gift and in the necessary acknowledgement of that gift on the part of those who chose to subject themselves to the authority of the leader. One could certainly also consider Mary's quality of being the mother of the Son of God as a charisma that grounded her authority. Yet, since the evidence in ancient sources that would have to be considered as a basis for such an examination is ample, such a study of Mary's charismatic authority has to remain as a topic for a separate study. On charismatic authority, see Max Weber, *The Theory of Social and Economic Organization*, trans. A. M. Henderson and Talcott Parsons (Glencoe, IL: Free Press, 1947), 358–81.

[39] Deil S. Wright, *Understanding Intergovernmental Relations*, 3rd ed. (Pacific Grove, CA: Brooks–Cole, 1988).
[40] For subsequent discussions of Wright's innovative perspective, see, e.g., Robert Agranoff and Beryl A. Radin, "Deil Wright's Overlapping Model of Intergovernmental Relations: The Basis for Contemporary Intergovernmental Relationships," *Publius: The Journal of Federalism* 45 (2015): 139–59.
[41] Wright, *Understanding*, 40, and Agranoff and Radin, "Deil Wright's Overlapping Model," 140, offer a very helpful visualization of the three models discussed here.

formulated at the lower levels may be turned into practice, yet in modified forms.[42] Quite decisive in this third model is, moreover, that it addresses rather effectively and in a dynamic way a reality in which the number of actors in a set of relationships of power is greater than two.[43] In addition, this model takes seriously that neither level involved is dominant over any or all of the others with regard to all issues, that is, on some issues, one level may be dominant, while on other issues, another level may take the lead.[44] Related to this observation, moreover, is an important additional dimension of the overlapping authority model. Whereas the coordinate authority model and the inclusive authority model function on the basis of assuming strictly vertical relationships, the overlapping authority model is able to integrate horizontal and vertical relationships with one another.[45]

Of the three models of intergovernmental administration, the model of inclusive authority and the model of overlapping authority serve well as possible models for describing the authority that different traditions ascribe to Jesus' mother Mary. If one focuses on Mary's role as intercessor, that is, as one who turns to God through her words and prayers of intercession, the inclusive authority model might offer the best paradigm to characterize the various dimensions of that role as they emerge from ancient texts. In her role as intercessor, as the one who hears the prayers for intercession from the Christian faithful as her constituency, the many, mostly women and children, in need, and who then brings those intentions and requests before God through her own prayers of petition and intercession, Mary appears to be the only mode of access humans have who wish to reach God. In this model, Mary clearly exercises inclusive authority. She has a central and necessary role in a thoroughly hierarchical setup of authority. Not only does she emerge as the only way of access to God that the faithful have, but she also depends explicitly on the hierarchical authority with which she is endowed, from the top down. Upon closer examination of the role Mary is ascribed in scenes of miracle-working in the Syriac *History of the Blessed Virgin Mary*, the *Arabic Infancy Gospel*, expansions on traditions advanced in Byzantium, and related texts and contexts, however, it seems that this model does not suffice to describe how the Christian faithful understand and believe to experience Mary's role. The evidence of those sources suggests that the more fitting model of authority is another one. Wright's third administrative or intergovernmental model that articulates the distribution of power and authority as one of overlapping competencies or overlapping authority offers the basis for a more accurate way to capture the whole spectrum of the locus and identity of Mary's power of leadership through mediation that the Syriac, Arabic, and Byzantine sources we have at our disposal envision. In the imagination of ancient Syriac-, Arabic-, and Greek-speaking authors, the figure of Mary was able to emerge as

---

[42] On the relevance of bargaining and negotiation in a wider context of situational authority in the overlapping authority model, see also Brendan F. Burke, "Understanding intergovernmental relations, twenty-five years hence," *State and Local Government Review* 46 (2014): 63–76.
[43] See also Agranoff and Radin, "Deil Wright's Overlapping Model," 146–8.
[44] See Burke, "Understanding," 66.
[45] One might compare here observations in M. L. Bello, "Intergovernmental Relations in Nigeria: An Assessment of Its Practice at the Local Government Level," *Journal of Poverty, Investment and Development* 4 (2014): 68.

a leader of the faithful, who through mediation not only influenced but also effectively commanded her own share of her son's power. She depended on divine power to execute the petitions she brought before God. She also depended on the faithful coming to her with their requests. Yet these dependencies neither confined nor determined her and her actions. On her own, and not merely through verbal statements of intention, she could take initiative in both directions and was thought to actually have done so. Most prominently, when the faithful turned to her with their requests and needs, she was the one who decided which actions of assistance were most appropriate and needed to be carried out. She did not delegate decision-making to the divine power above or rather outside her own realm of authority. She clearly guided and brought into action what was to be done, how, and when. Her mediation, combined with intercession, was not merely an ontological mediation, such that she was to be considered a mediator through the physicality of her giving of her body in the conception of and giving birth to Jesus, the Son of God. Her mediation was and is understood to remain an active, self-directed act of exercising multidirectional and powerful leadership.

9

The Constriction of Female Leadership

Tracing a Trend in the Early Reception of Miriam and Mary Magdalene

Erez DeGolan and Miriam-Simma Walfish

[I]t sometimes happens that the story of a story is as fascinating as the story itself. [1]

Introduction

The anthropologist Michael Jackson suggests that through stories, "we are each given three lives." The first is our awareness of our life as we live it; second, there are the stories told about us by others, those with whom we interact—such stories constitute the way we are experienced by the world we occupy. "Finally," adds Jackson, "there is our afterlife as a barely remembered name, a persona, an element in myth."[2] This "third life," our disembodied endurance as stories, is both productive and destructive. It is destructive because any "third life" erodes a forever-gone "first life"; it changes the lives of those remembered dramatically, in irreversible ways. But it is also productive: stories about figures who are gone join repositories of stories, which shape the lives of those who remember.

This essay tells a story about stories. It describes certain post-scriptural stories, or, following Jackson, the "third life" of the Hebrew Bible's Miriam and New Testament's Mary Magdalene. Specifically, it compares certain strands of stories about Miriam that appear in late antique rabbinic texts to those of Mary Magdalene that appear in Pope Gregory the Great's sermons, and in the *Golden Legend* (*Legenda Aurea*).

The "third lives" of Miriam and Mary are themselves stories about stories, that is, biblical stories. Both the Hebrew Bible and the New Testament depict Miriam and Mary Magdalene as prominent characters, or even leaders (broadly construed), who are present and active at critical junctures in the biblical narrative. Miriam is instrumental

---

We would like to thank Karen King, whose eye-opening course "The Gospel of Mary" exposed us to much of the secondary literature used in this article.
[1] Michael Jackson, *The Politics of Storytelling* (Copenhagen: Museum Tusculanum, 2013 [2002]), 228.
[2] Ibid., 249.

to Moses's survival,[3] and the biblical text portrays her as a leader and a prophet in the exultation scene after the Israelites cross the Red Sea.[4] Likewise, the gospels report that Mary Magdalene witnessed the crucifixion[5] and that she was present after the resurrection of Jesus.[6] At the same time, the scriptures also report negatively on these characters. The Hebrew Bible narrates that God inflicted Miriam with leprosy, as a punishment,[7] and the NT reports that Mary Magdalene was possessed by seven demons.[8]

The inherent tension within the scriptures, which portray the women both positively and negatively, coupled with the opaque, gapped, nature of the texts, gave rise to diverse interpretations of the women's stories. Storytellers use the gaps in the scriptural narratives as a springboard for stories that explore the women's leadership; they also, however, amplify the negative sides of Miriam and Mary, often by focusing the attention on their feminine bodies. Our interest in exploring these different directions is to offer a critique of the frames through which interpreters of the scriptures approach the stories about the two women. Particularly, we ponder how gender norms impacted the ways in which the prominent female characters were portrayed by male interpreters of scripture. We argue that the reception of the two women by later interpreters was shaped by the gender norms operative in these male readers' culture. In one strand, the status of Miriam and Mary and Magdalene as leaders is affirmed but redirected, while the other strand suppresses traces of this leadership by highlighting the negative, bodily portrayal of each.

We begin by discussing postbiblical stories that depict Miriam and Mary Magdalene as leaders but whose leadership is confined to the private sphere and whose impact is primarily centered on the realms of procreation and fertility. In the second section, we explore how the women's stories work as a leadership tool in the hands of male leaders. We show that sermonic texts use the stories about the sins of Miriam and Mary Magdalene to prescribe moral standards and that such retellings describe the feminine body as bearing the marks of sin. Interestingly, while these didactic texts refer to sins that both men and women may perform, their treatment of the Miriam and Mary Magdalene creates distance between men and sins of slander and sexual impropriety, and instead portrays women the epitome of these sins. In this way, women heroines are evoked to reaffirm women's sinfulness.

Spheres of Influence

The traditions explored in this section take as their starting point the two women's leadership roles in the Hebrew Bible and the NT. The portrayal of the two women in postbiblical literature, however, is notably gendered. As we shall see, interpreters confined and constricted the women's leadership through their creative reading of the

---

[3] See Exod 2:1–8.
[4] See Exod 15:20–21.
[5] See Matt 27:56; Mark 1:40; and John 19:25.
[6] See Matt 28:1; Mark 1:9; Luke 24; John 20:1.
[7] See Numbers 12.
[8] Luke 8:1–3; Mark 16:9.

biblical text. We trace the ways in which postbiblical exegetes paint Miriam and Mary as leaders who influence the realms marked as "feminine:" fertility and procreation. Moreover, in the traditions we consider, the two women fulfill their leadership role only when acting in the nonpublic spatial sphere. Thus, we suggest that postbiblical interpretations of Miriam and Mary were driven not only by the scriptural accounts but also by the gender norms of their own time and place.

Procreation as Leadership

In the Hebrew Bible, Miriam plays a supporting role in the narrative about Moses's survival in infancy. She first enters the stage at the banks of the Nile, from where she watches Moses's reed basket float on the river (Exod 2:4). After Pharaoh's daughter rescues the baby, Miriam shrewdly arranges for her mother to be hired as the infant's wet nurse (Exod 2:7).

Rabbinic interpreters assign Miriam much greater agency and expand her centrality to the narrative. In rabbinic imagination, Miriam is instrumental in bringing about the birth of Moses and securing the continuation of procreation among the Israelites. Her role in the rabbinic narrative of Israel's salvation cannot be understated; if it were not for Miriam, neither Israel's liberator nor its children who await liberation would even exist.

According to one tradition, for example, Miriam was one of the midwives mentioned in Exodus 1. In the biblical narrative, these midwives, named Shiphrah and Pu'ah, disobey Pharaoh's order to kill all male Israelite babies (Exod 1:15-17). Perhaps on account of the midwives' single appearance in the text and their ambiguous ethnic identity,[9] the rabbis assert that, in fact, Shiphrah and Pu'ah were known Israelite figures. Thus, the rabbis associate the midwives with Miriam and her mother, Yokhebed:

> Shiphrah [who is Yokhebed. She was called by this name because during] her time the Israelites were fruitful and they multiplied.[10] Pua'h—this is Miriam. And why was she called Pua'h? Because she cried and then delivered the baby. (b.Sotah 11b)

By injecting Miriam into the midwives' narrative, this tradition broadens Miriam's meritorious portrayal. Not only was she involved in reuniting infant Moses and his mother, the rabbinic Miriam was also one of the Hebrew midwives who stood up against the Egyptian king. In doing so, Miriam challenged Pharaoh's authority and saved the Israelites with her own hands. Thus, she prefigures her brother's role in Jewish tradition; she too is a savior of the oppressed nation.

---

[9] The biblical text refers to the midwives as "the Hebrew midwives," or, as "the midwives of the Hebrews." The Hebrew construction *hameyaldot ha'ivriyot* enables both readings, as the word "Hebrews" can function grammatically either as an adjective or as a noun in construct form. It is unclear to the rabbis, as well as to modern readers, whether they are Israelites or Gentiles.

[10] This is a pun on Shiphrah's name, which has aural similarity to the past conjugation of the Hebrew phrase "be fruitful and multiply" from Gen 9:7, together with the explanatory prefix "that." In the Hebrew: *Shē-Paru Uravu*.

This positive portrayal of Miriam, however, appears in a specific context—that of procreation. Portraying Miriam in this way is not unique to this story. In another tradition,[11] which we shall explore below, Miriam stimulates procreation among the Israelite community. Likewise, the Talmud offers an interpretation of Miriam's words against Moses in Numbers 12 in a story that argues that what Miriam actually discussed with Aaron was her concern that Moses was not engaging in sexual activity (and thus procreation) with his wife.[12]

In her study of the depictions of Miriam in rabbinic literature, Devora Steinmetz shows that the rabbis consistently characterize Miriam as having "one fundamental concern, the continuity of family."[13] The rabbis, then, portray Miriam as a high-caliber leader, parallel to her brother insofar as she ensures survival; at the same time, they constrict her influence to the specifically feminine sphere of procreation. In this regard, it is noteworthy that the tradition above describes Miriam as "crying" when she delivers Israelite babies. In rabbinic culture, as in contemporary society, crying is a gendered activity associated with women.[14] The rabbinic pun on the midwife's name, therefore, also frames Miriam's heroism in gendered terms.

Such framing is detectable in texts about Mary Magdalene as well; some exegetes of the New Testament's Mary confine her role to the theme of procreation in ways that resonate with rabbinic accounts of Miriam. An apt example of this tendency appears in Mary's hagiography in the *Golden Legend (Legenda Aurea)*, a thirteenth-century Latin collection containing tales of Christian saints compiled by Jacobus de Voragine (d. ca. 1298).[15] As we shall see, the *Golden Legend* develops Mary's character and expands her role beyond what is explicitly stated in the NT, but it does so primarily when she affects the feminine sphere of fertility. Not unlike the rabbinic homilies, gender assumptions are central to such figuration of Mary.

The *Legend* recounts Mary Magdalene's life trajectory from sinfulness to penance and conversion and, consequently, to righteousness.[16] The main focus is on how Mary arms others with the "armor of penance,"[17] shepherding nonbelievers through the path she has chosen, into the arms of Christ. In one section of the story, Mary Magdalene ends up in Marseilles along with some other Christians.[18] The narrative focuses on Mary's role in the conversion of the local governor's family. In one scene, Mary confronts the governor and his wife and urges them to convert. The couple then tells her, "We are prepared to do whatever you tell us to if you can obtain a son from us

---

[11] b.Sotah 12a; see below
[12] *Sifre Bamidbar* 99.
[13] Devora Steinmetz, "A Portrait of Miriam in Rabbinic Midrash," *Prooftexts* 8 (1998): 38.
[14] See, e.g., Charlotte Elisheva Fonrobert, "When the Rabbi Weeps: On Reading Gender in Talmudic Aggadah," *Nashim: A Journal of Jewish Women's Studies and Gender Issues* 4 (2001): 61.
[15] Eamon Duffy, "Introduction," in Jacobus de Voragine, ed., *The Golden Legend: Readings on the Saints*, trans. William Granger Ryan (Princeton, NJ: Princeton University Press, 2012), xi. We consider the *Legend*'s Mary Magdalene and its dialogue with the rabbinic Miriam not out of interest in textual relationships between the texts (which, most likely, do not exist). Instead, we are interested in a parallel phenomenon: the ways in which biblical heroines' third lives are informed by the gender norms of their composers.
[16] Ibid., 374–6.
[17] Ibid.
[18] Ibid., 376.

from God."[19] Mary Magdalene rises to the challenge and prays to God. God hears her prayers and the wife of the governor conceives. The greatness of Mary Magdalene is manifested in her ability to engender a pregnancy (through God).

Sadly, the governor's wife dies in childbirth. Her corpse, together with the newly born baby, are abandoned on the shore of an unknown land. The readers are led to assume that the newborn son has also died. On his journey back from Jerusalem, however, the governor learns that his son has survived and, even more miraculously, that his wife has come back to life. These miracles, the *Legend* reports, occurred thanks to Mary Magdalene; the text stresses that the governor's son survived because "Mary Magdalene had preserved [him] unharmed."[20] This thrust in the story, similar to the rabbinic tradition about Miriam explored above, links Mary to procreation and continuity. The governor's wife thanks Mary for her service as a midwife, with words that resonate with Miriam's story: "O blessed Mary Magdalene! ... you did me a midwife's service."[21] The *Legend*'s Mary Magdalene, like the rabbinic Miriam, is celebrated for her life-giving vitality.

In the traditions examined here, both Mary Magdalene and Miriam play a crucial role in the history of the Israelite nation or of the Christian ecclesia. At the same time, gender assumptions determine the realms that they influence: birth and continuity. We contend that gender assumptions not only direct the *themes* with which the women leaders are associated but also characterize the *spatial placement* of their characters in the postbiblical stories.

Leadership and Space: Where Are Women Leaders Effective?

In *Poetics of the Flesh,* Mayra Rivera writes, "My visible body affects which areas of the world I may inhabit."[22] Rivera draws our attention to the relation between the how bodies are perceived and the spaces they occupy in the world. A current example that concretizes this notion is the controversy over the access of transgender individuals to public bathrooms. The ways in which bodies are perceived may impact an individual's freedom of movement. Thinking with Rivera, we examine the physical spaces that Miriam and Mary Magdalene occupy in postbiblical stories. We note that these stories place women leaders place them only in spaces where—in the interpreters' view—it is appropriate for the feminine body to act.

For the rabbis, as we have seen, Miriam is a catalyst of Israel's salvation. Miriam fulfils this role, however, through action in nonpublic spaces. A well-known elaboration of the first chapter of Exodus illustrates this point. Building upon Pharaoh's command to throw the Israelite male babies into the Nile (Exod 1:22), the rabbis imagine Amram as persuading Israelite men to divorce their wives in order to prevent the birth of babies whose death has been decreed:

---

[19] Ibid., 377.
[20] Ibid., 379.
[21] Ibid.
[22] Mayra Rivera, *Poetics of the Flesh* (Durham: Duke University Press, 2015), 114.

"And there went a man of the house of Levi"—where did he go? Rabbi Judah the son of Rabbi Zavina said: [it means that] he went because of his daughter's advice. (Rabbi Judah) recited a tradition: Amram [Moses' father] was great in his generation [i.e., an authoritative figure amongst the community], and since he heard about Pharaoh the evil's decree "cast every male to the Nile" (Ex. 1:22), he said [to himself and to the community]: we labor [i.e., procreate] in vain! He got up and divorced his wife. [Following his actions] everyone got up and divorced their wives.

While Exodus blames Pharaoh for persecuting the Israelites, in this midrash, the immediate threat is internal. Amram, Miriam's father and a leader in the Israelite community ("great in his generation"), doubles down on Pharaoh's decree, deeming any attempt of procreation useless ("we labor in vain!"). He decides, therefore, to divorce his wife (Moses's future mother); as a result, other Israelite men divorce their wives too, and procreation is cut short. The foe in this story is still Pharaoh, but the actual risks to continuity are Amram's actions and the despair of the Israelites.

Next, the midrash describes Miriam's intervention:

His daughter [Miriam] told him: Father, your decree is harsher than that of Pharaoh as Pharaoh decreed only regarding male, and you decreed regarding male and female; Pharaoh decreed only regarding this world, and you decreed regarding this world and the world-to-come [i.e., if they do not exist, they have no share in the eschatological future]; with regards to the evil Pharaoh, the outcome of his decree is questionable, while you, who is a righteous, your decree is surely will come to fruition, as it said "you shall decree a thing, and it shall be established for you" (Job 22:28). [In response. Amram] got up and brought his wife back. [Following his actions] everyone got up and brought back their wives. (*b.Sotah* 12a)

Here, Miriam changes her father's mind and saves the day. She does so, however, neither by rebelling against her father nor by demanding that he abolish his decree of celibacy. Instead, Miriam deploys powerful and sophisticated rhetoric. She is an astute rabbinic-like exegete, using both logic and scriptural evidence to buttress her argument; midrashically, she compares her father's righteousness to that of Job, claiming that his decree will have consequences both in this world and in the world to come.

Miriam exercises her leadership within the confines of her family. She does not contest the cessation of procreation in the public realm; she does not present her logic to the community at large. Indeed, it seems that, the community is unaware of Miriam's concerns until Miriam convinces her father; only her father can act and influence others to act. Her gender dictates where she can be effective, and her leadership is limited to private space.

According to this tradition, Miriam is instrumental to the birth of Moses and Israelite babies, and therefore to the liberation of the Israelites from Egypt. If it were not for her, Pharaoh's decree would have led to the complete annihilation of Israel, simply by suppressing the community's desire to procreate. Miriam's method of combating Pharaoh's decree, namely, to encourage procreation, recalls Steinmetz's point. This tradition clearly depicts Miriam as one who "understands the importance of childbearing" and has "concern for continuity."[23] But in addition to limiting Miriam's ability to the sphere of fertility, this rabbinic tradition also restricts Miriam's spatial presence to the home.

This same dynamic is present in other traditions. Within the same Talmudic pericope from which we quoted the previous text, the rabbis treat Exod 15:20, which states, "Then the prophet Miriam, *Aaron's sister*, took a tambourine in her hand; and all the women went out after her with tambourines and with dancing" (NRSV, emphasis ours). Perplexed by the fact the Miriam is referred to as Aaron's sister, rather than as Moses's sister, the rabbis conclude that Miriam's prophetic act must relate to the pre-Moses narrative. Hence, Miriam was a prophet only when she and Aaron were not yet the brother and sister of Israel's savior:

> "And Miriam the prophet, the sister of Aaron, took, etc." The sister of Aaron and not the sister of Moses? Rabbi Amram reported in the name of Rav, and some say Rabbi Nachman reported in the name of Rav: [this verse] teaches us that she prophesied when she was Aaron's sister [i.e., before Moses was born], saying: my mother is destined to give birth to a son who will set the Israelites free. When Moses was born, the house was filled with light, and Miriam's father got up and kissed Miriam on her head, saying: Daughter, your prophecy was actualized!
>
> But when they cast him [Moses] into the Nile, Miriam's father got up and struck her on her head, saying: Daughter, where is your prophecy [now]? Thus it is written: "And his sister stood afar off, to know what would be done to him" (Exod 2:4). (*b.Sotah* 12b–13a)

In this tradition, Miriam's role does not follow the usual depiction of prophecy in the Hebrew Bible. The rabbinic Miriam does not pronounce the words of God to the community in the manner of other prophets. Rather, in this tradition, the rabbis imagine a family member who shares a vision with her relative. In the biblical text, Miriam prophesies in public space, by leading the Israelite women in song and dance. In this rabbinic story, her prophetic activity is limited to the privacy of the family.

Furthermore, in this story, Miriam declares her prophecy only to her father; apparently no one else is present. Thus, Miriam, the communal prophet of Exodus 15, becomes an intimate, familial, prophet. As a heroine, Miriam is said to have had divine revelation, but as a woman, she can only deliver her message to her family. The feminine body can prophesy only in the intimate space of the home.

This Talmudic tradition reveals the degree to which Miriam's gender is operative in her depiction as a leader. First, the text transposes Miriam's prophesying from the public sphere to the private one. To recall Rivera, the visibility of Miriam's body determines the appropriate place for her effectiveness. Second, the text emphasizes the familial hierarchy and Miriam's subordination to her father by showing that the reception of her prophecy is contingent upon external signs. In other words, the text both elevates Miriam as a meritorious leader and deprives her of actual power. She

---

[23] Steinmetz, "A Portrait of Miriam," 45.

may be a prophet, but she is first and foremost a woman in a patriarchal household. Third, the Talmudic text implicitly limits Miriam's prophetic role to the time before Moses's birth. For the composers of this tradition, Miriam's prophetic role ends when the Israelites are transformed from slaves to a free nation.

In a similar manner, Mary Magdalene's leadership, as portrayed in the *Golden Legend*, is confined to private spaces. We return now to Mary Magdalene's interaction with the governor and his wife. At the beginning of the story, Mary Magdalene *does* operate in a public space: "Then the governor of that province came with his wife to offer sacrifice and pray the gods for offspring. Magdalene preached Christ to him and dissuaded him from sacrificing."[24] Her public leadership role, however, ends with the announcement of her humiliating failure. Thereafter, she can no longer preach in public but rather must appear in a vision to the governor's wife to advance her agenda; her rebuke of the governor was not effective and did not lead him to change his ways. The appearance to the wife, however, also fails. Only when Mary Magdalene reveals herself in a vision to both the governor and his wife is change achieved. As in the case of Miriam, Mary Magdalene of the *Golden Legend* has to mobilize a male's body to generate action. And like Miriam, Mary Magdalene's leadership is effective only in the private sphere. She must penetrate the intimacy of the family—the bed of the governor and his wife—to actualize her leadership.

As the story about the governor and his wife unfolds, it becomes apparent that Mary Magdalene's body, and her leadership, are confined to nonpublic spaces. Rivera's words resonate in the *Golden Legend* in a similar fashion to what we have explored regarding the story of Miriam. The husband, we are told, wanted "to go to Peter and find out whether what Magdalene preached about Christ was true."[25] Like Amram, the kissing/striking father of Miriam, the governor seeks confirmation for the words of the female leader. For the governor, only Peter—a male leader—can provide proofs and validate the message. Peter travels freely from Rome to Jerusalem and leads the governor in a guided tour through "all the places where Christ had preached and performed Miracles."[26] We later discover, however, that Mary Magdalene and the governor's wife accompanied Peter and the governor in their journey. In the words of the governor's wife,

> [I am] just coming from the pilgrimage from which you yourself are returning. And as blessed Peter conducted you to Jerusalem and showed you all the places where Christ suffered ... I, with blessed Mary Magdalene as my guide and companion, was with you and committed all you saw to memory.[27]

The previous section of the story portrayed the governor as simultaneously accepting and also questioning Mary Magdalene's leadership. His doubts about her lead him to seek validation through Peter who, unlike Mary Magdalene, can provide him

---

[24] de Voragine, *Golden Legend*, 377.
[25] Ibid., 378.
[26] Ibid., 379.
[27] Ibid.

with "thorough instruction in the faith."[28] While the story initially implies that Mary Magdalene was absent from Rome and Jerusalem, it turns out that she can, and does, travel miraculously to Jerusalem. As a female leader, however, her travel in the public sphere must take place invisibly. Although the *Golden Legend* seeks to depict Magdalene as a meritorious saint, her gender determines the places that her body inhabits and how she can inhabit them.

Thus far, we have focused on the role of Miriam and Mary Magdalene's gender in their depiction as heroines and leaders. We have argued that, in the traditions examined here, the women's gender affects their portrayal in two ways. As Steinmetz has shown, Miriam's leadership is characterized by the rabbis primarily in relationship to procreation and fertility. This is true in the *Golden Legend*, too, as Mary Magdalene performs miracles that are associated with fertility. Second, drawing on Rivera's work, we showed that gender also determines the spaces where the two leader women perform their leadership. In the surveyed texts, both Miriam and Mary Magdalene, as leaders, are confined to intimate, nonpublic, spheres. In other words, in the surveyed stories, the women's leadership is effective only where women's bodies can be appropriately present, namely, in intimate family spaces.

Leading by (Sinful) Example: When a Female Leader Becomes a Moral Paradigm

We now turn to another way in which the bodies of Miriam and Mary and Magdalene are mobilized by later interpreters. Some rabbis and church fathers turn to them as moral exemplars. For others, however, these Mary and Miriam epitomize everything that is wrong with women. Their bodies are indelibly marked by sin, and for that reason their leadership is dismissed.

This section will chart the reception of Miriam in the early rabbinic midrash *Sifre Zuta*[29] and will compare it to the reception of Mary Magdalene in a sermon of Pope Gregory, from the turn of the seventh century. We will first explore the ways in which Pope Gregory and the rabbis shift the discourse about Mary and Miriam from the characters themselves to the ways in which their stories can be used as models of sinful actions to be avoided. We will explore how this frame affects the characterization of the women's sin and penance, highlighting especially the portrayal of the marks the sins leave on their flesh and bodies. We will argue that by projecting the sins of slander and lust onto the bodies of women, male religious leaders subtly, and perhaps even unconsciously, distance themselves from these sins and minimize the power of female leadership. The ultimate effect of this distancing in the third life of Mary and Miriam is to negate the positive claim that these once powerful women had on male lives. As Jane Schaberg states in her discussion of Mary Magdalene, "The counterweight of her sinfulness had made it safe to speak of her power and authority."[30]

---

[28] Ibid.
[29] For more information on *Sifre Zuta*, see H. L. Strack and Günter Stemberger, *Introduction to the Talmud and Midrash*, trans. and ed. Markus Bockmuehl (Minneapolis, MN: Fortress, 1992), 266–70.
[30] Jane Schaberg, *The Resurrection of Mary Magdalene: Legends, Apocrypha, and the Christian Testament* (New York: Continuum, 2002), 89.

Miriam and Mary as Universal Moral Paradigms

The third life of Miriam begins already in the Hebrew Bible, when Deut 24:9 enjoins: "Remember what the Lord, your God, did to Miriam on the way, when you went out of Egypt." The rabbis, taking their lead from the biblical text, hear in this "Remember" a moral injunction. The (primarily male) audience is to remember what God had done to Miriam so that we might know how to behave. Deuteronomy 24 refers back to Numbers 12, in which the narrator reports that

> **1** Miriam and Aaron spoke against Moses because of the Cushite woman whom he had married (for he had indeed married a Cushite woman). **2** and they said, "Has the Lord spoken only through Moses? Has he not spoken through us also?" And the Lord heard it. … **6** And he said, "Hear my words: When there are prophets among you, I the Lord make myself known to them in visions; I speak to them in dreams. **7** Not so with my servant Moses; he is entrusted with all my house. **8** With him I speak face to face—clearly, not in riddles; and he beholds the form of the Lord. Why then were you not afraid to speak against my servant Moses?"
> (Num 12:1–2; 6–8, NRSV)

Following this speech, God's presence departs from the Tent of Meeting and Miriam is stricken with leprosy. The rabbis delve into Numbers 12 in an attempt to ascertain precisely what it was that Miriam did to merit the wrath of God, instantiated in the form of leprosy. Rather than parse God's speech, which seems to indicate that the issue at hand is the challenging of Moses's authority, the rabbis identify Miriam and Aaron's speech (vv. 1–2) as the catalyst for her leprosy and as a model of speech which others should remember to avoid. In *Sifre Zuta*, the rabbis hold up Miriam and Aaron as a warning:

> And behold, the matter is analogous: Just as these spoke against their younger brother and did not speak poorly about him, rather simply compared him to the other prophets, they nonetheless were punished, a person (man) who speaks negatively about his fellow in his presence all the more so. And so it says, "Remember what the Lord your God did to Miriam" (Deut 24:9)—that she sinned with her mouth and yet her whole body suffered.

In this midrash, the rabbis state that the content of Miriam and Aaron's speech was not problematic, but they contend that it was the very act of speaking about another person that was negative. The rabbis frame their comparison using the typically rabbinic phrase "all the more so." Miriam and Aaron were righteous, and their speech was not categorically wrong, yet they deserved punishment. Vigilance in speech, therefore, is even more necessary for you, the audience, the nonrighteous. The rabbis use the events of Numbers 12 as an occasion for moral teaching; the audience is to learn how not to behave, based on the biblical precedent.

Upon closer examination, however, the logic deployed by this teaching is not entirely smooth. Miriam and Aaron's actions are equated, and both are judged by the text as deserving punishment. Only Miriam, however, actually faces consequences. This imbalance is not, of course, manufactured by the rabbinic exegetes. *Sifre Zuta* only echoes the disjuncture in the biblical narrative, which mentions Aaron's participation in the event that led to Miriam's bodily affliction ("Miriam and Aaron spoke against Moses") but mentions no punishment inflicted upon him.

While this tradition ignores this logical difficulty, earlier paragraphs of *Sifre Zuta* do treat the mismatch between the culprits' punishments. One tradition, for instance, suggests that Aaron, too, was deserving of leprosy: "And Aaron too was fit for this [punishment], thus it says, "incensed with them," (Num 12:9) but he was wearing the [priestly] mantle which atones for slander" (*Sifre Zuta* 12:9). Here, Aaron's priestly post differentiates between his body and Miriam's. The imbalance of their roles explains the imbalance in the outcome of their deeds. Miriam's non-priestly, feminine, body is susceptible to leprosy, while the priestly gear makes Aaron immune to the punishment. At the same time, depicting Aaron's role as a priest as the armor that protects his body highlights Miriam's lack of a parallel leadership role that might have similarly protected her.

This teaching also promotes a view on the dynamics between body, sin, and punishment that explains the imbalance in Miriam and Aaron's *capacity* to be punished for speaking about Moses. The following source in the same midrashic pericope makes this dynamic even more explicit:

"And Aaron turned to Miriam" (Num. 12:10)—The Holy Blessed One said: If Aaron becomes leprous, a blemished priest may not sacrifice upon the altar. Rather, he will see his sister and will be shocked and he will rebuke himself of his own accord, as it says, "and Aaron turned to Miriam and behold she is leprous."

Aaron's priestly function once again protects his body. Because leprosy is a blemish that renders a priest unfit for service, God spares Aaron so that he can continue functioning as the high priest.[31] The rabbis do not see God as letting Aaron off the hook; God uses Miriam's body to dispense a moral teaching to Aaron. Like a warning sign, her visible affliction spurs Aaron's own self-reflection, leading him to correct his wrongful ways. This dynamic is analogous to the impact that the homilies of *Sifre Zuta* seek have on their audience. Following the biblical text, the rabbinic exegetes place Miriam at the heart of their discussion, which is intended for an implied audience of rabbinic men. She is deployed as a pedagogical instrument, teaching these men through her negative example. The audience is to "see" her affected body and, like Aaron, rebuke themselves of their own accord.

The complex ways in which *Sifre Zuta* investigates Numbers 12 expose the mixture of exegesis and gender norms in the construction of Miriam's "third life." The composers of the homilies explored above take the lead from the biblical narrative in their deployment of Miriam as a (negative) moral exemplar. The texts do not ignore Aaron's participation in the slander of Moses. Yet the exegetical direction taken by the homilies uses Miriam as a body that alerts Aaron (and men) not to sin.

---

[31] The biblical source from which the laws concerning blemished priests were developed is Lev 21:17.

A similar move is made in Gregory the Great's interpretation of the story of Mary Magdalene. In Homily 33, he holds Mary up as a model of repentance, saying, "For whose heart, however hardened, would not be so softened by the tears of this sinner that he follows her model of penitence?"[32] Gregory develops the character of Mary as the penitent par excellence whose every action demonstrates how true repentance is achieved. Like the rabbis, Gregory employs the story of Mary as a pedagogical tool, meant to instruct his listeners in how to achieve forgiveness.

Gregory the Great also uses Mary in this way in Homily 25, wherein he lays out the seven deadly sins and connects each one to a different, repentant gospel figure:

> Perhaps someone in the faith has fallen into sin—let him them look at Peter who wept bitterly, because he had denied him when he was afraid … Someone else, inflamed with the fire of passion, has lost the purity of his flesh—let him look at Mary, who in herself melted the fleshly love through the fire of the divine love. See, the almighty God has everywhere set people before our eyes who we must follow … So let us turn away from evil, above all from that which we ourselves have experienced. (Sermon 25.10)[33]

In this sermon, Peter and Mary are both employed as illustrative examples for how to achieve a state of repentance from sin. By grouping Mary with the other apostles in this sermon, Pope Gregory does ascribe to her a measure of leadership. Like Miriam, Mary is still on some level a leading agent in her status as a moral paradigm, but her leadership has shifted from the realm of the family even more inwardly, into realm of an individual's psyche.

Even this measure of leadership, however, tells only part of the story. As in *Sifre Zuta* above, Pope Gregory's treatment of Mary's story deeply enmeshes her sin and penitence with fleshly language. Whereas Peter's sin—his disbelief—is connected to his intellect and mind, Mary's sin is "fleshly love."

While there need not be anything inherently gendered about the use of Mary and Miriam as moral paradigms, the rabbis in *Sifre Zuta* and Pope Gregory treat Miriam and Mary differently than the way they treat the male leaders with whom they are paired. Moreover, their bodies are visibly present in both *Sifre Zuta* and Gregory's speech. Both Mary's and Miriam's bodies and the ways in which sin and penitence are marked on them get in the way of a non-gendered understanding of how each works as a moral paradigm; body and flesh suffuse these as well as later iterations of their stories.

Femininity and the Sinful Body

While both the rabbis and Pope Gregory treat their female subjects as moral examples from whom their male audiences can learn how to act, the fact that both women's

---

[32] The translation for Gregory's sermon here is from Esther A. De Boer, *The Mary Magdalene Cover-up: The Sources behind the Myth*, trans. John Bowden (London: T&T Clark, 2007), 172.
[33] Ibid., 180.

punishment and penance were enacted by or upon their bodies creates a link between sin, punishment, and the feminine body.

As we saw above, *Sifre Zuta* uses the bodily punishment to highlight the intensity of the punishment for slander: "She sinned with her mouth and yet her whole body suffered" (*Sifre Zuta* 12.9). The next paragraph sharpens the reason for this extreme reaction: "Because they (Miriam and Aaron) made (him) pale and blush (through their slander) they were defiled with intensely bright white lesions" (*Sifre Zuta* 12.0).[34] According to this logic, leprosy is the appropriate response to slander, because it uses the body as a canvas and paints it to mirror the effect the harmful words had on their recipient. For *Sifre Zuta*, this leprosy is not specifically feminine; it is the divine response to anyone who sullies their fellow's name. The fact that it is Miriam who is punished in the biblical text, however, inspires the last line in the midrash: "Remember what the Lord your God did to Miriam (Deut 24:9)—that she sinned with her mouth and yet her whole body suffered" (*Sifre Zuta* 12.9, quoted above). Thus, while the text begins by highlighting a measure-for-measure logic to explain the nature of the punishment that Miriam and Aaron deserve, the text ends by noting that only Miriam's body was afflicted and that it was afflicted entirely.

Highlighting the corporeality of the punishment opens up the way for a narrative strand that claims that not only did sin mark Miriam's entire body, but it did so permanently and indelibly. A midrash in *b.Sotah*, for example, connects Miriam with a woman named Azuvah who appears in a genealogy in Chronicles as the wife of Caleb.[35] This connection serves two purposes. The first relates to the rabbinic desire to domesticate Miriam; by linking Miriam and Azuvah, they successfully marry Miriam off, which echoes the strand we saw above, linking Miriam to the domestic sphere. The second effect, however, is more insidious. The name Azuvah means "abandoned." The rabbis here suggest that Miriam's leprosy causes her to be abandoned by marking her flesh permanently.

The poet Alicia Ostriker plays out this aspect of the third life of Miriam in her poem entitled "The Songs of Miriam." She states, "I peel the skin off myself in strips/I am going to die in the sand."[36] For Ostriker and *b.Sotah*, the marks on Miriam's flesh are not a penance, enabling her to reenter society in God's good graces. Rather, they serve as her societal death; her flesh is indelibly marked by her sin and she is abandoned to her lonely fate. The result of this fleshly marking is the complete othering of Miriam. This othering enables her sin to be seen as uniquely feminine. As such, this sin is something that men need not control within themselves but rather may police in others.

A more explicit articulation of this strand appears in *Midrash Tanhuma*, a collection of rabbinic teachings that (according to some scholars) dates from the late fourth century:[37]

---

[34] *Sifre Zuta* dances between talking about Miriam and talking about the sin that she and Aaron share. These early rabbis are uncomfortable with blaming Miriam exclusively and find ways to explain why Aaron was not punished even though he rightfully should have been.

[35] See 1 Chron 2:18.

[36] Alicia Ostriker, "Miriam's Songs," in *All the Women Followed Her*, ed. Rebecca Schwartz (Santa Clara County, CA: Rikudei Miriam, 2001), 13–15.

[37] For more information on *Tanhuma* midrashim, see Strack and Stemberger, *Introduction to the Talmud and Midrash*, 302–6.

Rabbi Judah b. Shalom said: You have nothing more difficult than woman ... Come and see that when God sought to create Eve, God calculated which place to create her from. God said: If I create her from the head, her spirit will be haughty, from the eye—she will be [overly] curious, from the mouth she will be a chatterbox, from the ear she will be an eavesdropper, from the hands she will be a thief, from the feet she will be a runabout. What did the Holy Blessed One do? He created her from the rib—from a modest place—so that she would be modest, sitting at home, as it says, "And God took one of his ribs ..." (Gen. 2:21).

And even so, they [i.e., women] did not escape these flaws ... [for example] God did not create her from the mouth so that she not be a chatterbox and yet Leah was a chatterbox...and so too, "And Miriam and Aaron spoke against Moses ..."

... Rabbi Judah b. Shalom said: And this that we have said about the most fitting of them [i.e., of women] and it is not necessary to say about other women.[38]

The midrash begins with the statement, "R. Yehudah b. Shalom states: there is nothing more difficult than the woman." R. Yehudah goes on to explain that when creating Eve, God deliberated about which body part of Adam's to use as Eve's core. God dismisses various body parts because of their potential to lead to various types of negative behaviors. Finally, "He created her from the rib, from a modest place so that she would be modest, sitting at home." In the end, however, despite God's careful planning, women display all of these negative traits. R. Yehudah invokes Miriam as evidence for this tragedy, noting, "He did not create her (Eve) from the mouth so that she would not be a chatterbox ... and behold (Num. 12), 'And Miriam spoke, and Aaron, about Moses.'"

Here, Miriam's sin has taken on quite a different character from earlier strands that use her sin as a negative example for men not to follow. Her sin is part and parcel of what makes all women "difficult." Eve contains a physical core of Adam's flesh, says R. Yehudah, but when this flesh takes on the form of a woman's body, it becomes unrecognizable. A rib should lead to modesty and yet the female body participates in all manner of negative social performance. Furthermore, by highlighting the fact that God did *not* create Eve out of Adam's mouth, the Midrash makes the claim that women's speech is not to be attributed to men and, implicitly, that men's speech is essentially different than that of women. Miriam's body, according to this logic, is living proof that women are at their core incapable of speaking in ways that are positive.

The final statement of Rabbi Judah b. Shalom highlights a stark contrast between *Sifre Zuta* (discussed above) and *Midrash Tanhuma*. Both midrashim see in Miriam the basis of a logical extrapolation. In *Sifre Zuta*, the fact that Miriam's punishment was for a relatively minor type of slander serves as a warning to the audience—if she who sinned in a minor way was punished, then you, the audience will certainly be punished for a more damaging type of slander! In *Sifre Zuta*, therefore, a primarily male audience is being taught a moral lesson by being compared unfavorably to Miriam.

Midrash Tanhuma employs a similar logical extrapolation to very different ends. Instead of comparing blameworthy men to the exalted Miriam, Rabbi Judah deploys

---

[38] *Midrash Tanhuma* (Warsaw) Parashat Vayeshev 6 (translations our own).

the same logic to implicate women. Miriam and other biblical women, says Rabbi Judah, are the best women there are. If they are not immune to sin, certainly no woman can be immune! This midrash essentially absolves men of the sin of slander but places full blame on Miriam and therefore puts a nail in the coffin of Miriam's role as leader. Here, Miriam is not considered a moral exemplar whose sin can teach men how to behave better. Miriam's sin of negative speech is not a sin that men need to control in themselves but is solely a feminine sin to be policed.[39]

Thus far, we have traced a trajectory in which Miriam's fleshly punishment described by the biblical narrator invites later interpreters to connect her sin to her flesh as well. *Midrash Tanhuma* seals this connection—if her sin is localized in her body, it is perforce wrapped up in her femininity. This trajectory reflects the circular dynamic exposed by Rivera—words about bodies change social relations and are formed by social perceptions.[40] In *Midrash Tanhuma*, words about Miriam's body participate in a broader discourse that dismisses women as sinful, but the specific exegesis is enabled by the words of biblical text that separate between Miriam and Aaron and paint Miriam's punishment as fleshly. The result is that Miriam is no longer only an example but has become a template of women's nature.

Pope Gregory also highlights the bodily nature of Mary's sin. In Homily 33, when he connects the Mary out of whom went seven demons (Luke 8:1–3; Mark 16:9) to the sinful woman who anoints Jesus in Luke 7, he says, "She whom Luke calls the sinful woman, whom John calls Mary, we believe to be the Mary from whom seven devils were ejected according to Mark. And what did these seven devils signify, if not all the vices?" The demons were, for Gregory, not external forces that had attacked Mary but were in fact sins she was wont to commit. Gregory goes on to explain how Mary's sinfulness had imprinted itself on her body:

> It is clear, brothers, that the woman previously used the unguent to perfume her flesh in forbidden acts. What she therefore displayed more scandalously, she was now offering to God in a more praiseworthy manner. She had coveted with earthly eyes, but now through penitence these are consumed with tears. She displayed her hair to set off her face, but now her hair dries her tears. She had spoken proud things with her mouth, but in kissing the Lord's feet, she now planted her mouth on the Redeemer's feet. For every delight, therefore, she had had in herself, she now immolated herself. She turned the mass of her crimes to virtues, in order to serve God entirely in penance.[41]

According to Gregory, Mary Magdalene had used her flesh, eyes, hair, and mouth to sinfully seduce men. Thus, when the gospels report positive actions she does with her body, his assessment has diminished her service, labeling it a penance for her fleshly sinfulness. In the gospels, Mary serves Jesus with their body and is praised by

---

[39] We are not arguing that the portrayal of women in *Midrash Tanhuma* stems directly from *b.Sotah*'s portrayal of Miriam's abandonment, just that they mirror each other as two sides of the same coin.
[40] Loosely paraphrasing Rivera, *Poetics of the Flesh*, 113–14.
[41] Translation in Susan Haskins, *Mary Magdalen: Myth and Metaphor* (London: Harper Collins, 1993), 96.

him for her service.[42] Pope Gregory, however, turns these virtues into former vices, transforming Mary from apostle into penitent. She is no longer a messenger; rather, her body is the message. When he talks about how Mary "displayed her hair to set off her face" or "used the unguent to perfume her flesh," he describes lust and sexual temptation using objects perceived as inherently feminine. Where the gospels discuss sin in general terms, Gregory has specified that these are sins of the flesh. It is thus no accident that Mary, a woman, is chosen to be the paradigm of the sin of lust.

In many ways, the penance Gregory attributes to Mary Magdalene resembles Miriam's leprosy. Both women are seen to have atoned with their bodies for sins they committed. By marking their bodies, their penance makes public and visible what was at first a private sin. This characterization of their penance intersects with another strand that downplays the penitential force of these women's stories and focuses instead on their sinfulness. This shift in focus represents the ultimate negation of their leadership.

In the third life of Mary Magdalene, as in *Midrash Tanhuma*, we also see a second view concerning the sins marked on the female body. In the nineteenth century, the term "magdalenism" emerged as a synonym for prostitution.[43] The very existence of this term shows that for this strand, all other aspects of Mary Magdalene's leadership have been eclipsed. Rather than embodying righteous penitence, as Mary does in Pope Gregory's speech, this term myopically focuses on the sin that Pope Gregory associates with Mary—that of lust. This reframing had devastating consequences for some women. In Ireland, women identified as sexually deviant (including victims of rape and incest) were confined to institutions called "Magdalen Laundries." There, they were employed (but not paid) as washerwomen who laundered the clothes of the convent.

While a revised understanding of Mary Magdalene did not in and of itself lead to this confinement, the connection of Mary to this institution demonstrates a number of factors regarding sexual sin. First, unlike in Pope Gregory's understanding, the Magdalen Laundries demonstrate that for some interpreters no complete penitence is ever possible for sexual sin. As a mother superior in charge of one such laundry explains, "very few of these who have lost their good name, and generally speaking, have contracted habits of intemperance, idleness, and other vices, will be able to resist temptation if exposed to the rough contract of the world again."[44] Sexual sin was perceived as permanent—nothing could wipe away its marks on these women's flesh. While this mother superior speaks in terms of temptation, there is something evocative about the laundering these women were charged with doing. In some ways, they were attempting, over and over, to bleach away the sin that had stuck to their bodies, to no avail.

---

[42] E.g., Luke 7:44–48.

[43] See, e.g., https://archive.org/details/magdalenismainq00taitgoog. The earliest reference to Mary Magdalene herself as a prostitute is in Odo of Cluny (tenth century). Sanctus Odo Abbas Cluniacensis II, Sermo II. Migne, P.L., vol. 133, col. 721. Thank you to Mary Ann Beavis for the reference.

[44] Rebecca Lea McCarthy, *Origins of the Magdalene Laundries: An Analytical History* (Jefferson, NC: McFarland, 2010), 148.

Fascinatingly, in her book *Origins of the Magdalene Laundries*, Rebecca Lea McCarthy connects the term magdalenism to Pope Gregory's sermons quoted above.[45] Just as the exegetical rhetoric of *Sifre Zuta* did not necessitate that of *Tanhuma* but paves the way for it, so too Pope Gregory's identification of Mary Magdalene with sexual sin opened a pathway for seeing in prostitution a sin that could not be expunged.

In conclusion, we have seen that the rabbis of *Sifre Zuta* and Pope Gregory transpose the actual leadership attributed to Miriam and Mary Magdalene in the biblical text into the moral realm. They hold up these women as moral paradigms whose own actions signal ways in which men should behave and sins they should avoid. Their treatment of these women, however, uses rhetoric that links their punishment and penance to their feminine flesh, implying that their sins are embedded there as well. The strand of this tale that we have just explored takes this statement to its logical conclusion—if sin is embedded in their flesh, it cannot be expunged.

This fleshly portrayal of women's sins allowed some men to take the easy way out. Rather than seeing sinful speech and sinful lust as universal human tendencies to be worked on in oneself, some succumbed to the temptation to paint these sins as inherently feminine. Indeed, as Rivera argues, "Words about bodies create social relations."[46]

Conclusion

Miriam's dance at the sea and Mary's witnessing of Jesus' resurrection serve as "shadows and traces," to use Jane Schaberg's term,[47] which indicate that both women were at one point seen as powerful religious leaders. Indeed, later commentators saw the two as central to the biblical narrative and therefore constructed an elaborate "third life" for both characters. Tracing these traditions, which postdate the women's lives by hundreds or thousands of years, provides an opportunity for exploring the interplay between exegesis and cultural norms around gender.

While other strands do exist, we have explored some that are central to the reception of each woman's story and that reframe the leadership that is associated with each. Perhaps threatened by the echoes of powerful female leadership, later male interpreters reconfigured the contours of their leadership according to how they viewed women's role in society. In their hands, Miriam and Mary became models of femininity with both positive and negative valences. In the first strand we explored, postbiblical stories about the leadership of Miriam and Mary Magdalene restricted their leadership both thematically and spatially. In their third life, these women leaders primarily exercise their leadership regarding issues related to procreation in the private arena.

A second strand, seen often in sermonic contexts, further constricts their leadership. While initially, these contexts provided a leadership platform of sorts in which the women could influence men and women to act morally, the use of bodily

---

[45] Ibid., 26–7.
[46] Rivera, *Poetics*, 113.
[47] Schaberg, *Resurrection*, 353.

inflected rhetoric opened the door for the sins with which these women were identified to be seen permanently associated with them. This identification led to the ultimate constriction of these women's leadership, as they became paradigms to avoid, shun, and even silence.

Jackson states that storytelling "does not necessarily help us understand the world conceptually or cognitively; [rather, stories change] … our *experience* of events that have befallen us by symbolically restructuring them."[48] Once we have been exposed to the retellings of the Miriam and Mary stories, the way we imagine these women will never be the same, no matter how hard we try to escape them. We may feel an ethical commitment to give new life to stories of Miriam leading the women in song at the sea and imagine how she may have led the community in other ways. We may wish to reimagine Mary as an integral part of Jesus' circle of apostles. But the shadows and traces of this leadership are not powerful enough to overcome the other Miriams and Mary Magdalenes whose stories we have recounted here. This fact, however, is not entirely negative. Modern-day prostitutes, for example, may take comfort in looking to Mary Magdalene as a religious role model. Examining the reception, the "third life," of Mary and Miriam invites us to attend to the ways in which their stories affect the life that we currently live.

---

[48] Jackson, *Politics*, 16.

10

Virgin Mary Co-Priest or Not

The Continuing Trend of Redaction and Revision in the Medieval Era

Judith M. Davis

While examining the "multiple oral and written traditions depicting Mary as a leader in the early church," Ally Kateusz observed that "later scribes systematically excised … markers of Mary's ecclesiastical leadership and ultimately replaced them with orthodox markers of female respectability."[1] In this chapter, I continue the discussion of a tradition that redacted and reduced Mary's agency, with special attention to her priestly heritage and activities, in a number of extracanonical "Marian biographies," texts depicting Mary as a woman worthy of divine motherhood and—in one remarkable *Life of Mary*—offering evidence of her priesthood. Beginning with the second-century *Protevangelium of James*, other extracanonical works sought to enhance and justify Mary's role in salvation history, expanding her sphere of influence and encouraging further speculation about her life. A desire to establish the priestly lineage of Christ led to the writing of genealogies—which perforce had to include Mary's, given the role of the Holy Spirit in Christ's conception and birth. A third-century letter ascribed to Julius Africanus attempted to reconcile the line of Jesus as it appears in Matthew 1 and Luke 3 by positing a genealogy for Mary.[2] One of the most notable traces her descent on her father's side from the tribe of Judah and on her mother's from the priestly tribe of Levi.[3]

A seventh-century writer made use of the information in these genealogies, combining it with other scriptural, liturgical, and extracanonical sources into the earliest complete *Life of Mary*. At first attributed to Maximus the Confessor (d. 662),

---

[1] Ally Kateusz, "Collyridian Déjà Vu: The Trajectory of Redaction of the Markers of Mary's Liturgical Leadership," *JFSR* 29 (2013): 75–92, esp. 92.

[2] Michel-Jean van Esbroeck, "Généalogie de la Vierge en géorgien," *AnBoll* 91 (1973): 347–56, esp. 347.

[3] Sebastian Brock, "The Genealogy of the Virgin Mary in Sinai Syr. 16," in *Universum Hagiographicum Mémorial R.P. Michel van Esbroeck, s.j. (1934–2003),*" ed. Sevir Boroscovic Cernecov (Saint Petersburg: Byzantinorossica, 2006), 58–71, esp. 67.

herein referred to as Ps-Maximus,⁴ this text remains extraordinary for its depiction of Mary as Christ's constant companion, with her own following of women; as the "primary source of the very Passion Narratives that pass her over in almost complete silence"⁵; as the first one to whom Jesus appeared after his resurrection; and as a leader in the early church. Mary's priestly ancestry fitted her for the role she played in the life of her Son as his partner in ministry; the same sacerdotal heritage enabled her to offer Him first to the Jewish community as she presented him in the Temple and then to all humankind as she celebrated the Passover with him before his death. Particularly striking is Ps-Maximus's portrayal of her role in Christ's Passion: at the Last Supper, "she offered the sacrifice herself as the priest and she was sacrificed; she offered and she was offered."⁶ The depiction of Mary in a priestly role parallel with her son's—together with descriptions of Mary's active participation in the life of Jesus and in the promulgation of his gospel—might have contributed to the virtual disappearance of much of this work for more than a millennium. The idea that Mary might be considered a co-priest with Christ also might have contributed to more recent redaction of words indicating that she played such a role.⁷

In light of Ps-Maximus's daring parallels between Mary's life and that of her son, I consider the following themes in later *Lives of Mary*: (1) Mary's genealogy and priestly ancestry; (2) her presentation in the Temple; (3) her experience of a *bât qôl*, or revelation before the Annunciation that she would be the mother of God (parallel to God's statement at Jesus' baptism, "This is my beloved Son"); (4) Mary's female disciples; (5) a parental relationship with Jesus parallel to her son's relationship to his divine father; and—most significantly—(6) Mary's priestly actions at the Last Supper, followed by her work, service, and authority after Christ's resurrection that affirm her ministry.

Scholars have emphasized that Ps-Maximus drew upon a tradition about Mary's power that "seems to have been a part of the life of the church during the first generations."⁸ For example, a "clearly identifiable early image of the Life of the Virgin

---

⁴ Michel-Jean van Esbroeck, trans., *Maxime le Confesseur: Vie de la Vierge*, 2 vols. (Leuven: E. Peeters, 1986), first published the text of the *Life*. Stephen J. Shoemaker wrote extensively about this Marian biography (see References), translating the Georgian text *The Life of the Virgin: Maximus the Confessor* (New Haven, CT: Yale University Press, 2012). Challenging the attribution to Maximus is Philip Booth, "On the *Life of the Virgin* Attributed to Maximus Confessor," *JTS*, NS 66, pt. 1 (2015): 149–203. Shoemaker acknowledged the difficulties regarding the authorship of the *Life* but defended his dating the work to the seventh or eighth centuries in Stephen J. Shoemaker, "The (Pseudo?-)Maximus *Life of the Virgin* and the Byzantine Marian Tradition," *JTS*, NS 67, pt. 1 (2016): 116–42.

⁵ Stephen J. Shoemaker, "The Virgin Mary in the Ministry of Jesus and the Early Church according to the Earliest *Life of the Virgin*," *HTR* 98 (2005): 441–67, esp. 449.

⁶ Van Esbroeck, 2:64. "Elle se sacrifiait elle-même comme le prêtre et elle était sacrifiée, elle offrait et elle était offerte." Translations of this and other quotations from the French are mine. I refer to van Esbroeck extensively because his edition and translation used the oldest manuscript of the work, Tbilisi A-40. Shoemaker did not have access to this manuscript and used later ones.

⁷ See Ally Kateusz, *Mary and Early Christian Women: Hidden Leadership* (New York: Palgrave Macmillan, 2019), 113–49; and Kateusz, "'She Sacrificed herself as the Priest': Early Christian Female and Male Co-Priests," *JFSR* 33 (2017): 45–67, esp. 49–51.

⁸ David R. Cartlidge and J. Keith Elliott, *Art and the Christian Apocrypha* (New York: Routledge, 2001), 23.

cycle is in a crypt in the Sainte-Marie-Madeleine basilica in Saint-Maximin La-Sainte-Baume in Provence, France. As seen in Figure 10.1, it is a stone slab upon which there is engraved the figure of a woman, veiled and *orans*.[9] There is also an inscription which reads 'MARIA VIRGO MINESTER DE TEMPULO GEROSALE'. Here we have a scene in the Life of the Virgin which represents a time in which the iconography classically associated with that particular scene has not yet been established."[10] The stone slab has been dated between 375 and 500 CE.[11] The earlier dating of this plaque would be consistent with fourth-century gold-glass artifacts that portray Mary in the same arms-raised pose,[12] such as shown in Figure 10.2.

Several early extracanonical texts attest to Mary's accompaniment of her son during his ministry. The *Gospel of Philip*, from the second or – century,[13] avers that "there were three who always walked with the lord: Mary his mother and her sister and Magdalene, the one who was called his companion."[14] The third-century *Gospel (Questions) of Bartholomew* affirms Mary's leadership of the apostles in prayer and places her at the altar in a startling personal narrative.[15] In Book II, the apostles ask Mary how she conceived Jesus. Mary first stands in prayer, the apostles behind her. When she hesitates to lead them, "they said to her: in you the Lord set his tabernacle ... Therefore you have more right than we to lead in prayer ... Then Mary stood up before them and spread out her hands to heaven, and began to pray."[16] For an image of Mary and the apostles portrayed in a sixth-century scene where the artist similarly portrayed her as their prayer leader, see Figure 7.3. Mary then tells the apostles that during her days in the Temple, she was visited by "one in the form of an angel" but "indescribable"

---

[9] Edmond le Blant, *Les sarcophages chrétiens de la Gaule* (Paris: Imprimerie Nationale, 1886), pl. 57, fig. 1.

[10] Cartlidge and Elliott, *Art and the Christian Apocrypha*, 38. I find it intriguing that Mary, clearly identified as virgin and minister of the Temple, occupies a niche in a church dedicated to the Magdalene. It is also interesting that the caption accompanying the figure identifies the site of the slab as the *Basilica of St. Mary Magdalene*, but the text on the same page identifies the site as the *Church of St. Maximin*, masculinizing the site itself. The actual site is the Basilica of the Magdalene in the *city* of St. Maximin of the Holy Balm.

[11] Michel Fixot, *La Crypte de Sainte-Maximin-La-Sainte-Baume, Basilique Sainte-Marie Madeleine* (Aix-en-Provence: Edisud, 2001), 32–3.

[12] Louis Perret, *Catacombes de Rome*, vol. 4 (Paris: Gide et J. Baudry, 1851), pl. 21, fig. 1. There is also a gold-glass image, seen in Figure 15.1, now in the Vatican museum, of "Maria orans" dating from about the fourth century, showing Mary praying, with MA on one side of her haloed head, RA on the other. She is wearing a large stola, and is flanked by two palm trees, symbols of victory over death. Gold-glass images were "etched in gold leaf [and] were fused between two layers of glass, usually into circular bottoms of drinking vessels." See Andrew Simsky, "Christian Gold-Glasses from the Vatican Museum," www.asimsky.livejournal.com/7005.html (accessed on June 6, 2018). For more, see Eileen Rubery, "From Catacomb to Sanctuary: The Orant figure and the Cults of the Mother of God and S. Agnes in Early Christian Rome, with Special Reference to Gold Glass," *StPatr* 73 (2014): 129–74.

[13] See R. McL. Wilson, trans., *The Gospel of Philip* (New York: Harper & Row, 1962), v–vi; Wesley W. Isenberg, trans., "The Gospel of Philip (II,3)," in *The Nag Hammadi Library in English*, ed. James M. Robinson, 4th rev. ed. Leiden: Brill, 1996), 139–60, esp. 139–41.

[14] *Gospel of Philip* 59.6–9 (Isenberg, *Gospel of Philip*, 141–60, esp. 145).

[15] *Gospel (Questions) of Bartholomew* 2.6–21 (Wilhelm Schneemelcher, ed., *New Testament 0Apocrypha, Volume One: Gospels and Related Writings*, trans. R. McL. Wilson, rev. ed. [Louisville, KY: Westminster/John Knox, 1990], 1:540–53, esp. 543–5, dating on 540); and Kateusz, "Collyridian," 80 for further discussion.

[16] *Gospel (Questions) of Bartholomew* 2.6–13 (Schneemelcher, *New Testament Apocrypha*, 545–6).

Figure 10.1 Maria Virgo Minester de Tempulo Gerosale. Stone plaque dated 375–500 CE, Sainte-Marie-Madeleine basilica in Saint-Maximin La-Sainte-Baume in Provence, France. Source: Edmond Le Blant, *Les sarcophages chrétiens de la Gaule* (Paris: Imprimerie Nationale, 1886), plate 57, fig. 1.

Figure 10.2 Mary (MARIA) portrayed arms raised on fourth-century gold glass from the catacombs of Rome. Source: Louis Perret, *Catacombes de Rome*, 5 vols. (Paris: Gide et J. Baudry, 1851), vol. 4, plate 21, fig. 1.

and ineffable; an earthquake and the shredding of the Temple veil identify the Being as God, who shares bread and wine with her as they stand at the altar, assuring her that in three years "I will send my word and you shall conceive my son."[17]

In his *Letter to Virgins*, the fourth-century Athanasius of Alexandria (d. 373) introduced a portrait of Mary by writing, "Now then, that *the life of Mary*, who engendered God, be with you all, *as it is written*, the image to which each one will conform her virginity."[18] An allusion to "a pattern for the life of a virgin" based on

---

[17] *Gospel (Questions) of Bartholomew* 2.15–21 (Schneemelcher, *New Testament Apocrypha*, 544–5). Kateusz, "Collyridian," 81–2, 90, notes that homilists "essentially sanitized this scene" and "most editors of Dormition homilies omitted it," perhaps because it "suggest[ed] Mary's high priesthood."

[18] Charles William Neumann, *The Virgin Mary in the Works of Saint Ambrose* (Fribourg: University of Fribourg, 1962), quotation on 19, citing Louis-Theodore Lefort, "Athanasius, *Lettre aux Vierges*," *Le*

Mary occurs in the *Gnomes* or *Maxims of the Council of Nicaea*, a fourth- or fifth-century Gnostic text.[19] This text, with its emphasis on Mary's beauty, reclusiveness, and asceticism, may have influenced the ninth-century *Life of Mary* by Epiphanius the Monk.

Another fifth- or sixth-century Syriac text incorporates the *Protevangelium* as well as a *Transitus Mariae*. The latter describes her standing and praying, offering incense.[20] Offering incense was a high prerogative of Jewish priesthood, and what seems like a simple if hieratic gesture indicates Mary's privilege—and sacerdotal function. This and other early extracanonical narratives attest to a tradition, fragmented as it is in many manuscripts, that regards Mary as an authoritative and hieratic woman backed by the power and authority of her son. Ps-Maximus's *Life of the Virgin* evidently relied upon that tradition.[21]

Both Ps-Maximus and the fragments cited above testify to the existence of narratives about Mary that were edited or eliminated or lost as the theological or political climates changed. In every version of her life from the ninth through the twenty-first centuries, homilists, theologians, translators, and editors redacted segments of the text that highlighted Mary's activities on behalf of her son and his mission, reducing her importance to the miraculous, virginal/biological motherhood that has been so accessible and acceptable to patriarchs through the ages.

George of Nicomedia (d. after 880) drew most "of his material [for his Holy Week homilies] from the earlier *vita*, including in particular the very features for which [the homilies] have become so famous: Mary's central role in the Passion and Resurrection and her ornate lamentations."[22] In his Homily 8 for the liturgy of Good Friday, George redacts the Last Supper scene, limiting Mary to the care of Christ's female disciples; on the other hand, he elaborates the Marian lament of the *vita*, emphasizing at length the sufferings of both mother and son. Ps-Maximus describes Mary's active and central participation in the life of the early church, commissioning disciples, preaching, and

---

Muséon 42 (1929): 197–275, esp. 255; to this quote Neumann adds on 19, "The reference to a written life of Mary has suggested to some scholars an apocryphal [sic], many of which were in vogue in the fourth century."

[19] Hans Achelis, "The Gnomai of the Synod of Nicea [sic]," *JTS* 2 (1901): 128. See also Alistair C. Stewart, ed. and trans., *The Gnomai of the Council of Nicaea* (Piscataway, NJ: Gorgias, 2015).

[20] Agnes Smith Lewis, ed. and trans., *Apocrypha Syriaca: The Protevangelium Jacobi and Transitus Mariae*. (London: Cambridge University Press, 2012), 20, and before her death, Mary calls for "censers of incense" with which to pray, 29. In the oldest Dormition manuscript, Mary "was four times depicted burning incense," per Kateusz, "Collyridian," 85.

[21] Hans Urs von Balthasar wrote to van Esbroeck that his French translation of the *Life of the Virgin* "gives us [an author] who is involved in a brighter tradition—known and unknown"; van Esbroeck quoted him and agreed, stating that Ps-Maximus was "deeply involved in a tradition which preceded him before the year 600. This is true not only in the sense that lost Lives are supposed to explain the emergence of [this] text. It also indicates that many fragments of longer texts which were saved could really have belonged to larger compositions": Michel-Jean van Esbroeck, "Some Earlier Features in the *Life of the Virgin*," *Marianum Ephemerides Mariologiae* 159–60 (2001): 297–308, esp. 298.

[22] Stephen J. Shoemaker, "A Mother's Passion: Mary at the Crucifixion and Resurrection in the Earliest *Life of the Virgin* and its Influence on George of Nikomedeia's Passion Homilies," in *The Cult of the Mother of God in Byzantium: Texts and Images*, ed. Leslie Brubaker and Mary B. Cunningham (Burlington, VT: Ashgate, 2011), 53–67, esp. 55.

taking care of "every need and ministry of the Christians."[23] In contrast, although George depicts Christ telling his mother that she will have a position of respect and authority among the disciples after his death, her actions are limited to the events of her son's death and burial.[24] In George's homily for Holy Saturday, *On the Immaculate Virgin's Vigil at the Tomb*, Mary holds vigil alone and is the first to see the risen Christ, but that is all; George omits Mary's apostolic work.

Epiphanius the Monk (d. ca. 800) wrote a *Treatise on the Life and Years of the Most Holy Mother of God*, notable mainly for its brevity and imaginative fervor. Although the monk repeats and embroiders Ps-Maximus's genealogy of Mary, any reference to Mary as "priestly" is metaphorical. Epiphanius does include the *bât qôl*: one night, praying at the doors of the sanctuary, Mary sees a light brighter than the sun and hears a voice saying, "You will be the mother of my Son."[25] He gives us the first recorded description of Mary, a trope that would become popular in the Middle Ages;[26] he also emphasizes Mary's piety, fasting and praying.[27] However, she is not present at the Last Supper; after the Crucifixion she does not visit the sepulcher because she is overcome by grief. As Shoemaker remarks, "Mary is almost completely absent from her own biography."[28] She does not resemble in the least the heroic woman of the Georgian narrative but reflects the obedient, pious, devoted virgin of the Gnomic/pseudo-Matthew tradition.

Simeon Metaphrastes (late tenth century) wrote a *Life of the Virgin* for her feast day, August 15, in his *Menologion* or collection of saints' lives.[29] A recent translation[30] allows a comparison with Ps-Maximus and a contrast with Simeon's contemporary John the Geometer. Although Simeon follows the sequence of episodes in the Georgian *Life*, the

---

[23] Shoemaker, *Life*, 124–5, citation 125.
[24] Shoemaker, "Mother's Passion," 61: "and through her he will remain in their midst, and she will be their mediator, offering ready reconciliation with her son."
[25] Guillermo Pons, ed. and trans., *Vida de Maria by Eipphanius the Monk* (Madrid: Ciudad Nueva, 1990), 50.
[26] Epiphanius's *Life*, and his physical description of Mary, influenced a number of medieval writers. One notable example is the work of an anonymous thirteenth-century cleric but attributed to Albert the Great: the *Mariale sive CCXXX quaestiones super Evangelium 'Missus Est.'* This work describes Mary's wisdom and intellectual gifts, virtues, and accomplishments. The author—and his contemporaries—describe Mary as a beautiful young woman. The *Mariale* appears in volume 37 of the *Opera Omnia* edited by Auguste and Émile Vorgnet (Paris: Ludovicum Vivès, 1898). For a discussion of the authorship, see Hilda Graef and Thomas A.Thompson, *Mary: A History of Doctrine and Devotion*, combined edition (Notre Dame, IN: Ave Maria, 2009), 210–16.
[27] The source of Mary's asceticism—described in the seventh-century *Ps-Matthew*, chapter 6—may have been the *Gnomes* or *Maxims* of the Council of Nicaea as interpreted by Athanasius: "Mary never beheld the face of any strange man. She lived retired in her own house, waited upon by her mother only. She never saw her own body naked, and many things remained for her unknown … She slept little and prayed much, her face turned eastwards"; Achelis, "Gnomai," 128.
[28] Shoemaker, "Virgin Mary in the Ministry," 457.
[29] The complete title of his work on Mary is "A Discourse including the Facts Relative to the Life of Our Lady the Most Holy Mother of God, Beginning with Her Venerable Birth and Upbringing, and of the Divinely Glorious Birth of Christ our God; and all That Happened Up until Her Vivifying Death, Followed by the Account of Her Precious Garment Showing How the Christians Came to Possess This Great Treasure." Simon Claude Mimouni, "Les *Vies de la Vierge*: État de la question," *Apocrypha* 5 (1994): 211–48, quote on 237.
[30] Georges Gharib, trans.," Vita de Maria," in *Testi Mariani del Primo Millennio 2: Padri e altri autori bizantini (VI–XI sec.)*, ed. Georges Gharib-Hermano, M. Toniolo, Luigi Gambero, and Gerardo Di Nola (Rome: Città Nuova Editrice, 1989), 980–1019.

53 abbreviated chapters of this work are less than half the length of Ps-Maximus's 124 chapters—and only one-fifth of John the Geometer's.[31] Simeon's condensed version leaves little room for Mary's activities, and there is no intimation of her priestly heritage or role. Omitting Mary's genealogy and Temple experience, Simeon instead meditates on Christ's birth and moves rapidly to Cana and then to the Passion, where he does say that Mary was always near her son, even when his disciples fled. In chapter 27, the Last Supper, Jesus asks her to "take care of the women *who were serving at table*."[32] Chapter 32 elaborates on her immense suffering at the Passion, but she does take charge of Jesus' burial (Chapter 33). The remaining twenty chapters abbreviate the Ps-Maximus, omitting Mary's preaching and direction of the early church.

John the Geometer (d. ca. 990) produced a *Discourse of Farewell on the [Occasion of] the Dormition of the Most Glorious Mother of God, Our Lady*, a panegyric to the life of Mary. Only the final portion, which recounts Mary's last days on earth, has been edited;[33] I therefore depend on van Esbroeck's descriptions of the work.[34] He advances cogent arguments for regarding the work of Ps-Maximus as the source for the Geometer's narrative, and it seems highly likely that it served as a source for the Metaphrast as well.[35] John the Geometer interprets Mary's physical presence throughout Christ's public life, passion, death, and resurrection as a metaphysical identification with her son in a parallel to Christ's hypostatic union with his heavenly Father. He also presents her as a coredeemer with Jesus. Paradoxically, then, he eliminates any mention of her priestly heritage and her presence at the Last Supper.[36] He limits her role at

---

[31] Mimouni, "Les *Vies*," 238, quoting Martin Jugie, "Sur la vie et les procédés littéraires de Syméon Métaphraste. Son récit de la vie de la Sainte Vierge," *Échos d'Orient* 22 (1923): 5–10.

[32] Gharib, "Vita de Maria," 1000. Emphasis mine.

[33] Van Esbroeck, *Vie*, 2:xix. He concludes that Maximus was the source of the Geometer's work (xviii–xxix). The edited and translated segment of the Geometer's Life, based on Vatican gr. 504, appears in Antoine Wenger, *L'Assomption de la T.S. Vierge dans la tradition byzantine du VIe au Xe siècle. Études et documents* (Paris: Institut Français d'Études Byzantines, 1955), 185–201, for introduction and commentary, and 363–415 for the Greek text and translation. Wenger's tripartite text includes an account of the Dormition, beginning with the apparition of the angel who announces Mary's approaching passing to the transfer of her burial vestments to Constantinople. The second part is a theological reflection on the mystery of Mary's dormition and a celebration of the (feast)day of August 15. The third is a prayer of thanksgiving to Christ the Redeemer and Mary Coredeemer and a concluding presentation of the work to Mary, the glory of the Trinity. See also Mimouni's discussion of John the Geometer in Mimouni, "Les *Vies*," 228–32; and (somewhat condensed) in Mimouni, *Les Traditions anciennes sur la Dormition et l'Assomption de Marie* (Leiden: Brill, 2011), 94–101. Mary B. Cunningham, "The Life of the Virgin Mary According to Middle Byzantine Preachers and Hagiographers: Changing Contexts and Perspectives," *Apocrypha* 27 (2016): 140, notes that "Fr. Maximos Constans and Prof. Christos Simeledes are currently preparing a critical edition of the [Geometer's] text, based on work that was completed by A. Wenger but never published."

[34] Van Esbroeck, *Vie*, 2:xx, says, "John the Geometer revised the text which Euthemius [the Hagiorite] translated into Georgian." His discussion of the Geometer covers pp. xx–xxvi.

[35] Wenger, *Assomption*, 193; Wenger argues that Jean's text depends on Simeon's, rather than the other way around (194). Shoemaker, "Virgin Mary in the Ministry" 460, states that "as van Esbroeck and I have both demonstrated, [Maximus] clearly served as the primary source for the Lives of Simeon and John." I agree, especially since both tenth-century writers eliminate depictions of Mary's physical following of her son and her many activities on his behalf both before and after his death and resurrection.

[36] Van Esbroeck, *Vie*, 2:xxii, notes that "John the Geometer ... omits Mary's priestly role ... and writes solely in terms of the masculine." He adds, "distancing himself from the theology implied by the phrase, 'a second sacrificiant' [the Virgin], ... the theological context, among the most interesting

Pentecost to directing the fasting and prayer—in contrast to Ps-Maximus, who associates the presence of the Holy Spirit at the Annunciation with Mary's openness to the Spirit throughout her life, making her a singular participant in the events of Pentecost.[37] Like the Metaphrast, John neglects to mention her female disciples, her leadership before Pentecost, her assertiveness—despite her sorrow—in following Jesus throughout the Passion, and her preaching after Christ's ascension, preferring to stress her universal motherhood and compassion. Although he does describe her directing the work of the apostles and inspiring members of the early church, it is significant that the influential twentieth-century interpreter of the Geometer's work, Jean Galot, criticizes John's including those activities as an "exaggeration of Mary's functions in assimilating them with the functions of the vicar of Christ [the Pope]."[38]

It may be significant to note that about the time that John and Simeon were writing, at least one image of a priestly Mary was available to the public: the Byzantine icon displayed at Constantinople and throughout the Eastern empire during the liturgy of the Feast of the Encounter or Hypapante (Presentation of Jesus in the Temple) on February 2. "With a canopy and an altar, the icon evokes the temple simply. Mary stands at bottom center [in front of the altar], offering her son to Simeon who leans forward to receive him."[39] Joseph stands behind Mary holding the offering of two doves, while Anna, her hands raised in prayer or prophecy, stands behind Simeon.

> The hands of both Mary and Simeon are covered, respectively with the edges of her *maphorion* and his robe. The motif … derives from a Byzantine gesture that was intended to convey profound respect and humility when giving or accepting a sacred object … *Mary is shown as assuming a sacerdotal role which will be consummated at the sacrifice of Calvary.*[40]

[of its kind], corresponds to the fact that in the account of the Last Supper, the term 'sacrificiant' is equally applied to the Virgin, which is precisely what the Geometer has eliminated" in van Esbroeck, *Vie*, 1:xv.

[37] Shoemaker, *Life*, 121–4.

[38] Jean Galot, "La plus ancienne affirmation de la corédemption mariale : Le Témoignage de Jean le Géomêtre," *RSR* 45 (1957): 205. This, despite the fact that Galot does not cavil at John's hyperventilating descriptions of Mary, who sometimes seems "semidivine" and "so unequivocally approximated to the Godhead" per Graef, *Mary*, 155–6.

[39] This icon is described by Dorian Llywelyn, SJ, "The Life of Mary and the Festal Icons of the Eastern Church," *Marian Studies* 60 (2009): 231–52, 242.

[40] Ibid., 243, emphasis mine. This icon from the *Menologion* of Basil II dates from about 1000 CE: www.iconreader.wordpress.com/2013/01/17/presentation-of-christ-temple-and-church (accessed on June 6, 2018). Llywelyn remarks that "the basic elements in the illustration for the Feast can be found in just about every Eastern icon … The basic lineaments of the icons of the twelve major feasts are earlier by a few centuries than that manuscript, and the Feast itself was being celebrated in Jerusalem by 450" (electronic communication September 18, 2014). Other images show Mary wearing the pallium, a liturgical vestment representing episcopal priestly power worn, from the sixth century on, only by bishops, only with the permission of the pope and only at Mass. So far, I have found only Western images dating from the seventh century (www.womanpriests.org/mrpriest/gallery.asp) (accessed on June 6, 2018). There are examples of Mary wearing the pallium on coins dating from the eleventh century.

An example of such an icon can be found in the Basil II *Menologion*, an illustrated manuscript of the tenth century.[41]

Recent scholarship has noted additional icons of Mary that depict her in priestly garb, not only as a priest of the Old Testament, wearing the ephod of the Hebrew high priest, but as a presider of the NT, wearing a deacon's garb, a stole, or a maniple (communion cloth).[42] In representations of the Deesis, a tripartite icon showing Christ between Mary and John the Baptist, there is "the idea of the priesthood of Christ Himself, as well as the related liturgical meaning of the Virgin Mary and John the Baptist co-officiating with Him."[43]

Mary's priestly role was not so much overlooked as simply ignored by major twentieth-century writers about the life of Mary. Three important clerical Marian scholars—Martin Jugie, Antoine Wenger, and Jean Galot—were doctrinally focused and thereby biased in their analyses of early Marian literature. Jugie claims that John [the Geometer] teaches the Immaculate Conception (not Church dogma until 1854).[44] Both he and Wenger defend the bodily assumption of Mary (which became Church dogma in 1950), and Galot's treatment of the work of John the Geometer aims at establishing proof of Mary as Mediatrix.[45] Like his colleagues, Galot effectively ignores any evidence of Mary's priestly ancestry, the period of her life in the Temple, her female disciples, and above all her offering her son to God during the Last Supper and on Calvary.[46] Absent from the voluminous writings of all three is any indication of Mary's fitness for, and practice of, leadership in Jesus' ministry and in the early church. Their preoccupation with the Dormition—and selected texts, at that—may well reflect a fear of engaging elements of the tradition that suggest Mary's agency.

In the twenty-first century, Luigi Gambero presents an overview of Marian lives, placing them in a new literary genre which he calls the "biographic homily."[47] Gambero engages Ps-Maximus's work ("The Georgian *Life of Mary*") in addition to that of John the Geometer, Epiphanius, and Simeon Metaphrastes without a single reference

---

[41] See https://en.wikipedia.org/wiki/Menologion_of_Basil_II#media/File:Menologion_of_Basil_037.jpg (accessed on June 7, 2018).

[42] Alexei Lidov, "The Priesthood of the Virgin Mary as an Image-Paradigm of Christian Visual Culture," *IKON* 10 (2017): 9–26, esp. 14, remarking that some icons date from the sixth, seventh, and eighth centuries. See also Kateusz, *Mary and Early Christian Women*, 67–99.

[43] Lidov, "Priesthood of the Virgin Mary," 11.

[44] See Martin Jugie, *L'Immaculée Conception dans l'Écriture sainte et dans la tradition orientale* (Rome: Officium Libri Catholici, 1952), 29.

[45] Jugie dedicated his 747-page tome, *La Mort et l'Assomption de la Sainte Vierge: Étude historic-doctrinale* (Città del Vaticano: Biblioteca Apostolica Vaticana, 1944), to the "gloriously reigning protector of the families of the Assumption," Pope Pius XII, who proclaimed the dogma in 1950. Wenger was concerned with the Dormition segment only in relation to the Assumption.

[46] Galot's politics are evinced in his essay that appeared in *Theology of the Priesthood*: "Women and the Priesthood: A Theological Reflection," which begins, predictably, with the statement, "The tradition of the Church, firm and unchanging, rests on the fundamental fact which is Christ's own decision: Jesus chose only men to exercise the priestly ministry." See www.ignatiusinsight.com/features2007/jgalot_priesthd_aug07.html.

[47] Luigi Gambero, "Biographies of Mary in Byzantine Literature," *Marian Studies* 40 (2009): 31–50, esp. 31. Gambero mentions "Mary's presence at the baptism of her Son and during his entire public life," 39.

to Mary's priestly character—as does Simon Mimouni.[48] Shoemaker in his recent translation of Ps-Maximus's *Life of the Virgin* consulted Michel van Esbroeck's 1986 French translation, but did not use the eleventh-century manuscript (Tbilisi A-40), the oldest available[49]—the manuscript that was van Esbroeck's primary source. Instead, he relied upon others, including Jerusalem 108, which van Esbroeck himself said was censored in the Last Supper scene of Mary's priesthood.[50] A suggestive contrast between the two editions can be found in chapter 14, in the description of Mary's *bât qôl*. Van Esbroeck's edition situates Mary "between the doors of the altar"[51] while Shoemaker's places her "right in front of the doors of the sanctuary."[52] In van Esbroeck's edition, Mary is closer to the altar; significantly, she is on her way into the Holy of Holies where she will hear God's voice.[53] Another difference between the editions occurs in chapter 98, where van Esbroeck's describes John the Evangelist preaching in the company of women who became "apostles" as they suffered, several dying a martyr's death.[54] Shoemaker's speaks of the women becoming "*co-apostles*"; he adds in a footnote, "Of course the meaning is the same in either case."[55]

The contrast between the two editions is most poignant at the beginning of the Last Supper scene in chapter 74. On one hand, Shoemaker's reads,

> As we said, [Mary] was always inseparable from her Lord and king and son. And she held authority: as the Lord did over the twelve disciples and then the seventy, so did the holy mother over the other women who accompanied him ... The holy Theotokos was the leader and director of them all [the women]. *For this reason*, when the ... supper took place and *he sacrificed himself as a priest and was sacrificed, he offered and was offered*[56] ... and he gave them the exalted mysteries, the signs of the divine Passover.[57]

Van Esbroeck's edition, on the other hand, reads,

> I have said that she is always inseparable from the Lord and king her son, and as the Lord had his direction over the twelve apostles and then the seventy, so his mother had [the direction] of the other women who accompanied him ... The holy Theotokos was their guide and their mentor. *That is why*, during the supper

---

[48] Both Mimouni's essay on the lives of the Virgin ("Les *Vies*") and his book on the traditions of the Dormition and the Assumption, *Traditions*, are devoid of any references to her presence at the Last Supper.
[49] Shoemaker, *Life*, 4.
[50] Van Esbroeck, *Vie*, 2:xxxvii.
[51] Ibid., 10, "entre les portes de l'autel."
[52] Shoemaker, *Life*, 46.
[53] Van Esbroeck, *Vie*, 2:10.
[54] Ibid., 86.
[55] Shoemaker, *Life*, 125, n. 14. Emphasis added.
[56] In a footnote to this passage, Shoemaker comments on van Esbroeck's translation: "He would understand the Virgin as somehow sacrificing herself and being sacrificed at the Last Supper. This interpretation is not impossible, since, as van Esbroeck notes, there are no indications of gender at this point in the text, as is very often the case in Georgian"; Shoemaker, *Life*, 102, n. 1.
[57] Shoemaker, *Life*, 102.

[when] the great mystery took place, *she offered the sacrifice herself as the priest and she was sacrificed; she offered and she was offered.*[58]

Van Esbroeck notes that here "Maximus clearly means to say that among the women (*auprès des femmes*) Mary took the role of priest at the very moment [of Christ's words]"; he does mention Vat.gr. 504, which offers a different reading, and says, "the insistence on *the men* [in that manuscript] could well mean that the original said that the Virgin officiated in a parallel fashion with the women."[59]

In either case, Mary's sacrifice—her offering—has profound theological implications. With her *fiat* at the Incarnation, Mary offers to bear the child Jesus and then offers him to Simeon in the Temple. At the Last Supper, she offers her son and herself in the same Spirit "as the culmination of the Incarnation."[60] She is portrayed as a priest.

Speaking of the principles undergirding his translation, which was based largely on Tbilisi A-40, van Esbroeck points out a parallel between chapter 128 and chapter 74. In chapter 128,

> the Virgin is presented as she who sacrifices second for the Father, after Christ who sacrifices first; this passage corresponds to the [offering] in Chapter 74, where we see the Virgin sacrificing on her own behalf as a priest during the Last Supper, with the community of women. Curiously, the Jerusalem [MS 108, or "J"] manuscript, censored this passage; once again it coincides here with John the Geometer. But the correspondence between chapters 74 and 128 is too close to allow for the tempered contraction of manuscript J. Again [in this manuscript], we find the reflex of a theologian a little uneasy to see attributed to the Virgin prerogatives assumed above all by the Savior himself.[61]

Van Esbroeck translates Ps-Maximus's statement in chapter 128 regarding Mary as follows: "a human being clothed in Godhead next to God incarnate, a second sacrifice of our [human] nature to God, after the first who sacrificed himself one time for all."[62] By contrast, Shoemaker's edition reads, "a *devout* human being [next to] the incarnate God, a second offering of our nature to the Father after the first one who was himself sacrificed one time on behalf of all."[63]

---

[58] Van Esbroeck, *Vie*, 2:63–4:
> j'ai dit qu'elle est toujours inséparée du Seigneur et roi son fils, et comme le Seigneur avait sa direction sur les douze apôtres et ensuite les soixante–dix, ainsi la sainte mère sur les autres femmes qui l'accompagnaient, ... La sainte Theotokos était leur guide et leur tutrice. C'est pourquoi lorsque le repas, le grand mystère se déroulait, *elle se sacrifiait elle–même comme le prêtre et elle était sacrifiée, elle offrait et elle était offerte*. (Emphasis added)

[59] Ibid., xxii.

[60] Shoemaker, *Life*, 32. "It bears repeating," he says, "that the Greek Fathers understood the sacrifice of the Crucifixion not as a singularly redemptive act but instead primarily as the Incarnation, in which the Immortal God finally vanquishes death by death."

[61] Van Esbroeck, *Vie*, 2:xxxvii.

[62] Ibid., 115: "un être humain revêtu de Dieu auprès de Dieu incarné, un second sacrifice de notre nature auprès du Père, après le premier qui s'est sacrifié lui–même une fois pour toutes."

[63] Shoemaker, *Life*, 154. Emphasis mine.

In his article, "The Virgin Mary in the Ministry of Jesus," Shoemaker questions van Esbroeck's presentation of "Mary at the Last Supper in the role of a priest who offers herself as a sacrifice of reconciliation, an image more traditionally associated with her son's sacrifice and its repetition in the Eucharist. Is it possible that the *Life* has elevated Mary ... to the status of a *coredemptrix*, whose coredeeming activity is present even in the Eucharist?"[64] Despite admitting the possibility that Mary "*somehow* at the Last Supper offered herself as a reconciling sacrifice," he goes back to John the Geometer to support his proposal that "Jesus [is] the subject of the parallel passage [in chapter 128]."[65] In his commentary regarding the *Life*, Shoemaker does not address the importance of Mary's autonomy and offerings.

In three earlier articles, Shoemaker had considered both Mary of Nazareth and Mary Magdalene in Christian traditions, finding it possible and even probable that they were conflated and/or confused in early gnostic writings. In one of those articles, Shoemaker states that in contrast to Mary Magdalene, "from an historical-critical vantage, the involvement of Christ's mother in his public ministry is quite improbable."[66] More recently, in "The Virgin Mary's Hidden Past" (2009), Shoemaker tempers that statement somewhat, observing that Ps-Maximus's *Life* "brings Mary and other women to the fore at seemingly every opportunity" and that "at the Last Supper, the Virgin takes charge of the female disciples during the sacred meal, serving in a parallel fashion to her son at the institution of this sacrament."[67] Two 2011 articles, "Mary at the Cross, East and West" and "A Mother's Passion," deal with affective piety as transmitted through Ps-Maximus and George of Nicomedeia.[68] Shoemaker acknowledges Ps-Maximus's "augmenting several of [Mary's] more minor appearances, thus portraying [her] both as a central figure in her son's ministry and as the leader of the nascent Church."[69] Concentrating on the Passion, however, he does not discuss her priestly activity at the Last Supper according to van Esbroeck's edition, merely "noting that the Virgin was placed in charge of her son's female disciples during the sacred meal."[70] "Mary at the Cross" focuses on Ps-Maximus's Marian laments and their influence on the aspects of George's homilies that "dramatically portray the Virgin's sufferings with great emotion" and stress "Mary's emotional bond with her divine Son"[71] that are transmitted across continents through the centuries. The focus on Marian piety etherealizes Mary's agency and ignores her priestly status.

Over the course of centuries, then, various theologians and translators excised the attested tradition of Mary's authoritative and hieratic roles—her accompaniment

---

[64] Shoemaker, "Virgin Mary in the Ministry," 447.
[65] Ibid., 448 and 449. The emphasis on "somehow" (448) is mine.
[66] Stephen J. Shoemaker, "Jesus' Gnostic Mom: Mary of Nazareth and the 'Gnostic Mary' Traditions," in *Mariam, the Magdalen and the Mother*, ed. Deirdre Good (Bloomington: Indiana University Press, 2005), 159.
[67] Stephen J. Shoemaker, "The Virgin Mary's Hidden Past: From Ancient Marian Apocrypha to the Medieval *Vitae Virginis*," *Marian Studies* 40 (2009): 1–30, esp. 19.
[68] Stephen J. Shoemaker, "Mary at the Cross, East and West: Maternal Compassion and Affective Piety in the Earliest Life of the Virgin and the High Middle Ages," *JTS*, NS 62, Pt 2 (October 2011): 570–606; and Shoemaker, "Mother's Passion," 53–67.
[69] Shoemaker, "Mother's Passion," 55.
[70] Ibid., 57.
[71] Shoemaker, "Mary at the Cross," 586.

of Jesus and leadership of his female followers, her co-offering of her son at the Last Supper, and her preeminence in directing the apostles and other members of the early church. These men instead emphasized her humility, her motherhood, and her extravagantly emotional lament over the death of Jesus. They overlooked icons and mosaics, depicting her in deacon's robes or even in the attire of an Old Testament high priest, and chose instead to emphasize her virginal motherhood, her devotion to her son, her fasts and prayers. Even contemporary commentators tend to focus on her piety and devotion, those orthodox markers of female respectability, in a continuing trend of redaction and revision.

11

The Memory of Mary's Mission According to "Guadalupan Sermons" of the Seventeenth and Eighteenth Centuries

J. L. Manzo

The story of Mary of Guadalupe had a profound impact on the history of the evangelization of Latin America. Since her apparition in the mid-sixteenth century to Juan Diego, the Roman Catholic Church has recognized Mary of Guadalupe as Patroness of Mexico, entrusted to her intercession the future of the Latin American Church, invoked her as the Mother of our faith, and granted her a liturgical office.[1] But long before Our Lady of Guadalupe found a more precise historical and theological reference in the Latin American Episcopal documents and in the Pontifical Magisterium, Guadalupan sermons of the sixteenth and seventeenth centuries recognized how the local Church was invigorated by the outline of historical experience and the theological doctrines evoked by the *Virgen Morena* (Dark Madonna). In this essay, we consider the theological message of the Guadalupan sermons of Rev. Jose Vidal de Figueroa (1661) and Friar Antonio López Murto (1792). Before turning to the thought of these writers, we look at the "Guadalupan Event."

Mary of Guadalupe Appears to Juan Diego

The popularity of the appearance of Mary of Guadalupe grew with the first public account of the event written by Miguel Sánchez, a diocesan priest of Mexico City, entitled *Imagen de la Virgen Maria, Madre de Dios de Guadalupe* in 1648.[2] In Sánchez's account, Mary of Guadalupe appeared for the first time to the Mexican peasant Juan Diego at the Hill of Tepeyac on December 9, 1531.[3] Speaking to Juan Diego in his

---

[1] In 1754, Pope Benedict XIV approved her patronage and granted her own mass and feast for December 12. Pope Pius X proclaimed her the patroness of Latin America in 1910. She was given the title "Queen of Mexico" and "Empress of the Americans" by Pope Pius XII in 1945. Pope John XXIII prayed to her as "Mother of the Americas" in 1961.
[2] Lisa Sousa, Stafford Poole, and James Lockhard, eds., *The Story of Guadalupe. Luis Laso de las Vega's Huei tlamahuçolica of 1649* (Stanford, CA: Stanford University Press, 1998), 1.
[3] The Hill of Tepeyac belongs to the Villa de Guadalupe, a suburb of Mexico City.

native Nahuatl language, the Mary of Guadalupe identified herself as "mother of the true God through whom one lives" and instructed him to have Bishop Zumárraga build a shrine at that site in her honor.[4] Juan Diego then sought out the bishop and related Mary's message. The bishop was kind to him but did not believe his words. On the same day, Juan Diego saw Mary of Guadalupe again and she asked him to keep insisting.

On Sunday, December 10, Juan Diego talked to Bishop Zumárraga for the second time, and the bishop instructed him to return to the Hill of Tepeyac and ask Mary of Guadalupe for a miraculous sign to prove her identity. Juan Diego returned immediately to Tepeyac and, encountering Mary of Guadalupe for the third time, reported the bishop's request for a sign, to which she replied, "Very well, my son, you will return here tomorrow so that you may take to the bishop the sign which he asked for."[5]

The following day, Monday, December 11, Juan Diego's uncle Juan Bernardino felt sick and Diego was obliged to attend to him. In the very early hours of Tuesday, December 12, his condition deteriorated and Juan Diego set out to Tlatelolco to get a priest to hear his uncle's confession and minister to him on his deathbed. To avoid being delayed by Mary of Guadalupe and ashamed at having failed to meet her the day before, Juan Diego chose another route around the hill. As he was coming down the hill, Mary of Guadalupe appeared to him for the fourth time and asked him, "What is happening, my son, the smallest of my children? Where are you going?"[6] After informing Mary of his uncle's imminent death, she gently chided him for not having had recourse to her, with the words that have become the most famous phrase of the Guadalupan Event: *No estoy yo aqui que soy tu madre?* ("Am I not here, I who am your mother?"). After assuring him of his uncle's recovery, Mary of Guadalupe instructs Diego to gather flowers from the normally barren top of the Hill of Tepeyac. Juan followed her instructions, and he found Castilian roses blooming there. Mary of Guadalupe arranged the flowers in Juan Diego's *tilma*, or cloak, and when he spread opened his *tilma* before Bishop Zumárraga on December 12, the flowers fell to the floor, and on the fabric was the image of Mary of Guadalupe.

Today, this fabric image is preserved in a magnificent basilica on Mount Tepeyac, on the outskirts of Mexico City. The image of our Lady revealed in Diego's *tilma* is Mexico's most popular religious and cultural symbol. Her image is duplicated in paintings or statues venerated at home. She is also found on the side of buildings or worn as a medallion around the neck of young and old alike as a symbol of protection, hope, healing, and strength.

Beside the influence that the first written record of the event had on the popularity of the legend of Mary of Guadalupe, sermons that were preached, published, and circulated in the seventeenth and eighteenth centuries became the basis for the evangelization of the Mexican people and the cause for a great devotion to Mary. This took place at the time when the Protestant Reformation took issue with Mary's role

---

[4] Jeanette Rodríguez, *Our Lady of Guadalupe. Faith and Empowerment among Mexican-American Woman* (Austin: University of Texas, 1994), 31.
[5] Ibid., 33.
[6] Ibid., 34.

as *Mediatrix*, arguing that intercessory prayer diminished Christ's glory. The sermons expressed the conviction that Mary of Guadalupe was divinely chosen as missionary, apostle, and founder of the faith in the Americas. They proclaimed the unshakable conviction that the Indigenous were a new, divinely elected people who were the recipients of God's love through Mary's apparition.[7]

Mary of Guadalupe, Evangelizer and Apostle to the Americas

The first Guadalupan sermon was published in 1661, thirteen years after the publication of Sánchez's work. It was preached by Jose Vidal de Figueroa, parish priest of Tejupilco, in Mary's sanctuary on December 12, 1660.[8] The sermon proclaims Mary of Guadalupe as the light bearer who brought the light, Christ, to an idolatrous and sinful culture whose bloodthirsty gods demanded human sacrifices.[9] After juxtaposing Juan Diego, who suffered the spiritual captivity of idolatry, with St. John the Baptist, who suffered physical captivity at the hand of Herod Antipas, Vidal de Figueroa makes a bold statement about Mary of Guadalupe. Relying on the Neoplatonic notion that all creation emanates first in the divine mind prior to their physical being, he argues that the image imprinted on Juan Diego's *tilma* is an original reproduction of Mary, who is a model of God himself. He says, "God first painted Mary in his mind when he selected her for his mother, to subsequently reveal it on the image of Mary of Guadalupe."[10] Thus, when God revealed Mary to the Indigenous, he desired them to conform to the image of the faithful portrait of the divine idea of Mary. Mary, as the most perfect of God's creatures, is the most perfect created likeness of the perfection of God and consequently an image after God himself.

As a human prototype of the divinity, the image of Mary of Guadalupe becomes the divine instrument for restoring the dignity of the Indigenous and the means to restore the image of God deformed in them due to abuse and idolatry. The inhumane treatment of the *Conquistadores* who subjected them to hunger, thirst, physical abuse, poverty, and who sought to wipe out every vestige of their civilization in the name of Jesus Christ, caused them to fall into a state of powerlessness and helplessness. The image of Mary of Guadalupe, which appears to the humble Juan Diego as an Indigenous expecting mother, with her mature eyes, low gaze, and a smile of compassion, told them that she was one with them and worthy of her protection.[11] This teaching is captured on a sermon by Francisco de San Cirilo:

---

[7] Francisco Raymond Schulte, *Mexican Spirituality: Its Source and Mission in the Earliest Guadalupan Sermons* (Lanham, MD: Rowman & Littlefield, 2002), ix, 78–109.
[8] José Vidal de Figueroa, *Teórica de la prodigiosa imagen de la Virgen Santa María de Guadalupe de México* (México, D.F.: Juan Ruyz, 1961), 1–18.
[9] Anonymous, "Of Aztec Human Sacrifice," in *A Handbook on Guadalupe* (New Bedford, MA: Franciscan Friars of the Immaculate, 1997), 138–40.
[10] David A. Brading, *Mexican Phoenix. Our Lady of Guadalupe Image and Tradition across Five Centuries* (Cambridge: Cambridge University Press, 2001), 96.
[11] Rodríguez, *Our Lady of Guadalupe*, 23–4.

The sacred Virgin presents herself to an Indian who was walking along with his mind on matters other than seeking her. She speaks to him with affectionate words, humbling herself to the point of treating him as a son and promising him the good offices of a Mother. She makes known to him the outstanding dignity that is his and she offers him her powerful patronage for the remedy of his necessities. And was this not to soothe the Mexicans that they might become more docile to the Faith and conserve it with firmness?[12]

Mary of Guadalupe comes to Juan Diego as a loving mother; she is an expression of the mercy and compassion of God.

Vidal de Figueroa expands his analysis of the apparition by suggesting to the Indigenous that Mary was predestined for the evangelization of the Americas to reveal God's love to them. He is quick to say that Mary's apparition happened "as a plan for the fullness of times, to sum up all things in Christ, in heaven and on earth (Eph 1:10 [NAB])."[13] He quotes Eph 3:8-11 to say that to Mary was given

> La de anunciar a los gentiles la inescrutable riqueza de cristo, y esclarecer cómo se ha dispensado el Misterio escondido desde los siglos en Dios, creador de todas las cosas, para que la mutlíforma sabiduría de Dios sea ahora manifestada a los Principados y a las Potestades en los cielos, mediante la Iglesia conforme previo designo eterno que realizó en Cristo Jesús, Señor nuestro (… to preach to the Gentiles the inscrutable riches of Christ, and to bring to light what is the plan of the *mystery hidden from ages past in God* who created all things, so that the manifold wisdom of God might now be made known through the church to the principalities and authorities in the heavens. This was according to the eternal purpose that he accomplished in Christ Jesus our Lord.)[14]

God ignored the American hemisphere when the rest of the world was evangelized because the apparition of Mary of Guadalupe takes place according the "mystery hidden from ages past in God"[15] to sum up all in Christ through Mary at the divinely appointed time and in the divinely ordained order. Chance was not a factor in the Guadalupan event; instead, God waited until the most fitting time for Mary's evangelical mission.

Continuing with his explanation of Mary of Guadalupe's missionary activity, Vidal de Figueroa states,

> [Mary, as presented in the Guadalupan image], brought in her arms not the Word made flesh but rather the Son of God transformed in light. Mary appears in Mexico without the Child God in her arms but rather surrounded by light; because the most stupendous thing about the miracle is how ancient the mystery

---

[12] Schulte, *Mexican Spirituality*, 71.
[13] Brading, *Mexican Phoenix*, 97.
[14] P. Pedro Alarcón Méndez, *El amor de Jesús vivo en la Virgen de Guadalupe* (Bloomington, IN: Palibrio, 2013), 364-5.
[15] Ibid.

is, since it brings its origin from all eternity, when the Son of God was the light *erat lux vera* (John 1:9).¹⁶

Mary of Guadalupe is a missionary who personally proclaims the Son of God transformed in light, but if her mission is to reveal the Son, why is there no representation of the divine child? The answer is hidden in the meaning of the light symbols encrypted in the *tilma* and Vidal de Figueroa's own scriptural interpretation of that light.

The image of Mary of Guadalupe shows the divine child not on her arms but in her womb. Her pregnancy is shown by the maternity tassel (or *cinta*) around her waist. *Estoy en cinta* means "I am pregnant." Underneath the tassel, an image of the *Nahui Ollin*, a four-petal flower, is visible. It was for the Indigenous people a symbol of the Sun God. The Sun God was for them the true, omnipotent, eternal deity who was the sovereign Lord of the universe and life. Thus, Mary of Guadalupe is the mother of the living God.¹⁷

The picture of Mary of Guadalupe that arose miraculously on the *tilma* has her surrounded by the light that emanates from the stars, the moon, and the sun. The stars adorn the bluish-green mantle that wraps around her body. For the Aztecs, they represented heaven and the seat of the gods. Mary stands over the crescent moon, a symbol of fecundity, birth, and life. Lastly, she is encircled by solar rays. These were symbols of the highest God, Huitzilopochtli, whom the Aztecs revered as the greatest life-giving force on earth. The Aztec symbols convey unambiguously that Mary of Guadalupe is the Queen of the Cosmos, Mother of Child Sun/the child of light, the one true God.¹⁸

For Vidal de Figueroa, the motifs of light pertaining to the world of the Aztecs carry still deeper theological meaning: They point to the Child's divine preexistence. "The most stupendous thing about the apparition is its ancient mystery, it brings its origin from all eternity when the Son of God was the true light."¹⁹ The phrase "true light" harkens back to John 1:9. John affirms that Jesus, the true light, which enlightens everyone, was coming into the world. Through the mediation of Mary of Guadalupe, the identity of the true God was shown to the Indigenous through cultural symbols that turned upside-down their Indigenous beliefs.

Another sermon that uses the motif of light to describe Mary's role to the Americas was delivered by Friar Antonio López Murto in the parochial church of San Luis Potosi on September 14, 1792. He stated,

> I will make you a light to the nations that salvation may reach to the ends of the earth (Isa 49.6). With these words the Lord announced through Isaiah the glorious purposes, salutary ends and admirable designs with which his First Born came to this world. In them the Evangelist Prophet introduces the Eternal Father, who talks

---

¹⁶ Brading, *Mexican Phoenix*, 97; Vidal de Figueroa, *Teórica*, 8; and Schulte, *Mexican Spirituality*, 79.
¹⁷ Rodríguez, *Our Lady of Guadalupe*, 29.
¹⁸ Eduardo Chávez, *Our Lady of Guadalupe and Saint Juan Diego. The Historical Evidence* (Lanham, MD: Rowman & Littlefield, 2006), 21.
¹⁹ Schulte, *Mexican Spirituality*, 79.

with his beloved Son. To those whom you find in the midst of gloom, you should find brightness, you shall fill them with light, you shall scatter the shadows that encompass them: To those in darkness: show yourself!

When Mary, that sweet Mary, that loving Mother of the Americas, prepared herself mercifully to go down from Heaven to our land, we can piously venture that her Son would have said to her almost with the same words of the Prophet: I send you to the Indies that you may be the salvation of all, that you may establish peace to the Gentiles.

Mary was the light of the Gentiles that came to banish and push away their darkness, bring health, salvation and life to these farthest parts of the earth. The Guadalupana is that bright Sun from whose heat and radiance no inhabitant of Americas can hide. The Guadalupana is the one through whom the mystery of the Cross, all lights, is adored.[20]

To introduce the role of Mary of Guadalupe as an apostle to the Americas, López Murto quotes Isa 49:6, which describes one of the most important extensions of the task of the suffering servant: to bring light to those in darkness. The suffering servant whom God address through the prophet has been identified in Christian thought to be Jesus Christ. This is in part due to texts that tell how the devout Simeon, filled with the Holy Spirit, seeing the infant Jesus in the Temple and taking Him into his arms, blessed God and said, "For my eyes have seen your salvation ... a light for revelation to the Gentiles" (Luke 2:30–32 [NAB]). López Murto, like the evangelist, traces the active presence of the Light to Israel and especially in creation. Jesus is the true light that came into the world so that those in darkness, that is, under the estrangement from God caused by sin, may receive the divine light.

After identifying Jesus as our saving light, López Murto turns to address Mary's role. The homily describes how Mary who dwells in heaven was commissioned by the risen Christ in a way like His own commission by the Father: "I send you to the Indies that you may be the salvation of all, that you may establish peace to the Gentiles."[21] How is Mary to bring salvation and peace (the eschatological reconciliation between God and people) to the Gentiles? Mary of Guadalupe's apostleship is to reveal the mystery of the Cross and, thus, to show that the people of the Indies were included in the spiritual benefits promised to Israel. If different parts of the world own their evangelization to the Apostles of Christ (Peter received Rome; Andrew, Achaia; James, Spain; Thomas, India; John, Asia) who were preachers of the faith and teachers to the nations, Mary of Guadalupe was allotted the Americas: "Who has been [American's] light? Who has been [America's] Aurora? Who has been [America's] apostle? Who has been [America's] moon? Who has been [America's] sun? The Guadalupan is the one through whom the Christian religion shines in our land."[22] From these words comes the reassuring conviction that as God has provided missionaries for the Church in

---

[20] Antonio López Murto, *La luz saludable de la América* (México, D.F.: la imprenta madrileña de Don Felipe de Zúñiga y Ontiveros, 1792), 1–17; Schulte, *Mexican Spirituality*, 79.
[21] López Murto, *La luz saludable*, 1–17.
[22] Ibid., 84.

previously known lands, to Mary belonged the mission of proclaiming her son Jesus to the Indigenous. The light of the good news was divinely destined to dawn upon the people of America in the Aurora of Mary of Guadalupe as a sign of God's special love for them.

In the Catholic tradition, there is a plethora of portraits of Mary capturing her multivalent history. Undoubtedly, the apparition to Mary Guadalupe inspired sermon contributed to her iconic status. She is *Mediatrix* with respect to the plan of salvation, apostle to the Americas, symbol of the downtrodden and oppressed, motherly protection and love, and benefactor. Her many attributes make her one of the most enigmatic women in the Christian tradition.

Section Three

Recovering Receptions of the Marys in Literature, Art, and Archaeology

12

Mary of Nazareth and Nazareth Archaeological Excavations 1997–2015

Richard Freund

What Archaeology Is Really About

The photo in Figure 12.1 is intended to show just how complicated it is to excavate in a continuously occupied city like modern Nazareth. One can see the modern buildings, the modern roads, businesses, houses, and the holy sites all built upon for centuries. Even when there are opportunities to excavate and permissions given by the local homeowner, religious authorities, and national body of archaeological oversight, it is a balancing act as traditional archaeology is both destructive and expensive, and often does not get to the desired stratum without multiyear projects that may upset the locals (just living their daily lives) and tourists that are wanting to see the city's sites. Despite all of this, we have persisted working in Nazareth since 2003, especially around the GOCOA and the Mary's Well area but also in other parts of Nazareth. My research group uses multisystem high-tech noninvasive, subsurface tracking and mapping to identify what is often "unseen" in a modern cityscape.

Searching for an individual using geoscience and archaeology is fraught with problems. What we are really doing in accumulating data about the period to give a fuller picture of a historical person of this period—in this case, Mary of Nazareth, and in some cases, excavating down to the Roman period when she would have lived. Most people think that archaeology is about architecture, artifacts, and material culture. It is about these elements, but they are not an end in themselves. Ultimately they provide us with a more systematic analysis of the people of a region, area, city, or village in various periods and in this case does give us a better understanding of what the life of Mary of Nazareth might have been like.

Nazareth is a village in Galilee mentioned twenty-three times in the New Testament and is a major part of the designation of Jesus as "Jesus of Nazareth" in all four Gospels and in the book of Acts. The village is not mentioned in the Hebrew Bible, nor do Jewish and non-Jewish Second Temple period writings have any information on the village. It is assumed this is because it was a small village that did not warrant too much notice. From the material culture alone it is possible to surmise that many small villages existed in Galilee in the Hellenistic period, many of which were resettled during the reign of Alexander Janneaus and not mentioned in other earlier writings.

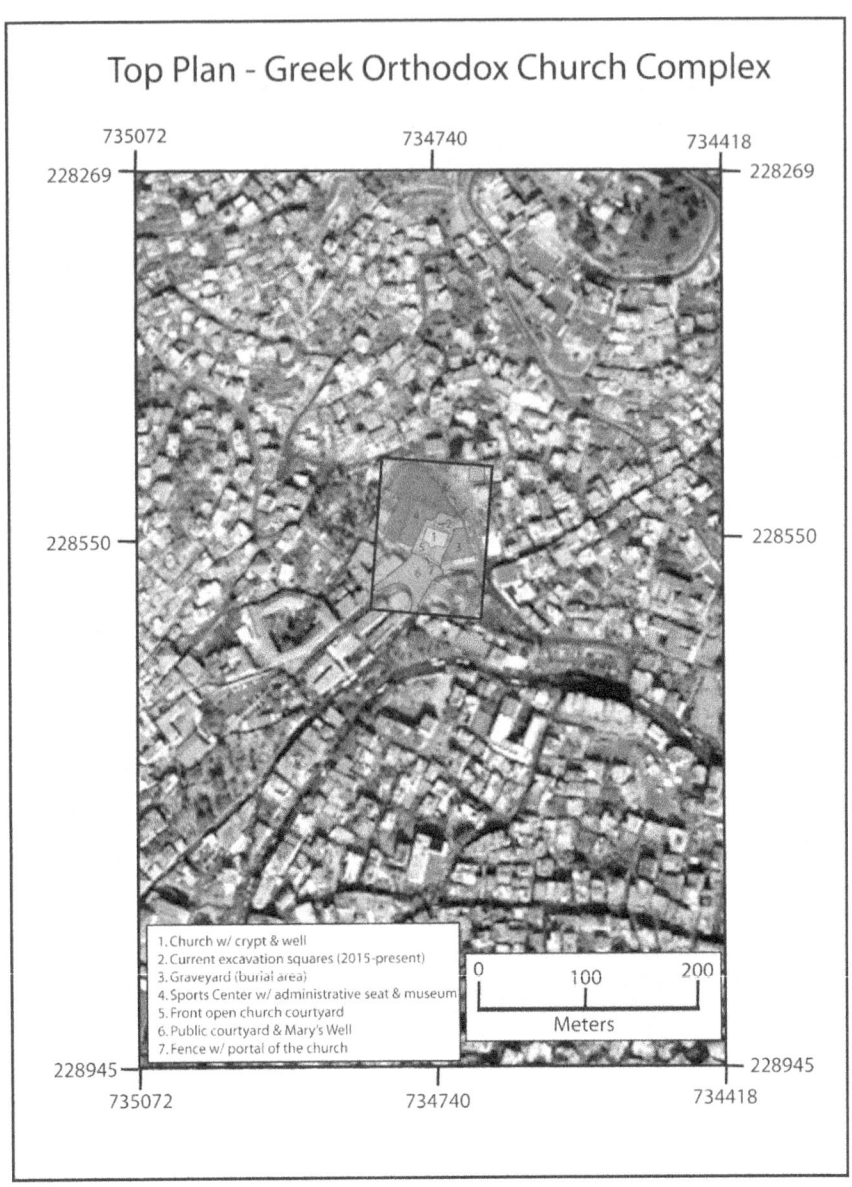

Figure 12.1 The area of Nazareth and the Greek Orthodox Church of the Annunciation (GOCOA). Courtesy of Professor Philip Reeder, Duquesne University, on behalf of the Scribante Family Nazareth Excavations Project at the University of Hartford.

Archaeology provides a missing piece to the full picture of the Galilee both in Nazareth and in other small villages.

The New Testament has Mary as a Jewish woman of the first century BCE who married a Jewish *tekton* (usually translated as carpenter; it is better translated as a contractor/builder) named Joseph (Matt 13:55) and they lived in Nazareth. Clues to the life that Mary led would require us to look at the status of Jewish men and women in the Galilee in this period in small villages (not a Jerusalem or Tiberias, for example), the types of institutions that might have existed in Nazareth (and in these small villages of the region), the types of artifacts that Jews would have used in this time period, and the comparisons with the rest of Galilee in the period. The comparisons between the archaeological discoveries made in Nazareth would be compared with the discoveries of other small villages in Galilee in this period.

Comparing a Biblical Site with Archaeological Data: Illumination, Background Attestations, Direct Correlations

The whole debate over how biblical archaeology is "done" by trying to scientifically assess sites associated with biblical events is both a methodological as well as an intellectual endeavor. It is not any different, however, than other areas of the world with ancient literary accounts (think Greece, India, and China) and how nationally/traditionally recognized sites are assessed with the relatively new discipline of archaeology. When I hear that an archaeologist is looking for the burial place of Ghengis Khan in Mongolia, I assume that he is using literary texts to direct the work. Not every site yields all three possibilities for comparison, but most traditions around the world have compared their literary traditions with the archaeological sites associated with their literary texts. Most of the time, at least "illumination" and "background" are in play, and "direct correlation" between a text and an artifact may also be a factor.

For this chapter, I will be using the first two but not the third. The first type of comparison is called "illumination" and is most well known. "Illumination" means that material culture that is found at a scene/site/region where the "literary" character is purported to have lived "illuminates" aspects of the literary account. In the case of Mary of Nazareth, we have three different types of literary accounts:

1. Canonical and noncanonical Gospels
2. Early Christian writings and Byzantine period witnesses
3. Byzantine and medieval Pilgrim accounts from Nazareth

We were comparing the noncanonical accounts about the meeting of Mary at the Well of Nazareth with the Angel Gabriel with our findings at what is called "Mary's Well" today. It is a very specific designation that appears, for example, in the *Protoevangelium* (or "Proto-Gospel") of James. We started by doing a site survey, which followed and collaborated with the excavations of Mary's Well done by the Israel Antiquities Authority in the late 1990s.[1]

The *Protevangelium* was composed in the late second century CE and combined the infancy narratives of Matthew and Luke with other traditions, including stories of Mary's own birth and life. The *Protevangelium* was exceptionally popular among Christians in the Byzantine and medieval periods, with hundreds of manuscripts of the text extant in a variety of languages. It figured and influenced Christian liturgy and teachings about Mary. The *Protevangelium* was transmitted in the West as part of the *Gospel of Pseudo-Matthew*, which added to it details of the Holy Family's sojourn in Egypt and, in some manuscripts, stories of Jesus' childhood taken from the *Infancy Gospel of Thomas*. Other *Pseudo-Matthew* manuscripts incorporate a different telling of Jesus' birth from an otherwise lost gospel that scholars call the *Book about the Birth of the Savior*. In the East, the *Protevangelium* was translated into Syriac and expanded with a different set of stories set in Egypt to form the *Life of the Blessed Virgin Mary*, which was later translated into Arabic as the Arabic Infancy Gospel.

Nazareth today is a modern city in the Natufa Valley in Galilee, Israel. Unlike some of the other cities on the Sea of Galilee associated with the life of Jesus, Nazareth does not sit upon the major road systems north and south or east and west. It was within walking distance of a well-known Greco–Roman period city, Sepphoris, that has been extensively excavated. The area of Nazareth is riddled with natural and artificially enhanced caves and was the site of very ancient burial (Qafzeh caves). Bronze Age pottery finds near the local well (later known as "Mary's Well") suggest that it was settled in this period.

The archaeological record in the north is affected by the differing populations. The "depopulation" of the north of Israel of Israelites in the period of the Assyrian Exile (eighth century BCE) raises serious question about the status of small villages like Nazareth in the Persian and Greco–Roman periods. After the Greek conquests of the Seleucid and Ptolemaic dynasties (fourth to third centuries BCE) and the repopulation of Galilee with Judeans by the Jewish King Alexander Jannaeus in the second century BCE, the coin record demonstrates a clear "Judaization" by the second century BCE.[2] This brings us up to the period when the families of Mary and Joseph would be found in Nazareth, the first century BCE, and might even explain the need for them to follow the census from the Judean city of Bethlehem where their families may have been from before coming to Nazareth. The fact that this city may have been settled by Levite families is supported by genealogical literary pieces embedded in the canonical NT in Luke and Matthew, and the existence of a well around which the village would have been settled would have facilitated the observance of ritual bathing rules in a place so far from either the coast or the Sea of Galilee. This history is confirmed by the Mary's Well excavations that have specifically found second-century BCE and Alexander Janneaus, Hellenistic, and early-Roman-period coins, pottery, and glass.

[1] Y. Alexandre, *Mary's Well, Nazareth: The Late Hellenistic to the Ottoman Periods* (Jerusalem: IAA Reports 49, 2012).

[2] Isaiah Gafney, "The Historical Background," *Jewish Writings of the Second Temple Period: Apocrypha, Pseudepigrapha: Qumran Sectarian Writings, Philo, Josephus*, ed. Michael E. Stone (Philadelphia, PA: Fortress, 1984), 13-17.

The multiple attestations to the well of Nazareth in second-century CE texts leads one to conclude that the well was a well-enough known fixture to become a literary piece in some of the Annunciation accounts. There is no indication in the canonical Gospels that this event happened at a well. Luke 1:26–28 simply states that the angel appeared in an undetermined location. The *Protevangelium* account, though, suggests that there were two visitations of the angel Gabriel—one at the well and another at Mary's home.

According to the *Gospel of Pseudo-Matthew*, ch. 9:

> And on the second day, while Mary was at the fountain to fill her pitcher, the angel of the Lord appeared to her, saying: Blessed are you, Mary; for in your womb you have prepared an habitation for the Lord. For, lo, the light from heaven shall come and dwell in you, and by means of you will shine over the whole world.[3]

The *Protevangelium of James*, chap. 11, has the expansive "annunciation" account at the well and then includes a second visitation at home:

> And she took the pitcher, and went out to fill it with water. And, behold, a voice saying: Hail, you who hast received grace; the Lord is with you; blessed are you among women! And she looked round, on the right hand and on the left, to see whence this voice came. And she went away, trembling, to her house, and put down the pitcher; and taking the purple, she sat down on her seat, and drew it out. And, behold, an angel of the Lord stood before her, saying: Fear not, Mary; for you have found grace before the Lord of all, and you shall conceive, according to His word. And she hearing, reasoned with herself, saying: Shall I conceive by the Lord, the living God? And shall I bring forth as every woman brings forth? And the angel of the Lord said: Not so, Mary; for the power of the Lord shall overshadow you: wherefore also that holy thing which shall be born of you shall be called the Son of the Most High. And you shall call His name Jesus, for He shall save His people from their sins. And Mary said: Behold, the servant of the Lord before His face: let it be unto me according to your word.[4]

The *Infancy of Thomas* text in chap. 11, draws Jesus and Mary both into an ongoing use of the well:

> And when He was six years old, His mother gave Him a pitcher, and sent Him to draw water, and bring it into the house. But He struck against someone in the crowd, and the pitcher was broken. And Jesus unfolded the cloak which He had on, and filled it with water, and carried it to His mother. And His mother, seeing the miracle that had happened, kissed Him, and kept within herself the mysteries which she had seen Him doing.[5]

---

[3] http://www.newadvent.org/fathers/0848.htm (accessed on June 20, 2018).
[4] http://www.newadvent.org/fathers/0847.htm (accessed on June 20, 2018).
[5] http://www.newadvent.org/fathers/0846.htm (accessed on June 20, 2018).

The common thread here is the centrality of the "spring/well" and "the pitcher" that provides an important context confirmed by archaeology.

By the Crusader period (Saewulf, Fetellus, Theoderich, twelfth century), the well is mentioned with decoration and a structure. Saewulf, an early twelfth-century pilgrim, adds details to the elaborate structure of a well with marble and square columns and that Jesus himself would gather water from this well. No bathhouse is specifically mentioned although the elaborate architectural pieces that are mentioned are suggestive of something much more sophisticated than just a well. By the fourteenth century, however, *The Travels of Sir John Mandeville*, chap. 13 ("Galilee") includes the additional information that the well had a place to bath attached to it:

> After go men by the hill beside the plains of Galilee unto Nazareth … here nigh is Gabriel's Well, where our Lord was wont to bathe him, when he was young, and from that well bare he water often-time to his mother. And in that well she washed often-time the clouts of her Son Jesu Christ. And from Jerusalem unto thither is three journeys. At Nazareth was our Lord nourished. Nazareth is as much to say as, "Flower of the garden"; and by good skill may it be clept flower, for there was nourished the flower of life that was Christ Jesu.[6]

It is common that ancient and medieval accounts borrow from one another (even as the scribes do as they copy these manuscripts), so ancient accounts may contain the same information, but in the case of the Mary's Well site, there are additions and elaborations that show elements that can indeed be verified in archaeology. Granted this is a tradition far removed from the first century, but it provides an insight into what was known at the site before the modern period. One such element is the "bathing" or possibly a bathhouse that is noted by Mandeville here and is borne out by the geoscience and archaeology.

Our Work in Nazareth: 2003–2012

Bathhouses are found in the Roman and Byzantine periods in ancient Israel, and comparisons can be made to their construction. In the Islamic period through and including the Crusades, bathhouses were parts of most villages where there was abundant water such as in Nazareth. The excavations of Mary's Well by the IAA indicated that there was indeed a bathhouse located adjacent to Mary's Well during the Islamic and Crusader periods. It was subsequently destroyed, but the remains may have been in use for quite some time. In addition, in many cases, a bathhouse for which there is evidence in an early medieval context may indicate that the site had been used even earlier as a bathhouse complex (Byzantine and Roman periods).

Jews would have had begun using a form of a ritual bath (*mikveh*), which was usually (but not always) attached to a bathhouse from the Greco-Roman period

---

[6] https://archive.org/stream/travelsofsirjohn00manduoft/travelsofsirjohn00manduoft_djvu.txt (accessed on June 20, 2018), p. 75.

onward. Ritual bathing and the need for a Jewish community to be centered around the well may be associated with a particular type of Jewish practice associated with priests and Levites. Levites and Kohanim (priests) apparently continued to keep the biblical and later developing ritual purity bathing laws even though they did not actually work in the Temple of Jerusalem. All of the material culture found in and around the present-day Mary's Well, from a modern bathhouse to ancient ceramic piping and stone channels that lead from a water source that begins in a cave behind the present GOCOA to the public well, all suggest that the well was only a part of a larger complex. The archaeological finds that were discovered in the Well all contribute to a sense of a community living close to the main water source and that from the ancient to modern period it was seen as more than just a place for drinking water. In the northern Galilee site known as Banias, for example, the spring begins in a cave and became from the Hellenistic period onward a type of sacred spring of Pan only to be absorbed into the world of the NT (as Caesarea Philippi). It is possible that the same was true at Nazareth's ancient spring that emerged from a cave as well. The topography of the area near Mary's Well also suggests that the grading of the lower village of Nazareth down to the location of the Roman Catholic Church of the Annunciation at the bottom of a hill, and the existence of cistern-like caves nearby while approaching the church, shows that attempts were made to divert the abundant rain into other water resources and cisterns as the village grew.

The periods of the pilgrim narratives continue from the Byzantine period until the premodern period. The sixteenth-century Jewish traveler account of Rabbi Moshe Bassola of Ancona, for example, mentions that the locals speak about the bathhouse: "We came from Kfar Kana [a village near Nazareth], arriving the next day in Nazareth, where the Christian Jesus lived. The citizens told me that there existed a hot bathhouse where the Mother of Jesus immersed herself."[7] In the 1664 map of Nazareth in Eugene Roger's *La Terre Sainte* (Paris), there is an illustrated map of the holy places and there is a structure directly adjacent to the public well that resembles a bathhouse; the image continues through the early eighteenth century in illustrated maps of Nazareth.[8] The open square structure pictured in the illustrated maps of Nazareth nearby Mary's Well may very well reflect the remnants of a bathhouse. In fact, in the 1870s, the "bathhouse" was "re-" built by the Kawar family of Nazareth in what appears to be the same place where earlier bathhouses had been built and located on as the square pool area pictured in the early illustrations. Our work has revealed that the area was originally a bathhouse at least as early as the Crusader and Mamluk periods, but perhaps even earlier. This fits a pattern of bathhouses that were rebuilt in the Crusader period over Byzantine and even Roman bathhouses. At the Byzantine bathhouses discovered and excavated at Emmaus[9] and Bet Zur in central Israel, for example, the structures were rebuilt in the Crusader period and help us analyze the remains inside of the bathhouse found nearby the Nazareth Mary's Well site. Thus,

---

[7] I. Ben-Zvi, *Maso't Eretz–Israel le–Rabbi Moseh Basola* (Jerusalem: Mosad Byaliq, 1938), 38.
[8] Eugene Roger, *La Terre Sainte* (Paris: Antoine Bertier, 1664), 58.
[9] R. A. Freund, *Digging through the Bible* (Lanham, MD: Rowman & Littlefield, 2008), 363.

our first working hypothesis about the greater Mary's Well area was that there was a bathhouse attached from its earliest periods to the public well (see Figure 12.2).

We started our work tracing the water sources and the Well's iterations and additions because they "illuminated" the existing literary accounts of the Well and the account of the Annunciation to Mary. We did this primarily using geoscience since the areas are occupied by businesses that did not want us to dig up the floors of their shops but were interested in knowing the history of the locations of their shops. They allowed us (with government permits and local permissions) to do our work and collect our data, and we shared the information with them and the government archaeological authorities.

Nazareth seems to be documented starting in the early Byzantine period. A fourth-century CE inscription written about by Michael Avi Yonah the first mention of Nazareth as a Jewish village in Galilee.[10] The reference is important since it alludes to it as a site to which priests went after the destruction of the Temple in 70 CE. They may have come to an already existing village with Levites as well. Among many other Byzantine-era writings, there is a rabbinic source—Midrash Ecclesiastes 2.8—that also holds that Nazareth was a priestly city. The fact that the NT genealogies in Luke and Matthew give Jesus a priestly family background (on his mother's side) creates a new background piece that a small separate Jewish (priestly) settlement may have been expressly created there during the Hasmonean period—explaining the journey of the Holy Family to Bethlehem from which they may have come.

The University of Hartford Mary's Well and Bathhouse, and the GOCOA Geoscience and Archaeology Projects

We used different forms of noninvasive geoscience, such as ground-penetrating radar (GPR) and electrical resistivity tomography (ERT), followed by archaeology in our work in businesses, streets, cisterns, and churches. GPR has been successful in helping to locate tombs, shallow graves, buried walls, tunnels, and other voids, as well as mapping historic-period fortifications, defining the outlines of buried features such as buildings and providing an immediate image of the site stratigraphy without having to put a spade in the ground (see Figure 12.3).

We used GPR together with ERT, a second, noninvasive, geo-electrical subsurface mapping technique that we used in Nazareth over the past fifteen years. GPR can detect large anomalies under the ground and uses FM radio waves to penetrate the different surfaces. ERT, which uses electricity, can detect different types of materials below the surface and can map to greater depths than GPR (see Figure 12.4).

The ERT metal electrodes do not necessarily have to go into the ground to conduct the electricity and when working with a delicate floor; for example, in the GOCOA in Nazareth, the geophysicists used a conductive gel and metal mediator of the electricity (aluminum foil), and were able to achieve results without destroying the marble floors there.

---

[10] MichaelAvi Yonah, "A List of Priestly Courses from Caesarea," *Israel Exploration Journal* 12 (1962): 137-9.

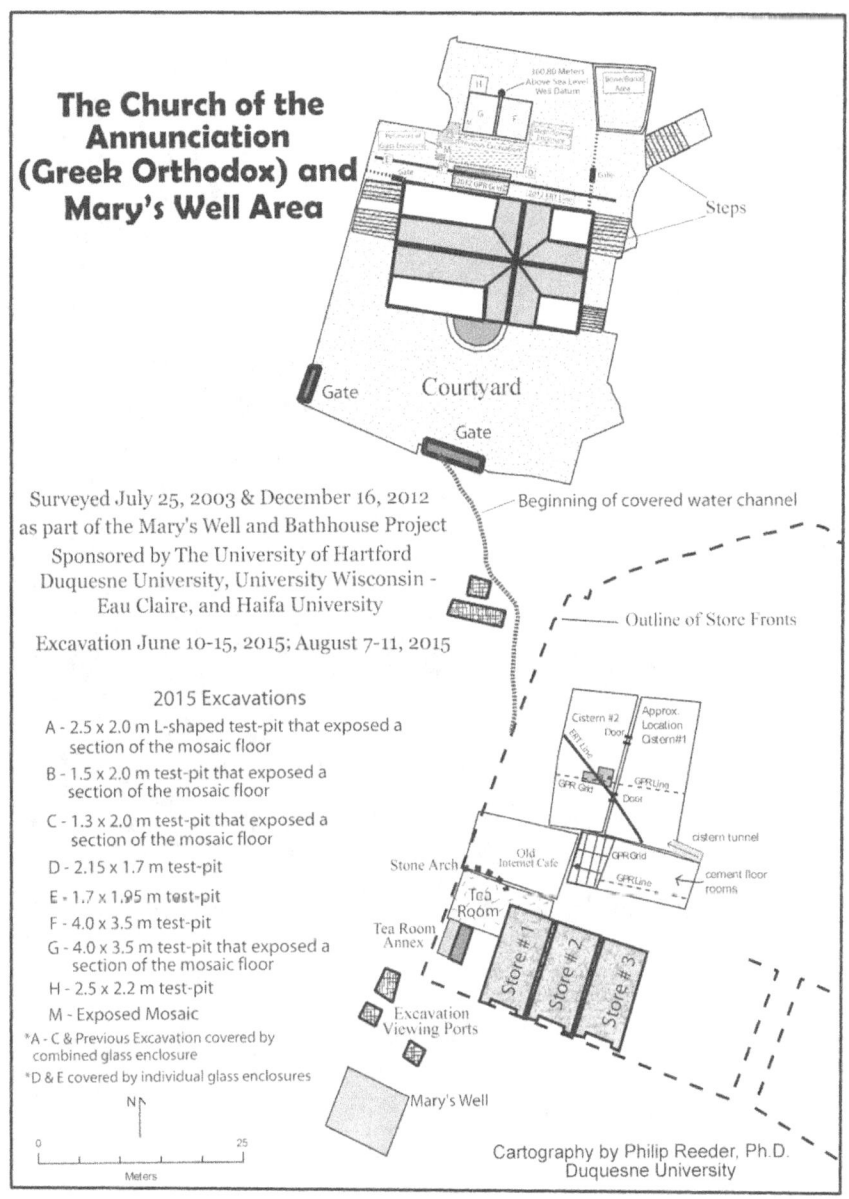

Figure 12.2 The map of Mary's Well, the Bathhouse, and the GOCOA. Courtesy of Professor Philip Reeder, Duquesne University, on behalf of the Scribante Family Nazareth Excavations Project at the University of Hartford.

Figure 12.3 GPR work by Harry Jol, University of Wisconsin-Eau Claire, in the bathhouse adjacent to Mary's Well. Notice on the wall the arch (to the left of the GPR operator's shoulder) indicating where an earlier building ceiling would have been located. The bottom of the arch is over 15 feet below the present street level. Courtesy of the Scribante Family Nazareth Excavations project at the University of Hartford.

Figure 12.4 ERT array on the floor of the GOCOA. Courtesy of the Scribante Family Nazareth Excavations Project at the University of Hartford.

Data are collected through a linear array of electrodes coupled to a DC (usually a car battery) resistivity transmitter/receiver and an electronic switching box using an electrode array. This equipment was on loan to us from a private industry (gas and oil) and would generally not be available for use by archaeological teams or universities. The collection process is driven by a laptop that is also used for data recording, and the software can interpret the data to create an image that is meaningful both to the geophysicist and the public. Conducting the electrical charge through the ground to the materials below is allowed through the natural materials below the surface that can help direct the signal as it is collected (soil, stone, clay, etc.). Our geophysicists have done this in some of the most extreme conditions around the world. While GPR cannot function in the rain and with extreme construction going on around the site of investigation, both rain and some types of construction do not affect ERT work (and rain can enhance the electrical current in the ground). These two geoscience technologies have given us a tremendous advantage in searching for, learning, and collecting about and mapping an area (that it often too sensitive or complicated for traditional excavation) that may or may not ever be excavated.

Why We Map Before We Excavate: Digital Mapping

All of the GPR and ERT data is mapped onto a digital map, which then gives us a "strata" perspective on what was below the surface thousands of years ago and how deep it is buried. As we worked in Nazareth and over time with the local religious and political authorities, we were allowed to map more sensitive locations, including the GOCOA that sits near the Mary's Well and bathhouse complex and is the source of water that feeds the public well there. The map of the ancient course of the water is important since it traces the development of the relationships between the Church, the public well, and the bathhouse, and also gives us an understanding of the relationship to the rest of the village below. Our maps contain very specific GPS designations about where excavations might be done if the area would become accessible. This is one of the goals of geoscience in a place such as Nazareth: to collect as much data as possible in a very specific location to minimize the damage done with traditional excavation.

Mary's Cave and The Sisters of Nazareth Convent Caves and Tunnels near the Basilica

Down the street from Mary's Well and the COAGO is another site where we were invited to investigate "Mary's Cave" (today designated as the "Holy Cave") that was introduced to us by the Greek Orthodox Bishop of Nazareth, Kyriakos (under his residence). The natural cave has an artificial combination cistern and naturally dug cave construction, which has been further dug out and has (now blocked) tunnels. The association with the family of Jesus, the cave house of Joseph and Mary, and Mary's Well spawned multiple pilgrimage sites that were being visited during the early fifth and sixth centuries. Willibald, who visited Nazareth about 725 CE, apparently found only the area where the Basilica is now located.[11] The foundations of the GOCOA and the Roman Catholic Church were most likely planted in the Byzantine period during Queen Helena's visit to the Holy Land. The letter of Constantine to Eusebius and other bishops (book 3, chapter 46) enabled the search for the holy sites in places such as Nazareth and the building, rebuilding, and restoring of holy sites from the events in the life of the holy family from the time of Jesus, and is seen as the "Magna Carta" for what became the Holy Land.[12]

The Rediscovery of the GOCOA, Geoscience and Archaeology

Two surveys were conducted on December 17 and 18, 2012, at the COAGO with authorization and cooperation from the Municipality of Nazareth and facilitated by the Greek Orthodox Bishop of Nazareth, Kyriakos, and the successive heads of the Arab Orthodox Council, Dr. Azmi Hakim, Mrs. Afaf Touma, and the Israel Antiquities Authority. We traced and also surveyed, to the back of the GOCOA and onto an open plaza, an ancient part of the building. On June 10, 2015, in an area that we had earlier surveyed with GPR and ERT, we opened a layer that contained pottery shards from the Byzantine period, and among other things, some tiny tesserae or mosaic pieces (0.5 cm × 0.5 cm each). Also discovered were some iron nails and glass fragments. Under that layer and at a depth of approximately 1.5 meters below the open plaza surface behind the present church was discovered a part of a decorated mosaic floor with tesserae measuring 25 tesserae per decimeter square. The mosaic design consists of precisely organized rhombus shapes and lines with a repeating black pattern on a white background that is found in other Byzantine churches throughout the country. The C14 analysis of the plaster remains dated the floor to the fifth to the seventh century CE.

Each side of the rhombus has seven smaller black dart/arrow shapes in a line from corner to corner delineating the larger rhombus shape. The connecting chevrons of the rhombus shape is a well-known Roman motif found throughout the period and is prominent in Byzantine floors of both synagogues and churches of the period. In the center of each large rhombus is a small black rhombus consisting of an outline of twelve tesserae pieces, then a single inner row of red tesserae, and finally a row of white tesserae forming an almost "hidden" cross shape with four white tesserae and a single black tessera in the center. After exposing the mosaic floor, the excavated area was expanded to the west of the square until black lines indicating the edge of the mosaic floor pattern were discovered (see Figure 12.5).

---

[11] https://books.google.com/books?id=kKDl50V8nooC&pg=PT576&lpg=PT576&dq= Willibald+and+Nazareth&source=bl&ots=_w6KxdR4Fx&sig=Bnlwu-L3z3z7qUReIYJBVfwYWwg&h (accessed on June 20, 2018).

[12] Constantine's letter to Eusebius and other bishops, respecting the building of churches, with instructions to repair the old and erect new ones on a larger scale, with the aid of the provincial governors, XLVI, http://www.ccel.org/ (accessed on July 23, 2019).

Figure 12.5 The ancient mosaic floor of the GOCOA by Mary's Well, Nazareth. Courtesy of the Scribante Family Nazareth Excavations Project at the University of Hartford.

After the discovery of the mosaic floor, another four squares were opened. Each measured approximately 1.5 m × 1.5 m and labeled B, C, D, and E. The finds included many new sections of the mosaic, coins, pottery, glass, and marble parts of a table that resemble others found at altars in other churches. In squares B and C, the previously mentioned mosaic floor continued. At the edge of the mosaic floor in squares B and C, a wall structure measuring more than 6.5 meters in length was exposed, and the size would suggest that it was part of a large public building. When we compare the floor with the many other examples of churches around the country from the Byzantine period, it is clear that we are dealing with a church associated with the Annunciation at the Well from the earliest period of church construction in the Holy Land.

In square G, remains of an even earlier ancient floor were located deeper than the mosaic. This floor, made of pink plaster, contains fragments of charcoal; a charred sample from this area (C14) was analyzed by the Weizmann Institute. The test results showed that the charcoal fragments are from the late Roman period, indicating that the site may have been in use before the Byzantine period. The work will continue, but our hypothesis is that there was some form of shrine on the site on or before the Byzantine period.

What We Now Know about Mary from Geoscience and Archaeology in Nazareth

The sites we have worked on in and around Mary's Well demonstrate that Mary in Nazareth fulfilled many of the prerequisites for Jewish Galilean life and culture:

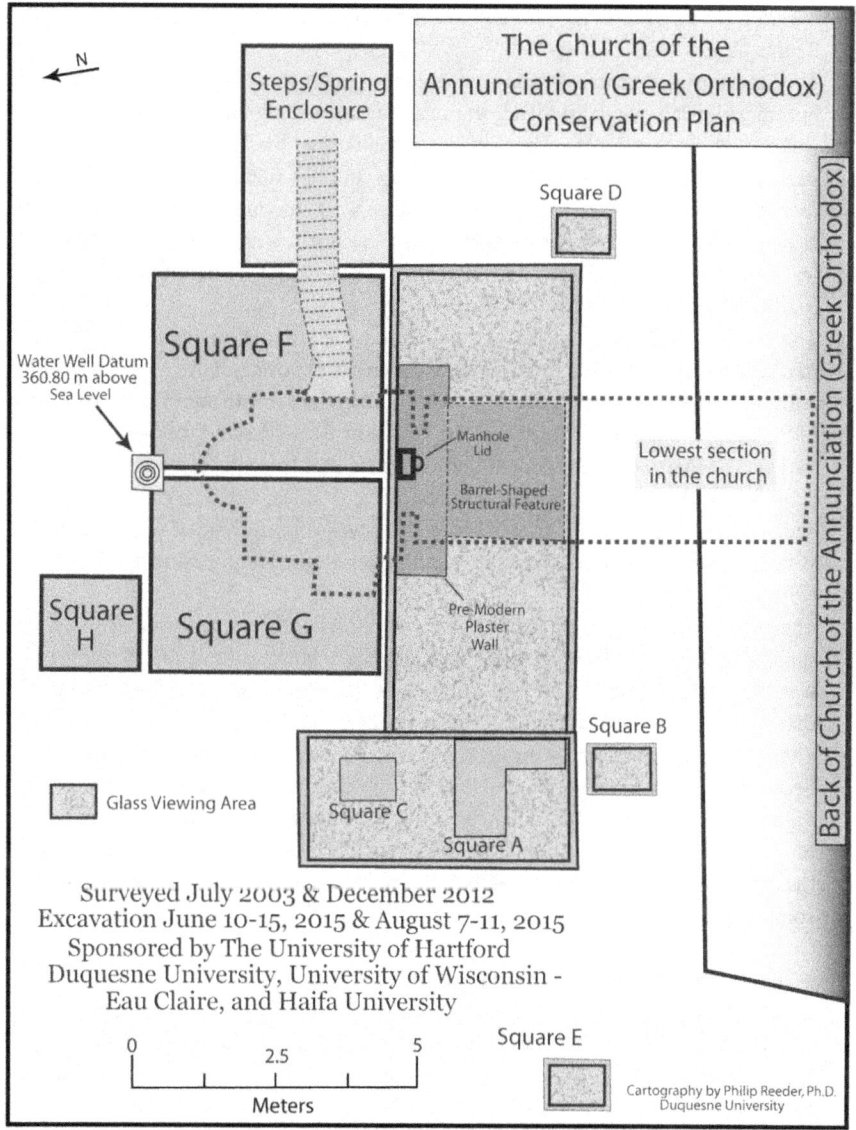

Figure 12.6 The map of our excavations, showing the excavated areas, the present back of the church, and the possible ancient church inset. Courtesy of Professor Philip Reeder, Duquesne University, on behalf of the Scribante Family Nazareth Excavations Project at the University of Hartford.

- Nazareth had a settlement centered around an ancient well perhaps as early as the Bronze Age.
- The literature and especially the archaeology suggest that this ancient village became a Jewish village in the Hasmonean period and by the first century CE was probably resettled (as other villages in Galilee) in the Hasmonean period perhaps with Levites (ex-Judeans) who had a special ritual interest in the water resources available there. Others in the village were drawn to it because of the close proximity to the larger Roman city of Sepphoris, which meant that there was ample work for builders, contractors, and a road system that led from the Mediterranean to the Sea of Galilee and beyond.
- The village was Jewish because it contained a variety of distinctive Jewish ethnic markers such as elements in burial caves, coins, and pottery.[13]
- Although there is a single large well in town, this does not mean that the runoff of the rains did not allow for the creation of house cisterns and mikvaot (ritual baths). The hydrology assessment demonstrates that from the elevation of the COAGO at Mary's Well down to the area of the Basilica, a typical configuration of ancient villages built in an area of limestone caves with individual water collection systems is seen. Water collection in small-area cisterns and for ritual bathing would be possible.
- The pottery of Mary's Well, for example, contained pottery forms that are specifically associated with "Jewish" pottery, Kfar Hananya (and Kfar Shikhin) ware,[14] which originate from well-known Jewish "supervised" clay forms in Galilee that were used by Jews during the Roman period in the area.[15]
- The ancient mosaic floor of the GOCOA is particularly important not only because it is associated with an ancient church and the public well in Mary's name but also because the similarity of the decoration of the rhomboid squares is found throughout the country with this particular design. These may be some of the earliest symbols associated with Mary and need to be carefully assessed with color and design. The design of the Byzantine mosaic floor with the interlocking chevrons and the extended arms multicolored stone "X" is accented only by a single central stone. The design may not be unique to Mary, but it is found in both the GOCOA and at the Roman Catholic excavations of the area of the Basilica. The design of the chevrons and rhombi is found also in synagogues of the same period at Bet Alpha, Jericho, and elsewhere in churches in Kursi, Bet Safafa, Hippos, Shiqmona, and Shavei Tzion, among many others. The period of construction may suggest that even in the Byzantine period, there were some shared design styles in synagogues and churches.

---

[13] Nurit Feig, "Nazareth Burial Caves," *Atiqot* 10 (1990): 67–79.
[14] The chapter titled "Distribution Maps of Archaeological Data from the Galilee: An Attempt to Establish Zones Indicative of Ethnicity and Religious Affiliation" on this by M. Aviam is found in *Religion, Ethnicity and Identity in Ancient Galilee: A Region in Transition*, ed. J. Zangenberg, H. W. Attridge, D. Martin (Tübingen: Mohr Siebeck, 2007), 115-32. This form of pottery is specifically associated with Jews, similar to the limestone ware.
[15] The pottery in the caves, especially the types of oil lamps, indicate a Jewish population. The "Sabbath" oil lamps and Herodian oil lamps, and even ossuaries found in the burial caves, distinguish the population as Jewish practices.

The design of the mosaic in the GOCOA had chevrons and rhombi, and the makings of a cross is like the one at Ramat Rachel (near Jerusalem) where Prof. Aharoni worked and was designated by him in the church he excavated there as "decorated with simple geometric mosaics: squares and rhombi, hexagons in blue, red cubes on a white background." Aharoni added in his description that there were "little crosses in the centre." This is before the period of the lavish and large displays of the relatively new symbol of the cross. These were simple attempts at creating a sense of continuity between the Roman and Jewish designs that eventually morphed into the cross image in the Byzantine period. Though it is hard to know how far Mary's fame extended in the early centuries, the unknown origin of the designation of Mary as the "Stella Maris" (known from the fourth century onward—the Star of the Sea/Water) may be a play on words of the "star" of Mary (Maria/Maris) but may ultimately allude to her connection with the eponymous well of Nazareth.

13

The Dormition of Miriam in Rabbinic Literature

Michael Rosenberg

In this chapter, I consider a passage in the Babylonian Talmud (also known as the "Bavli") that describes the death of the biblical Miriam as miraculous and her lifeless body as untouched by decay or worms. I argue that the passage reflects rabbinic participation in a discourse in which contemporaneous Christian traditions about the Dormition of Mary arose. Both rabbinic and Christian circles display a marked increase in creativity regarding the deaths of these similarly named women in late antiquity, especially beginning in roughly the late fourth/early fifth centuries CE.

The passage appears at Tractate Bava Batra, folio 17a:[1]

A. Our rabbis taught [in a *baraita*]:[2]
B. [There were] six over whom the angel of death did not exert control. And who are they? Abraham, Isaac, and Jacob; Moses, and Aaron, and Miriam.
C. Abraham, Isaac, and Jacob, as it is written about them: *In all* (Gen 24:1), *from all* (Gen 27:33), *all* (Gen 33:11).
D. Moses, and Aaron, and Miriam,[3] as it is written about them: *By the mouth of God* (Num 33:38; Deut 34:5).
E. But behold, [regarding] Miriam it is not written *by the mouth of God*!
F. Rabbi Eleazar said: Miriam also died by a kiss, which comes from the [shared language of] *there* with [the passage describing the death of] Moses (Num 20:1,

---

[1] Translation based on the standard Vilna printing, with relevant variants noted where appropriate, based on the transcriptions found in the Saul and Evelyn Henkind Talmud Text Databank (www.lieberman-institute.com). All translations of rabbinic texts in this article are my own.

[2] MS Vatican 115 lacks the introductory marker "Our rabbis taught" both here and in line G as well. However, given that these two *beraitot* are part of a longer chain of similarly structured traditions, and the first of these is introduced by the phrase in this manuscript, it likely is the case that the reader is meant to understand all of them as similarly marked as tannaitic. Moreover, the language (Hebrew) and style of these traditions all reflect typical tannaitic style.

[3] MS Vatican 115 does not have the name "Miriam" here, but that is clearly an error, perhaps a result of mistaken "correction," based on the coming (and obvious) query about the phrase *by the mouth of God* not appearing in the Bible with reference to Miriam. Both the opening claim that six figures are to be discussed, and the Talmudic objection, make clear that Miriam indeed belongs in this text.

Deut 34:5). And why was *by the mouth of God* not stated regarding her? Because the matter is disgraceful.

G. Our rabbis taught [in a *baraita*]:

H. [There were] seven over whom the worm did not exert control. And who are they? Abraham, Isaac, and Jacob; Moses, Aaron, and Miriam; and Benjamin son of Jacob.

I. Abraham, Isaac, and Jacob, as it is written about them: *In all, from all, all.*

J. Moses, Aaron, and Miriam,[4] as it is written about them: *By the mouth of God.*

K. Benjamin son of Jacob as it is written: *And to Benjamin he said, "The beloved of God shall dwell forever beside [God]"* (Deut 33:12).

L. And some say also David, as it is written: *Also my flesh will dwell surely* (Ps 16:9).

M. And the other (i.e., the view that does not include David in this list) [thinks that] that was a request that he was making.

The passage comprises two texts that the editors of the Talmud assert to be *beraitot*, that is, rabbinic texts that date to the tannaitic period (roughly the early third century CE or earlier in Palestine). The first *baraita* describes six biblical characters over whom the angel of death did not exert control (*lo' shalat bahen malakh hamavet*). These six characters come in two groups of three—the patriarchs Abraham, Isaac, and Jacob, and the siblings Miriam, Aaron, and Moses. For Aaron, Miriam, and Moses, the phrase *by the mouth of God*, which appears in the descriptions of both Aaron's and Moses's deaths, provides evidence of the inability of the angel of death to wield power over them.

To this, the later, anonymous editor of the Talmudic passage immediately objects (line E): that phrase does not actually appear in the Torah's description of Miriam's death! A statement attributed to the early fourth-century sage Rabbi Eleazar provides a resolution to this objection: Miriam also died by a divine kiss, as implied by a word common to the description both of her death and that of Moses. However, the Torah only alluded to Miriam's miraculous death rather than state it outright because, presumably due to an assumption of a male-figured divinity and Miriam's being female, it would be unseemly to be so explicit.

A second *baraita* immediately follows this exchange, stating that seven biblical characters did not suffer decay to their corpses following their deaths. Here we have the six figures from the previous *baraita*, and additionally, Benjamin, the son of Jacob and brother of Joseph. The same verses are invoked for the initial six, and Deut 33:12 supports the claim for Benjamin. A brief discussion ensues about whether King David was similarly immune to the normal indignities of death.

Several curiosities warrant our attention. To begin with, we should not take the presence of Miriam as one of the six or seven illustrious figures in these two *beraitot* for granted. That a thoroughly masculinist authorship such as that of the Babylonian Talmud would think of including a woman in this list of biblical heroes is in and of itself surprising. Even allowing for such an inclusion—after all, one woman out of six

---

[4] MS Escorial G-I-3 lacks the name "Miriam" here, again, likely a mistake resulting from the cognitive dissonance of her name followed by "as it is written about [her]," followed by a phrase never applied to her in the Bible. See n. 3 above regarding a similar phenomenon in the first *baraita*.

or seven characters does not exactly merit high feminist praise—the choice of Miriam rather than some other female figure is intriguing.[5]

In addition to its perhaps surprising invocation of Miriam as a uniquely meritorious woman, the passage raises several source critical red flags. The Talmud labels each of these traditions as a *baraita*. However, there is good reason to believe that several aspects of these *beraitot* are the handiwork specifically of Babylonian author/editors working in the generations after the tannaitic period.

To understand the development and significance of these two *beraitot*, it is best to begin with the second (lines H–L). Despite the Talmud's claim of tannaitic origins for this tradition, no parallel exists in extant tannaitic corpora such as the Mishnah or tannaitic works of midrash. That does not mean that we can, willy-nilly, declare this a falsely labeled tradition. Several decades of scholarship in rabbinic literature, however, have made clear that not everything claimed by the Bavli to be of tannaitic provenance is indeed so.

Indeed, in this case, our *baraita* does find a parallel, but not in a tannaitic corpus. Rather, the closest parallel appears in the so-called minor tractate of *Kallah rabbati*:

Seven ancestors lay down with the honor of the world/eternal honor (*bikhvod ha'olam*) and the worm did not exert control over them: Abraham, Isaac, and Jacob, and Amram the father of Moses, and Benjamin the son of Jacob, and Jesse the father of David, and Chileab, and some say also David, as it says: *Then my heart was joyous and my being is glad, also my flesh will dwell surely*. (Ps 16:9)[6]

As in the Talmud's *baraita*, here we have seven figures not subject to consumption by worms, but Moses, Aaron, and Miriam are gone from the equation, with Amram the father of Moses and two other figures appearing in their stead. Dating the traditions in *Kallah rabbati* is difficult, but scholars have generally argued that it (or at least its last seven chapters, where this tradition is found) was redacted after the Babylonian Talmud.[7] It is therefore possible that the *Kallah rabbati* passage may be a reworking of our *baraita* from the Talmud and the Bavli's version would be the earliest attestation of this tradition.[8]

---

[5] Of course, the grouping of Miriam, as one of a trio of siblings, with Aaron and Moses has strong precedent, not only from Mic 6:4, but from early rabbinic texts as well, as, e.g., in *Sifre Deuteronomy* 338, which describes Mt. Nebo as the burial site for the three siblings, who are united as well by the fact of their deaths not resulting from transgression.

[6] *Kallah rabbati* 3.22, translation based on Michael Higger, ed., *Massekhtot kallah vehen massekhet kallah, massekhet kallah rabbati* (New York: Moinester, 1936), 245-6.

[7] See David Brodsky, *A Bride without a Blessing: A Study in the Redaction and Content of Massekhet Kallah and Its Gemara* (Tübingen: Mohr Siebeck, 2006), 182–200, who argues that the language of *Kallah rabbati* chapters 3–9 likely dates from no earlier than the latest strata of the Babylonian Talmud, and likely later.

[8] Also possible is that *Kallah rabbati*, even if redacted later, preserves an earlier version of the *baraita* found in the Bavli. Reasons for both possibilities can be mustered; on the one hand, the more obscure figures mentioned in *Kallah rabbati* might be more likely to be replaced by the better-known trio of Moses, Aaron, and Miriam. Conversely, the redactor(s) of *Kallah rabbati*, in keeping with the work's dearth of female voices and characters, may have sought to excise the appearance of Miriam in this illustrious list (I am thankful to the anonymous reviewer for this framing). For reasons I explain in the next paragraph, I think dependence of *Kallah rabbati* on the Babylonian Talmud is more likely than the reverse in this case.

If so, then a tradition attributing impermeable corpses to seven figures, one of whom is Miriam, is unattested prior to the Babylonian Talmud. Such a conclusion is surely speculative, but it may find support from a finding of Jeffrey Rubenstein. Discussing a story of a sage who died and whose corpse became the subject of inter-town dispute, Rubenstein argues that the rabbinic story—which appears in both the Babylonian Talmud and the roughly contemporaneous *Pesiqta deRav Kahana*—is best understood in the light of Christian texts about contention regarding possession of the bodies of holy men.[9] Rubenstein highlights several striking points of similarity, but the one most relevant to this study is the incorruptibility of the holy body: not even a hair on the rabbinic sage's body endures decay. Rubenstein points out the similarity of this detail to a description in Evagrius Scholasticus's *Life of Simeon the Stylite*.[10] Like the sage story discussed by Rubenstein, the Babylonian "*baraita*" reveals that rabbinic author/editors of the fifth century CE and later were, like their Christian contemporaries, invested in the notion that holy bodies could be impervious to decay; one of those holy bodies, significantly, is Miriam.

The interest both in Miriam and in non-decomposing corpses likely reflects rabbinic awareness of ideas found in Christian contexts, a likelihood buttressed by the Bavli's introduction, immediately following this second *baraita*, of yet another *baraita*, this one with characters that more neatly overlap with those who appear in the *Kallah rabbati* text:

N. Our rabbis taught [in a *baraita*]:
O. Four died because of the counsel of the serpent. And who are they? Benjamin son of Jacob; Amram the father of Moses; Jesse the father of David, and Chileab the son of David …

---

[9] Jeffrey Rubenstein, "A Rabbinic Translation of Relics," in *Crossing Boundaries in Early Judaism and Christianity: Ambiguities, Complexities, and Half-Forgotten Adversaries: Essays in Honor of Alan F. Segal*, ed. Kimberly B. Stratton and Andrea Lieber (Leiden: Brill, 2016), 314–32.

[10] Ibid., 326. See also Jeffrey Rubenstein, "Hero, Saint, and Sage: The Life of R. Elazar b. R. Shimon in Pesiqta de Rab Kahana 11," in *The Faces of Torah: Studies in the Texts and Contexts of Ancient Judaism in Honor of Steven Fraade*, ed. Michael Bar-Asher Siegal, Tzvi Novick, and Christine Hayes (Göttingen: Vandenhoeck & Ruprecht, 2017), 523, where he suggests that the Palestinian version of the story, in which the deceased sage's body is infiltrated by a single worm "may be a parody of [Christian holy man] accounts, as if the rabbinic storyteller wished to insist that even the holiest 'holy man' could not be completely sin-free, and therefore worm-free." In neither article does Rubenstein explicitly contrast this potential parody with the Babylonian version, in which the worm, rather than "nibbling behind his ear," merely exits the ear, with no mention of damage to the body, and in which the continued vitality of the sage's ear uniquely appears. I would suggest, however, that it may well be that while both the Palestinian and Babylonian versions of the story engage with ideas known to us from early Christian texts about holy men and the decay of their corpses, these versions differ in *how* they engage these ideas, with the Palestinian version resisting this notion and the Babylonian one appropriating it (though see Daniel Boyarin, *Carnal Israel: Reading Sex in Talmudic Culture* [Berkeley: University of California Press, 1993], 209, who reads the image of the worm crawling out of the ear in the Babylonian story as itself "a satire or parody on hagiographies." But note that to do so, Boyarin has to assume the worm implies a body "full of worms," against the narrative purpose of the image in the story). If so, then we truly find a similar phenomenon in the story Rubenstein studied to the one I am describing here, where not only late, but specifically Babylonian, rabbinic sources express interest in the incorruptibility of the bodies of holy people.

This *baraita*[11] provides yet another list, this time of four men who apparently died sinless, their deaths a result solely of the transgression caused by the serpent in the Garden of Eden.[12] A number of themes here—for example, the consequences of the serpent and the possibility of human sinlessness—are significant as well in Paul's conception of human sinfulness,[13] and two of the characters in this *baraita* are tied to the Davidic (that is, messianic) line—Jesse, King David's father, and Chileab, his fairly obscure son.[14] Scholars have already noted the possible interplay of this text with Pauline ideas about the consequences of sin in the Garden.[15] This third *baraita* thus heightens our sense that we are in the midst of a passage somehow particularly engaged with ideas popular in Christian circles.[16]

[11] As with the previous one, this *"baraita"* also has no parallel in known tannaitic works (see Yaakov Elman, "Righteousness as its Own Reward: An Inquiry into the Theologies of the Stam," *PAAJR* 57 (1990–1), 41. Elman argues that the parallel pericope at bShab 55a–b in which this *baraita* also appears is an example of late Babylonian resistance to measure-for-measure theology (ibid., 40–5), thus implying that he likely believes it to be a Babylonian *"baraita."*

[12] Though the *baraita* does not explicitly call these men sinless, such is the reasonable interpretation—an interpretation that also derives support from the Talmud's use of this *baraita* elsewhere (bShab 55a–b) as an attack on the notion that a person's death always results from some sin. See also *Sifre Deuteronomy* #338, which states that Mt. Nebo is so called because "these three who died not through transgression were buried on it—Moses, Aaron, and Miriam."

[13] See, e.g., the brief and clear description in Gary A. Anderson, *The Genesis of Perfection: Adam and Eve in Jewish and Christian Imagination* (Louisville, KY: Westminster/John Knox, 2001), 209–210.

[14] Urbach, in an attempt to blunt the force of the *baraita* as an embrace of something like "original sin," suggests that the obscurity of these figures serves to "[annul] the significance of the episode, and hence takes away the basis of Paul's doctrine of redemption" (Ephraim E. Urbach, *Hazal: pirqe emunot vede'ot* [Jerusalem: Magnes, 1969], 377=Urbach, *The Sages: Their Concepts and Beliefs*, trans. Israel Abrahams [2 vols., Jerusalem: Magnes, 1975], 427).

[15] Israël Lévi, "Le péché originel dans les anciennes sources juives," *Annuaires de l'École pratique des hautes études* 20 (1906): 9–10; Urbach, *Hazal*, 376–7=*Sages*, 427. See, however, Elman, "Righteousness," 42, n. 19, who argues that, at least with regard to the statement about sinless death against which this *baraita* appears as an attack, Urbach has missed the point, since that statement is not about "original sin" but rather the suffering of the righteous more generally. Elman's argument, however, does not really affect our reading of the *baraita*; the editors of the discussion at bShab 55a–b already offered the same interpretation—correct or not—of the statement about sinless death, evidenced by their presumption that this *baraita* was a relevant attack.

[16] The appearance of the same obscure figures as those found in *Kallah rabbati*'s version of the Talmud's second *baraita* about impervious corpses also suggests another way of conceiving the development of this tradition, namely, that even though *Kallah rabbati* postdates the Talmud, in this case it preserves an earlier tradition, one which the Babylonian Talmud has reworked so as to include Miriam (alongside her brothers Aaron and Moses). Indeed, the notion of *lectio difficilior* would suggest that that is a particularly likely description of what has occurred, since it is more likely that a later editor would replace the relatively marginal figures Amram, Jesse, and Chileab with the more significant triumvirate of Aaron, Miriam, and Moses than the opposite phenomenon occurring. See also *Derekh eretz zutah* 1.17, a parallel to *Kallah rabbati* 3.22, in the edition of Michael Higger, ed., *The Treatises Derek Erez, Pirke Ben Azzai, Tosefta Derek Erez* (New York: Moinester, 1935), 67–8. Higger's base text has there "Moses, and Aaron, Miriam," though he cites mss. Oxford 59, Oxford 2339 (Opp. Add 4 to 128), Oxford 2257, Adler 1909, Adler 2237, the Vilna printing, the Venice printing, a manuscript from the library of A. Epstein, and a Yemenite manuscript in the collection of the Jewish Theological Seminary of America, all with the intriguing variant of "Moses, Aaron, and Amram their father" (or in the case of MS Oxford 59, "Amram"). Moreover, MS Oxford 2339 was, in Higger's estimation, the best manuscript of this work, which generally served as the base text for his edition. The fact that he deviated from his usual base text in producing his edition in this case likely reflects the influence of the Bavli's version on him (see also the emendation of the Vilna Gaon, found in the Vilna printed edition of *Derekh eretz zutah*, who similarly emends "Amram" to "Miriam"). A number of intriguing possibilities arise from this textual situation, potentially highlighting the

A similar though not identical phenomenon is at work in the Talmud's treatment of Miriam in the first *baraita* (lines B–D), which states only that Miriam was not touched by the angel of death. Unlike the second *baraita*, this text, also labeled as tannaitic, finds a parallel in David Tzvi Hoffman's reconstruction of the tannaitic midrash *Mekhilta Deuteronomy* (which he titled *Midrash tannaim*), seemingly corroborating the claim that this tradition dates to the second century or earlier in Palestine. To be sure, use of Hoffman's attempt to reconstruct a lost midrashic work is beset with difficulties, since he drew his reconstruction from what he determined to be citations of *Mekhilta Deuteronomy* in the medieval work *Midrash hagadol* and only a few leaves found in the Cairo Genizah.[17] It thus may be that this "*baraita*" as well is entirely a late Babylonian production. But even if we accept Hoffman's reconstruction, the differences between the *baraita* as it appears there and the Babylonian Talmud's version are instructive, again highlighting the especial significance of Miriam in post-tannaitic Babylonian rabbinic culture. Here is how the *baraita* appears in Hoffman's reconstructed work:

A. *By the mouth of God*. By a kiss. This teaches that the death of Moses was from the mouth of the Holiness.
B. I have only the death of Moses; whence the death of Aaron as well? It says: *As your brother Aaron died on Mount Hor* (Deut 32:50).
C. Behold, we learn from the death of Moses to the death of Aaron. But the matter is not thus; rather, [we learn] from the death of Aaron to the death of Moses:
D. Just as the death of Aaron was from the mouth of the Holiness, so too the death of Moses was from the mouth of Holiness.[18]
E. I have only the death of Moses and Aaron; whence the death of Miriam as well? It says: *Also* (Num 27:13). The death of Miriam as well.
F. Whence the death of Joshua as well? It says…
G. I have only the death of Joshua; whence the death of the righteous as well…[19]

The *baraita* as found in *Midrash tannaim* focuses on the comparison of the deaths of Moses and Aaron, with lines A–D entirely about the two brothers. Only in line E do we come to Miriam. Unlike the Bavli's version of the *baraita*, in which a word in the

---

way in which Miriam in particular is a contested figure in this tradition. Unfortunately, the relative dating of *Derekh eretz zutah* is unclear enough that I leave this speculation for others to take on. In any event, whether we treat the *baraita* as the reworking by the Bavli's editors of earlier material so as to include Miriam (alongside Moses and Aaron), or as a creation of those Bavli's editors, interest in Miriam's non-decomposing body has its origins in this late Babylonian milieu.

[17] David Zvi Hoffman, *Midrash tannaim ʿal sefer dəvarim* (Berlin, 1908), iii–v; Menahem Kahana, "The Halakhic Midrashim," in *The Literature of the Sages* (2 vols.), ed. Shmuel Safrai (Philadelphia, PA: Fortress, 2006), 2:100–1. Although some more testimonies to *Mekhilta Deuteronomy* have appeared since the publication of Hoffman's edition (see Kahana, "The Halakhic Midrashim," 101–2), none covers the section of *Mekhilta Deuteronomy* relevant here.

[18] I have translated in accordance with the words as they appear in Hoffman's edition; however, Hoffman suggests emending lines C–D, such that they read: "Behold, we learn from the death of Aaron to the death of Moses. But the matter is not thus; rather, [we learn] from the death of Moses to the death of Aaron: Just as the death of Moses was from the mouth of the Holiness, so too the death of Aaron was from the mouth of holiness." Hoffman, *Midrash tannaim*, 225, n. 8.

[19] Ibid., 225–6 (commenting on Deut 34:5).

biblical description of Miriam's death hinted at its miraculous nature, in the *Midrash tannaim* version, we must turn to a verse about Moses's death (i.e., the word "also" in Num 27:13) for evidence of Miriam's special status. No explicit claim is made here, as in the Babylonian Talmud's version, that Miriam's death merited the descriptor *by the mouth of God*. Moreover, the version in *Midrash tannaim* immediately moves on to argue that even Joshua's death was by means of a divine kiss, and even the righteous more generally, thus minimizing Miriam's significance by comparison.[20] By contrast, the later, Babylonian version of this tradition not only highlights Miriam but also emphasizes the immediacy of divine involvement in her death, applying to her a verse about God's direct involvement that the Pentateuch itself does not.

Notice also how the Babylonian Talmud's commentary on the *baraita* (line E) emphasizes and elaborates on the Miriam tradition, first by noting that the verse cited in support of her miraculous death (*by the mouth of God*) does not actually appear in the pericope of her death, and then with Rabbi Eleazar's response that it is implied, at one and the same time highlighting the biblical imbalance between Miriam and her two brothers but also rectifying it and putting her on an equal footing with them. Indeed, of the six characters mentioned in the *baraita*, only Miriam receives any extended discussion, increasing Miriam's visibility as a character with a particularly honored passing.[21]

The Babylonian passage thus highlights rabbinic interest in Miriam's death. Such interest is of course not unique to rabbinic Babylonia. *Sifre Deuteronomy* already introduces Miriam, again alongside her brothers, as a figure who died on Mt. Nebo, which, the midrash tells us, is so called because these three died "not from sin" (*shelo' miyde 'averah*).[22] A tradition that the miraculous well that provided Israel with water in the desert disappeared when Miriam died also appears already in tannaitic literature.[23] But the Babylonian treatment of Miriam expands on and emphasizes these Miriam traditions, applying to Miriam a biblical claim of direct divine involvement in her death and ascribing to her the miraculous non-decaying body of the "holy man [*sic*]."

Only one Palestinian tradition reveals this level of interest in Miriam's death. In the Palestinian Talmud (also known as the "Yerushalmi"), redacted near the year 400 CE, we find the following:

> Rabbi Hiyya b. Ba said: The sons of Aaron died on the first of Nissan. And why was their death mentioned in [the passage regarding] Yom Kippur (Lev 16:1)? To teach you that just as Yom Kippur atones for Israel, so too the death of the righteous atones for Israel.

---

[20] Indeed, the *baraita* is closely paralleled in *Sifre zuta* as well, another reconstruction of a lost tannaitic midrash (27:12), and there, Miriam is entirely absent, i.e., the midrash moves from the death of Aaron to the death of Joshua.

[21] Regarding the rabbinic tendency to consider Miriam's stature vis-à-vis other biblical characters, see Miriam Sherman, "A Well in Search of an Owner: Using Novel Assertions to Assess Miriam's Disproportionate Elaboration among Women in the Midrashim of Late Antiquity" (PhD dissertation, University of California, San Diego, 2006), 124–7.

[22] *Sifre Deuteronomy* 338.

[23] *Mekhilta deRabbi Yishmael*, Tractate *Devayisa'* 5; Tosefta *Sotah* 11:1.

Rabbi Ba b. Bina said: Why did the text juxtapose the death of Miriam (Num 20:1) with the passage about the heifer (Num 19:1–22)? To teach you that just as the ash of the heifer atones for Israel, so too the death of the righteous atones for Israel.

Rabbi Yudan b. Rabbi Shalom said: Why did the text juxtapose the death of Aaron (Deut 10:6) with the breaking of the tablets (Deut 10:2)? To teach you that the death of the righteous is as difficult for the Holy One as the breaking of the tablets.[24]

The Yerushalmi claims that Miriam provides through her death atonement for Israel. This notion of death providing vicarious atonement certainly has precedents in early Jewish literature.[25] However, in the context specifically of *rabbinic* Jewish literature, the idea has currency only from the time of the Palestinian Talmud (i.e., roughly 400 CE) and later.[26] To be sure, a number of tannaitic passages discuss death as a means of atonement, but in those cases, it is always the atonement of the deceased at stake, never of another.[27] Thus, the passage represents a theological motif that, though not unprecedented in Jewish texts, is new to rabbinic ones.[28]

---

[24] pYom 1:1 (38b). My translation is based on the Venice printing.

[25] See, e.g., 4 Macc 6:28–29, 17:20–22, discussed by Daniel Stöckl Ben Ezra, *The Impact of Yom Kippur on Early Christianity: The Day of Atonement from Second Temple Judaism to the Fifth Century* (Tübingen: Mohr Siebeck, 2003), 116–17. See also the texts cited at Ra'anan Boustan, *From Martyr to Mystic: Rabbinic Martyrology and the Making of Merkavah Mysticism* (Tübingen: Mohr Siebeck, 2005), 157, nn. 24–5. See as well David Frankel, "The Death of Moses as a Sacrifice of Atonement for the Sins of Israel: A Hidden Biblical Tradition," in *The Actuality of Sacrifice: Past and Present*, ed. Alberdina Houtman et al. (Leiden: Brill, 2014), 47–67, who argues that a strand in the Deuteronomic source already has such a notion about the death of Moses.

[26] A number of scholars try to find examples of this theme in tannaitic literature, but each example is problematic. Sanders, Hengel, and Boustan all point, e.g., to *Mekhilta deRabbi Yishmael*, Tractate *Pisha* 1 (E. P. Sanders, *Paul and Palestinian Judaism: A Comparison of Patterns of Religion* [Philadelphia, PA: Fortress, 1977], 191, n. 50; Martin Hengel, *The Atonement: The Origins of the Doctrine in the New Testament*, trans. John Bowden [Philadelphia, PA: Fortress, 1981], 63–4; Boustan, *From Martyr to Mystic*, 158). However, the passage does not suggest that their deaths functioned as expiation but rather that they were willing to die in order to save the people, irrespective of the sinfulness of the people (a point highlighted by the fact that the prophet Jonah serves as the paradigm in that midrash, and it is Jonah—not the other denizens of the boat—who has transgressed!). In any event, Sanders cites this passage as an *exception* to his claim that "vicarious suffering is not a major theme in Tannaitic literature" (*Paul and Palestinian Judaism*, 191, n. 50). Boustan also notes that tannaitic literature generally assumes "measure-for-measure punishment" rather than allowing for vicarious atonement (*From Martyr to Mystic*, 158). Hengel (*The Atonement*, 64) and Boustan (*From Martyr to Mystic*, 158) also both marshal *Sifre Numbers* 131 as an example of vicarious suffering, but that interpretation requires conflating two adjacent *midrashim* that are not necessarily dependent on each other; a simpler reading to my mind is simply that Phineas is rewarded for risking his own life. Hengel (*The Atonement*, 63) points to *Sifre Deuteronomy* 333, but there again, the claim of atonement through another's death is tenuous; that passage seems to suggest death atoning for the martyrs themselves, not necessarily for others. By contrast, death providing atonement for others appears with relative frequency in post-tannaitic texts, especially in the Babylonian Talmud. See Stöckl Ben Ezra, *Impact of Yom Kippur*, 130; and Boustan, *From Martyr to Mystic*, 159–62.

[27] See, e.g., mYom 8:8; tYom (Kippurim) 4:8–9; mSan 6:2. Note that mSan 2:1, while curious in its attribution to those comforting a high priest in morning with the phrase "we are your atonement," does not make any clear claim about the atoning power of death—for the deceased or anyone else.

[28] Already in the first century, Josephus notes the juxtaposition of Miriam's death with the ritual of the red heifer, but he derives from it not a notion of vicarious atonement but rather the narrative-legal point that Moses performed the red heifer ritual following Miriam's death to purify the people

The tradition appears in a variety of post-tannaitic Palestinian works of midrash,[29] as well as the Babylonian Talmud, albeit with some differences in the latter.[30] The relatively widespread appearance of salvific death at this point in rabbinic history at least raises the specter of early Christian notions.[31] We, of course, must be wary of simplistic—and false— bifurcations that label ideas that appear in Christian texts as by definition "intrusions" into some previously "pure" "Judaism." My point is not that the notion of the righteous person's death atoning for Israel is some Christian "influence" on rabbinic texts; to the contrary, this notion appears in a number of places.[32] Rather, I am highlighting that rabbinic interest in the atoning power of the death of the righteous is a prominent theme only in works dating from roughly 400 CE and later, and that one of the earliest attested[33] examples appeals specifically to Miriam.

The Bavli is thus not unique in the rabbinic canon in describing Miriam's death as significant, or in doing so in ways that potentially allude to Christian intertexts. The Bavli is, however, unique in the emphasis it places on that significance. Like the Palestinian Talmud and works of midrash, it describes Miriam's death as atoning. Only the Bavli, however, asserts that the Torah describes her death as *by the mouth of God*,[34] and only in the Babylonian Talmud do we find a claim that Miriam's body was immune to decomposition.[35]

That the Babylonian Talmud would devote special attention to Miriam's death is to some extent unsurprising. Miriam Sherman has demonstrated through statistical analysis that Miriam experiences a startlingly disproportionate amount of midrashic expansion in rabbinic literature relative to other female biblical characters. Moreover, Sherman shows that, while Miriam's prestige rises disproportionately in rabbinic literature generally, her rising star is especially noteworthy in the Babylonian Talmud specifically.[36]

(*Antiquities* 4.6). This post-tannaitic tradition thus introduces this idea to a juxtaposition that earlier Jewish authors had already highlighted.

[29] *Leviticus Rabbah, aharei mot*, par. 20; *Pesikta de Rav Kahana* 26:11 (*aharey mot*); *Midrash Tanhuma* (Buber) *ahare* 10; *Midrash Tanhuma* (Warsaw) *ahare* 7.

[30] bMQ 28a. The difference in the Bavli tradition most likely relevant to my concerns here is that in the Babylonian version, Aaron's death, like Miriam's, serves as evidence for the notion that the death of the righteous brings atonement, rather than, as in the Palestinian tradition, the idea that the death of the righteous is difficult for God. I hope to explore the significance of this difference in a more extensive treatment of these sources in the future.

[31] For scholars who already note the possibly allusive nature of this text to ideas current in contemporary Christian circles, see: Galit Hasan-Rokem, *Web of Life: Folklore and Midrash in Rabbinic Literature*, trans. Batya Stein (Stanford, CA: Stanford University Press, 2000), 125; Boustan, *From Martyr to Mystic*, 162–3 (implicitly); Frankel, "The Death of Moses," 66–7.

[32] See, e.g., Boustan, *From Martyr to Mystic*, 155–64.

[33] By "earliest attested," I mean to express my caution; the Miriam tradition appears in the Yerushalmi, the earliest work in which we find this notion. Of course, it is possible that a tradition appearing in, e.g., Leviticus Rabbah or even the Babylonian Talmud might have earlier roots, despite being attested only in a work redacted later.

[34] Compare David Daube, *The New Testament and Rabbinic Judaism* (London: Athlone, 1956), 7, n. 3, for a cursory claim of a similar, though not identical, development. Daube, however, relies on *Targum pseudo-Jonathan* for evidence of what he views as the earliest tradition, a problematic usage in light of the late redaction of that work.

[35] Though see above, n. 16, regarding the manuscript variants of *Derekh eretz zutah*.

[36] Sherman, "A Well in Search of an Owner." Sherman demonstrates that even when one controls for the different amounts of biblical material found for various women in the Hebrew Bible, and

Sherman in her dissertation, and Avraham Grossman in a brief and far less exhaustive article in Hebrew, both understandably speculated about the possibility that rabbinic discussions of Miriam reflect rabbinic awareness of and interest in Mary the mother of Jesus.[37] The Babylonian rabbinic depiction of Miriam's death is likely an example of such a tradition, formulated in some kind of relationship to the growing production of and interest in Marian Dormition traditions. The Babylonian claim that Miriam's corpse was incorruptible sounds similar to versions of Marian Dormition narratives in which the Virgin ascends to heaven untouched by death. Similarly, the claim that "the angel of death did not exert power of them," alongside the prooftext *by the mouth of God*, implies not immortality but, rather, the direct involvement of God, as opposed to the intermediary angel of death.[38] The image is reminiscent of depictions, both in text and art, of Jesus personally escorting his mother to heaven.[39]

The uptick in rabbinic description of Miriam's death, then, aligns with a similar growth of Christian interest in Mary's. This does not mean that these midrashic elaborations of Miriam's death represent some sort of Christian intrusion into a previously hermetically sealed rabbinic canon. I have already noted that some of these ideas appear in less fully developed form in earlier rabbinic texts. Rather, as Shaul Shaked has so helpfully articulated regarding a different comparative question,

> the new developments, probably stimulated by internal factors and prepared for by a set of indigenous ideas, no less than by the effect of pressure from without, took the direction and character which they did, not by mere accident, but as a result of the fact that the Iranian pattern was at hand and quite well known.[40]

---

even accounting for the tendency of rabbinic literature to expand greatly on biblical details, the Rabbis' creativity in describing Miriam significantly outpaces that regarding any other female character. Though there is certainly more subjectivity involved in determining how much creativity any particular authorship presents with regard to some topic than Sherman seems to admit, the difference in the Babylonian Talmud's treatment of Miriam is so significant that it seems safe to accept, even if one might quibble with any particular interpretation Sherman offers.

[37] Ibid., 328–66; 431–5; Avraham Grossman, "Ben miryam lemaria: ketzad hayyetah miryam lidmut ha'ishah ha'idi'alit besifrut hazal?," in *Tiferet Leyisrael: Jubilee Volume in Honor of Israel Francus*, ed. Joel Roth, Menahem Schmelzer, and Yaakov Francus (New York: Jewish Theological Seminary of America, 2010), 183–94 (Hebrew pagination). For a similar argument regarding medieval rabbinic culture, see Ephraim Shoham-Steiner, "The Virgin Mary, Miriam, and Jewish Reactions to Marian Devotion in the High Middle Ages," *AJS Review* 37 (2013): 75–91.

[38] The phrase cannot mean that these characters did not die, since their deaths are explicitly described in the Hebrew Bible (contra Ishay Rosen-Zvi, *Demonic Desires: "Yetzer Hara" and the Problem of Evil in Late Antiquity* [Philadelphia: University of Pennsylvania, 2011], 184, n. 101), though such an interpretation would make for an even more surprising similarity—to Dormition narratives in which Mary ascends to heaven still alive.

[39] See, e.g., Ally Kateusz, "Ascension of Christ or Ascension of Mary?: Reconsidering a Popular Early Iconography," *JECS* 23 (2015): 273–303.

[40] Shaul Shaked, "Iranian Influence on Judaism: First Century B.C.E. to Second Century C.E.," in *Introduction: the Persian Period*, ed. W. D. Davies and Louis Finkelstein, CHJ 1 (Cambridge: Cambridge University Press, 1984), 309. My thanks to Shana Schick for bringing this elegant articulation of this point to my attention. Shaked's formulation in concise form prefigures Peter Schäfer's more thoroughly worked out theory exploring the interplay of notions already embedded in a tradition and the transformations that result when that tradition participates in a broader contemporary discourse; see Peter Schäfer, *Mirror of His Beauty: Feminine Images of God from the Bible to the Early Kabbalah* (Princeton, NJ: Princeton University Press, 2002).

The increased rabbinic interest in Miriam's death beginning in the year 400 CE, and especially in the rabbinic center in Sasanian Persia, marks this literature as participating in a discourse shared with Christians. Earlier rabbinic texts already reveal a nascent interest in elaborating on the biblical depiction of Miriam's death. But only in post-tannaitic texts, written in the years when interest in the Virgin Mary was on the rise, does this early interest expand in ways that suggest awareness of and, indeed, attraction to those Marian traditions. It may well be, then, that rabbinic literature, and the Babylonian Talmud in particular, is an untapped resource for studying the growth of Marian traditions in late antiquity.

14

Dormition Urtext?: Oldest Dormition Wall Painting Combines the Great Angel and Women with Censers

Ally Kateusz

Introduction

In 2002, a team of conservators working in the church of the Deir al-Surian monastery, about an hour southwest of Cairo, uncovered an extraordinary wall painting. It portrayed Mary, the mother of Jesus, on her deathbed surrounded by women swinging censers. In addition, a Great Angel with brilliant red-tipped wings stands by her. Twelve men sit in the background, as if sleeping. This painting is confidently dated prior to the year 925, making it one of the two very oldest scenes of the Dormition of Mary.[1] The other, a tiny sixth-century pottery token from Palestine, appears to be the same scene, for it also depicts three people at Mary's head, each of whom appears to be wearing a *maphorion*, that is, a woman's cloak with a hood.[2] For the painting, see Figure 14.1.

Art is conservative, that is, art sometimes preserves narrative motifs that are otherwise lost, or nearly lost. It is easier for scribes to excise passages in manuscripts than it is to replace art on the upper levels of church walls such as where this scene was painted. I argue that this painting likely represents a lost Dormition narrative, a source that underlies the three main Dormition textual traditions that survive today.

At the time the wall was painted, the monastery was populated at least in part by Syrian monks, who began arriving around the year 800 and over the next two centuries

---

[1] Karel Innemée and Youhanna Nessim Youssef, "Virgins with Censers: A 10th Century Painting of the Dormition in Deir Al-Surian," *BSAC* 46 (2007): 69–85, esp. 69–70.
[2] For this token, see L. Y. Rahmani, "Eulogia Tokens from Byzantine Bet She'an," *Atiqot* 22 (1993): 109–19, 113–15, fig. 10; note that Rahmani posited that the faces were bearded a decade before this painting was uncovered, yet now the painting demonstrates that it was women with head coverings—an explanation consistent with the photo of the token as well as Rahmani's sketch of it. For more discussion regarding this token, see Ally Kateusz, "Ascension of Christ or Ascension of Mary?: Reconsidering a Popular Early Iconography," *JECS* 23 (2015): 273–303, esp. 295, n. 73. For more dating discussion of the token, see Stephen J. Shoemaker, "The (Re?)Discovery of the Kathisma Church and the Cult of the Virgin in Late Ancient Palestine," *Maria: A Journal of Marian Studies* 2 (2001): 21–72, 45–8.

Figure 14.1 Women swing censers at Mary's deathbed. Wall painting. Dated before 925. Deir al-Surian, Egypt. Photo courtesy of Karel Innemée.

collected a rich library of Syriac manuscripts.³ The top border of the painting is written in Syriac, but the inscriptions are Coptic within its larger composition, a composition that fills the whole wall with the ascension/assumption of Mary, as well as Mary and Jesus seated side by side.⁴

How extraordinary the painting is becomes clear when it is compared to an example of the later iconography of the Dormition of Mary, which depicts Mary surrounded by men. The oldest example of this later iconography is dated to the late tenth century, but it rapidly became popular in both East and West.⁵ See the ivory carving in Figure 14.2, one of the older examples, dated to the tenth and eleventh centuries. The wall painting itself was plastered over around the thirteenth century, approximately the same time that the later iconography was painted in the northern semidome.⁶

In the wall painting, a Great Angel with beautiful red-tipped wings stands in the center of the scene. In the later iconography, as seen on the ivory, Jesus replaces the Great Angel. In the wall painting, women swing censers around Mary. In the ivory, a man swings a censer. Finally, in the painting, six women are around Mary's deathbed and twelve men are seated in the background. No women, however, are on the ivory—only men are around Mary's bed. Each of the three motifs—the Great Angel, the women swinging censers, and the women around Mary—appear in various Dormition manuscripts. Each of these three motifs, however, was redacted in the later Dormition narrative tradition, as well as in its later iconography. The trajectory of this redaction suggests that the Deir al-Surian painting may have a very old Dormition narrative behind it, a narrative with all three of these elements.

The Three Main Dormition Textual Traditions

In his 2002 book about Dormition narratives, Stephen J. Shoemaker discusses the three main Dormition textual traditions.⁷ The first of these is the "Palm of the Tree of Life" tradition, sometimes called the *Liber Requiei*, which in its oldest layer described a "Great Angel" giving Mary a sacred book. The popular homilies attributed to John of Thessalonica, as well as others, replaced the book with a palm branch and say the Great Angel gave Mary a *palm* branch, hence the name, Palm tradition.⁸ Later scribes,

---

³ Karel Innemée, "Dayr al-Suryan: New Discoveries," in *Claremont Coptic Encyclopedia*. Online. Claremont, CA: Claremont Graduate University, 2016, 1–50, 1. http://ccdl.libraries.claremont.edu/cdm/ref/collection/cce/id/2137 (accessed on May 15, 2018).
⁴ Innemée and Youssef, "Virgins with Censers," 70, 72; for the elements of the larger composition, see Innemée, "Dayr al-Suryan," 30–2, figs. 27–9. For more on the iconography of the ascension/assumption of Mary, see Kateusz, "Ascension of Christ or Ascension of Mary?"
⁵ J. Myslivec, "Tod Mariens," in *Lexikon der christlichen Ikonographie IV*, ed. Engelbert Kirschbaum et al. (Rome: Herder, 1972), cols. 333–8.
⁶ Innemée, "Dayr al-Suryan," 34, fig. 33.
⁷ Stephen J. Shoemaker, *Ancient Traditions of the Virgin Mary's Dormition and Assumption* (Oxford: Oxford University Press, 2002), 32, fig. 1; 46, fig. 2; 57, fig. 3. After these three main categories, he designates the few manuscripts that do not fall into one of these three as "atypical," etc.
⁸ John of Thessalonica, *Homily on the Dormition* 3 (Brian E. Daley, trans., *On the Dormition of Mary: Early Patristic Homilies* [Crestwood, NY: St. Vladimir's Seminary, 1998], 57–70, 49).

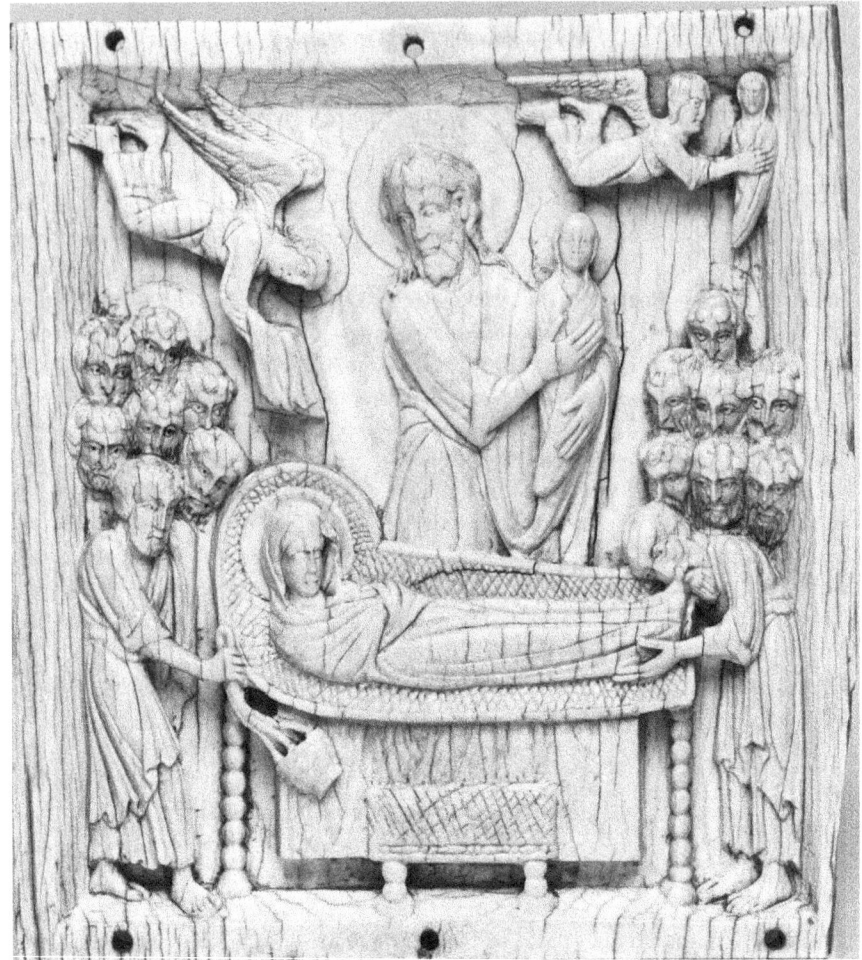

Figure 14.2 Twelve men surround Mary on her deathbed. Peter swings a censer. Tenth- to eleventh-century ivory. Image: The Walters Art Museum, Baltimore. Acquired by Henry Walters, 1926. Accession no. 71.135 (CC0).

apparently concerned about the early Jewish and gnostic motif of Jesus as a Great Angel, often replaced the Great Angel with Jesus, or alternatively harmonized this angel with the canonical angel who spoke to Mary at the Annunciation, "the angel Gabriel."[9] Shoemaker says, "The unmistakable efforts of later redactors to efface the primitive Angel Christology also attest to its antiquity."[10] Shoemaker proposes that an important fifth-century Syriac fragment sometimes called the "Obsequies" is probably

---

[9] Agnes Smith Lewis, ed. and trans., "*Transitus Mariae*," in *Apocrypha Syriaca: The Protevangelium Jacobi and Transitus Mariae* (StSin 11; London: C. J. Clay, 1902), 20.

[10] Shoemaker, *Ancient Traditions*, 215–18, quotation on 217.

the oldest remnant of this tradition; its value, however, is limited because the entire narrative is missing before the handful of folios that preserve the ending, after Mary has already died.[11] Shoemaker proposes that the oldest nearly complete recension of this text tradition is in a fourteenth-/fifteenth-century Ethiopic manuscript; indeed despite how late it is, this manuscript preserves the Great Angel giving Mary a book and telling her to give it to the apostles. It was translated first into Latin by Victor Arras and then by Shoemaker into English. Shoemaker calls it the Ethiopic *Liber Requiei*.[12] Given the confusing nomenclature, I call this text tradition the *Palm* tradition.

Shoemaker's second listed Dormition text tradition is what he calls the "Bethlehem" tradition because it describes Mary going to Bethlehem. Michel van Esbroeck called it the "Bethlehem and Incensing" tradition because of its frequent descriptions of censers, incense, and censing.[13] Most important with respect to the wall painting, its text describes both Mary and women around her with censers. Later scribes often excised these scenes with the result that subsequent recensions usually include fewer and fewer passages of women with censers. The oldest recension of this text tradition is the under script of a fifth-century Old Syriac palimpsest, which is the very oldest nearly complete Dormition manuscript in any of the three text traditions. This manuscript was edited and translated by Agnes Smith Lewis, who published it as the *Transitus Mariae*.[14] It preserves more passages depicting Mary with agency than any other Dormition manuscript, including that Mary raised her arms and led the apostles in prayer,[15] healed with her hands,[16] sprinkled, sealed, exorcised[17]—and preached the gospel, and set out the censer of incense to God.[18] Also of interest since the oldest Palm Dormition text described the Great Angel giving Mary a book of mysteries and telling her to give it to the apostles, the palimpsest text describes Mary giving women evangelists small books, or writings, to take to their home cities around the Mediterranean.[19] I have previously demonstrated the trajectory of scribal redaction with respect to these markers of Mary's liturgical leadership and further demonstrate it in Chapter 7 in this volume.[20] Shoemaker sometimes calls this text tradition the Six Books, so called because the narrator says that the apostles wrote six books; I also often

---

[11] William Wright, "The Obsequies of the Holy Virgin," in *Contributions to the Apocryphal Literature of the New Testament: Collected and Edited from Syriac Manuscripts in the British Museum*, trans. William Wright (London: Williams and Norgate, 1865), 42–51.

[12] Shoemaker, "Ethiopic *Liber Requiei*," in Shoemaker, *Ancient Traditions*, 290–350, 290; and for the Latin, see Victor Arras, *De Transitus Mariae Aethiopice*, vol. 1 (CSCO 342–3; Louvain: Secrétariat du Corpus SCO, 1973).

[13] Michel-Jean van Esbroeck, "Les textes littéraires sur l'Assomption avant le Xe siècle," in *Les actes apocryphes des apôtres*, ed. François Bovon (Publications de la faculté de théologie de l'Université de Genève 4; Geneva: Labor et Fides, 1981), 265–85, 273.

[14] Smith Lewis, "Transitus Mariae," 12–69. Note that Smith Lewis used a second manuscript to fill in lacunae in the palimpsest text, which is distinguished by a smaller font.

[15] Ibid., 32.

[16] Ibid., 34, 35, 48.

[17] Ibid., 34.

[18] Ibid., 46–7.

[19] Ibid., 34.

[20] Ally Kateusz, "Collyridian Déjà Vu: The Trajectory of Redaction of the Markers of Mary's Liturgical Leadership," *JFSR* 29 (2013): 75–92.

call it the Six Books. In this chapter, however, I am going to call this text tradition as van Esbroeck described it: The *Censers* tradition.

The third tradition Shoemaker calls the *Coptic* tradition, which I also call it. Shoemaker's analysis of Coptic Dormition homilies attributed to Evodius of Rome is especially relevant to the iconography of the wall painting.[21] Shoemaker discovered that the oldest layer of the Dormition narrative in the Coptic described only women, no men, at Mary's deathbed. According to the narrator, Jesus had come down from heaven to take his mother back up with him after she died—and Jesus took the men outside, where the men fell asleep. Per the original narrative, which is witnessed in various seams across both Coptic and Palm manuscripts, after Mary died, Salome and Joanna went outside and told Jesus that his mother had died. Jesus then came back inside, while the men remained outside sleeping.[22] The women took care of Mary's body, placed it on her bier, and then the women woke up the men.[23] The wall painting appears to preserve the memory of this scene because the women are with Mary at her deathbed and the men are seated in the background, as if waiting outside, with several men resting their chin on their hand as if asleep. Shoemaker demonstrates that subsequent scribes redacted the women's agency by replacing the women with men. Quite humorously, in some later recensions, the *men* surround Mary's deathbed and the *men* announce to Jesus that his mother has died—*and then the men wake up!*[24]

To recap, thus, between the eighth century and the year 925, a painter painted a wall mural in the Deir al-Surian church that included three of the oldest narrative elements from each of the three main Dormition traditions—elements that later scribes redacted or excised. Almost all later art of the Dormition of Mary also redacted these same elements. Later artists depicted Jesus at Mary's deathbed, not the Great Angel. They depicted men around Mary, not women. They depicted a man swinging the censer, not women.

Redaction Analysis of Passages Depicting Women with Censers

To demonstrate the trajectory of scribal redaction with respect to women using incense and censers, I will provide a redaction analysis of several passages across the text of three

---

[21] Stephen J. Shoemaker, "Gender at the Virgin's Funeral: Men and Women as Witnesses to the Dormition," *StPatr* 34 (2001): 552–8.

[22] Stephen J. Shoemaker, "The Sahidic Coptic Homily on the Dormition of the Virgin Attributed to Evodius of Rome: An Edition from Morgan MSS 596 & 598 with Translation," *AnBoll* 117 (1999): 241–83, 275, specifies on the Savior went in with the women: "And Salome and Joanna came to us and said to the Savior, 'Our Lord and our God, your mother and the mother of us all has died.' Then the Savior arose immediately and went in to the place where she was lying." Shoemaker, "Gender at the Virgin's Funeral," 553, incorrectly states that "Christ re-enters with the apostles."

[23] Shoemaker, "Gender at the Virgin's Funeral," 556; for the text, which is in the oldest Greek Palm manuscript (eleventh century), see Shoemaker, "Earliest Greek Dormition Narrative," in Shoemaker, *Ancient Traditions*, 351–69, 366.

[24] Shoemaker, "Gender at the Virgin's Funeral," 555–6; see also Ethiopic *Liber Requiei* 71 (Shoemaker, "Ethiopic *Liber Requiei*," 326).

published manuscripts in the Censers/Six Books tradition. The first is that of the fifth-century palimpsest, the very oldest nearly complete Dormition manuscript, as detailed above. The second is the second-oldest nearly complete Dormition manuscript so far published, a late sixth-century Syriac manuscript published in 1865 in the *Journal of Sacred Literature and Biblical Record* by William Wright.[25] The third is a late medieval manuscript with an Ethiopic translation translated into Latin by Marius Chaine and into English by Shoemaker, which, despite the age of the manuscript itself, Shoemaker privileges as an old recension.[26]

To demonstrate this scribal redaction, I have selected three detailed passages preserved in the fifth-century palimpsest that portray Mary with a censer and incense. The first passage depicts Mary going to pray at her son's tomb, carrying spices, and throwing incense upon a censer.[27] The second depicts her praying with a censer in front of her. The third describes her preaching the gospel to the Governor of Jerusalem and telling him that after the angel of the Annunciation departed, she set out the censer of incense to God.[28] See Figure 14.3.

As can be seen, the fifth-century palimpsest preserves the most complete text, text redacted differently by each later scribe. In the first passage—the scene of Mary taking the censer and incense to her son's tomb—the scribe behind the medieval Ethiopic translation excised Mary's agency in throwing incense on the censer, and even the censer itself, but preserved the *smell* of incense. The sixth-century scribe, however, excised everything, even the smell.[29] In the second passage, however, the two scribes' excisions were opposite in severity. The sixth-century scribe preserved the scene of Mary praying in front of a censer, while the scribe behind the Ethiopic translation excised it. Both later scribes, however, excised all of the third passage, which included Mary's preaching to the governor of Jerusalem to whom she described setting out the censer of incense to God.[30] The pattern of these excisions demonstrates that indeed the oldest manuscript preserves the most original text. The two later scribes sometimes excised the same passages, but the proof is in the way that sometimes one excised a passage whereas the other did not, and vice versa.

The next chart contains excerpts from a long passage about the women who lived with Mary, women whom she taught, and who served her, including bringing censers and incense to Mary. The text of all three manuscripts includes the last passage, which

---

[25] William Wright, trans., "The Departure of My Lady Mary from This World." *Journal of Sacred Literature and Biblical Record* 7 (1865): 129–60. For its dating, see William Wright, trans., *Contributions to the Apocryphal Literature of the New Testament: Collected and Edited from Syriac Manuscripts in the British Museum* (London: Williams and Norgate, 1865), 8. This manuscript is in the British Library, catalogued as BL, syr. Add. 14 484, f. 16r.–45r.

[26] Stephen J. Shoemaker, "The Ethiopic Six Books," in *Ancient Traditions of the Virgin Mary's Dormition and Assumption* (Oxford: Oxford University Press, 2002), 375–96, and 142–67 for discussion; also Marius Chaine, *Apocrypha de Beata Maria Virgine* (Rome: Karolus de Luigi, 1909), 17–42; this manuscript is Paris BN éthiop. 53, per Mimouni, *Dormition*, 242 n. 13.

[27] Smith Lewis, "Transitus Mariae," 24–5.

[28] Ibid., 46–7.

[29] Ethiopic Six Books 26–7 (Shoemaker, *Ancient Traditions*, 378–9); Wright, "Departure of My Lady Mary," 135–6.

[30] Wright, "Departure of My Lady Mary," 146; Ethiopic Six Books 40 (Shoemaker, *Ancient Traditions*, 389).

5th-c. Syr. palimpsest	6th-c. Syr. ms	Medieval Ethiop. ms
On the Friday Mary had prepared herself to go to the tomb of the Lord, and she was **carrying sweet spices and fire**. And while she was praying and had lifted up her eyes and gazed at heaven, suddenly the doors of heaven were opened and a *scent of myrrh went up*, which **the Lady Mary had thrown on the censer.**	Passage omits all fragrance	On Friday Mary came to pray at the tomb of Golgotha, and as she prayed, she raised her eyes to heaven with the *fragrant perfume of fine incense.*
Now the Lady Mary was standing and praying, the **censer of incense** being placed in her hand.	Now my Lady Mary was standing and praying, and the **censer of incense** was set before her.	omitted
[The governor] said to her: "I desire to learn from thee, Lady."… Mary said: "Hearken and recieve my words [she preaches the gospel]… And after the salutation with which he announced (this) to me, the angel departed from me. **And I arose, and set forth the censer of incense to God.**"	omitted	omitted

Figure 14.3 Redaction analysis: Mary with a censer and incense. Chart comparison of three manuscripts. © Ally Kateusz.

said that on Friday the women brought Mary a censer so that she could pray or make an offering.[31] With one exception, the other passages follow the same pattern as in the previous chart, that is, the two later scribes excised different parts. A passage only in the Ethiopic text, however, demonstrates that an even longer narrative source must

[31] Smith Lewis, "Transitus Mariae," 25; Wright, "Departure of My Lady Mary," 136; and Ethiopic *Six Books* 27 (Shoemaker, *Ancient Traditions*, 379).

be behind all three manuscripts. In this case, the fifth century palimpsest preserves a passage describing that Mary kept special clothing in a chest, but not how she used these clothes[32]—yet the Ethiopic text, while omitting the chest, nonetheless refers to the special clothes and preserves that Mary wore these vestments when she made an offering to God.[33] See Figure 14.4.

The pattern of excisions in these two charts demonstrates that later scribes and copyists apparently had considerable latitude to abbreviate the text before them. The pattern of excisions suggests that scribes cut what they or their masters considered "offensive to pious ears,"[34] or "objectionable,"[35] or "heretical."[36] Such excisions may have been an effort to sanitize a text such as the Dormition narrative, which was read in the church on certain holy days of the year.

Women with Censers in the Dormition Narrative

The Dormition text of the fifth-century palimpsest, as well as of the sixth-century Old Syriac and medieval Ethiopic manuscripts, depicted women taking censers and incense to Mary while she was alive, but did not depict women with censers at her deathbed, as seen in the wall painting. A Coptic homily attributed to Theodosius of Alexandria, however, does preserve women with censers around Mary's deathbed. According to this homily, Mary had a dream in which her son told her that she was going to die, and when she woke up and told the people around her about the dream, they began to weep. Then came a knocking on the door. When they opened the door, "There came in many virgins from the mount of Olives, having choice censers and lamps."[37]

The medieval Ethiopic Palm manuscript that describes the women around Mary's deathbed also suggests that the narrative originally included the women carrying censers, for it preserves that a wondrous smell came around Mary on her deathbed—"a sweet, pleasant smell, like the odour of Paradise"[38]—and everyone fell asleep, except for the women. The oldest Greek Palm narrative preserves a similar passage. It says there was "a sweet-smelling fragrance so that everyone was driven off to sleep by the exceedingly sweet smell, except for only the three virgins ... The three virgins attended to Mary's body and placed it on a bier. After that they woke up the apostles."[39]

---

[32] Smith Lewis, "Transitus Mariae," 24.
[33] Ethiopic *Six Books* 26–7 (Shoemaker, *Ancient Traditions*, 378–9, quotation on 379).
[34] Bruce Metzger, *The Text of the New Testament: Its Transmission, Corruption, and Restoration* (New York: Oxford University Press, 1968), 120.
[35] Eldon J. Epp and Gordon D. Fee, *Studies in the Theory and Method of New Testament Textual Criticism* (Grand Rapids, MI: Eerdmans, 1993), 14.
[36] François Bovon and Christopher R. Matthews, eds. and trans., *The Acts of Philip: A New Translation* (Waco, TX: Baylor University Press, 2012), 8.
[37] Theodosius of Alexandria, *Discourse on the Falling Asleep of Mary* 3 (Forbes Robinson, trans., *Coptic Apocryphal Gospels* [Cambridge: Cambridge University Press, 1896], 90–127, quotation on 99).
[38] Ethiopic *Liber Requiei* 66 (Shoemaker, "Ethiopic *Liber Requiei*," in *Ancient Traditions*, 290–350, 325).
[39] Greek *Liber Requiei* 33, 37 (Shoemaker, *Ancient Traditions*, 351–69, 364, 366).

5th-c. Syr. palimpsest	6th-c. Syr. ms	Medieval Ethiop. ms
These virgins were with the Lady Mary night and day, that they might minister unto her, and **bring to her the censer of sweet spices.**	omitted	omitted
Mary told them everything; and they spread her couch and washed her feet, and folded her garments, and **arranged sweet spices.**	omitted	She told them everything that they wanted to be taught by her. … And they washed her feet and **made her clothes fragrant with incense.**
And she opened a chest and **they took out her garments and the censer,** and put everything in order.	omitted	omitted
omitted	omitted	The blessed Mary summoned the virgin women and said to them, "**Bring incense and clothing so that I may make an offering to God."**
And on the Friday the Blessed one was distressed, and said to them: "**Bring nigh unto me the censers of incense, for I wish to pray"** … and **these vigins brought nigh unto her the censers.**	And on the Friday my Lady Mary was distressed, and said to them: "**Bring nigh unto me the censer of incense, for I wish to pray"** … and **they brought nigh unto her the censer of incense.**	And on Friday at dawn, Mary became ill, and she said to the virgins, "**Bring me a censer, because I want to make an offering"** … and **they brought her one, and she placed incense in the censer.**

Figure 14.4 Redaction analysis: Women with censers and incense. Chart comparison of three manuscripts. © Ally Kateusz.

Thus, using three different text traditions, we can assemble fragments of the underlying source narrative that described women with censers around Mary on her deathbed. The Censers tradition preserves women bringing censers and incense to Mary but not to her deathbed. The Coptic preserves women with censers arriving at Mary's deathbed. The Palm retains the sweet scent at Mary's deathbed and that the women were awake while the men slept.

Historicity of Women with Censers

Is there a kernel of historicity about early Christian women's liturgical use of censers and incense that is evinced by the wall painting and its underlying narrative? The mere fact that the women with censers were replaced in both art and narrative suggests that something about the scene later became a concern. Did this later concern correspond to a change in women's liturgical roles? Below I will provide evidence that suggests women in the early Christian era had a role associated with censers and incense, a liturgical role that later became restricted to men.

The origin of liturgical censing in Christian churches is not well understood.[40] Yet the North African theologian Tertullian (ca. 155–240) was the first to record that Christians used incense in their funerals; he claimed that as much incense was used "in the burying of Christians as in the fumigating of the gods."[41] Given that in Mediterranean cultures women had the primary role for preparing and lamenting the dead, it seems likely that Christian women were doing this censing. It thus would be consistent for an author of the Dormition narrative to describe women with censers around Mary's deathbed—just as the painting illustrates and just as the Coptic Dormition homily ascribed to Theodosius of Alexandria describes. The cultural tradition of women censing the dead could also account for the narrative tradition that described Mary taking censer and incense to her son's tomb.

In the early Christian era, chapels and basilicas were often built over the tomb or relics of a holy person, most famously the Anastasis over Christ's tomb and Old Saint Peter's over Peter's bones.[42] It seems possible that the liturgical censing that Christian women performed for the dead may have moved inside along with these saintly relics. Although later church practice might lead us to suppose that women never used censers liturgically, ancient narrative and art indicate that the practice was both very early, and also, later suppressed.

In Orthodox and Catholic churches today, women generally are not permitted to use the censers. Regardless of the modern practice, the late ninth-/early tenth-century *typikon* for the Easter Week liturgies in Jerusalem, which likely was taken from an older liturgical model, specified that women censed the holy sepulcher, that is, women censed the tomb of Christ in the Anastasis, the fourth-century rotunda church also called the Church of the Holy Sepulcher.[43] The iconography on a sixth-century pyx suggests that women had clerical roles associated with censing in the Anastasis centuries earlier.

The ivory sculptor carved two women with censers approaching the altar and also three arms-raised women around the back of the pyx as part of a liturgical procession

---

[40] Susan Ashbrook Harvey, *Scenting Salvation: Ancient Christianity and the Olfactory Imagination* (Berkeley: University of California Press, 2006), 11–90.
[41] Tertullian, *Apology* 42 (*ANF* 3:49).
[42] André Grabar, *Martyrium, recherches sur le culte des reliques et l'art chrétien antique*, 2 vols. (Paris: Collège de France, 1946), esp. 1:293–313, 400–10.
[43] For discussion, see Allie M. Ernst, *Martha from the Margins: The Authority of Martha in the Early Christian Tradition* (VS Supplements 98; Leiden: Brill, 2009), 152–8; and Valerie A. Karras, "The Liturgical Functions of Consecrated Women in the Byzantine Church." *Theological Studies* 66 (2005): 96–116, 109–15.

to the altar; in Christian iconography, the arms-raised pose is a liturgical pose.[44] The ivory pyx is as old as any art depicting a Christian man with a censer, and it is the oldest to depict anyone, man or woman, with a censer at a Christian altar[45]—and it depicts two women at the altar and a liturgical procession with only women participants. For several reasons, the altar on this sixth-century ivory pyx is thought to represent the altar in the Anastasis, not the least of which is that the round shape of the pyx suggests the Anastasis rotunda.[46] This identification is also due in part to the many sixth-century artifacts that depicted two Marys, one swinging a censer, walking toward what scholars agree depicted the Anastasis shrine over Jesus' tomb.[47] For the round ivory pyx, see Figures 14.5a and b.

This sixth-century liturgical procession led by women with censers lends credibility to a report that in the early fifth century, women with censers led another procession—the joyous procession that took place after the Council of Ephesus in 431 affirmed the title of Theotokos for Mary.[48] It also evokes a second report from 312, when Eusebius of Caesarea described the dreamlike consecration of a church in Tyre with a ritual that similarly included incense and raised hands at the altar.[49] In any case, Tyre is about a hundred miles from Jerusalem, and given the ivory pyx, it seems quite possible that the ritual involving censers and raised hands at the altar for the consecration of the Tyre church may have been performed by women.

The pilgrim Egeria's diary of her travels to Jerusalem in 381 is the oldest surviving definite report of incense used in the liturgy[50]—and Egeria described the Sunday morning service at the Anastasis, the same church apparently sculpted on the pyx. Egeria said on Sunday mornings the Anastasis rotunda was as crowded with people as it was at Easter. She wrote that the presbyters and deacons recited psalms and prayers, and that afterward "they take censers into the cave of the Anastasis, so that the whole Anastasis basilica is filled with the smell."[51]

---

[44] Alexi Lidov, "The Priesthood of the Virgin Mary as an Image-Paradigm of Christian Visual Culture," *IKON* 10 (2017): 9–26, esp. 10.

[45] See Princeton's Index of Christian Art for a review of the oldest dated artifacts; see another woman depicted with a censer in mosaics dated 539–540 in the Qasr el Lebya church.

[46] For discussion, see Archer St. Clair, "The Visit to the Tomb: Narrative and Liturgy on Three Early Christian Pyxides," *Gesta* 18 (1979): 127–35, 129–31, figs. 7 and 8; and Goldschmidt, who argues it is the Anastasis altar, in part from the sixth-century Piacenza pilgrim's description that it was carved from the stone that had sealed the cave, in A. Goldschmidt, "Mittelstüke fünfteiliger Elfenbeintafeln des V–VI Jahrhunderts," *Jahrbuch fur Kunstwissenschaft* (1923): 30–3, esp. 33. Also see Kurt Weitzmann, *Age of Spirituality: Late Antique and Early Christian Art, Third to Seventh Century: Catalogue of the Exhibition at the Metropolitan Museum of Art, November 19, 1977, through February 12, 1978* (New York: Metropolitan Museum of Art, 1979), 581, fig. 520, who curiously argues it might be the altar in some other nearby church.

[47] See André Grabar, *Les ampoules de Terre Sainte (Monza - Bobbio)* (Paris: C. Klincksieck, 1958), plates 9, 11–13, 16, 18, 26, 28, and 47; Martin Biddle, *The Tomb of Christ* (Thrupp, UK: Sutton, 1999), figs. 17–19 and 26; and St. Clair, "Visit to the Tomb," figs. 1 and 4.

[48] John I. McEnerney, *St. Cyril of Alexandria: Letters 1–50* (Washington, DC: Catholic University of America, 1987), 107.

[49] Eusebius, *Ecclesiastical History* 10 4.68.

[50] Harvey, *Scenting Salvation*, 77.

[51] *Diary of Egeria* 24.8–10 (John Wilkinson, trans., *Egeria's Travels*, 3rd ed. [Oxford: Oxbow Books, 1999], 144).

Figure 14.5a Women with censers at the Anastasis altar. Ivory pyx dated 500s. Metropolitan Museum of Art, New York City. Gift of J. Pierpont Morgan, 1917. Accession no. 17.190.57a, b (CC0).

Figure 14.5b Women in liturgical procession to the Anastasis altar (back of pyx).

Could Egeria have been describing a liturgical ritual such as depicted in the *typikon* and on the censer? Mid-fourth-century funerary epigraphs from near Jerusalem attest that female deacons were active in churches near Jerusalem when Egeria was there.[52] In addition, women deacons then may have had roles even more important than female "deacons" today, because the third- or fourth-century Syriac *Didascalia apostolorum*, which itself was compiled from even older sources, paired a male deacon and a female deacon, and ranked them above presbyters. The *Didascalia* stated that the male deacon was the type of the Christ and the female deacon the type of the Holy Spirit—whom fourth-century and earlier scribes in Ancient Syria described as feminine-gendered and mother[53]—and then listed *presbyters* as the type of the apostles.[54] Women deacons thus appear potentially to have had very important roles in the Jerusalem Church while Egeria was there.

Yet if Egeria saw women clergy censing, such as sculpted on the pyx, her diary does not specifically reflect that women participated in the ritual. Three reasons could explain this seeming omission. First, a later copyist could have excised Egeria's mention of women clergy censing in order to make her account harmonize with later practice. The above two charts witnesses this trajectory of redaction with respect to women with censers, and even modern editors have been known to conceal the presence of female deacons. For example, Hans Förster recently documented that a feminine title for people in a procession in the White Monastery was translated in 1958 as people "who refrain from the use of women" when it actually means "women serving as deacons."[55] Second, in the East, the masculine-gendered *diakonos* was used for both female and male deacons through the tenth century;[56] thus, we cannot assume that in the fourth century, Egeria would have grammatically distinguished male and female deacons like we do today. Third, and most interesting of all, Egeria may not have mentioned women clergy at the Anastasis because it was nothing new. In addition to the ivory pyx, which portrays women at the altar, according to John Wilkinson, Egeria wrote as if she herself sometimes took part in making the Offering, that is, the second part of the Eucharist.[57] While in some cases Egeria wrote, "The presbyters made the Offering there at our request"[58]—in other cases, such as at a church with a stone altar where she believed

---

[52] Aimé Georges Martimort, *Deaconesses: An Historical Study*, trans. K. D. Whitehead (San Francisco, CA: Ignatius, 1986), 35–58; Ute E. Eisen, *Women Officeholders in Early Christianity: Epigraphical and Literary Studies*, trans. Linda M. Maloney (Collegeville, MN: Liturgical, 2000), 158–62, esp. 160.

[53] For Holy Spirit as feminine gendered, see Sebastian Brock, *Holy Spirit in the Syrian Baptismal Tradition* (The Syrian Churches 9, enlarged 2nd ed.; Pune, India: Anita Printers, 1998), 19–26; Susan Ashbrook Harvey, "Feminine Imagery for the Divine: The Holy Spirit, the Odes of Solomon, and Early Syriac Tradition," *SVTQ* 37 (1993): 111–39, 111–22; Robert Murray, *Symbols of Church and Kingdom: A Study in Early Syriac Tradition*, rev. ed. (Piscataway, NJ: Gorgias, 2004), 312–20; and Ally Kateusz, *Finding Holy Spirit Mother* (Holt, MO: Divine Balance, 2014).

[54] Syriac *Didascalia apostolorum* 9 (Alistair Stewart-Sykes, trans., *The Didascalia apostolorum: An English Version with Introduction and Annotation* [Turnhout: Brepols, 2009], 150–1).

[55] Förster, Hans, "'Sich des Gebrauchs der Frauen enthalten': Eine Anfrage an die grammatikalische Struktur einer Interzession für Verstorbene im Grossen Euchologion aus dem Weissen Kloster," *ZAC / JAC* 9 (2006): 584–91.

[56] Valerie A. Karras, "Female Deacons in the Byzantine Church," *Church History* 73 (2004): 272–316, 280.

[57] Wilkinson, *Egeria's Travels*, 57 and 110, n. 1.

[58] *Diary of Egeria* 4.8 (Wilkinson, *Egeria's Travels*, 112).

Elijah had offered sacrifice, she instead wrote for the second Eucharist of Sunday, "We made the Offering there."[59] Wilkinson notes that in those instances, Egeria did not mention *receiving* communion, and he concludes, "Egeria seems to think that her presence at the Eucharist means that she is taking part in the sacrifice."[60]

Further affirming that indeed Egeria may have been accustomed to taking part in the sacrifice, the two oldest artifacts to depict Christians in the liturgy in a real church portray women and men in parallel flanking the altar.[61] These two artifacts, both discovered in the twentieth century, are usually dated to the decades around 430, approximately fifty years after Egeria was in Jerusalem. One, an ivory reliquary box dug up in Croatia, depicts the sanctuary in Old Saint Peter's Basilica (Figure 14.6).[62] The other, a huge sarcophagus front dug up in Istanbul, depicts the sanctuary in the second Hagia Sophia (Figure 14.7).[63] Art historians agree that both artifacts portray men and women with their arms raised flanking the ciborium over the altar.

The ciborium on the ivory reliquary box is of particular interest because it is not square but in the shape of a trapezoid, or half-hexagon, as is the shape of the ciborium over the altar sculpted on the ivory pyx. Galit Noga-Banai argues that during the Christianization of Rome, architects in the city of Rome used visual motifs from Jerusalem, so the half-hexagon ciborium over Peter's tomb in Old Saint Peter's may have been constructed to mirror the ciborium over Christ's tomb in the Anastasis.[64] Old Saint Peter's was built around a second-century shrine composed of an approximately 8-foot by 8-foot wall embedded with a stone mensa, which subsequent excavations beneath the high altar of the modern Saint Peter's Basilica conclusively demonstrated was the same seen under the ciborium on the ivory; for example, Vatican excavator Englebert Kirschbaum said the ivory scene was "so striking even in its details as to confirm conclusively its interpretation as the Constantinian apse in Saint Peter's."[65] Even an arched niche behind the mensa on the second-century shrine matched the arched niche behind the table on the ivory. In addition to the arms-raised women and men flanking the ciborium, almost all art historians identify a veiled woman (right) and a man (left) facing each other across the stone tabletop.[66]

---

[59] *Diary of Egeria* 4.3–4, 4.8 (Wilkinson, *Egeria's Travels*, 111), also 111 n. 4.

[60] Wilkinson, *Egeria's Travels*, 57.

[61] For more detail on these two artifacts, as well as others both literary and iconographic, see Ally Kateusz, "'She Sacrificed Herself as the Priest': Early Christian Female and Male Co-Priests," *JFSR* 33 (2017), 45–67, esp. 51–66.

[62] Ibid., 56–63.

[63] Ibid., 54–6.

[64] Galit Noga-Banai, *Sacred Stimulus: Jerusalem in the Visual Christianization of Rome* (Oxford: Oxford University Press, 2018), esp. 129–71.

[65] Engelbert Kirschbaum, *The Tombs of St. Peter and St. Paul*, trans. John Murray (New York: St. Martin's, 1959), 60.

[66] Kateusz, "'She Sacrificed Herself as the Priest,'" 63; Fabrizio Bisconti, "La Capsella di Samagher: Il quadro delle interpretazioni," *Il cristianesimo in Istria fra tarda antichità e alto Medioevo* (2009): 217–31, esp. 230–1; Davide Longhi, *La capsella eburnea di Samagher: iconografia e committenza* (Ravenna: Girasole, 2006), 109–12; Margherita Guarducci, *La capsella eburnea di Samagher: un cimelio di arte paleocristiana nella storia del tardo impero* (Trieste: Società istriana di archeologia, 1978), 126–7; Carlo Cecchelli, *La vita di Roma nel Medioevo, volume 1: Le arti minori e il costume* (Rome: Palandi, 1951–2), 208; Giuseppe Wilpert, "Le due più antiche rappresentazioni della Adoratio Crucis," *Atti della Pontificia Accademia romana di archeologia*, series 3, memorie 2 (1928): 135–55, esp. 148; Henri

Figure 14.6 Pola ivory reliquary box carved with a liturgical scene depicting the sanctuary of Old Saint Peter's Basilica in Rome, ca. 430s. Men and women flank the mensa in parallel. Museo Archeologico, Venice. © Alinari Archives-Alinari Archive, Florence.

Figure 14.7 Sarcophagus front with liturgical scene in the second Hagia Sophia, Constantinople, ca. 430s. Man and woman on opposite sides of the altar. Photo courtesy of Ally Kateusz and Archeological Museum of Istanbul.

With respect to the sarcophagus front, Johannes Deckers and Ümit Serdaroğlu, who excavated it, concluded from the design of its column capitals that it represented the sanctuary of the second Hagia Sophia, which had the same type of capitals.[67] The man and woman flanking the ciborium over the altar with its early Christian cross appear to affirm the historicity of a report in the *Letter of Cosmas*, which said that Princess Pulcheria—who at the age of 14 was made regent for her 7-year-old younger brother, Theodosius II—was accustomed to standing in the holy of holies of the second Hagia Sophia with her younger brother. According to this letter, the new Patriarch of Constantinople, Nestorius, stopped Pulcheria from entering the Holy of Holies, saying only priests could enter—at which for her justification, Pulcheria invoked Mary, the Theotokos.[68] Three years later, the Council of Ephesus in 431 affirmed the title of Theotokos for Mary and exiled Nestorius, after which presumably Pulcheria resumed her custom—a custom that appears to have continued in Constantinople, if mosaics installed a century later in the holy of holies of San Vitale in Ravenna are any indication. On the left of the altar, these mosaics depict Emperor Justinian holding the gold paten for the bread, and on the right, Empress Theodora holding the gold chalice for the wine.[69] The image of Theodora holding the chalice with both hands resonates with the image of the woman sculpted at the mensa tabletop in Old Saint Peter's, whom various art historians have suggested is lifting some kind of container with both hands.[70]

In short, both of these artifacts appear to validate Wilkinson's conclusion that Egeria thought she was taking part in the sacrifice, because they depict women flanking altar tables along with men, suggesting that during this early era, women, as well as men, took part.[71] Thus, the depictions of women using censers in the Dormition narratives appear to be consistent with what we know about the origins of the liturgical use of censers in the church, as well the role of women in the liturgy during the early Christian era. This evidence includes both contemporary accounts, such as that of

---

Leclercq, "Pola," in *Dictionnaire d'archéologie chrétienne et de liturgie*, vol. 14, part 1, ed. Fernand Cabrol and Henri Leclercq (Paris: Letouzey et Ané, 1939), cols. 1342–46, esp. 1345; Alexander CoburnSoper, "The Italo-Gallic School of Early Christian Art," *Art Bulletin* 202 (1938): 145–92, esp. 157; Pericle Ducati, *L'arte in Roma dalle origini al sec. VIII* (Bologna: Cappelli, 1938), 380; Pietro Toesca, *Storia dell'arte italiana*, vol. I (Turin: Unione, 1927), 322; Anton Gnirs, "La basilica ed il reliquiario d'avorio di Samagher presso Pola," *Atti e memorie della società istriana di archeologia e storia patria* 24 (1908): 5–48, esp. 34, 36–7, fig. 28.

[67] Johannes G. Deckers and Ümit Serdaroğlu, "Das Hypogäum beim Silivri-Kapi in Istanbul," *Jahrbuck für Antike und Christentum* 36 (1993): 140–63, 161.

[68] *Letter to Cosmas* 6 (François Nau, trans., *Histoire de Nestorius d'après la lettre à Cosme et l'Hymne de Sliba de Mansourya sur les docteurs grecs* [Patrologia Orientalis 13; Paris: Firmin-Didot, 1916], 275–86, esp. 279).

[69] Otto G. von Simson, *Sacred Fortress: Byzantine Art and Statecraft in Ravenna* (Princeton, NJ: Princeton University Press, 1987), 23–39, esp. 30–1, regarding Theodora's image in the holy of holies, and see plates 2–4 and 10 for Justinian, and plates 4, 10, 18, and 19 for Theodora.

[70] Longhi, *Capsella eburnea*, 100; Anna Angiolini, *La capsella eburnea di Pola* (Bologna: Pàtron, 1970), 29; Tilmann Buddensieg, "Le coffret en ivoire de Pola: Saint-Pierre et le Latran," *Cahiers archéologiques* 10 (1959): 157–95, 163; and Jelena Bogdanović, *The Framing of Sacred Space: The Canopy and the Byzantine Church* (New York: Oxford University Press, 2017), 185, although note she sees a Roman priest (masc.) wearing a veil.

[71] For more argument regarding the eucharistic role of women, including literary references from the second to the eighth centuries that described women and men officiating in the eucharistic ritual, see Kateusz, "'She Sacrificed Herself as the Priest,'" esp. 45–51.

Tertullian and Egeria, as well as the portrayal of women with censers at the Anastasis altar, plus the artifacts that depict women flanking the altar table in parallel with men at other important basilicas. Later scribes redacted passages that depicted women with censers, and later artists replaced women with men in iconography, most clearly in the iconography of the Dormition of Mary. This censorship, along with the other evidence, strongly suggests that there is more than just a kernel of historicity behind these early depictions of women using censers liturgically. Depictions of women using censers in the Dormition narrative appear to have corresponded to women's roles in the early church. Later scribes and artists harmonized their texts and art with later practice which restricted the liturgical use of censers to men.

In conclusion, all three elements of the Deir al-Surian wall painting of the Dormition of Mary are found across two or more of the Dormition text traditions. Shoemaker demonstrated that the original source depicted women as the active agents at Mary's deathbed, passages most fully preserved in the Coptic but also seen in bits and pieces in the Palm tradition. The Censers tradition preserves more markers of female liturgical authority than any other tradition, but the element of women carrying censers to Mary's deathbed appears to be preserved primarily in the Coptic, most prominently the homily of Theodosius of Alexandria. The text of the fifth-century palimpsest in the Censers tradition, however, preserves several other passages that depicted women bringing censers to Mary while she was alive, and the Palm tradition preserves the sweet scent of incense at Mary's deathbed, as well as the women there. Finally, the Jewish and gnostic element of the Great Angel is preserved only in a few manuscripts in the Palm tradition, because most scribes either replaced the Great Angel with Jesus (Palm and Coptic) or gave this angel the canonical name of Gabriel (Censers). All of the three main later Dormition text traditions, thus, preserve different narrative elements seen in the Deir al-Surian wall painting.

The presence of highly redacted narrative elements across multiple later manuscripts in all three Dormition text traditions strongly suggests that the iconography preserved in the remarkable Deir al-Surian wall painting, as well as in the tiny sixth-century Palestinian pottery token, preserves a scene in a Dormition source narrative. This scene portrayed Jesus as the Great Angel, the women liturgically censing Mary on her deathbed, and the men sleeping outside. It seems quite likely that the source narrative also contained other passages with narrative elements that survive only in bits and pieces across surviving manuscripts.

15

Mary in the Qur'an and Extracanonical Christian Texts

Deborah Niederer Saxon

Despite the privileging of males in the contexts from which these writings emerged, the ancient texts of both Christians and Muslims accord special status to Mary (*Maryam* in Arabic), the mother of Jesus. The NT mentions her by name nineteen times, and the Qur'an does so thirty-four times.[1] Chapter 19 from the Qur'an is even titled "Maryam." References to Mary in the Qur'an emphasize her strength of character and her active engagement with the divine and those around her. Simultaneously, however, the Qur'an depicts the vulnerability of Mary in the context of a patriarchal society. Interestingly, these Muslim portrayals of Mary evoke similar representations in Christian texts from the early centuries of the Common Era that also reflect patriarchal norms.

This chapter examines the role of Mary at four major moments in these texts: when she is a young child who is dedicated to and grows up in the Jewish temple in Jerusalem, when she receives the message (or Annunciation) that she will become the mother of Jesus, when she gives birth to Jesus, and when she serves as a leader near the end of or just after Jesus' life on earth. The chapter then uses these references as a starting point to explore the idea that Mary can be considered a prophet in both traditions despite considerable reluctance to categorize her in this way in either. It also probes the deeper significance of her spiritual role for certain distinguished medieval scholars and mystics of Andalusia and juxtaposes their reflections with the depictions of Mary that emerge in extracanonical Christian texts that have resurfaced from the desert sands of Egypt only in the last century. The paper then considers the implications of these varied, often marginalized perspectives for our contemporary context.

Both the NT and the Qur'an include narratives of the Annunciation and the Nativity.[2] While Mary is already a teenager by the time we meet her in the NT, the Qur'an

---

[1] Mary is the only woman referred to by name in the Qur'an, and its references to her by name constitute fewer than half of the total number of times it refers to her, as sometimes only an identifying phrase is used. See Miri Rubin, *Mother of God: A History of the Virgin Mary* (New Haven, CT: Yale University Press, 2009), 83; Jane I. Smith and Yvonne Y. Haddad, "The Virgin Mary in Islamic Tradition and Commentary," *MW* 79 (1989): 161–87, esp. 162; Barbara Freyer Stowasser, *Women in the Qur'an, Traditions, and Interpretation* (New York: Oxford University Press, 1994), 67, 69.

[2] See Luke 1:26–38; 2:6–7; Matt 1:18–25 for the NT passages. The Qur'anic passages are cited below.

includes a narrative about her early life that emphasizes her special role, something that it holds in common with a Christian extracanonical text, the *Protevangelium of James*.³ In chapter 3 of the Qur'an, Mary's mother dedicates her to the Lord even before Mary is born: "My Lord! I vowed to **You** what is in my womb—that which is dedicated—so receive **You** this from me (Q 3:35).⁴ After giving birth, Mary's mother says, "I commend her to Your protection (Q3:36).⁵ Likewise, in the *Protevangelium*, when "a messenger of the Lord" tells Mary's mother Anna that she will bear a child (4.1–2),⁶ Anna promises to dedicate her child to God. According to the Qur'an, as Mary grows up in the temple under the care of Zechariah, the text carefully notes that the Lord accepts her graciously and even provides sustenance for her when she is alone in the sanctuary:

> So her Lord received her with the very best acceptance. And her bringing forth caused the very best to develop in her. And Zechariah took charge of her. Whenever Zechariah entered upon her in her sanctuary, he found her with provision. (Q3:37)⁷

When Zechariah questions Mary about this, she is not afraid to speak up and firmly tells him that it comes from God (Q3:37).⁸

The *Protevangelium of James* provides a striking parallel to this narrative, beautifully describing Mary's dedication to the temple at the age of 3:

> The priest welcomed her, kissed her, and blessed her: The Lord God has exalted your name among all generations. In you the Lord will disclose his redemption to the people of Israel during the last days. And he sat her down on the third step of the altar, and the Lord showered favor on her. And she danced, and the whole house of Israel loved her. (7.7–10)⁹

This text also indicates her receiving special provision: "She was fed there like a dove, receiving her food from the hand of a heavenly messenger" (8.2).¹⁰

---

³ Schliefer notes that the Qur'an does not claim to be

> a chronicle, and for this reason we should not expect to find in it a detailed biography of any of the great historical and prophetic figures it mentions. Muslim scholars have characteristically analyzed not the detailed facts of her life, but the 'meaning of Mary', as this indeed seems to be the focus of the texts given in the Qur'an. (Aliah Schliefer, *Mary: The Blessed Virgin of Islam* [Louisville, KY: Fons Vitae, 1997], 21)

On p. 22, Schliefer continues, "As for the stories which may be classed simply as fictional, these are valuable not as sources of fact, but as further illustrations of the Marian idea in traditional Islam; in other words, they serve the same purpose as a novel or a poem which intensifies meaning and animates its heroes and heroines."

⁴ Laleh Bakhtiar, *The Sublime Quran: English Translation: Revised Edition* (Chicago, IL: Kazi, 2012), 49.
⁵ Ibid.
⁶ Ronald F. Hock, *The Infancy Gospels of James and Thomas* (Santa Rosa, CA: Polebridge, 1995), 37.
⁷ Bakhtiar, *Sublime Quran*, 49.
⁸ Ibid.
⁹ Hock, *Infancy Gospels*, 45.
¹⁰ Hock, *Infancy Gospels*, 47. For further discussion the variety of ways the *Protevangelium* was circulating in Coptic- and Arabic-speaking Christian contexts—in liturgies, homilies, historical

The next significant moment in Mary's life is the Annunciation. In addition to the well-known scene in Luke (1:26–38), the *Protevangelium* describes Mary's being visited by a "heavenly messenger" (11.5)[11] who tells her that "you've found favor in the sight of the Lord of all. You will conceive by means of his word (11.5).[12] He goes on to say that "the power of God will overshadow you. Therefore, the child to be born will be called holy, son of the Most High" (11.7).[13] In the Qur'an, the text describes Mary as receiving "good tidings of a Word from Him" and then states, "His name is the Messiah—Jesus Son of Mary—well-esteemed in the present and in the world to come and among the ones that are brought near" (Q3:45).[14] In the Maryam Sura, the Annunciation is explained in this way:

> And remember Mary in the Book when she went
> apart from her people to an eastern place.
> Then, she took to herself a partition away from them,
> so we sent Our Spirit to her and he presented him-
> self before her as a mortal without fault.
> She said: Truly, I take refuge in The Merciful from
> **you**; *come not near me* if you had been devout.
> He said: I am only a messenger from **your** Lord
> that I bestow on **you** (f) a pure boy.
> She said: How will I have a boy when no mortal
> touches me, nor am I an unchaste woman?
> He said: Thus, *it will be.* **Your** Lord said: It *is* for
> Me insignificant. And: We will assign him as a sign
> for humanity and as a mercy from Us.
> And it had been that which is a decreed command.
> So she conceived him and she went apart with him to
> a farther place. (19.16–22)[15]

Notice that Mary does not accept these pronouncements passively. In fact, she rather assertively questions how this can be. In Luke 1:34, she says, "How can this be, since I have never been with a man?"[16] Similarly, in the *Protevangelium*, the text reads, "But as she listened, Mary was doubtful and said, 'If I actually conceive by the Lord, the

---

accounts, art, and oral traditions, see Cornelia Horn, "Mary between Bible and Qur'an: Soundings into the Transmission and Reception History of the *Protevangelium of James* on the Basis of Selected Literary Sources in Coptic and Copto-Arabic and of Art-Historical Evidence Pertaining to Egypt," ICMR 18 (2007): 509–38. Horn carefully notes that there were "permeable boundaries" (510) between Muslim and Christian communities that allowed for Islamic tradition to interpret the figure of Mary—that literary traditions were "not merely transferred" (511) but, rather, that there was "active exchange" (510) between the two communities.

[11] Hock, *Infancy Gospels*, 53.
[12] Ibid.
[13] Ibid.
[14] Bakhtiar, *Sublime Quran*, 50.
[15] Ibid., 286–7.
[16] The translation comes from Priests for Equality (Organization), *The Inclusive Bible: The First Egalitarian Translation* (Lanham, MD: Rowman & Littlefield, 2009), 677.

living God, will I also give birth the way women usually do?" (12.6).[17] In the Qur'an, she commands the messenger to keep his distance and voices her skepticism clearly while simultaneously declaring that she is not unchaste.

Others through the centuries have wrestled with the same question. The Qur'an explains her becoming pregnant in this way: "And she who guarded her private parts, then, We *breathed* into her Our Spirit and We made her and her son a sign for the worlds" (emphasis added) (Q21:91).[18] In Q66:12, the text states this again: "And Mary, the daughter of Imran (Aaron), who guarded her private parts, so We *breathed* into it of Our Spirit and she established as true the Words of her Lord and His Books and she had been among the ones who are morally obligated" (emphasis added).[19] However, these statements have proven to be open to interpretation. Just exactly where and how the divine spirit is breathed into and enters Mary's body has been a subject of much speculation.[20]

One rather surprising view in Christian thought is the idea that the spirit breathes into Mary's ear. This idea seems to have originated in Ancient Syria. In a fourth-century homily, "Panegyric Recited on the Birth of Christ," Ephrem the Syrian includes this detail, and the same detail is part of the *Armenian Gospel of the Infancy*, a sixth-century text that is likely a translation of an earlier, no longer extant, Syriac text.[21] Certain church leaders such as Athanasius and Theodotus also mention this conception through the ear.[22] An extracanonical Christian text, the *Gospel of Philip*, takes a different approach, "Some said Mary became pregnant by the Holy Spirit. They are wrong and do not know what they are saying. When did a woman ever get pregnant by a woman?" (55.22–23).[23]

Likewise, many have commented on this matter in Islamic writings.[24] One particularly interesting explanation is that of Abū Bakr al-Qurtubī, a thirteenth-century Muslim commentator from Cordova. Using hermaphroditic imagery, he speculates that although normally liquid in the father's back and liquid in the mother's uterus combine to create a child, Mary's body contained liquid both in her back and in her uterus and that the two mixed when Gabriel blew the divine spirit into her

---

[17] Hock, *Infancy Gospels*, 53.
[18] Bakhtiar, *Sublime Quran*, 311.
[19] Ibid., 549.
[20] It is worth noting that the term "Trinity" is not used anywhere in the NT. In the extracanonical texts of the early centuries mentioned in this chapter (the dating of these texts and the sources upon which they draw being subject to considerable debate), it cannot necessarily be assumed that the writers thought of the spirit in terms of the doctrine of the Trinity. The Qur'an speaks of Allah breathing spirit into the first human being (as described below), but of course, the spirit is not a member of a trinity. For a beautiful explanation of the various ways in which the Qur'an describes the spirit and its interaction with human beings, see Michael Sells, "Sound, Spirit, and Gender in the Qur'ān," in *Approaching the Qur'ān: The Early Revelations*, ed. Michael Sells (Ashland, OR: White Cloud, 2007), 199–223.
[21] Abraham Terian, *The Armenian Gospel of the Infancy: With Three Early Versions of the Protevangelium of James* (Oxford: Oxford University Press, 2008), xxv, n. 45.
[22] Ibid.
[23] Marvin Meyer, trans., "The Gospel of Philip," in *The Nag Hammadi Scriptures: The International Edition*, ed, Marvin Meyer (New York: HarperCollins, 2007), 161–86, esp. 164.
[24] See Smith and Haddad, "The Virgin Mary," 167, for particularly intriguing discussion of various Islamic commentators' theories regarding the conception.

body.²⁵ Michael Sells also discusses one of the passages describing the spirit's breathing into Mary (Q21:19) and points out important intertextual connections and resonances between it and the passage describing the creation of Adam (Q15:29, Q38:72). The Arabic phrasing of the two passages is almost the same word for word.²⁶ Likewise, he points out that in Q19:17, the text reads, "So we sent to her our spirit which took the appearance before her as a human shaped."²⁷ The particular phrase "as a human (that had been) shaped" (*basharan sawiyyan* in Arabic) is the very same used to describe the human form receiving the breath of spirit and coming to life.²⁸ Sells goes on to explain, "These parallels—between the breathing of the spirit into the shape of Adam and the breathing of the spirit into Mary—link the two processes in a way that is never explicit, but is nevertheless robust."²⁹

Similarly, the passage in which Jesus forms a bird of clay and breathes life into it (Q3:49)³⁰ reminds the hearer/reader of such associations as well. It immediately brings to mind the verses in which Jesus forms birds of clay and claps his hands to bring them to life in the *Infancy Gospel of Thomas* (2:1–7).³¹ The passage in the Qur'an, however, has Jesus *breathe* life into the clay bird (Q3:49)³² thereby reminding the hearer or reader of God's breathing life into Adam (Gen 2:7)³³ (Q15:29; Q32:9, Q38:71–72)³⁴ and the spirit's breathing into Mary in order for her to conceive Jesus (Q21:91, Q66:12).³⁵

The third major moment in the life of Mary that this chapter examines is the birth of Jesus. At this juncture, her vulnerability becomes pronounced. Mary withdraws from other human beings and gives birth in a place where she experiences complete isolation. She then cries out in desperation as she lacks both material and emotional sustenance. A messenger of the Lord responds by saying,

> Feel not remorse! Surely your Lord made under **you** (f) a brook. And shake toward **you** (f) the trunk of the date palm tree. It will cause ripe, fresh dates to fall on **you**. So eat and drink and **your** eyes be refreshed. (Q19:24–26)³⁶

The implication is that she is crying, and "refreshed" can therefore be translated simply as "consoled," or "comforted." Notably, the messenger of the divine listens

---

²⁵ See the extended discussion and citations in ibid.
²⁶ Sells, "Sound, Spirit, and Gender," 211.
²⁷ Ibid., 212.
²⁸ Ibid.
²⁹ Ibid.
³⁰ Bakhtiar, *Sublime Quran*, 51.
³¹ Hock, *Infancy Gospels*, 105–7.
³² Bakhtiar, *Sublime Quran*, 51.
³³ *Adam* is a Hebrew word that has most often been translated into English as "man." E.g., the NRSV reads, "Then the Lord God formed man from the dust of the ground, and breathed into his nostrils the breath of life; and the man became a living being." Another possible translation is "earth creature" as this being is created from *adamah*, or "earth." Priests for Equality, *Inclusive Bible*, 6, translates as follows: "So YHWH fashioned an earth creature out of the clay of the earth, and blew into its nostrils the breath of life. And the earth creature became a living being."
³⁴ Bakhtiar, *Sublime Quran*, 243, 395, 439.
³⁵ Ibid., 311, 549.
³⁶ Ibid., 287.

compassionately to this woman who is in desperate circumstances, speaks directly with her, and intervenes on her behalf.[37]

Though there is no mention of a date tree in Christian accounts of the Nativity, a date palm is associated with God's protection when Mary, Jesus, and Joseph flee to Egypt. This narrative, of course, also recounts a time when Mary is extremely vulnerable. In chapter 20 of the *Gospel of Pseudo-Matthew*, Mary is tired and sits down to rest under a date palm. She remarks that she wishes they could eat the dates. Joseph says that he is more concerned about finding water not only for themselves but also for their animals. Jesus speaks up and asks the date palm to bend its branches so that she can be refreshed. It immediately does so, and then it waits for Jesus' next order. Jesus tells it to stand back up, and "open from thy roots a vein of water which has been hid in the earth." When it complies, "a spring of water exceedingly clear and cool and sparkling" flows forth.[38]

This story is also part of the Ethiopic *Liber Requiei*, which Stephen J. Shoemaker privileges as an early recension of the Dormition narrative. According to its text, Mary sits to rest under a date palm and asks Joseph to find something for them to eat. He is tired, too, and says that there is nothing to eat but the dates of the palm and that it is too tall for him to climb.[39] Jesus speaks up and asks the trees to "incline" themselves so that his father and mother can satisfy their hunger, and the trees immediately do so.[40] Though the Qur'an does not discuss the flight into Egypt in any detail, it appears to be the subject of Q23:50: "And We made the son of Mary and his mother a sign, and We gave them refuge on a hillside, a stopping place, and a spring of water."[41]

The image of Mary between two palms that appear to represent date palms is found in fourth-century gold glass from the Christian catacombs of Rome, as seen in Figure 15.1.[42] The artists appears to have illustrated bunches of dates hanging down from the fronds. Mary's name is broken into MA on one side of her head and RA on the other, but several other pieces of fourth-century gold glass, which have

---

[37] Though a full comparison exceeds the scope of this paper, the figure of Hagar comes to mind as she, too, speaks with and receives provision from the divine at two different times while she is isolated alone in the desert with her son (once while she is pregnant and once after he is born) (Gen 16:7-19; 21:15-19). In the second case, the divine specifically provides water just as water is provided for Mary and her son. This second event is also recounted in the hadith collection, Ṣaḥīḥ al-Bukhārī as narrated by Ibn Abbas. See the citations and commentary in Riffat Hassan, "Islamic Hagar and Her Family," in *Hagar, Sarah, and Their Children*, ed. Phyllis Trible and Letty M. Russell (Louisville, KY: Westminster/John Knox, 2006), 149-67, 152-5.

[38] *The Gospel of Pseudo-Matthew* (ANF 8:376-77).

[39] Ethiopic *Liber Requiei* 5-6 (Stephen J. Shoemaker, trans., "The Ethiopic *Liber Requiei*," in *Ancient Traditions of the Virgin Mary's Dormition and Assumption* [OECS; Oxford: Oxford University Press, 2006], 290-350, esp. 292-4).

[40] Ethiopic *Liber Requiei* 7 (Shoemaker, *Ancient Traditions*, 294); in section three on p. 291, trees also incline themselves to venerate a book Mary is carrying on the Mount of Olives, and she attributes this miraculous happening to Jesus.

[41] Bakhtiar, *Sublime Quran*, 325. See Schliefer, *Mary the Blessed Virgin*, 38-41, for discussion of Islamic commentary on the flight into Egypt. Interestingly, Leila Ahmed mentions a recurring vision of Mary just outside Cairo in 1967 that drew thousands of people and notes that the site of the appearances was a chapel where tradition says that the Holy Family rested; Leila Ahmed, *Women and Gender in Islam: Historical Roots of a Modern Debate* (New Haven, CT: Yale University Press, 1992), 216. Also see Smith and Haddad, "Virgin Mary," 161.

[42] Louis Perret, *Catacombes de Rome*, 5 vols. (Paris: Gide et J. Baudry, 1851), vol. 4, pl. 21, fig. 1.

Figure 15.1 Mary (MARA) portrayed arms-raised between date palms. Fourth-century gold glass from the Christian catacombs of Rome. Source: Louis Perret, *Catacombes de Rome*, 5 vols. (Paris: Gide et J. Baudry, 1851), vol. 4, plate 21, fig. 7.

a similar iconography of a woman with her arms raised, are titled MARIA, such as seen in Figure 10.2. Thus, most scholars accept this artifact as likely representing Mary also.[43] I would argue that the date palms associated with MARA in this artifact further supports the identification of Mary given the association of Mary and date palms in multiple narratives.

Finally, we find mention of Mary near the end of or just after Jesus' life on earth in both Islamic and Christian texts. In an account of the events of Jesus' life and death written by Ibn al-Athīr, Jesus finds Mary at the cross, explains that "nothing but good

---

[43] Eileen Rubery, "From Catacomb to Sanctuary: The Orant Figure and the Cults of the Mother of God and S. Agnes in Early Christian Rome, with Special Reference to Gold Glass," *StPatr* 73 (2014): 129–74, esp. 149–58; for a photo of the artifact, which today is in the Vatican Museum, and which the author identifies as Mary, see Caroline H. Ebertshauser et al., *Mary: Art, Culture, and Religion through the Ages*, trans. Peter Heinegg (New York: Crossroad, 1998), image and detail on 63.

has befallen me," and then commands Mary to "gather the Apostles" who then go out as messengers spreading the message with which Jesus entrusts them.[44] Likewise, in the NT, Mary is specifically named as present at Pentecost (Acts 1:14) where the apostles are gathered and go out to preach after being filled with the spirit. Similarly, in the Christian *Gospel of Mary*, there is a somewhat similar scene in which an unspecified Mary—identified as neither mother nor Magdalene, nor Mary of Bethany—speaks to a group of disciples who are already gathered, exhorting them to be courageous who then go out to spread the good news (presumably herself included) (19,1–5).[45] Yet other scenes, in the extracanonical Dormition narrative and *Gospel (Questions) of Bartholomew*, identify specifically Mary the mother of Jesus with the apostles after Jesus' death, including leading the apostles in prayer, as Ally Kateusz and Judith M. Davis detail in their chapters in this volume, and also as seen in Figure 7.3.

Over time, Islamic tradition's elevation of Mary intersects with that of the honor accorded to Fatima, daughter of the prophet Muhammad.[46] Sometimes Muslims refer to Fatima as "the greater Mary."[47] Fatima, too, is yet another woman who is a crucial link in the chain of divine revelation. For Shia Muslims in particular, she is the mother of those constituting the line of successors to Muhammad who serve as the imams through the centuries. One striking example is a hadith found in many sources relating the story of Muhammad's coming to Fatima's home and asking for something to eat. She tells him that she does not have any food, but shortly after he leaves, a neighbor provides her with a small portion of meat and a couple of loaves of bread, and Fatima sends Muhammed a message to return. She does not think there will be enough for everyone, but she wants him to be able to eat even if she and her husband and sons cannot. When she uncovers the bowl of food, however, it contains a huge amount—enough to feed Muhammed, Fatima and her family, all of Muhammed's wives, and even the neighbors. Fatima gratefully thanks God, and then Muhammed quotes *Mary's* words in the Qur'an regarding the provision she received from a divine source while growing up in the temple in Jerusalem: "It comes from God. Verily, God provides sustenance to whom He pleases without measure" (Q3:37). Muhammed goes on to say, "Praise be to God Who has done for you something akin to what He did for the Lady of the Israelites."[48]

---

[44] Schliefer, *Mary the Blessed Virgin*, 41, n. 84. Tha'labī also mentions these details.

[45] This is the wording in the Coptic manuscript of the *Gospel of Mary* (19,1–5); see Karen King, trans., "The Gospel of Mary with the Greek Gospel of Mary," in *The Nag Hammadi Scriptures*, ed. Marvin W. Meyer and Wolf-Peter Funk (New York: HarperOne, 2007), 737–47, 745. In one of the two Greek fragments of the *Gospel of Mary*, Levi alone goes out to spread the good news. In the other fragment, the relevant sentence is missing. See King, "*Gospel of Mary*," 747. Of course, many scholars believe the Mary in this text to be the Magdalene; however, the point here is not to resolve who the literary figure "really" is but rather to point out the remarkable role that a woman close to Jesus plays in leadership.

[46] Smith and Haddad, "The Virgin Mary," 179–81; Stowasser, *Women in the Qur'an*, 80.

[47] Jane D. McAuliffe, "Chosen of All Women: Mary and Fatima in Qur'anic Exegesis," *Islamochristiana* 7 (1981): 19–28.

[48] The story and the quotes above come from the version narrated by Abū Ya'lā as found in these sources: Ibn Kathīr, Tafsīr, I, 360; Badawī, Batūl, 16; Zamaksharī, Kashāf, I, 143; Tha'labī, Qiṣāṣ 209. See Schliefer, *Mary the Blessed Virgin*, 26–7. See Smith and Haddad, "The Virgin Mary," 179–81, for further discussion of associations between Mary and Fatima.

Furthermore, Mary's status is so elevated that although women are not usually considered prophets in Islam, a notable minority have argued that Mary should be an exception. Contemporary scholars such as Hosn Abboud, Michael Sells (who stops short of saying that Mary is a prophet but strongly implies it), and Loren D. Lybarger all advocate for this position.[49] Abboud has made the powerful argument that Mary is a prophet because in the Qur'an Jesus is repeatedly named "the son of Maryam." This matrilineal naming implies that both are prophets coming from a certain genealogical line, "the offspring" of Adam, Noah, Abraham, and Israel (Q19:58).[50] In turning to the world of close intertextual analysis, Michael Sells demonstrates the remarkable similarities in vocabulary and phrasing between the passage involving the spirit's breathing into Mary and the conception of Jesus (Q21:91) and the passage describing the Night of Destiny (*Laylat al-Qadr*) when the night itself is partially personified as a female figure from whom Muhammed receives revelation.[51] He also points out parallels with the Day of Reckoning in which the earth itself is personified as a woman in labor and when the mother of the one who is found lacking will be *hāwiya* ("a mother who has lost her child").[52] Sells concludes his analysis by saying,

> Through an intricate webbing of echoes, allusions, and resonances ... across a variety of passages, the Qur'an echoes an experience of *bushrā* (bearing of good news) similar to that found in the *xaire kexaromene* (Hail, blessed one) of Luke 1:28. When we compare the various Quranic texts tied together through these resonances and hear their undertones of gender dynamic, we arrive at a sustained gender figure in which a series of partially personified female referents (the earth, the *hāwiya*, the night of *qadr*) and a related female character (Maryam) are found at the center of the experiences of prophecy, creation, and the day of reckoning.[53]

Most recently, Loren D. Lybarger has used a literary approach to argue that Maryam functions as a prophet.[54] Lybarger explains that Mary's very body becomes a site of

---

[49] Such perspectives are found in earlier centuries as well. E.g., Ibn Hazm of Cordoba, a prominent member of the short-lived but prolific eleventh-century Zahirites and one whose views have challenged the boundaries of mainstream Islamic thought, reasoned that Mary was a prophet. He argued that she received knowledge from the divine that was just as valid as that received by prophets who were men. In particular, he pointed out that the Qur'an refers to Joseph the son of Jacob (considered a prophet in Islam) as a "man of truth" and to Mary as "a woman of truth." See Stowasser, "Chapter of Mary," in *Women in the Qur'an, Traditions, and Interpretation* (New York: Oxford University Press, 1994), 77.

[50] Hosn Abboud, "'Idhan Maryam Nabiyya' ('Hence Maryam is a Prophetess'): Muslim Classical Exegetes and Women's Receptiveness to God's Verbal Inspiration," in *Miriam, the Magdalen, and the Mother*, ed. Deirdre Good (Bloomington: Indiana University Press, 2005), 183–96, esp. 186.

[51] Sells, "Sound, Gender, and Spirit," 205–9.

[52] Ibid., 213–17.

[53] Ibid., 219–20.

[54] Loren D. Lybarger, "Gender and Prophetic Authority in the Qur'anic Story of Maryam: A Literary Approach," *JR* 80 (2000): 240–70; especially noteworthy is her argument on p. 261 where she argues that Mary fits the model of a prophet as outlined by M. Waldman even though Waldman applies it only to men.

revelation, a "gynocentric metaphor" par excellence.[55] Since conceiving of Mary as a prophet has never been the norm, the very fact that it has been the subject of such discussion is remarkable.[56]

The same is true in the Christian tradition. The NT depicts Mary as a strong, assertive figure. Her prophetic voice rings out clearly in the Magnificat (Luke 1:46–55), and she is the one who urges Jesus to reveal his power and perform his first miracle of turning water into wine at the wedding in Cana (John 2:1–11). Most importantly, the book of Acts specifically names her as present at Pentecost (1:14) when the flames of the Holy Spirit descend. However, she is not actually called a prophet. Since she acts and speaks as a prophet would, one cannot help but wonder if it is her gender alone that has kept interpreters from designating her as such.

Finally, at each of the four major moments described in this paper, Mary's intimate relationship to the spirit is evident. Christians eventually developed the doctrine of the Trinity, and most (though not necessarily all) have believed through the centuries that Mary was impregnated by God's very self. Muslims reject this thinking and associate the spirit with inspiration or revelation. However, the term that is used by both is simply "spirit." Moreover, the Christian texts of the early centuries do not necessarily reject but neither do they necessarily reflect the doctrinal certainties of later centuries. Through the centuries, the depictions of the intimate connections between Mary and the spirit have prompted deeper reflections about its specific nature. Ibn ʿArabī, the prolific scholar and mystic of twelfth- and thirteenth-century Cordova, equates Mary with Wisdom (*Sophia*) and describes her as the one who links the human and the divine—one who mediates the material and the spiritual—that which is readily comprehended versus that which can only be intuited. Indeed, it is into her very body that the spirit enters, and the physical and spiritual meld.[57] He elaborates by saying, "She both veils and reveals God, providing the medium by which he comes into concrete existence in terms of human perception":[58]

> Just as a Feminine had been existentiated by a Masculine without the mediation of a mother, namely, Eve created by Adam and standing in a passive relation to Adam, so it was necessary that a Masculine should be borne by a Feminine without the mediation of a father; and so Jesus was borne by Maryam.[59]

---

[55] Ibid., 242. Lybarger defines a "gynocentric metaphor" as "any metaphor or image evoking the special experience of women. Any image involving reference to the womb and childbirth, for instance, would be gynocentric."

[56] See Schliefer, *Mary the Blessed Virgin*, 73–94; Smith and Haddad, "The Virgin Mary," 177–9; Stowasser, "Chapter of Mary," 69, 77, for a discussion of the opinions of other commentators regarding whether Mary is a prophet.

[57] Smith and Haddad, "Virgin Mary," 182.

[58] Henri Corbin, *Creative Imagination in the Sufism of Ibn ʿArabī* (Princeton, NJ: Princeton University Press, 1969), 145–53. See also Smith and Haddad, "Virgin Mary," 182.

[59] See Smith and Haddad, "Virgin Mary," 183n113 who cite p. 163 of Corbin's work but also refer the reader to *Ibn ʿArabī's Futūḥāt*, I, 136, [chapter 10], 2:31 and 4:24.

This is a novel idea, but such an interpretation is possible in Islam, for there is no need for a pure and innocent Mary to replace a sinful Eve as there is no doctrine of original sin.[60]

This conceptualization bears a strikingly similarity to the way a woman named Mary functions in the *Gospel of Mary*. In this writing, Jesus tells Mary that one sees "a vision" with the *nous* ("mind")—that which is neither the soul nor the spirit but which negotiates between the two. This "mind" is filled with *pneuma*, or spirit, by Christ and is "the treasure" (10.15–23).[61] Mary is the one whose mind correctly perceives spiritual truth and therefore mediates these two realms. The Savior indicates this when he tells her, "Blessed are you because you are not wavering when you see me. For where the mind is, there is the treasure."[62]

In conclusion, this chapter serves as an outline noting many interconnections that can serve primarily as a starting point for further reflection about the ways in which Islamic tradition intersects Christian tradition in thinking through the symbolic meaning and significance of Mary, the mother of Jesus, and the role she plays at various times in her life in the Qur'an and Islamic commentary and tradition as well as in Christian texts—particularly those extracanonical ones that fill in certain details regarding her reception history.[63] These portrayals of Mary have broad significance for thinking through contemporary women's roles as they portray Mary positively as a woman with tremendous strength of character and an assertive character who dances on the steps of the temple, speaks up and defends herself to Zechariah when questioned about the provision she has received, questions the messenger who says

---

[60] See George Anawati, "Islam and the Immaculate Conception," in *The Dogma of the Immaculate Conception: History and Significance*, ed. E. D. O'Connor (Notre Dame, IN: University of Notre Dame, 1958), 447–61; R. J. McCarthy, "Mary in Islam," in *Mary's Place in Christian Dialogue*, ed. Alberic Stacpoole (Wilton, CT: Morehouse–Barlow, 1982), 205–8; Smith and Haddad, "Virgin Mary," 172, n. 51.

[61] Esther A. De Boer, *The Gospel of Mary. Listening to the Beloved Disciple* (London: A&C Black, 2005), 20, 79–80. As noted above, many scholars argue that the Mary in this gospel is the Magdalene. See Ann Graham Brock, *Mary Magdalene, the First Apostle: The Struggle for Authority* (HThS 51; Cambridge, MA: Harvard University Press, 2003); Karen L. King, *The Gospel of Mary of Magdala: Jesus and the First Woman Apostle* (Santa Rosa, CA: Polebridge, 2003); Jane Schaberg, *The Resurrection of Mary Magdalene: Legends, Apocrypha, and the Christian Testament* (New York: Continuum, 2002). For the argument that this Mary could be the mother of Jesus and discussion of the difficulty of sorting out which Mary is which in this and other extracanonical texts, see Stephen J. Shoemaker, *Mary in Early Christian Faith and Devotion* (New Haven, CT: Yale University Press, 2016), 74–104. As noted above, Mary's role contains rich spiritual meaning regardless of which Mary she is. For discussion of the way in which Mary functions as an exemplar of "the care of the soul/self" and one who engages in the open-hearted, frank speech characteristic of the person who has engaged successfully in the therapy of emotions, see Deborah Niederer Saxon, *The Care of the Self in Early Christian Texts* (The Bible and Cultural Studies; New York: Palgrave Macmillan, 2017), 133–55, 191, 196.

[62] De Boer, *Gospel of Mary*, 20. Ibn 'Arabī also discusses Mary in terms of her achieving spiritual perfection, noteworthy even apart from her role as the mother of Jesus, that reflects an understanding similar to that of the ancient *Gospel of Mary*. He discusses her perception of the Oneness of God and of God as the Unity of the Many. See the discussion in Schliefer, *Mary the Blessed Virgin*, 91, n. 280.

[63] This is a different approach regarding similarities between the Qur'an and Christian extracanonical texts than that of the first Western scholars who wrote about these within the framework of an Orientalist perspective and denigrated both kinds of writings in the process. See, e.g., William Tisdale, *The Original Sources of the Qur'an*, repr. (London: Society for Promoting Christian Knowledge, 1911), 140–3.

she will become pregnant, makes her needs known to the divine when isolated in the desert, asks for provision when fleeing into Egypt, and draws others together to encourage them to spread good news. Her vulnerability does not turn her into a passive victim whose voice is lost to the hearers/readers of the narratives in which she plays a major role. In short, contemporary listeners and readers of these narratives can enter into them by taking note of the way in which she rises to meet challenges, wrestles even with the divine, and exhorts others to right action. In addition, the compassion of the divine comes through clearly—one who listens to, provides for, and empowers a marginalized figure. Hearers/readers then have the opportunity to heed the implicit call to respond likewise. In short, the narratives describing Mary and the roles she plays are not merely accounts of a figure who has increasingly been portrayed as "meek and mild" in the later centuries of Christianity.[64] Neither are they simply sweet stories to be trotted out during Christmas or Ramadan. They provide the hearers/readers with clear models regarding appropriate responses to the marginalization of one's self or others. In a globalized world full of turmoil, the stories of women with Mary's strength of character and strong voice matter more than ever.

---

[64] For the reception history of Mary throughout the centuries, there are many good sources that include Jaroslav Pelikan, *Mary Through the Centuries: Her Place in the History of Culture* (New Haven, CT: Yale University Press, 1996); Rubin, *Mother of God*; and Marina Warner, *Alone of All Her Sex: The Myth and the Cult of the Virgin Mary* (New York: Alfred K. Knopf, 1976).

16

The Origin and Manifestations of the Smiling Virgin Mary

Jin H. Han

Amid the Marian representations that are saturated with the theme of grief, the idea of Mary's smile evokes no conceptual resistance, and it is inviting to imagine her smiling as a young girl, expectant maiden, or nursing mother. For most of the two millennia of the Common Era, however, the report of her smile has been sparse until recent centuries. This shift invites a query as to whether the trope of the smiling Mary is a modern pop-religious phenomenon encouraged under the twentieth- and twenty-first-century papacies of the Marian popes, who have promoted *hyperdulia* of Mary more than previous pontiffs had done. This article explores Mary's smile attested to in the Marian imagination from earlier centuries and discovers that it represents much more than passing endearing moments sought in the modern world where suffering and pain persist. Over the centuries, her motherly smile continues to disarm tangling complex theological debates on Mary, inviting a renewed reception of the story of Mary and Jesus in terms of down-to-earth human experiences.

Mater Dolorosa

Among many artistic representations of Mary the mother of Jesus at the foot of the cross (John 19:25–27), Marian grief finds a gripping example in the thirteenth-century *Stabat Mater Dolorosa* ("The Sorrowful Mother Stood"), a medieval hymn that depicts her suffering at the crucifixion of Jesus. Its song text, variously attributed to Innocent III (d. 1216), St. Bonaventure (d. 1274), or Jacopone da Todi (d. 1306), is set to music by famous composers including Giovanni Pierluigi da Palestrina (1590), Antonio Vivaldi (1712), Domenico Scarlatti (1715), Giovanni Battista Pergolesi (1736), Joseph Haydn (1767), Gioacchino Antonio Rossini (1832, 1842), Antonín Dvořák (1880), and Giuseppe Verdi (1897). This emphasis on grief is also inscribed all over Michelangelo's marble statue *Pietà* (1498–9) in Saint Peter's Basilica, Vatican. This life-size sculpture of Mary threatens to overwhelm the space with sorrow, while she "avoids our look and internalizes her sorrow."[1]

A childlike question as to why Mary is sad evokes the full weight of the gospel tradition. According to the Lukan infancy narrative, her grief does not begin with the death of Jesus. At the presentation of the Child in Luke 2, Simeon adds to his prayer of *Nunc Dimittis* and says, "This child is destined for the falling and the rising of many in Israel, and to be a sign that will be opposed so that the inner thoughts of many will be revealed—and a sword will pierce your own soul too" (vv. 34–35 NRSV). Simeon's pronouncement is prefaced with the presentative *idou* ("behold"). Translators struggle with the implicature of the particle, which modern cognitive linguistics recognizes as a device that "substantially enriches the knowledge of the listener."[2] One who hears the sentence learns more than she or he could bear to know about the child's destiny, which will have a profound impact on the mother.

In later iconography, Simeon's piercing prophecy is graphically represented with the seven swords or seven sorrows of Mary.[3] In the West, it is incorporated in the religious devotions of the Servite Order, and they underscore her mourning. An Eastern counterpart finds expression in the Russian iconic tradition that features a sword that "is piercing Her heart: *The Mother of God is weeping over the world*."[4] A twelfth-century painting of the Virgin and Child in the south aisle at the Church of the Nativity, Bethlehem, has two letters (*A* and *W* signifying the alpha and the omega) flanking the Latin metrical verse, *Virgo celestis confer solatia mestis* ("Virgin of Heaven, Grant Comfort to the Sorrowful").[5] The prayer calls upon the one whom the worshipper perceives to be the most familiar with grieving.

The Annunciation Revisited

Mary the mother's pain is indeed a ubiquitous theme in the Marian reflection of the church, but the gospel tradition is not without glimpses of her beaming smile that intersects her sorrow and suffering. One may discover this as early as in the account of the Annunciation in Luke 1:26–38, which marks the beginning of God's measure of redemption, although iconographical studies usually focus on other

---

[1] William E. Wallace cited in Judith Dupré, *Full of Grace: Encountering Mary in Faith, Art, and Life* (New York: Random House, 2010), 211, with the picture of Michelangelo's *Pietà* on 210. Her youthful face designed "to reflect her age when she bore Jesus, because it was the only way to show her virginity," may have been based on "Dante's *Paradiso*, a favorite literary work of Michelangelo's, which proposes that all persons, including Mary herself, are reborn in Christ" (ibid.).

[2] Joseph Vachek, *The Linguistic School of Prague* (Bloomington: Indiana University Press, 1966), 89–90.

[3] The seven sorrows are as follows: Simeon's prophecy (Luke 2:34–35), flight to Egypt (Matt 2:13), Jesus in the temple (Luke 2:43–45), Jesus on the via dolorosa (Mark 15:16–21 and parallels), crucifixion (John 19:25), piercing of the side (vv. 31–37), descent from the cross (Matt 27:57–59), and the burial (John 19:40–42).

[4] Sergius Bulgakov, *Churchly Joy: Orthodox Devotions for the Church Year* (Grand Rapids, MI: William B. Eerdmans, 2008), 10–11 (italics in the original).

[5] R. W. Hamilton, *The Church of the Nativity, Bethlehem: A Guide* (Jerusalem: Government of Palestine, Dept. of Antiquities, 1947), 78, fig. 14.

artistic details such as what activity Mary is engaged in when the angel visits her. For example, in the Byzantine style, the Virgin is often shown as being engaged in the domestic affairs like weaving with purple wool, whereas in the West, Mary, rarely portrayed as weaving, is seated at a lectern, where she ponders over the Scriptures, displaying an intellectual posture (e.g., *The Annunciation* by Barthélémy d'Eyck, ca. 1444).[6]

In the Annunciation proper in Luke, Gabriel says, "Greetings [*chaire*], favored one *kecharitōmenē*! The Lord is with you" (1:28). In Greek, both the salutation [*chaire*] and the appellation [*kecharitōmenē*] share the etymological root that signifies "joy." A number of uncial manuscripts including Codex Alexandrinus as well as most minuscules add "Blessed are you among women" (*eulogēmenē su en gynaixin*) and evoke a scene of jubilation. The appearance of Gabriel to Mary provides an auspicious overtone for the scene by recalling the role of an interpreting angel, who comes to the aid of the distressed Daniel in the Old Testament (see Dan 8:15–26 and 9:21–27, for example). The angel's address also echoes other verses including Zeph 3:14 and Zech 9:9a, which call upon Daughter Zion to rejoice.

Within the immediate context of the Gospel of Luke, the *angelus interpretans* has just announced Elizabeth's pregnancy with John the Baptist to Zechariah (Luke 1:11–13, 19). In that elated scene, Gabriel says to Zechariah, "You will have joy (*chara*) and gladness (*agalliasis*), and many will rejoice (*charēsontai*) at his birth" (v. 14). The appearance of the angel that serves as the harbinger of joy (*agalliasis*; v. 14) and "this good news" (v. 19) anticipates the Visitation (vv. 39–45), which reports that the fetus in Elizabeth's womb leaps with quickening joy (v. 44; *eskirtēsen en agalliasei*).

The third evangelist reports that Mary is "much perplexed" (*dietarachthē*, an emphatic derivative based on *tarassō*) by the angel's words and "pondered what sort of greeting this might be" (v. 29). The consternation of unexpected pregnancy associated with this passage is occasionally compared to the scenes of disciples frightened by Jesus walking on the water (Mark 6:50; *etarachtēsan*, an aorist passive of *tarassō*; see also Matt 14:26) or by the appearance of the post-resurrection Jesus (Luke 24:38, *tetaragmenoi*, perfect-participle form of *tarassō*). However, the arrangement of the story (*dispositio*, as the ancient rhetoricians would call it) indicates that, on Mary's part, her perplexing has to do more with the angel's greeting than with the message she is yet to receive (1:30–33). Gabriel's salutation (*mē phobou*, which recalls the Hebrew *'al tirā'*: "Do not fear")[7] signals theophany (or angelophany in this instance). *In nuce*, Gabriel's message in v. 30 conveys not terror but "favor" (*charin*), a lexeme etymologically related to "greetings" (*chaire*) and "favored one" (*kecharitōmenē*) in v. 28.

In the Gospel according to Luke, the joy of the Annunciation gives way to the *Magnificat* (vv. 46b–55), in which Mary intones, "My soul magnifies the Lord, and my spirit rejoices" (*ēgaliassen* from *agalliao*, which echoes *agalliasis* of v. 14) "in God my

---

[6] See Christine Gallisot-Ortuno, "L'iconographie de l'Annonciation," in *Quelques figures de maternités: fétiches, déesses–mères, mystère de l'incarnation et pots pansus*, ed. Jean-Roche Bouiller (Milan: Silvana, 2009), 25–6, illus. A and C.
[7] E.g., Gen 15:1; 21:17; 26:24; Judg 6:23.

savior" (vv. 46b–47). In her song of praise, "her *'delight'* sets the tone and atmosphere for the new era that is dawning."[8]

Mary's Smile Sighted

Mary's smile, decidedly apropos against the backdrop of the Lukan account of the Annunciation, enters iconography, albeit intermittently. In the medieval vista dominated by the magisterial image of the *Regina Coeli* (the Queen of Heaven), her pleased facial expression offers gentle depth, and the display of affection toward her baby invokes a graceful sense of her presence for others. One may encounter this appealing smile in the Annunciation scene of the twelfth-century window at Chartres, in which "Mary, standing, her eyes wide open, turned toward the angel, smiling serenely but slightly troubled, holds her right hand raised as in defense but ready to bless."[9]

The Late Middle Ages leaves remarkably rich trails of Mary's smile, and Peter Barnet, art historian, attributes it to "significant changes in attitudes toward the Virgin that occurred during the thirteenth century."[10] From this period, the widely known Romanesque statue of *la Virgen Blanca* ("the White Virgin") stands at the altar of the Cathedral of Toledo, Spain—with a smile on her face.[11] In addition, the ivory statuette of Mary and the Christ Child from northern France of the mid-thirteenth century (1240–50), now in the Art Institute of Chicago, presents a smiling Mary with the Christ Child. In the left hand, he holds a bird, presumably a goldfinch,[12] and blesses with his right hand—and "both figures have wide, blank, string eyes and a stylized smile."[13] Another ivory statue of smiling Mary (dated slightly later; housed in Musée National du Moyen Age, Thermes de Cluny, Paris) represents a quintessential example of the ivory sculptures in which "Gothic ivory workers produced sculptures in the round striking in their similarity to contemporary monumental statuary" (Figure 16.1).[14]

Superb ivory craftsmanship of the thirteenth century plays an important role in the rendition of Mary's smile. Paul Williamson of the Victoria and Albert Museum in London says, "When carving larger figures from ivory, it was difficult to disguise the natural curve of the tusk: many of the most talented ivory carvers maximized this

---

[8] Joseph A. Fitzmyer, SJ, *The Gospel According to Luke (I–IX)* (AB 28; Garden City, NY: Doubleday, 1981), 360 (emphasis added).

[9] Eugene LaVerdiere, *The Annunciation to Mary: A Story of Faith, Luke 1:26–38* (Chicago, IL: Liturgy Training Publications, 2004), 80–1.

[10] Peter Barnet, "Enthroned Virgin and Child," in *Images in Ivory: Precious Objects of the Gothic Age*, ed. Peter Barnet (Detroit, MI: The Detroit Institute of Arts, 1997), 118, cat. no. 2.

[11] Nicholas J. Santoro, *Mary in Our Life: Atlas of the Names and Titles of Mary, the Mother of Jesus, and Their Place in Marian Devotion* (Bloomington, IN: iUniverse, 2011), 657.

[12] In this instance, the goldfinch represents the passion of Christ based on a legend that speaks of a bird "that fluttered down to His head and pulled out a thorn that was ranking in His brow" (Herbert Friedmann, *The Symbolic Goldfinch: Its History and Significance in European Devotional Art* [The Bolligen Series; Washington DC: Pantheon Books, 1946], 9).

[13] Richard H. Randall Jr., *The Golden Age of Ivory* (New York: Hudson Hill, 1993), 34, pl. 1 (cat. no. 1).

[14] Xavier Dectot, "Madonna and Child," *Musée nationale du Moyen Age: The Cluny Thermae* (Paris: Réunion des musées nationaux, 2003), 76.

Figure 16.1 Smiling Madonna and Child in elephant ivory, Musée de Cluny. Photo courtesy of Jungyoon Han.

feature, however, giving their Virgins a pronounced *déhanchement* not seen in larger sculpture before the middle of the thirteenth century." He counts among the best examples Mary of the Sainte-Chapelle (ca. 1250–60; Louvre),[15] which is also known as "la plus belle de les Vierges"[16] and "one of the first great Parisian products made in the newly popular material of elephant ivory."[17] Another ivory statue, one from the Abbey Church of Saint-Denis (the third quarter of the thirteenth century) in the Taft Museum, Cincinnati, Ohio, presents Mary, who "stands with her weight on the right leg, smiling serenely at the Child she holds on her left arm and offering him a wide, flat flower."[18] Barnet offers a detailed assessment of the piece, when he says,

> The artist of the Taft ivory conveys the intimate communication between the Virgin and her child. The Virgin sways slightly, her right leg bent and her weight on her left leg. Cloaked about her shoulders and held in place by cords across her chest, her mantle gathers in sweeping folds to her left hip and then cascades to the ground in deeply cut folds. The mantle falls in long, shallow folds down the back of the statuette, gracefully suggesting the Virgin's contrapposto stance. Under the mantle she wears a simple robe, with a narrow belt at her waist. The child, perched on the Virgin's left arm, reaches with his right arm for a rose that the Virgin holds out for him. He kicks his left foot and tilts his head, glancing at his mother, while still clutching a small apple in his left hand."[19]

Mary's smile is also shown on the central panel of the early fourteenth-century *Maestà*, in which "Duccio changed his imagery of the Virgin and the Virgin's garments to a more western and a softer, more motherly interpretation."[20] A statue made of walnut from the second quarter of the fourteenth century, located in Suermondt-Ludwig-Museum, Aachen, presents the Virgin Mary with a delightful motherly smile (Figure 16.2). A standing Virgin, whose "body forms an S curve, as she supports the Christ Child on her veiled right arm and hand," is smiling in a fifteenth-century Austrian statute in fruitwood (Figure 16.3).[21] Presented in the International Style, the "Soft Style," or "Beautiful Style," it is in "a special category of small-scale sculptures intended for private devotional use in an intimate setting, such as a bedroom or a small domestic chapel."[22] In *Madonna and Child* by Joos van Cleve (ca. 1485–1541), "a slight

---

[15] Paul Williamson, "Symbiosis across Scale: Gothic Ivories and Sculpture in Stone and Wood in the Thirteenth Century," in *Images in Ivory: Precious Objects of the Gothic Age*, ed. Peter Barnet (Detroit, MI: The Detroit Institute of Arts, 1997), 42, fig. III–3.

[16] Louis Grodecki, *Ivoires français* (Paris: Larouose, 1947), 89, pl. 26.

[17] Peter Barnet, "Gothic Sculpture in Ivory: An Introduction," in *Images in Ivory: Precious Objects of the Gothic Age*, ed. Peter Barnet (Detroit, MI: The Detroit Institute of Arts, 1997), 11–12, figs. 1–4.

[18] Randall Jr. *The Golden Age of Ivory*, 34–5, colorplate 2 (cat. no. 3).

[19] Peter Barnet, "Virgin and Child with Two Angels from Saint-Denis," in *Images in Ivory: Precious Objects of the Gothic Age*, ed. Peter Barnett (Detroit, MI: The Detroit Institute of Arts, 1997), 125–56, cat. no. 5.

[20] Jaroslav Folda, *Byzantine Art and Italian Panel Painting: The Virgin and Child Hodegetria and the Art of Chrysography* (New York: Cambridge University Press, 2015), 287; pl. 47A.

[21] Barbara Drake Boehm and William D. Wixom, *Mirror of the Medieval World* (New York: The Metropolitan Museum of Art, 1999), 175, cat. no. 213; see also https://www.metmuseum.org/art/collection/search/469898 (accessed on September 13, 2018).

[22] Boehm and Wixom, *Mirror of the Medieval World*, 175.

Figure 16.2 Smiling Virgin Mary, statue of walnut wood, ca. 1325–50. Photo Ann Bredol-Lepper; courtesy of Suermondt-Ludwig-Museum, Aachen.

Figure 16.3 Smiling Virgin and Child, statue of fruitwood carved in Austria ca. 1410. Metropolitan Museum of Art, The Cloisters Collection, 1985, Accession no. 1985.214 (CC0).

smile suggests emotions at which we can only guess while her expression is apparently just as contemplative."[23] One may compare it to *Virgin Annunciate* (ca. 1475-6) by Antonello da Messina (Galleria Regionale della Sicilia, Palermo), which "presents the Virgin in a tranquil, clearly structured composition," displaying "the hint of a smile … upon her lips while at the same time suggesting composed seriousness."[24] One finds a light smile on Leonardo da Vinci's *Madonna Benois* (Hermitage, St. Petersburg) as well. In this piece that the artist began working on in 1487, Mary "is shown in a very familiar attitude," revealing as "the innovative aspect of this small painting … the intimacy in which the two figures are developed."[25] The same ambience of affinity is unmistakable in Albrecht Dürer's *Mary on the Sickle of the Moon* (around 1511) in Landesmuseum, Hanover, Germany, in which a smiling mother is holding her baby, and the crown made of stars hovers over her.[26]

Even in instances in which Mary herself may show neither palpable signs of grief nor any visible emotive features, a smile is found on the face of other characters portrayed in the scene. It goes without saying that the smiling Christ Child makes a seamless part of many Marian images including the triptych with Virgin and Child by Master of Frankfurt (active ca. 1490 – after 1518), housed in Museo Civico, Pistoia.[27] A smiling Gabriel—*l'Ange au Sourire* (also known as *le Sourire de Reims*; carved in 1235-45)—forms a fitting feature in the scene of the Annunciation, as one can observe in the west portal of the cathedral at Rheims, in which the angel waits to receive Mary's response, and "Mary, serene and dignified, shows no anxiety."[28] In this scene, "the angel's smile on the central portal of the Cathedral at Rheims … awakens the humble devotion of Mary, the loving servant of God."[29] In the Virgin's coronation portrayed in the ivory work from the third quarter of the thirteenth century, two smiling angels gently turn to each other, lifting up their open hands (located in Musée Mayer van den Bergh, Antwerp, Belgium).[30]

---

[23] Reindert L. Falkenburg, *The Fruit of Devotion: Mysticism and the Imagery of Love in Flemish Paintings of the Virgin and Child 1450-1550*, trans. Sammy Herman (Amsterdam: John Benjamins, 1994), 87, fig. 61.

[24] Klaus Krüger, "Mute Mysteries of the Divine Logos: On the Pictorial Poetics of Incarnation," in *Image and Incarnation: The Early Modern Doctrine of the Pictorial Image*, ed. Walter S. Melion and Lee Palmer Wandel (Leiden: Brill, 2015), 78-9, fig. 2.1.

[25] Simona Cremante, *Leonardo da Vinci: The Complete Works* (Newton Abbot, UK: David and Charles, 2006), 108.

[26] Barbara Vinken, "Das Konzept Madonna," in *Madonna: Frau-Mutter-Kultfigure*, ed. Katja Lembke (Dresden: Sandstein, 2015), 14-15, fig. 2.

[27] Falkenburg, *The Fruit of Devotion*, pl. 6. See also pl. 24, Joos van Cleve (ca. 1485-1541), *Virgin and Child*, location unknown; pl. 27, Joos van Cleve, Virgin and Child, Städelsches Kunstinstitut, Frankfurt am Main; pl. 37, Master of the Legend of St. Catharine (active ca. 1500-25), *Virgin and Child*, location unknown; pl. 54, Joos van Cleve, *Virgin Child and St Anne*, Galleria Estense, Modena; pl. 57, Jan Joest (ca. 1460-1519), *Virgin and Child and St Anne*, Columbus Gallery of Fine Arts, Columbia, OH; and pl. 75, Joos van Cleve, Virgin and Child with St Joseph, The Currier Gallery of Art, Manchester, NH.

[28] LaVerdiere, *The Annunciation to Mary*, 30; for the photo of the scene, see Michael Camille, *Gothic Art, Glorious Visions* (New York: Harry N. Abrams, 1996), 80.

[29] Gertrud Schiller, *Iconography of Christian Art*, vol. 1, trans. Janet Seligman (Greenwich, CT: New York Graphics Society, 1971), 39.

[30] Gudrun Sporbeck, "Deux anges provenant d'un Couronnement de la Vierge Paris, troisième quart du XIIIe siècle," in *Un trésor gothique la châsse de Nivelles*, ed. Anne de Margerie (Paris: Réunion des musées nationaux, 1996), 354-5, cat. 39, fig. 50.

Numerous studies have examined the famous Gothic smile represented on an early thirteenth-century sculpture on the Fürstenportal of Bamberg Cathedral in Bamberg, Germany.[31] On the right side of Christ, the smiling saints rise from the dead. Among the blessed, one encounters Kaiser Heinrich and Kunigunde.[32] They smile as they are led by an angel. On the left, the damned include a bishop, a king, and a money changer. They are smiling, too, while being chained and taken to hell by the devil.[33] In this scene of the Last Judgment, Mary smiles before Christ the Judge.[34]

Mary's Smile Cited

The Virgin's smile makes its irenic appearance in vision reports in literature and hagiography, as well. Among examples, in the early fourteenth century, is *Paradiso* by Dante, who depicts Mary's smile adoringly (31.133–38):

> I saw there, a Beauty that was delight, in the eyes of all the other saints, smiling at their dances and their songs. And if I had words as rich as my imagination, I would still not dare to attempt the smallest part of her delightfulness.

Mary's smile can also be postulated in John Milton, *Paradise Regained*, 1.227–30:

> These growing thoughts my Mother soon perceiving
> By words at times cast forth inly rejoyc'd,
> And said to me apart, high are thy thoughts
> O Son, but nourish them and let them soar.

A few centuries later, the adoration of Mary's smile develops with the statue of *Notre Dame de la Sourire* ("Our Lady of the Smile") in the home of Blessed Louis and Blessed Zelie Martin (St. Thérèse's parents). Edmé Bouchardon molded the figure with the silver collected from the parish, hence "Our Lady of the Old Silverware." The original was destroyed during the French Revolution, but its replicas were available around

---

[31] For the photos of the images on the Fürstentor, see Wilhelm Pinder, *Der Bamberger Dom und seine Bildwerke* (Berlin: Deutscher Kunstverlag, 1927), pl. 9 (das Fürstentor), pl. 11 (Bogenfeld des Fürstentor, das Jüngste Gericht), pl. 30 (Die Seligen aus dem Jüngsten Gericht Fürstentor), pl. 31 (Engel und Papst aus dem Fürstentor Gericht Fürstentor), pl. 32 (die Seligen aus dem Jüngste Gericht), pl. 33 (Geizhals und König unter den Verdammten aus dem Jüngste Gericht), pl. 34 (ein verdammter aus dem Jüngsten Gericht), and pl. 35 (ein Bischof unter den verdammten Jüngstes Gericht). See also Bruno Neundorfer, *Der Dom zu Bamberg: Mutterkirche des Erzbistums* (Bamberg: St. Otto-Verlag, 1987), 22 (Gruppe der Seligen vom Tympanon des Fürstenportals; Gruppe der Verdammmten aus dem Bogenfeld des Fürstenportals), 23 (das Fürstenportal), 25 (Tympanon des Fürtenportals), and 26 (Ein König unter den Verdammten; Kaiser Heinrich in der Gruppe der Seligen). For the history of restoration of the Fürstenportal, see Tilmann Breuer, "Das Fürstenportal: Geschichte seiner Instandsetzung bis 1980," in *Fürstenportal des Bamberger Domes*, ed. Manfred Schuller (Bamberg: Bayerische Verlagsanstalt, 1993), 7–18.
[32] Neundorfer, *Der Dom zu Bamberg*, 26.
[33] Ibid., 22–8.
[34] Wilhelm Boeck, *Der Bamberger Meister* (Tübingen: Katzmann, 1960), 108, fig. 7.

Paris, and Louis Martin brought home a copy. St. Thérèse reports the statue's smile in her poem:[35]

> O Thou who came to smile on me at dawn of life's beginning!
> Come once again to smile on me. Mother! The night is near.

St. Thérèse states that when she was 10, she was healed by that smile.[36] Writing of the "ravishing smile of the Blessed Virgin,"[37] she recalls, "It seems to me the Blessed Virgin must have looked upon her little flower and *smiled* at her, for wasn't it she who cured her with a *visible smile*?"[38]

These instances of Mary's smile in literature and popular piety jibe with the papal reflections on Mary's smile. For example, Pius XI (1922–39) prays in his encyclical, *Miserentissimus Redemptor*, "And now lastly may the most benign Virgin Mother of God smile (*arrideat*) on this purpose and on these desires of ours; for since she brought forth for us Jesus our Redeemer, and nourished Him, and offered Him as a victim by the Cross, by her mystic union with Christ and His very special grace she likewise became and is piously called a reparatress (*Reparatrix*)."[39] Pius XII (1939–58), who calls Mary *Coredemptrix* (three times during his papal reign), links Mary's beauty with her smile and says in a radio address (*nuntius radiophonicus*) on December 8, 1953, to Italian Catholic Action (*Azione Cattolica Italiana*),

> Mary's glance! Mary's smile! Mary's sweetness! The majesty of Mary, Queen of heaven and of earth! ... Mary is the most beautiful of all God's creatures ... Do you not think that Jesus' countenance, that countenance which the angels adore, must have reproduced in some way the lines of Mary's countenance? For every son's countenance mirrors his mother's. *Pulchra ut luna*. Blessed is he who can see you, Mother of our Lord, who can find his happiness with you; may we be able, Mary, to remain with you, in your house to serve you forever.[40]

John XXIII (1958–63), *né* Angelo Giuseppe Roncalli, recalls what he saw at the church of Santa Maria in Rome on August 10, 1904, the day of his ordination:

> When all was over and I raised my eyes [being prostrate upon the floor for ordination], having sworn the oath of eternal fidelity to my superior, the Bishops,

---

[35] Francis Mary, ed., *St. Thérèse: Doctor of the Little Way* (New Bedford, MA: Franciscan Friars of the Immaculate, 1997), 72.
[36] Ibid., 72.
[37] Ibid., 141.
[38] Ibid., 142 (italics in the original).
[39] Pope Pius XI, "Encyclical on Reparation to the Sacred Heart 'Miserentissimus Redemptor,'" *AAS* 20 (1928): 178; the English translation is taken from https://w2.vatican.va/content/pius-xi/en/encyclicals/documents/hf_p-xi_enc_19280508_miserentissimus-redemptor.html (accessed on March 25, 2018).
[40] Cited in Paolo M. Siano, "Mary 'Mediatrix of All Graces' in the Papal Magisterium up to the Pontificate of Paul VI," in *Mary at the Foot of the Cross VII: Coredemptrix, Therefore Mediatrix of All Graces: Acts of the Seventh International Symposium on Marian Coredemption*, ed. Peter Damian Fehlner (New Medford, MA: Academy of the Immaculate, 2008), 86.

I saw the blessed image of Our Lady to which I confess I had not paid any attention before. She seemed to smile at me from the altar and her look gave me a feeling of sweet peace in my soul and a generous and confident spirit.[41]

The papal reflections on Mary's smile again resonate in the homily Benedict XVI (2005–13) delivered at the Mass for the Sick at Lourdes, France, on September 15, 2008, in which he calls attention to Mary's smile:

Christians have always sought the smile of our Lady, this smile which medieval artists were able to represent with such marvelous skill and to show to advantage. This smile of Mary is for all; but it is directed quite particularly to those who suffer, so that they can find comfort and solace therein. To seek Mary's smile is not an act of devotional or outmoded sentimentality, but rather the proper expression of the living and profoundly human relationship which binds us to her whom Christ gave us as our Mother.[42]

The pontiff underscores that her smile, "a true reflection of God's tenderness, is the source of invincible hope."[43] As Paul VI says in his apostolic exhortation, *Marialis Cultus* (February 2, 1974), a paradigmatic pronouncement for Marian representations, "it should be considered quite normal for succeeding generations of Christians in differing sociocultural contexts to have expressed their sentiments about the Mother of Jesus in a way and manner which reflected their own age" (2.36).[44] In the midst of those numerous modalities of portrayals of Mary, her smile emerges as a common thread. The instances and intimations of her smile in iconography and elsewhere firmly establishes that the smiling Mary is neither a mere encapsulation of fleeting moments of relief from pain and suffering nor a magisterial ecclesial directive fueled by the Marian popes of recent times. From the beginning and through the centuries, her smile reveals the human side of the story of Jesus and fosters reflections on the clear, albeit often subdued, felicity that flows out of the love of the mother who gave birth to her son and saw him killed brutally on the cross, and, according to tradition, witnessed the continuation of life and hope beyond death.

---

[41] Cited in Janice T. Connell, *The Secrets of Mary: Gifts from the Blessed Mother* (New York: St. Martin's, 2009), 104.
[42] Mike Aquilina and Kris Stubna, *Take Five: Meditations with Pope Benedictus XVI* (Huntington, IN: Our Sunday Visitor, 2009), 71.
[43] Ibid., 71.
[44] Pope Paul VI, "Apostolic Exhortation for the Right Ordering and Development of Devotion to the Blessed Virgin Mary 'Marialis Cultus' (February 2, 1974)," *AAS* 66 (1974), 147; the English translation is taken from http://w2.vatican.va/content/paul-vi/en/apost_exhortations/documents/hf_p-vi_exh_19740202_marialis-cultus.html (accessed on March 25, 2018).

17

From *Holy Grail* to *The Lost Gospel*

Margaret Starbird and the Mary Magdalene Romance

Mary Ann Beavis

Likely the most influential Mary Magdalene scholar today is not a biblical scholar, feminist theologian, or church historian but Margaret Starbird, a popular writer of speculative history. Two of her books are cited in Dan Brown's *The Da Vinci Code*: *The Woman with the Alabaster Jar* and *The Goddess in the Gospels*.[1] The two other books cited in *Da Vinci*, *The Templar Revelation* and *Holy Blood, Holy Grail*, were written by a mixed bag of esoteric theorists, novelists, documentarians, and occult researchers whose sensational theories about the marriage between Jesus and Mary Magdalene are traceable to a twentieth-century hoax about a royal bloodline that has been thoroughly discredited by its many critics.[2]

Margaret Starbird, however, is avowedly not a sensationalizing conspiracy theorist, and she does have some academic credentials, although not in biblical studies; her BA and MA from the University of Maryland focused on comparative literature, medieval studies, and German, and she studied theology for one year at Vanderbilt Divinity School.[3] By her own admission, it wasn't until the publication of *Da Vinci* in 2003 that her books began to sell in droves,[4] especially to women. From the autobiographical sections in her writings, it is clear that she is a genuine seeker after the (or at least her) truth about Jesus and Mary Magdalene; her mission is a personal, spiritual quest to

---

[1] Henry Lincoln, Michael Baigent, and Richard Leigh, *Holy Blood, Holy Grail* (New York: Dell, 1983); Dan Brown, *The Da Vinci Code* (New York: Doubleday, 2003); Lynn Picknett and Clive Prince, *The Templar Revelation: Secret Guardians of the True Identity of Christ* (London: Bantam, 1997); Margaret Starbird, *The Woman with the Alabaster Jar: Mary Magdalene and the Holy Grail* (Santa Fe, NM: Bear, 1993); Starbird, *The Goddess in the Gospels: Sacred Union in Christianity* (Santa Fe, NM: Bear, 1998); Starbird, *Mary Magdalene: Bride in Exile* (Rochester, VT: Bear, 2005).

[2] E.g., Richard Barber, *The Holy Grail: The History of a Legend* (Harmondsworth: Penguin, 2005), 27, 45, 96–7, 138.

[3] See http://www.margaretstarbird.net/margarets_bio.html (accessed on March 24, 2015).

[4] Public presentation at the Faith and Feminism Conference, Ebenezer Lutheran Church (herchurch), San Francisco, November 2009.

restore the "lost bride," the sacred feminine, to Christianity.[5] Although she agrees with the claim of *Holy Blood, Holy Grail* that Jesus and the Magdalene were married, she places no importance on the alleged bloodline of the holy couple "except as it applies to the full humanity of Jesus."[6] Her epistemology begins with her own experience of something missing in her received faith and a sense of her own God-given task to revise the NT to embrace not just the mystical marriage of Christ and the Church but also of the historical Jesus and his wife Mary Magdalene.[7] The storyline of *The Da Vinci Code* is significantly dependent on Starbird's articulation of what I call the "Mary Magdalene Romance," which is much more influential on the way that the hypothesis of Jesus' marriage is understood in popular culture than the discredited royal bloodline theories. This Romance holds that Mary Magdalene and Jesus were married, and that after Jesus' death, the distraught Magdalene fled from Judea, pregnant with a daughter, Sara, whom she gave birth to in southern Gaul. Starbird has transformed the suppressed history of a messianic lineage to a love story between Jesus and Mary Magdalene, emblematic of "sacred union" in Christianity.[8]

The wide-ranging evidence Starbird marshals to support her convictions ventures far beyond the bible, but many of her arguments are grounded in scripture, and she is sometimes frustrated by biblical scholarship's lack of engagement with her interpretations.[9] For example, in *Bride in Exile*, she notes that biblical scholars have failed to embrace her suggestion that the 153 fishes of the post-resurrection scene in John 21:11 have a numerological significance that, interpreted through the lens of Pythagorean geometry, point to the role of the Magdalene in the life of Jesus. Starbird's arguments are grounded in the fact that the Greek letters of *hē Magdalenē* add up to 153, signifying the identity of the "lost bride" of Jesus. She insists that the gematria behind this calculation is not numerology in a New Age sense but "a literary device used by educated philosophers of the Pythagorean tradition—both Jew and Greek—to enhance the meaning of important phrases in their texts."[10] Even the Jesus Seminar, she notes, "were apparently aware that the gematria existed but decided not to examine it, although they spent many months establishing which quotes from the gospels were actually spoken by Jesus."[11] She correctly insists that the symbolic numbers of the Greek canon are worthy of examination "to see what added insights they reveal about the original teachings of Jesus"[12]—or, at least, about the intent of the NT writers.

---

[5] See Starbird, *Magdalene's Lost Legacy: Symbolic Numbers and the Sacred Union in Christianity* (Rochester, VT: Bear, 2003), 1–6; *Alabaster Jar*, XIII–XXIV; *Goddess in the Gospels*, 5–28, 65–79, esp. 73–4.

[6] Starbird, *Alabaster Jar*, 178.

[7] Starbird, *Goddess in the Gospels*, 73–4.

[8] See Sacred Union in Christianity, Margaret Starbird's website: http://www.margaretstarbird.net/blog.html (accessed on March 30, 2015).

[9] The very few exceptions I have run across are Esther A. De Boer, who briefly refers to Starbird in *The Gospel of Mary: Listening to the Beloved Disciple* (London: A&C Black, 2005), 4, 118; De Boer, *The Mary Magdalene Cover-Up: The Sources Behind the Myth* (London: T&T Clark, 2005), 4, 6; and Marvin Meyer (with Esther A. De Boer), *The Gospels of Mary: The Secret Tradition of Mary Magdalene, the Companion of Jesus* (San Francisco, CA: HarperSanFrancisco, 2003), 122.

[10] Starbird, *Bride in Exile*, 149.

[11] Ibid.

[12] Ibid.

What Starbird does not notice, of course, is that although the enumeration of the fishes likely had some deeper significance for the Johannine evangelist, it does not appear in a saying of Jesus[13] but in the narrative details. The symbolic significance of the 153 fish has been pondered by interpreters since Ante-Nicene times[14] and in innumerable Johannine commentaries ever since. The usual explanation of the number is that it symbolizes the unity of the church, based on Jerome's claim that there are 153 varieties of fish in the world.[15] Augustine suggested that the number was the sum of 10, representing the Law, plus the Holy Spirit, represented by the number 7 (cf. Isa 11:2-3), for a total of 17: "and when this number is used for the adding together of every serial number it contains, from one up to itself, the sum amounts to 153."[16] In other words, 153 is the sum of the numbers 1 through 17, a triangular number, for Augustine, signifying all those who share in divine grace.

Historically, numerology has figured in biblical interpretation for a very long time; some of it was even intended by the original authors.[17] In a commentary on John, I would add a reference to Starbird's interpretation as a matter of interest (like Augustine's or Jerome's), if not the most plausible explanation of the reference.[18] Even if the evangelists intended to allude to the Magdalene by the reference to the 153 fish, it would not mean that she was the literal Bride of Jesus; for example, it might aptly refer to her role as resurrection witness (John 20:11-18). However, it might be very significant that, as Starbird observes, in Pythagorean geometry, 153 stands for the "golden ratio," signifying the square root of three and the intersection between two overlapping circles of equal radius.[19] This figure is known as the *vesica piscis*, "the bladder of the fish," a possibly significant number in a passage about a miraculous catch of fish (John 21:1-14). Starbird connects the *vesica piscis* with the astrological Piscean Age and speculates that there is a "strong probability that the very earliest Christians who knew her best intended to designate the Magdalene as the Virgo counterpart of

---

[13] The material under investigation in Robert W. Funk, Roy W. Hoover, and the Jesus Seminar, *The Five Gospels: The Search for the Authentic Words of Jesus* (New York: Scribner [Polebridge], 1996), which Starbird cites in *Bride in Exile*, 149, n. 9. The commentary in *The Five Gospels* (468) does not attempt to explain the numerical reference.

[14] See, e.g., Joel C. Elowsky, ed., *Ancient Christian Commentary, John 11-21* (Downers Grove, IL: InterVarsity, 2007), 381-3.

[15] See Jo-Ann A. Brant, *John* (Paideia Commentaries on the New Testament; Grand Rapids, MI: Baker Academic, 2011), 282.

[16] Elowsky, *John 11-21*, 381 (Augustine, *Tractates on the Gospel of John* 122.8-9).

[17] However, as Mikeal C. Parsons ("Exegesis 'By the Numbers': Numerology and the New Testament," *PRSt* 35 [2008]: 25-43) notes, the reason why many NT scholars have regarded alleged numerical symbolism with caution is that it can lead to "the extremes of allegorical interpretation" (26); the numbers used in the biblical writings can easily be manipulated to support the outcomes favored by the exegete.

[18] In a book that focuses specifically on numerology (*Lost Legacy*), Starbird adds the name "Mary" to her calculations, leading to a gematria of 345, which she associates with "the eternal feminine" and with Pallas Athene through calculations based on criteria that are obscure to me. More significantly, they are flawed by her use of the spelling *Mariam* for Mary Magdalene, as opposed to *Maria*. Of the fourteen Gospel references to the Magdalene, only four use the Semitic spelling *Mariam* (Matt 27:61; 28:1; John 20:16, 18); the preferred spelling is the Hellenized *Maria* (Matt 27:56; Mark 15:40, 47; 16:1, 9; Luke. 8:2; 14:10; John 19:25; 20:1, 11). The other two prominent Marys of the Gospel tradition, the mother of Jesus and Mary of Bethany, are always referred to as *Mariam*.

[19] Starbird, *Lost Legacy*, 139-40.

the Piscean Lord."[20] A more down-to-earth suggestion is that since there is evidence that some early Christians practiced a form of eucharist where the elements were bread and fish, and not the more usual bread and wine, the post-resurrection breakfast of bread and symbolically enumerated fish shared by Jesus and the disciples (John 21:9–14) could well be understood "in connection with the hope for resurrection or immortality or life in the messianic age."[21]

A more significant insight of Starbird's, recently confirmed by Joan Taylor in the *Palestine Exploration Quarterly*,[22] relates to the origin of the title "Magdalene." The overwhelming majority of scholars, including Mary Magdalene specialists, has been that the title *Magdalēnē* refers to Mary's place of origin, the town of Magdala. However, nowhere in the gospels is Mary identified as "Mary of Magdala" (like Jesus of Nazareth [e.g., Mark 10:47; 16:6] or Simon of Cyrene [Mark 15:21; Luke 23:26]); she is always "the Magdalene"—a title that may not refer to a place name at all. As Starbird noted in her 2005 *Bride in Exile*, there is no evidence of a town called Magdala/Migdal in the first century CE: the city on the site of present-day Migdal was consistently called Tarichea by Josephus and other ancient writers, including Strabo, Pliny the Elder, and Suetonius.[23] The only first-century references to a "Magdala" appear in a single variant of Mark 8:10 and one of Matt 15:39; in both verses, the preferred readings are Dalmanutha (Mark) and Magadan (Matthew).[24] Starbird suggests that after Tarichea was destroyed in the Jewish War (70 CE), the place was renamed Magdala ("Tower").[25] Beginning in the fourth century, Christian pilgrims mistook the renamed town for the birthplace of Mary Magdalene.[26]

Professor Taylor's article, published in 2014 (nine years after Starbird's book), independently of Starbird's writings, comes to very similar conclusions: "No place named Magdala is mentioned in the earliest manuscripts of the New Testament or in other contemporaneous writing. The site called 'Magdala' in Israel today, some 5 km north of Tiberias and just north of Mount Arbel, continues a Byzantine identification, from the 5th or 6th centuries CE."[27] In fact, as Taylor observes, the term Magdala ("Tower") would be an odd place name, since it should appear with another name, "to indicate 'the Tower of Something', like the Tower of London."[28] The term is much more likely to be a nickname or title, as it is rendered in Syriac translations of the Gospels, where Mary is always referred to as "the Tower-ess."[29] Taylor surmises that

---

[20] Ibid., 141. Although the mother of Jesus has been identified as virgin, Starbird does not entertain the possibility that she is the Virgo counterpart because it does not fit into her sacred marriage paradigm (ibid., 142).

[21] Richard H Hiers, "The Bread and Fish Eucharist in the Gospels and Early Christian Art," *PRSt* 3 (1976): 21–48.

[22] Joan Taylor, "Missing Magdala and the Name of Mary 'Magdalene'," *PEQ* 146 (2014): 205–23.

[23] Starbird, *Bride in Exile*, 52–5. Strabo, *Geography of Palestine* 16.2, 42; Pliny the Elder, *Natural History* 5.71; Suetonius, *Lives of the Caesars, Titus* 4.

[24] Esther A. De Boer, *Mary Magdalene: Beyond the Myth* (London: Bloomsbury, 1997), 23.

[25] Starbird, *Bride in Exile*, 58–9; cf. De Boer, *Mary Magdalene*, 23.

[26] Starbird, *Bride in Exile*, 56.

[27] Taylor, "Missing Magdala," 205.

[28] Ibid., 208. Cf. Judg 8:17; 9:46, 49; Neh 3:1, 11; 12:38, 39; Song 4:4; 7:4; Jer 31:38; Zech 14:10; Luke 13:4.

[29] Ibid., 208.

the designation "Magdalene" or "Tower-Woman" was Mary's Galilean nickname (like *Kepha*, the Rock, was Simon Peter's), which did not refer to Tarichea at all but possibly to another town (Migdal Nuniya [Tower of Fish] or Migdal Tsebaya [Tower of Dye]): "As such, beyond Galilee, Mary's distinctive name not only indicated her geographical origin but also her position as one of Jesus' closest disciples, and more. Perhaps, as Simon Peter was a Rock, she was in some way the woman of the 'Tower.'"[30] That is, Taylor has it both ways: *Magdalēnē* was both a vaguely defined place designation *and* a title ("Mary the Tower"). However, whatever Simon's nickname "the Rock" signified, nobody has ever suggested that he was from a place named after a rock[31]—it said something about his character or status, not about his home town. This is likely also true of the Magdalene. In fact, following the interpretation of Peter the Rock in Matt 16:18 ("on this rock I will build my church"), it seems plausible Mary the Tower was a similar architectural metaphor.

The interpretation of "Magdalene" as meaning Tower, rather than a place name, is not new. Jerome interpreted it as a title meaning "tower," symbolizing "the earnestness and glow of her faith" so that she was privileged to be the first to witness the risen Christ.[32] Starbird is very specific about the referent of the Tower metaphor; she argues that Mary was the *migdal-eder* ("Watchtower of the Flock") of Mic 4:8–11:

> And you, O tower of the flock,
>   hill of daughter Zion,
> to you it shall come,
>   the former dominion shall come,
>   the sovereignty of daughter Jerusalem.
> Now why do you cry aloud?
>   Is there no king in you?
> Has your counselor perished,
>   that pangs have seized you like a woman in labor?
> Writhe and groan, O daughter Zion,
>   like a woman in labor;
> for now you shall go forth from the city
>   and camp in the open country;
>   you shall go to Babylon.
> There you shall be rescued,
>   there the Lord will redeem you
>   from the hands of your enemies.
> Now many nations
>   are assembled against you,
>   saying, "Let her be profaned,
>   and let our eyes gaze upon Zion." (NRSV)

---

[30] Ibid., 222.
[31] There are actually very few biblical references to "rock" place names; cf. Judg 7:25; 15:8, 11; 20:45, 47; 1 Sam 23:28; Isa 20:26.
[32] Jerome, *Letter 127: To Principia*, http://www.newadvent.org/fathers/3001127.htm (accessed on May 14, 2018).

That is, for Starbird, the title Magdalene identifies her with Daughter Zion bereft of her king: "The desolate bride crying over her deceased bridegroom … the profaned and denigrated bride of Jesus forced into exile."[33] Starbird both allegorizes and historicizes this prophecy in terms of her distinctive construction of the Mary Magdalene Romance; for her, it refers to Mary the Tower, the Daughter of Zion who mourns for her messianic husband, Jesus, who must flee Israel in order to save herself and her child, borne of the grail of her womb.[34] This interpretation depends on Starbird's assumption that there is more than a grain of truth in the medieval *Golden Legend* (c. 1260) according to which after the crucifixion, Mary Magdalene (identified with Mary of Bethany), along with Martha, Lazarus, and many others, were set adrift by their enemies in a rudderless boat to be drowned. The saints were miraculously guided to the south of France, where Mary preached and worked miracles, and where she was buried.[35] Starbird's particular spin on this tradition is that she regards the legendary Egyptian maidservant of the Magdalene, St. Sara, as actually the child of Mary and Jesus;[36] the fact that the medieval French Cathars were the only Christian group to have harbored a belief that Jesus and Mary Magdalene were married bolsters her case.[37] In fact, St. Sara is widely regarded as a thinly Christianized version of a Roma deity (Sara-Kali) who is revered by Romani and Catholics alike in the seaside town of Saintes-Maries-sur-le-Mer, Provence.[38] Although Starbird's construction of the Micah prophecy, with its heady blend of legend, romance, and archetype ranges far beyond the limits of historical-critical exegesis into the realms of mythography,[39] it is possible that the prophetic image of the "Tower of the Flock," associated with Daughter Zion and messianic fulfillment, figures in the Magdalene title, where Mary is the "Tower" corresponding to the "Rock" of Peter.

One of Starbird's reasons for insisting (evidently quite rightly) that Mary was *not* from Magdala is that, like many generations of Western Christians, she regards Mary Magdalene and Mary of Bethany, sister of Martha and Lazarus, as the same woman. As I have argued elsewhere, there are some reception-historical grounds for making this identification, since as early as the Gospel of John the lines between the two Marys have been blurred, and, in post-biblical tradition, the "Mary Magdalene" who is supposed to figure in so many early Christian texts (including the *Gospel of Mary*) is often *not* identified as the Magdalene and shares many characteristics with the Mary of Bethany of Luke and John.[40] However, for Starbird, it is important for

---

[33] Starbird, *Bride in Exile*, 62.
[34] Ibid., 63.
[35] The *Golden Legend* actually attributes her title to the name of the castle Magdalo, a castle belonging to her parents (Jacobus de Voragine, *The Golden Legend: Readings on the Saints*, trans. William Granger Ryan [Waxkeep, 2013]). The *Legend* cites both Hegesippus and Josephus as sources of its narrative; no extant text of either ancient historian accords with Jacobus's account.
[36] Starbird, *Bride in Exile*, 101–4.
[37] Starbird, *Goddess in the Gospels*, 87; *Alabaster Jar*, 72–8. See also Mary Ann Beavis, "The Cathar Mary Magdalene and the Sacred Feminine: Pop Culture Legend vs. Medieval Doctrine," *JRPC* 24 (2012): 419–31. The *Legend* says that Jesus showed his great love of the Magdalene by exorcizing her of seven devils, and "He embraced her in all his love, and made her right familiar with him."
[38] Zina Petersen, "'Twisted Paths of Civilization: Saint Sara and the Romani," *JRPC* 26 (2014): 310–22.
[39] See Mary Ann Beavis, "The Deification of Mary Magdalene," *Feminist Theology* 21 (2012): 150.
[40] Mary Ann Beavis, "Reconsidering Mary of Bethany," *CBQ* 74 (2012): 281–97; Beavis, "Mary of Bethany and the Hermeneutics of Remembrance," *CBQ* 75 (2013): 739–55.

Mary the Tower to be the sister of Lazarus because of her erotic interpretation of John 12:1–7 (the Anointing at Bethany), where, in gratitude for the raising of her brother, Jesus' wife Mary anoints Jesus with expensive perfume and is commended by him for her prophetic act, anticipating his burial. Starbird connects this scene not only with Song 1:12 ("For the king's banquet, my nard gives forth its fragrance")[41] but also with the sacred marriages of Inanna and Dumuzi, Isis and Osiris, Anath and Baal,[42] and the ritual by which the royal priestess anointed the god-king of Sumer to prepare for his death and resurrection. This sacral allusion, Starbird suggests, would have been understood by anyone in the time of Jesus.[43] Possibly, "anyone" in ancient Sumer or Babylon, or even preexilic Jerusalem where the women mourned for Tammuz at the temple gate (Ezek 8:14), might have thought of the sacred marriage; this is highly unlikely of Jewish readers in first-century Judea. However, there may be mythic echoes buried in John 20:11–18, where the weeping Mary Magdalene meets with the risen Lord, the Bridegroom of the Gospel (John 3:29; cf. 2:1–11). Perhaps the ancient audience of John did perceive in Mary's weeping at the tomb an echo of the ancient goddesses mourning their murdered lovers (Inanna and Dumuzi, Ishtar and Tammuz, Isis and Osiris, Cybele and Attis, Venus and Adonis), like Daughter Zion suffering the loss of her anointed king (Mic 4:8–11). In subsequent, and even more extravagant, post-Starbird iterations of the Magdalene Romance, Mary morphs from bereaved spouse to full-fledged Gentile priestess of the Goddess: according to Lynn Picknett, the Magdalene was a Black devotee of Isis[44] and, more recently, for Simcha Jacobovici and Barrie Wilson in *The Lost Gospel*, a Phoenician priestess of Artemis.[45] Both cite Starbird as one of their authorities.[46]

In the light of Starbird's substantial popularity and influence, academic Mary Magdalene scholars would do well to be aware of her work. Works of esoteric history and fiction inspired by her iteration of the Mary Magdalene Romance are far more influential on popular audiences, especially women, than those of academic biblical scholars and theologians. In addition to her flashes of genuine exegetical acumen, the influence of her work speaks to concerns above and beyond the feminist construction of the Magdalene as faithful disciple and apostle to the apostles: the humanity of Jesus, the legitimacy of sexuality and family life, the embodiment of the female divine, the role of women in the church, and the suspicion that the church is suppressing information. It is true that feminist theologians have been addressing these issues at length for many years, but Starbird's critiques of theology and church, interwoven with the Mary Magdalene Romance, are much better known to nonacademic audiences than those of Rosemary Radford Ruether or Elisabeth Schüssler Fiorenza.[47] For nonacademic

---

[41] Starbird, *Alabaster Jar*, 41.
[42] Ibid., 42–3.
[43] Starbird, *Bride in Exile*, 49.
[44] Lynn Picknett, *Mary Magdalene: Christianity's Hidden Goddess* (New York: Carroll & Graf, 2003), 149–61. Picknett refers to Starbird on 66.
[45] Simcha Jacobovici and Barrie Wilson, *The Lost Gospel: Decoding the Ancient Text that Reveals Jesus' Marriage to Mary the Magdalene* (San Francisco, CA: HarperCollins, 2014), 112, 114, 190, 109.
[46] Picknett, *Mary Magdalene*, 66; Jacobovici and Wilson, *Lost Gospel*, 124, 141, 219–20.
[47] Classic works on this topic by these two highly influential feminist scholars are Rosemary Radford Ruether, *Sexism and God-Talk: Toward a Feminist Theology* (Boston, MA: Beacon, 1983, 1993),

readers, a published book, a TV documentary, or even a movie may be regarded as a credible source of information regardless of whether the publisher is a university press or the author has scholarly credentials; it's the content and message that counts. Magdalene scholars who are unaware of Starbird's ideas, or who are casually dismissive of them, run the risk of appearing to be uniformed, or worse, part of the corruption and cover-up the church (and the academy) is accused of (and sometimes merits), to church groups, university students, and women's spirituality groups (or even the media) they may encounter, and, as argued above, miss some valid and profitable avenues of exegetical inquiry.

8–11; Elisabeth Schüssler Fiorenza, "Mary Magdalene: Apostle to the Apostles," *Union Theological Seminary Journal* (1974): 22–4.

Afterword

The Future of Mariamic Studies

Mary Ann Beavis and Ally Kateusz

The essays in this book disrupt many of the scholarly commonplaces about the Marys that have filtered beyond the academy and into popular discourse. In Jewish tradition, the figure of Miriam, the sister of Moses and Aaron, far from receding into obscurity, developed in tandem with Mary of Nazareth *and* Mary Magdalene (Rosenberg, DeGolan and Walfish). Mary of Nazareth, more than simply the humble maid of Galilee, was an immensely powerful figure for some early Christians—liturgical leader, mediator, and counterpart of her son (Kateusz, Horn, Davis). The original "apostle to the apostles" was arguably not Mary Magdalene but Mary of Bethany (Goodacre) along with her sister Martha (Beavis). Maryam of Islam appears to have more relationship to the portrayal of Jesus' mother in extracanonical texts than in the canon (Saxon). Not only the Blessed Virgin, but in recent years Mary Magdalene, also has achieved near-deification (Beavis).

Nowhere is disruptive scholarship more in evidence here than with the figure of Mary called the Magdalene. On the one hand, some ancient authors did not identify their protagonist named Mary as Magdalene, mother, or Mary of Bethany (Hartenstein, Cwikla)—but on the other hand, some identified two Mary Magdalenes (Lyons-Pardue, Kateusz). Gregory the Great's pronouncement that Mary Magdalene and Mary of Bethany were one and the same is often identified as the turning point in the Magdalene's medieval reputation as a sinful woman, but his pronouncement was predated by centuries of similar conflation, a tendency that began in the gospels themselves (Goodacre, Beavis). Calling Mary Magdalene "Mary of Magdala" is to incorrectly reinforce a late misnomer, a misnomer that impedes her identification, because the town today known as Magdala was called Tarichaea in the first century, and not until the fifth century do we find the word "Magdala" in gospel manuscripts; a much more likely etymology of the title is that she was Mary the Tower (*migdal*) among the disciples, much like Peter was called the Rock (Beavis, Goodacre, Kateusz). A key question in understanding the historicity of the Magdalene within the Jesus movement is as follows: *Why did so many first- and second-century authors identify a woman (or women) as the Savior's apostle to the apostles?* (Hartenstein, Beavis).

Another disruptive stream, which flows across the three sections of this volume, is the leadership and authority of Jesus' mother, a phenomenon first seen in the canonical gospels, where sometimes she was elevated in a role that today we might expect of the Magdalene (Badley, Kateusz, Horn). As Cwikla notes, but Goodacre and Beavis discount, Stephen J. Shoemaker has contended that she may have been seen as the prominent disciple identified in the *Gospel of Mary*, *Dialogue of the Savior*, and other texts.[1] Certainly authors in Ancient Syria remembered Jesus' mother as a leader with extraordinary authority; Horn details her portrayal as a community leader and mediator with the divine; and Kateusz demonstrates that some writers portrayed her both as a liturgical leader and as the first witness to her son's resurrection with no apparent sense of contradiction in these two roles. In Ancient Syria, the continuing impact of the extracanonical narratives about her birth, life, and death is witnessed in archeological ruins of Christian basilicas (Freund), Jewish imagination (Rosenburg), and Islamic origins (Saxon). The social effect of narratives about Mary with liturgical leadership authority is suggested by the manner in which later scribes—ancient, medieval, and modern—censored those passages (Kateusz, Davis). Across centuries, competing church agendas are revealed in how Mary was portrayed. For example, in the twelfth century, a new iconography, the smiling virgin, sometimes replaced solemn presentations of Mary's power (Han), yet in the sixteenth century, colonial church writers invoked her ancient roles as protector of the oppressed, mediator, and apostle in order to facilitate the conversion of continents (Manzo).

Compared with Mary of Nazareth and Mary Magdalene, the elusive figure of Mary the sister of Martha—thusly identified because the designation "Mary of Bethany" is an academic construct, much like "Mary of Magdala"—has until recently received little scholarly attention. New reconsiderations of the evidence (Goodacre, Beavis) reveal that although from an early date she was sometimes conflated with the Magdalene and sometimes with an unnamed sexualized woman, the gospels nonetheless portray her in significant roles (Luke 10:38-42; John 11:1-3, 28-37; 12:1-8). Her guises as disciple, resurrection witness, myrrhbearer, and apostle were remembered by early Christians and have continued to influence Christian legend and iconography ever since.

The question of "which Mary" continues to matter. For the sake of historical and exegetical accuracy, it matters whether Mary of Nazareth, Mary Magdalene(s), Mary of Bethany, or another of the many Marys of early Christian tradition, including Miriam the sister of Moses, was portrayed in the ancient sources (Goodacre, Beavis, Hartenstein, Cwikla, Lyons-Pardue, Kateusz, Rosenberg, DeGolan and Walfish). From the standpoint of feminist interpretation, it is important to recognize the significance and contributions of these (and other) specific women as disciples, leaders, heroes, and archetypes, and not to bundle them all into one all-encompassing (generic or literary or composite) "Mary," as if ancient readers themselves believed there were no historical Marys. In fact, they remembered and honored several. Perhaps the disparate early Christian communities who treasured documents like the *Gospel of Mary* or the *Dialogue of the Savior* identified the unspecified Mary who spoke on their pages as

---

[1] Stephen J. Shoemaker, *Mary in Early Christian Faith and Devotion* (New Haven, CT: Yale University Press, 2016), 73–95.

the Mary they venerated most, as they may also have done with ambiguously named male figures, like James, John, and Judas.[2] Yet the keenest value of the historicity of texts such as the *Gospel of Mary* or the Dormition of Mary is that they each provide a window into the author's community, and that community's gender politics, concerns, and conflicts with other communities. How authors remembered their female protagonists named Mary, and how later authors redacted or reused their narratives, tells us a great deal about their cultural contexts. Less important is the biographical content, for authors' memories of their protagonists are notoriously misremembered and variegated, regardless of whether the protagonist is male or female, or whether the text is canonical or extracanonical. *Who was the historical Jesus* remains a perennial question in scholarly circles. *Who were the historical Marys*—Maria, Mariamne, and Miriam—is a similar mystery—and challenge.

The influence of the Marys on our culture is illustrated both by their multifaceted reception through the centuries (Badley, Manzo, Freund, Rosenburg, Kateusz, Saxon, Han, Beavis) and also by their suppression and contestation (Kateusz, DeGolan and Walfish, Davis). Miramic threads emanating from the ancient sources are seldom linear; more often they are intertwined, tangled, braided, spliced, and sliced. The range of perspectives on the Marys offered in the seventeen chapters of this anthology only scratch the surface of possible directions for future Mariamic research, for example, the liturgical roles of the Marys in ancient Judaism and Christianity; redaction analysis and the role of censorship in the formation of our modern perception of the historical Marys; the interplay between the Jewish, Christian, and Muslim receptions of Miriam/Maria/Maryam; and the promise of the Mariamic tradition for interfaith dialogue. We hope that this volume will provide an impetus for future research in these, and many other, directions.

---

[2] Or even, as a colleague facetiously suggested, Jesus, since Joshua/Jeshua/*Iēsous* was such a common Jewish man's name in antiquity (think of Jesus Sirach, Jesus Barabbas, Jesus Justus, Jesus son of Ananias, Jesus Bar Kochba).

References

Abbott, H. Porter. *The Cambridge Introduction to Narrative*. 2nd ed. Cambridge Introductions to Literature. Cambridge: Cambridge University Press, 2008.

Abboud, Hosn. "'Idhan Maryam Nabiyya' ('Hence Maryam Is a Prophetess'): Muslim Classical Exegetes and Women's Receptiveness to God's Verbal Inspiration." In *Miriam, the Magdalen, and the Mother*, 183–96. Edited by Deirdre Good. Bloomington: Indiana University Press, 2005.

Achelis, Hans. "The Gnomai of the Synod of Nicea [sic]." *JTS* 2 (1901): 121–9.

Agouridis, Savvas. "The Virgin Mary in the Texts of the Gospels." In *Mother of God: Representations of the Virgin in Byzantine Art*, 58–65. Edited by Maria Vassilaki. Milan: Skira editore, 2000.

Agranoff, Robert, and Beryl A. Radin. "Deil Wright's Overlapping Model of Intergovernmental Relations: The Basis for Contemporary Intergovernmental Relationships." *Publius: The Journal of Federalism* 45 (2015): 139–59.

Ahmed, Leila. *Women and Gender in Islam: Historical Roots of a Modern Debate*. New Haven, CT: Yale University Press, 1992.

Alarcón Méndez, P. Pedro. *El amor de Jesús vivo en la Virgen de Guadalupe*. Bloomington, IN: Palibrio, 2013.

Alexander, Loveday. "Fact, Fiction and the Genre of Acts." *NTS* 44 (1998): 380–99.

Alexander, Loveday. "Mapping Early Christianity: Acts and the Shape of Early Church History." *Int* 57 (2003): 163–73.

Alexander, Loveday. "Narrative Maps: Reflections on the Toponymy of Acts." In *Bible in Human Society: Essays in Honour of John Rogerson*, 17–57. Edited by R. M. D. Carroll, D. J. A. Clines, and P. R. Davies. JSNTSS. Sheffield: Sheffield Academic, 1995.

Alexandre, Y. *Mary's Well, Nazareth. The Late Hellenistic to the Ottoman Periods*. Jerusalem: IAA Reports 49, 2012.

Anawati, George. "Islam and the Immaculate Conception." In *The Dogma of the Immaculate Conception: History and Significance*, 447–61. Edited by E. D. O'Connor. Notre Dame, IN: University of Notre Dame, 1958.

Anderson, Gary A. *The Genesis of Perfection: Adam and Eve in Jewish and Christian Imagination*. Louisville, KY: Westminster/John Knox, 2001.

Angiolini, Anna. *La capsella eburnea di Pola*. Bologna: Pàtron, 1970.

Anonymous. "Of Aztec Human Sacrifice." In *A Handbook on Guadalupe*, 138–40. New Bedford, MA: Franciscan Friars of the Immaculate, 1997.

Apostolos-Cappadona, Diane. "On the Visual and the Vision: The Magdalene in Early Christian and Byzantine Art and Culture." In *Mariam, the Magdalene and the Mother*, 123–52. Edited by Deirdre Good. Bloomington: Indiana University Press, 2005.

Aquilina, Mike, and Kris Stubna. *Take Five: Meditations with Pope Benedictus XVI*. Huntington, IN: Our Sunday Visitor, 2009.

Arras, Victor. *De Transitus Mariae Aethiopice*, vol. 1. CSCO 342–3. Louvain: Secrétariat du CSCO, 1973.

Auer, Johann. *Unter deinen Schutz und Schirm. Das älteste Mariengebet der Kirche.* Leutesdorf am Rhein: Johannes-Verlag, 1967.

Aviam, M. "Distribution Maps of Archaeological Data from the Galilee: An Attempt to Establish Zones Indicative of Ethnicity and Religious Affiliation." In *Religion, Ethnicity and Identity in Ancient Galilee: A Region in Transition*, 115–32. Edited by J. Zangenberg, H. W. Attridge, D. Martin. Tübingen: Mohr Siebeck, 2007.

Avi Yonah, Michael. "A List of Priestly Courses from Caesarea." *Israel Exploration Journal* 12 (1962): 137–9.

Baert, Barbara. "Touching with the Gaze: A Visual Analysis of the *Noli me tangere*." In *Noli me tangere—Mary Magdalene: One Person, Many Images*, 43–52. Edited by Barbara Baert, Reimund Bieringer, Karlijn Demasure, and Sabine Van Den Eynde. Leuven: Peeters, 2006.

Barbara Baert, Reimund Bieringer, Karlijn Demasure, and Sabine Van Den Eynde, eds. *Noli me tangere—Mary Magdalene: One Person, Many Images.* Leuven: Peeters, 2006.

Bagatti, Bellarmino. *Excavations in Nazareth. Vol. 1: From the Beginning till the XII Century.* Jerusalem: Franciscan Printing Press, 1968.

Bagatti, Bellarmino. "La verginità di Maria negli apocrifi del II–III secolo." *Marianum* 33 (1971): 281–92.

Bakhtiar, Laleh. *The Sublime Quran: English Translation: Revised Edition.* Chicago, IL: Kazi, 2012.

Baldi, Donato, and Anacleto Mosconi. "L'Assunzione di Maria SS. negli apocrifi." In *Atti del congresso nazionale mariano dei Fratei Minori d'Italia*, 75–125. Studia Mariana 1. Rome: Commissionis Marialis Franciscanae, *1948*.

Baltsan, Hayim. *Webster's New World Hebrew Dictionary.* Cleveland, OH: Wiley, 1992.

Barber, Richard. *The Holy Grail: The History of a Legend.* Harmondsworth: Penguin, 2005.

Barnet, Peter. "Enthroned Virgin and Child." In *Images in Ivory: Precious Objects of the Gothic Age*, 118–19. Edited by Peter Barnet. Detroit, MI: The Detroit Institute of Arts, 1997.

Barnet, Peter. "Gothic Sculpture in Ivory: An Introduction." In *Images in Ivory: Precious Objects of the Gothic Age*, 2–17. Edited by Peter Barnet. Detroit, MI: The Detroit Institute of Arts, 1997.

Barnet, Peter. "Virgin and Child with Two Angels from Saint-Denis." In *Images in Ivory: Precious Objects of the Gothic Age*, 125–56. Edited by Peter Barnett. Detroit, MI: The Detroit Institute of Arts, 1997.

Barrett, C. K. *A Critical and Exegetical Commentary on the Acts of the Apostles.* 2 volumes. Edinburgh: T&T Clark, 1994–8.

Bass, Ardyth L. "Composition and Redaction in the Coptic Gospel of Mary." PhD dissertation, Marquette University, 2007.

Bauckham, Richard, and Stefano De Luca, "Magdala as We Now Know It." *Early Christianity* 6 (2015): 91–118.

Bauckham, Richard. *The Fate of the Dead: Studies on Jewish and Christian Apocalypses.* Leiden: Brill, 1998.

Bauckham, Richard. *Gospel Women: Studies of the Named Women in the Gospels.* Grand Rapids, MI: Eerdmans, 2002.

Bauckham, Richard. *Jude and the Relatives of Jesus in the Early Church.* Edinburgh: T&T Clark, 1990.

Bauer, Walter. *Das Leben Jesu im Zeitalter der Neutestamentlichen Apokryphen.* Tübingen: Mohr, 1909.

Baynes, Norman H. "The Supernatural Defenders of Constantinople." *AnBoll* 67 (1949): 165–77.
Beatrice, Pier Franco. "The 'Gospel According to the Hebrews' in the Apostolic Fathers." *NovT* 48 (2006): 147–95.
Beauregard, David. "Virtue Ethics in Michelangelo's the Last Judgment: Christ as Severity and Mary as Clemency." *Logos: A Journal of Catholic Thought and Culture* 19.2 (2016): 33–52.
Beavis, Mary Ann. "The Cathar Mary Magdalene and the Sacred Feminine: Pop Culture Legend vs. Medieval Doctrine." *JRPC* 24 (2012): 419–31.
Beavis, Mary Ann. "The Deification of Mary Magdalene." *Feminist Theology* 21 (2012): 145–54.
Beavis, Mary Ann. "The Influence of Feminist Theology on Canadian Women Artists." In *Feminist Theology with a Canadian Accent: Canadian Perspectives on Feminist Contextual Theology*, 291–306. Edited by Mary Ann Beavis, with Elaine Guillemin and Barbara Pell. Ottawa: Novalis, 2008.
Beavis, Mary Ann. "Mary of Bethany and the Hermeneutics of Remembrance." *CBQ* 75 (2013): 739–55.
Beavis, Mary Ann. "Reconsidering Mary of Bethany." *CBQ* 74 (2012): 281–97.
Beavis, Mary Ann. "Who Is Mary Magdalene?" In *Christian Reflection: A Series in Faith and Ethics. Women in the Bible*, 23–9. Edited by Robert B. Kruschwitz. Waco, TX: Baylor University Press, 2013.
Bedjan, Paul, ed. *S. Martyrii, qui et Sahdona quae supersunt omnia*. Paris: Harrassowitz, 1902.
Bello, M. L. "Intergovernmental Relations in Nigeria: An Assessment of Its Practice at the Local Government Level." *Journal of Poverty, Investment and Development* 4 (2014): 66–76.
Ben-Zvi, I. *Maso't Eretz-Israel le–Rabbi Moseh Basola*. Jerusalem: Mosad Byaliq, 1938.
Biddle, Martin. *The Tomb of Christ*. Thrupp, UK: Sutton, 1999.
Bisconti, Fabrizio. "La Capsella di Samagher: Il quadro delle interpretazioni." *Il cristianesimo in Istria fra tarda antichità e alto Medioevo* (2009): 217–31.
Blatz, Beate. "The Dialogue of the Saviour." In *New Testament Apocrypha, Volume One: Gospels and Related Writings*, 300–3. Edited by Wilhelm Schneemelcher. Translated by R. McL. Wilson. Rev. ed. Louisville, KY: Westminster/John Knox, 1990.
Blumell, Lincoln H. *Lettered Christians: Christians, Letters, and Late Antique Oxyrhynchus*. Leiden: Brill, 2012.
Boeck, Wilhelm. *Der Bamberger Meister*. Tübingen: Katzmann, 1960.
Boehm, Barbara Drake, and William D. Wixom. *Mirror of the Medieval World*. Published in conjunction with the exhibition "Mirror of the Medieval World," held at the Metropolitan Museum of Art, March 9–July 18, 1999. New York: The Metropolitan Museum of Art, 1999.
Bogdanović, Jelena. *The Framing of Sacred Space: The Canopy and the Byzantine Church*. New York: Oxford University Press, 2017.
Booth, Paul. "On the *Life of the Virgin* Attributed to Maximus Confessor." *JTS*, NS 66, pt. 1 (April 2015): 149–203.
Boring, M. Eugene. "Markan Christology: God-Language for Jesus?" *NTS* 45 (1999): 451–71.
Boustan, Raanan. *From Martyr to Mystic: Rabbinic Martyrology and the Making of Merkavah Mysticism*. Tübingen: Mohr Siebeck, 2005.

Bovon, François, and Christopher R. Matthews, eds. and trans. *The Acts of Philip: A New Translation*. Waco, TX: Baylor University Press, 2012.
Bovon, François, Bertrand Bouvier, and Frédéric Amsler, eds. and trans. *Acta Philippi: Textus*. Corpus Christianorum, Series Apocryphorum 11. Turnhout: Brepols, 1999.
Bovon, François. "An Introduction to the *Acts of Philip*." In *The Acts of Philip: A New Translation*, 1–30. Edited by François Bovon and Christopher R. Matthews. Waco, TX: Baylor University Press, 2012.
Bovon, François. "*Mary Magdalene in the Acts of Philip*." In *Which Mary? The Marys of Early Christian Tradition*, 75–89. Edited by F. Stanley Jones. SBLSS 19. Atlanta, GA: Society of Biblical Literature, 2002.
Boyarin, Daniel. *Carnal Israel: Reading Sex in Talmudic Culture*. Berkeley: University of California Press, 1993.
Boyarin, Daniel. "Hellenism in Jewish Babylonia." In *The Cambridge Companion to the Talmud and Rabbinic Literature*, 336-64. Edited by Charlotte Elisheva Fonrobert and Martin S. Jaffee. New York: Cambridge University Press, 2007.
Boyarin, Daniel. "Reading Androcentricism against the Grain: Women, Sex, and Torah-Study." *Poetics Today* 12 (1991): 29–53.
Boyarin, Daniel. *A Traveling Homeland: The Babylonian Talmud as Diaspora*. Philadelphia: University of Pennsylvania Press, 2015.
Brading, David A. *Mexican Phoenix. Our Lady of Guadalupe: Image and Tradition across the Five Centuries*. Cambridge: Cambridge University Press, 2001.
Brant, Jo-Ann A. *John*. Paideia Commentaries on the New Testament. Grand Rapids, MI: Baker, 2014.
Breuer, Tilmann. "Das Fürstenportal: Geschichte seiner Instandsetzung bis 1980." In *Fürstenportal des Bamberger Domes*, 7–18. Edited by Manfred Schuller. Bamberg: Bayerische Verlagsanstalt, 1993.
Brock, Ann Graham. "The Identity of the Blessed Mary, Representative of Wisdom in Pistis Sophia." In *Walk in the Ways of Wisdom: Essays in Honor of Elisabeth Schüssler Fiorenza*, 122–35. Edited by Shelly Matthews, Cynthia Briggs Kittredge, and Melanie Johnson-Debaufre. Harrisburg, PA: Trinity Press International, 2003.
Brock, Ann Graham. *Mary Magdalene, the First Apostle: The Struggle for Authority*. HThS 51. Cambridge, MA: Harvard University Press, 2003.
Brock, Ann Graham. "Setting the Record Straight—The Politics of Identification: Mary Magdalene and Mary the Mother in *Pistis Sophia*." In *Which Mary? The Marys of Early Christian Tradition*, 43–52. Edited by F. Stanley Jones. SBLSS 19. Atlanta, GA: Society of Biblical Literature, 2002.
Brock, Ann Graham. "What's in a Name: The Competition for Authority in Early Christian Texts." In *SBL 1998 Seminar Papers*, 106–24. Atlanta, GA: Society of Biblical Literature, 1998.
Brock, Sebastian. "The Genealogy of the Virgin Mary in Sinai Syr. 16." In *Universum Hagiographicum Mémorial R.P. Michel van Esbroeck, S.J (1934–2003)*, 58–71. Edited by Sevir Boriscovic Cernecov. Saint Petersburg: Byzantinorossica, 2006.
Brock, Sebastian. *Holy Spirit in the Syrian Baptismal Tradition*. The Syrian Churches 9. Enlarged 2nd ed. Pune, India: Anita Printers, 1998.
Brodsky, David. *A Bride without a Blessing: A Study in the Redaction and Content of Massekhet Kallah and Its Gemara*. Tübingen: Mohr Siebeck, 2006.
Brown, Dan. *The Da Vinci Code*. New York: Doubleday, 2003.
Brown, Raymond E. *The Birth of the Messiah: A Commentary on the Infancy Narratives in Matthew and Luke*. Rev. ed. Garden City, NY: Doubleday, 1993.

Brown, Raymond E. *The Gospel according to John XIII–XXI*. AB 29A. Garden City, NY: Doubleday, 1970.
Brown, Raymond E., Karl P. Donfried, Joseph A. Fitzmyer, and John Reumann. *Mary in the New Testament: A Collaborative Assessment by Protestant and Roman Catholic Scholars*. Philadelphia, PA: Fortress and Paulist, 1978.
Brubaker, Leslie, and Mary B. Cunningham. *The Cult of the Mother of God in Byzantium: Texts and Images*. Burlington, VT: Ashgate, 2011.
Bruce, F. F. *The Acts of the Apostles: The Greek Text with Introduction and Commentary*. 3rd ed. Grand Rapids, MI: Eerdmans, 1990.
Buddensieg, Tilmann. "Le coffret en ivoire de Pola: Saint-Pierre et le Latran." *Cahiers archéologiques* 10 (1959): 157–95.
Budge, Ernest A. Wallis, ed. and trans. *The History of the Blessed Virgin Mary and the History of the Likeness of Christ Which the Jews of Tiberias Made to Mock At*. 2 volumes. London: Luzac, 1899.
Bulgakov, Sergius. *Churchly Joy: Orthodox Devotions for the Church Year*. Translated by Boris Jakim. Grand Rapids, MI: William B. Eerdmans, 2008.
Burgon, John W. *The Last Twelve Verses of Mark: Vindicated against Recent Critical Objectors & Established*. Oxford: James Parker, 1871.
Burke, Brendan F. "Understanding Intergovernmental Relations, Twenty-Five Years Hence." *State and Local Government Review* 46 (2014): 63–76.
Butts, Aaron Michael. "Manuscript Transmission as Reception History: The Case of Ephrem the Syrian (d. 373)." *JECS* 25 (2017): 281–306.
Cameron, Averil. "The Theotokos in Sixth-Century Constantinople." *JTS* 29 (1978): 79–108.
Cameron, Averil. "The Virgin's Robe: An Episode in the History of Early-Seventh Century Constantinople." *Byzantion* 49 (1979): 42–56.
Camery-Hoggatt, Jerry. *Irony in Mark's Gospel: Text and Subtext*. SNTSMS. Cambridge: Cambridge University Press, 1992.
Camille, Michael. *Gothic Art, Glorious Visions*. New York: Harry N. Abrams, 1996.
Cartlidge, David R., and J. Keith Elliott. *Art and the Christian Apocrypha*. New York: Routledge, 2001.
Cecchelli, Carlo. *La vita di Roma nel Medioevo, volume 1: Le arti minori e il costume*. Rome: Palandi, 1951–2.
Cerrato, John A. *Hippolytus between East and West: The Commentaries and the Provenance of the Corpus*. Oxford: Oxford University Press, 2002.
Chaine, Marius. *Apocrypha de Beata Maria Virgine*. Rome: Karolus de Luigi, 1909.
Chávez, Eduardo. *Our Lady of Guadalupe and Saint Juan Diego: The Historical Evidence*. Lanham, MD: Rowman & Littlefield, 2006.
Chilton, Bruce. *Mary Magdalene: A Biography*. New York: Doubleday, 2005.
Connell, Janice T. *The Secrets of Mary: Gifts from the Blessed Mother*. New York: St. Martin's, 2009.
Connolly, R. H. "Jacob of Serug and the Diatessaron." *JTS* 8 (1906–7): 581–90.
Connolly, R. H. *Didascalia apostolorum: The Syriac Version Translated and Accompanied by the Verona Latin Fragments*. Oxford: Clarendon, 1929.
Conzelmann, Hans. *Acts of the Apostles: A Commentary on the Acts of the Apostles*. Translated by A. Thomas Kraabel James Limburg, and Donald H. Juel. Hermeneia: A Critical and Historical Commentary on the Bible. Philadelphia, PA: Fortress, 1987.
Corbin, Henri. *Creative Imagination in the Sufism of Ibn 'Arabī*. Princeton, NJ: Princeton University Press, 1969.

Cothenet, Édouard. "Traditions bibliques et apocalyptiques dans les récits anciens de la Dormition." In *Marie dans les récits apocryphes chrétiens*, 155–75. Edited by Édouard Cothenet. Paris: Médiaspaul, 2004.

Coyle, J. Kevin. "Twelve Years Later: Revisiting the Marys of Manichaeism." In *Mariam, the Magdalene, and the Mother*, 197–212. Edited by Deirdre Good. Bloomington: Indiana University Press, 2005.

Cremante, Simona. *Leonardo da Vinci: The Complete Works*. Newton Abbot, UK: David and Charles, 2006.

Cullman, Oscar. "The *Protevanglium of James*." In *New Testament Apocrypha, Volume One: Gospels and Related Writings*, 421–39. Edited by Wilhelm Schneemelcher. Translated by R. McL. Wilson. Rev. ed. Louisville, KY: Westminster/John Knox, 1990.

Cunningham, Mary B. "The Life of the Virgin Mary According to Middle Byzantine Preachers and Hagiographers: Changing Contexts and Perspectives." *Apocrypha* 27 (2016): 137–59.

Cureton, William. *Remains of a Very Antient Recension of the Four Gospels in Syriac*. London: John Murray, 1858.

Cwikla, Anna. "'Pray in the Place Where There Is No Woman': Mary in the Dialogue of the Saviour." MA thesis, University of Alberta, 2013.

Daley, Brian E., trans. *On the Dormition of Mary: Early Patristic Homilies*. Popular Patristics Series 18. Crestwood, NY: St. Vladimir's Seminary, 1998.

Dalton, O. M. *Catalogue of the Ivory Carvings of the Christian Era with Examples of Mohammedan Art and Carvings in Bone*. London: Longmans, 1909.

Dark, K. "Early Roman-Period Nazareth and the Sisters of Nazareth Convent." *AJ* 92 (September 2012): 37–64.

Daube, David. *The New Testament and Rabbinic Judaism*. London: Athlone, 1956.

Davis, Stephen J. *Christ Child: Cultural Memories of a Young Jesus*. Synkrisis: Comparative Approaches to Early Christianity in Greco-Roman Culture. New Haven, CT: Yale University Press, 2014.

De Boer, Esther A. *The Gospel of Mary: Beyond a Gnostic and a Biblical Mary Magdalene*. JSNTS 260. London: T&T Clark, 2004.

De Boer, Esther A. *The Gospel of Mary: Listening to the Beloved Disciple*. London: A&C Black, 2005.

De Boer, Esther A. *Mary Magdalene: Beyond the Myth*. London: Bloomsbury, 1997.

De Boer, Esther A. *The Mary Magdalene Cover-Up: The Sources behind the Myth*. Translated by John Bowden London: T&T Clark, 2007.

Deckers, Johannes G., and Ümit Serdaroğlu. "Das Hypogäum beim Silivri-Kapi in Istanbul." *Jahrbuck für Antike und Christentum* 36 (1993): 140–63.

DeConick, April D. *Holy Misogyny: Why the Sex and Gender Conflicts in the Early Church Still Matter*. New York: Continuum, 2011.

DeConick, April D. *Voices of the Mystics: Early Christian Discourse in the Gospels of John and Thomas and Other Ancient Christian Literature*. Sheffield: Sheffield Academic, 2001.

Dectot, Xavier. "Madonna and Child." In *Musée nationale du Moyen Age: The Cluny Thermae*, 76. Paris: Réunion des musées nationaux, 2003.

de Jonge, H. J. "The Chronology of the Ascension Stories in Luke and Acts." *NTS* 59 (2013): 151–71.

de Voragine, Jacobus, ed. *The Golden Legend: Readings on the Saints*. Translated by William Granger Ryan. Waxkeep, 2013.

Dindorf, Ludwig August, ed. *Chronicon Paschale*. Corpus scriptorium historiae Byzantinae 14.15. Repr. Bonn: Marcus & Weber, 1924.
Ditmore, Melissa Hope. *Prostitution and Sex Work*. Historical Guides to Controversial Issues in America. Santa Barbara, CA: Greenwood, 2011.
Donahue, Charles. *The Testament of Mary: The Gaelic Version of the Dormitio Mariae together with an Irish Latin Version*. New York: Fordham University Press, 1942.
Ducati, Pericle. *L'arte in Roma dalle origini al sec. VIII*. Bologna: Cappelli, 1938.
Dunn, J. D. G. "The Ascension of Jesus: A Test Case for Hermeneutics." In *Auferstehung—Resurrection: The Fourth Durham-Tübingen Research Symposium: Resurrection, Transfiguration and Exaltation in Old Testament, Ancient Judaism and Early Christianity*, 301-22. Edited by F. Avemarie and H. Lichtenberger. WUNT. Tübingen: Mohr Siebeck, 2001.
Dupré, Judith. *Full of Grace: Encountering Mary in Faith, Art, and Life*. New York: Random House, 2010.
Ebertshauser, Caroline H., Herbert Haag, Joe H. Kirchberger, and Dorothee Solle. *Mary: Art, Culture, and Religion through the Ages*. Translated by Peter Heinegg. New York: Crossroad, 1998.
Edwards, James R. *The Hebrew Gospel and the Development of the Synoptic Tradition*. Grand Rapids, MI: William B. Eerdmans, 2009.
Ehrman, Bart, and Zlatko Pleše. *The Apocryphal Gospels: Texts and Translations*. Oxford: Oxford University Press, 2011.
Ehrman, Bart D. *Peter, Paul, and Mary Magdalene: The Followers of Jesus in History and Legend*. Oxford: Oxford University Press, 2006.
Eisen, Ute E. *Women Officeholders in Early Christianity: Epigraphical and Literary Studies*. Translated by Linda M. Maloney. Collegeville, MN: Liturgical, 2000.
Eitenmiller, Melissa. "Mary, Mediatrix of All Graces." MA Theology thesis. Ave Maria University, 2016.
Eliade, Mircea. *The Sacred and the Profane: The Nature of Religion*. San Diego, CA: Harcourt, Brace, Jovanovich, 1959.
Elman, Yaakov. "Righteousness as its Own Reward: An Inquiry into the Theologies of the Stam." *PAAJR* 57 (1990-1): 35 67.
Elowsky, Joel C., ed. *Ancient Christian Commentary, John 11-21*. Downers Grove, IL: InterVarsity, 2007.
Emmel, Stephen, ed. *Nag Hammadi Codex III, 5: The Dialogue of the Savior*. Leiden: Brill, 1984.
Epp, Eldon J., and Gordon D. Fee. *Studies in the Theory and Method of New Testament Textual Criticism*. Grand Rapids, MI: Eerdmans, 1993.
Ernst, Allie M. *Martha from the Margins: The Authority of Martha in Early Christian Tradition*. VC Supplements 98. Leiden: Brill, 2009.
Esler, Philip G., and Ronald Piper. *Lazarus, Mary and Martha: Social-Scientific Approaches to the Gospel of John*. Minneapolis, MN: Fortress, 2006.
Fairclough, Norman. *Language and Power*. 2nd ed. Harlow, Essex: Pearson Education Ltd., 2001.
Falkenburg, Reindert L. *The Fruit of Devotion: The Mysticism and the Imagery of Love in Flemish Paintings of the Virgin and Child, 1450-1550*. Translated by Sammy Herman. Amsterdam: John Benjamins, 1994.
Farmer, William R. *The Last Twelve Verses of Mark*. SNTSMS 25. New York: Cambridge University Press, 1974.
Feig, Nurit. "Burial Caves at Nazareth." *Atiqot* 10 (1990): 67-79.

Ferrar, W. J., ed. and trans. *Eusebius's The Proof of the Gospel*. Eugene, OR: Wipf and Stock, 2001. Reprint of 2 volumes. London: SPCK, 1920.

Filipova, Alzebeta. "Santo, Vescovo e Confessore: L'immagine di Apollinare nei mosaici di Classe." In *L'évêque, l'image et la mort: Identité et mémoire au Moyen Âge*, 431–44. Edited by Nicolas Bock, Ivan Folletti, and Michele Tomasi. Rome: Viella, 2014.

Fitzmyer, Joseph A. *The Acts of the Apostles: A New Translation with Introduction and Commentary*. AB 31. New York: Doubleday, 1998.

Fitzmyer, Joseph A. *The Gospel According to Luke: Introduction, Translation, and Notes*. AB 28 and 28a. Garden City, NY: Doubleday, 1981–5.

Fixot, Michel. *La Crypte de Saint-Maximin-La-Sainte-Baume. Basilique Sainte-Marie-Madelaine*. Aix-en-Provence: Edisud, 2001.

Fleury, Katharina Mertens. "Maria mediatrix—*mittellos mittel aller súnder*." *Das Mittelalter* 15 (2010): 33–47.

Folda, Jaroslav. *Byzantine Art and Italian Panel Painting: The Virgin and Child Hodegetria and the Art of Chrysography*. New York: Cambridge University Press, 2015.

Fonrobert, Charlotte Elisheva. "When the Rabbi Weeps: On Reading Gender in Talmudic Aggadah." *Nashim: A Journal of Jewish Women's Studies and Gender Issues* 4 (2001): 61.

Forbes, Greg W., and Scott D. Harrower. *Raised from Obscurity: A Narrative and Theological Study of the Characterization of Women in Luke–Acts*. Translated with Foreword by Lynn H. Cohick. Eugene, OR: Pickwick, 2015.

Förster, Hans. "'Sich des Gebrauchs der Frauen enthalten': Eine Anfrage an die grammatikalische Struktur einer Interzession für Verstorbene im Grossen Euchologion aus dem Weissen Kloster." *ZAC / JAC* 9 (2006): 584–91.

Förster, Hans. *Transitus Mariae: Beiträge zur koptischen Überlieferung mit einer Edition von P. Vindob. K 7589, Cambridge Add 1876 8 und Paris BN Copte 12917 ff. 28 und 29*. Berlin: Walter de Gruyter, 2006.

Frankel, David. "The Death of Moses as a Sacrifice of Atonement for the Sins of Israel: A Hidden Biblical Tradition." In *The Actuality of Sacrifice: Past and Present*, 47–67. Edited by Alberdina Houtman, Marcel Poorthuis, Joshua Schwartz, and Yossi Turner. Leiden: Brill, 2014.

Frei, Hans W. *The Eclipse of Biblical Narrative: A Study in Eighteenth and Nineteenth Century Hermeneutics*. New Haven, CT: Yale University Press, 1974.

Freund, R. A. *Digging through the Bible*. Lanham, MD: Rowman & Littlefield, 2008.

Friedmann, Herbert. *The Symbolic Goldfinch: Its History and Significance in European Devotional Art*. The Bolligen Series. Washington, DC: Pantheon Books, 1946.

Funk, Robert W., Roy W. Hoover, and the Jesus Seminar. *The Five Gospels: The Search for the Authentic Words of Jesus*. New York: Scribner (Polebridge), 1996.

Gafney, Isaiah. "The Historical Background." *Jewish Writings of the Second Temple Period: Apocrypha, Pseudepigrapha: Qumran Sectarian Writings, Philo, Josephus*, 13–17. Edited by Michael E. Stone. Philadelphia, PA: Fortress, 1984.

Gallisot-Ortuno, Christine. "L'iconographie de l'Annonciation." In *Quelques figures de maternités: fétiches, déesses–mères, mystère de l'incarnation et pots pansus*, 25–8. Edited by Jean-Roche Bouiller. Milan: Silvana, 2009.

Galot, Jean. "La plus ancienne affirmation de la coredemption mariale: Le témoignage de Jean le Géomêtre." *RSR* 45 (1957): 187–208.

Galot, Jean. "Women and the Priesthood: A Theological Reflection." Excerpt from J. Galot, SJ. *Theology of the Priesthood*. Translated by Roger Balducelli. San Francisco, CA: Ignatius, 1985.

Gambero, Luigi. "Biographies of Mary in Byzantine Literature." *Marian Studies* 40 (2009): 31–50.
Gasquet, Aidano. *Codex Vercellensis*. Collectanea biblica Latina 3. Rome: Pustet, 1914.
Gaventa, Beverly Roberts. *Acts*. ANTC. Nashville, TN: Abingdon, 2003.
Genequand, Charles. "Vie de Jésus en Arabe." In *Écrits apocryphes chrétiens*, vol. 1, 207–38. Edited by François Bovon and Pierre Geoltrain. Bibliothèque de la Pléiade 442. Paris: Gallimard, 1997.
Gharib, Georges, trans. "Vita de Maria." In *Testi Mariani del Primo Millennio 2: Padri e altri autori bizantini (Vi–XI sec.)*, 980–1019. Edited by Georges Gharib-Hermano, M. Toniolo, Luigi Gambero, and Gerardo Di Nola. Rome: Città Nuova Editrice, 1989.
Gnirs, Anton. "La basilica ed il reliquiario d'avorio di Samagher presso Pola." *Atti e memorie della società istriana di archeologia e storia patria* 24 (1908): 5–48.
Goldschmidt, A. "Mittelstüke fünfteiliger Elfenbeintafeln des V–VI Jahrhunderts." *Jahrbuch fur Kunstwissenschaft* (1923): 30–3.
Good, Deirdre, ed. *Mariam, the Magdalene, and the Mother*. Bloomington: Indiana University Press, 2005.
Good, Deirdre. "Pistis Sophia." In *Searching the Scriptures: Volume 2: A Feminist Commentary*, 678–707. Edited by Elisabeth Schüssler Fiorenza. New York: Crossroad, 1994.
Goodacre, Mark. "Jesus' Wife, the Media and *The Da Vinci Code*." In *Fakes, Forgeries, and Fictions: Writing Ancient and Modern Christian Apocrypha: Proceedings from the 2015 York Christian Apocrypha Symposium*, 341–8. Edited by Tony Burke. Eugene, OR: Cascade, 2017.
Goodacre, Mark. "The Power of *The Passion of the Christ*: Reactions and Overreactions to Gibson's Artistic Vision." In *Jesus and Mel Gibson's* The Passion of the Christ: *The Film, the Gospels and the Claims of History*, 28–44. Edited by Robert Webb and Kathleen Corley. London: Continuum, 2004.
Goodacre, Mark. *The Synoptic Problem: A Way through the Maze*. London: Continuum, 2001.
Grabar, André. *Les ampoules de Terre Sainte (Monza – Bobbio)*. Paris: C. Klincksieck, 1958.
Grabar, André. *Martyrium, recherches sur le culte des reliques et l'art chrétien antique*. 2 volumes. Paris: Collège de France, 1946.
Graef, Hilda, and Thomas A. Thompson, SJ. *Mary: A History of Doctrine and Devotion*. 2 volumes. Combined ed. Notre Dame, IN: Ave Maria, 2009.
Green, Joel B. *The Gospel of Luke*. NICNT. Grand Rapids, MI: Eerdmans, 1997.
Grisar, Hartmann. *Die römische Kapelle Sancta Santorum und ihr Schatz: Meine Entdeckungen und Studien in der Palastkapelle der mittelalterlichen Päpste*. Rome: Laterano, 1908.
Grodecki, Louis. *Ivoires français*. Paris: Larouose, 1947.
Grossman, Avraham. "*Ben miryam lemaria: ketzad hayyetah miryam lidmut ha'ishah ha'idi'alit besifrut hazal?*" In *Tiferet Leyisrael: Jubilee Volume in Honor of Israel Francus*, 183–94 (Hebrew pagination). Edited by Joel Roth, Menahem Schmelzer, and Yaakov Francus. New York: Jewish Theological Seminary of America, 2010.
Guarducci, Margherita. *La capsella eburnea di Samagher: un cimelio di arte paleocristiana nella storia del tardo impero*. Trieste: Società istriana di archeologia, 1978.
Hamarneh, Sami K. "Cosmas and Damian in the Near East: Earliest Extant Monument." *Pharmacy in History* 27 (1985): 78–83.
Hamilton, R. W. *The Church of the Nativity, Bethlehem: A Guide*. Jerusalem: Government of Palestine, Dept. of Antiquities, 1947.

Hansbury, Mary, trans. *On the Mother of God. Jacob of Serug*, with an Introduction by Sebastian Brock. Crestwood, NY: St. Vladimir's Seminary, 1998.

Hanson, Mary Stromer. *The New Perspective on Mary and Martha*. Eugene, OR: Wipf & Stock, 2013.

Hartenstein, Judith. "Autoritätskonstellation in apokryphen und kanonischen Evangelien." In *Jesus in apokryphen Evangelienüberlieferungen: Beiträge zu außerkanonischen Jesusüberlieferungen aus verschiedenen Sprach- und Kulturtraditionen*, 423-44. Edited by Jörg Frey and Jens Schröter. WUNT 254. Tübingen: Mohr Siebeck, 2010.

Hartenstein, Judith. *Charakterisierung im Dialog. Maria Magdalena, Petrus, Thomas und die Mutter Jesu im Johannesevangelium im Kontext frühchristlicher Darstellungen*. NTOA 64. Göttingen: Vandenhoeck & Ruprecht, 2007.

Hartenstein, Judith. *Die zweite Lehre: Erscheinungen des Auferstandenen als Rahmenerzählungen frühchristlicher Dialoge*. Berlin: Akademie, 2000.

Harvey, Susan Ashbrook. "Feminine Imagery for the Divine: The Holy Spirit, the Odes of Solomon, and Early Syriac Tradition." *SVTQ* 37.2-3 (1993): 111-39.

Harvey, Susan Ashbrook. *Scenting Salvation: Ancient Christianity and the Olfactory Imagination*. Berkeley: University of California Press, 2006.

Hasan-Rokem, Galit. *Web of Life: Folklore and Midrash in Rabbinic Literature*. Translated by Batya Stein. Stanford, CA: Stanford University Press, 2000.

Haskins, Susan. *Mary Magdalen: Myth and Metaphor*. London: Harper Collins, 1993.

Hassan, Riffat. "Islamic Hagar and Her Family." In *Hagar, Sarah, and Their Children*, 149-76. Edited by Phyllis Trible and Letty M. Russell. Louisville, KY: Westminster/John Knox, 2006.

Hengel, Martin. *The Atonement: The Origins of the Doctrine in the New Testament*. Translated by John Bowden. Philadelphia, PA: Fortress, 1981.

Hiers, Richard H. "The Bread and Fish Eucharist in the Gospels and Early Christian Art." *PRSt* 3 (1976): 21-48.

Higger, Michael, ed. *Massekhtot kallah vehen massekhet kallah, massekhet kallah rabbati*. New York: Moinester, 1936.

Higger, Michael, ed. *The Treatises Derek Erez, Pirke Ben Azzai, Tosefta Derek Erez*. New York: Moinester, 1935.

Hock, Ronald F. *The Infancy Gospels of James and Thomas*. Santa Rosa, CA: Polebridge, 1995.

Hoffman, David Zvi. *Midrash tannaim 'al sefer dəvarim*. Berlin, 1908.

Hofrichter, Peter, ed. *Auf der Suche nach der Seele Europas: Marienfrömmigkeit in Ost und West. Studientagung der Pro Oriente-Sektion Salzburg aus Anlass ihres 20 jährigen Bestehens, 7. und 8. Oktober 2005*. Pro Oriente 30. Innsbruck: Tyrolia-Verlag, 2007.

Horn, Cornelia. "Ancient Syriac Sources on Mary's Role as Intercessor." In *Presbeia Theotokou: The Intercessory Role of Mary across Times and Places in Byzantium (4th-9th Century)*, 153-75. Edited by Leena Mari Peltomaa, Andreas Külzer, and Pauline Allen. Veröffentlichungen zur Byzanzforschung 39. Denkschriften der philosophisch-historischen Klasse 481. Vienna: Österreichischen Akademie der Wissenschaften, 2015.

Horn, Cornelia. "Christian Apocrypha in Georgia and in Literature on Georgians: Some Reflections on the Intersections of Apocrypha, Hagiography, and Liturgy." In *Proceedings of the Conference "Renaissance Humanism" in Honor of the 125th Anniversary of Shalva Nutsubidze*, Institute of Philosophy, Ivane Javakhishvili Tbilisi State University, Tbilisi, Georgia, December 12-13, 2013.

ფილოსოფიურ-თეოლოგიური მიმომხილველი / *Philosophical-Theological Reviewer* 3, 186–93. Tbilisi: Ivane Javakhishvili Tbilisi State University, 2013.
Horn, Cornelia. "From Model Virgin to Maternal Intercessor: Mary, Children, and Family Problems in Late Antique Infancy Gospel Traditions." Lecture delivered at the session "Late Antique Perspectives on *Apocryphal Acts of Apostles*" at the conference "Christian Apocryphal Texts for the New Millennium: Achievements, Prospects, and Challenges," organized by Pierluigi Piovanelli. University of Ottawa, Canada, Fall, 2006.
Horn, Cornelia. "Mary between Bible and Qur'an: Soundings into the Transmission and Reception History of the *Protoevangelium of James* on the Basis of Selected Literary Sources in Coptic and Copto-Arabic and of Art-Historical Evidence Pertaining to Egypt." *ICMR* 18 (2007): 509–38.
Horn, Cornelia. "Syriac and Arabic Perspectives on Structural and Motif Parallels regarding Jesus' Childhood in Christian Apocrypha and Early Islamic Literature: The 'Book of Mary,' the *Arabic Apocryphal Gospel of John*, and the Qur'ān." *Apocrypha* 19 (2008) 267–91.
Horn, Cornelia. "Traditions on Miracles of Mary in the Syriac Literary and Cultural Realm: Toward the *Status Quaestionis*." Paper delivered at the International Workshop Miracles of the Virgin Mary. Medieval Narratives through Time and Space, organized by Ewa Balicka-Witakowska and Anthony Lappin, Maynooth University. Maynooth, Ireland, March 29 to April 1, 2017.
Howard-Johnston, James. "The Siege of Constantinople in 626." In *Constantinople and Its Hinterland. Papers from the Twenty-Seventh Spring Symposium on Byzantine Studies, Oxford, April 1993*, 131–42. Edited by Cyril Mango, Gilbert Dagron, and Geoffrey Greatrex. Aldershot, Hampshire: Variorum, 1995.
Humphrey, Edith. Review of Ann Graham Brock, *Mary Magdalene: The First Apostle and the Struggle for Authority*. RBL [http://www.bookreviews.org] (2004).
Hurtado, Larry W. "The *Pericope Adulterae*: Where from Here?." In *The Pericope of the Adulteress in Contemporary Research*, 147–58. Edited by David Alan Black and Jacob N. Cerone. London: Bloomsbury T&T Clark, 2016.
Ilan, Tal. "Notes on the Distribution of Jewish Women's Names in Palestine in the Second Temple and Mishnaic Periods." *JJS* 40 (1989): 186–200.
Ilan, Tal. *Lexicon of Jewish Names in Late Antiquity: Part I Palestine 330 BCE–200 CE*. Vol. 1. 4 volumes. Texts and Studies in Ancient Judaism 91. Tübingen: Mohr Siebeck, 2002.
Innemée, Karel, and Youhanna Nessim Youssef. "Virgins with Censers: A 10th Century Painting of the Dormition in Deir Al-Surian." *BSAC* 46 (2007): 69–85.
Innemée, Karel. "Dayr al-Suryan: New Discoveries." In *Claremont Coptic Encyclopedia*, 1–50. Online. Claremont, CA: Claremont Graduate University, 2016. http://ccdl.libraries.claremont.edu/cdm/singleitem/collection/cce/id/2137/rec/1 (accessed on April 20, 2018).
Isenberg, Wesley W., trans. "The Gospel of Philip." In *The Nag Hammadi Library in English*, 139–60. Edited by James M. Robinson. 4th rev. ed. Leiden: Brill, 1996.
Jackson, Michael. *The Politics of Storytelling*. Copenhagen: Museum Tusculanum, 2013.
Jacobovici, Simcha, and Barrie Wilson. *The Lost Gospel: Decoding the Ancient Text that Reveals Jesus' Marriage to Mary the Magdalene*. San Francisco, CA: HarperCollins, 2014.
James, M. R. *The Apocryphal New Testament*. Oxford: Clarendon, 1953.
Jansen, Katharine Ludwig. *The Making of the Magdalen: Preaching and Popular Devotion in the Later Middle Ages*. Princeton, NJ: Princeton University Press, 2000.

Jelly, Frederick M. "Mary's Intercession: a Contemporary Reappraisal." *Marian Studies* 32 (1981): 76-95.
Jensen, Anne. *God's Self-Confident Daughters: Early Christianity and the Liberation of Women*. Translated by O. C. Dean Jr. Louisville, KY: Westminster, 1996.
Jensen, Robin M. "The Raising of Lazarus." *BRev* 11 (1995): 20-8, 45.
Jipp, Joshua W. "Luke's Scriptural Suffering Messiah: A Search for Precedent, a Search for Identity." *CBQ* 72 (2010): 255-74.
Johnson, Luke Timothy. *The Acts of the Apostles*. Edited by D. J. Harington, SJ. SP. Collegeville, PA: Liturgical, 1992.
Jones, F. Stanley, ed. *Which Mary? The Marys of Early Christian Tradition*. SBLSS 19. Atlanta, GA: Society of Biblical Literature, 2002.
Joosten, Jan. "The Dura Parchment and the Diatessaron." *VC* 57 (2003): 157-75.
Jugie, Martin. *L'Immaculée Conception dans l'Écriture sainte et dans la tradition orientale*. Città del Vaticano: Biblioteca Apostolica Vaticana, 1944.
Jugie, Martin. *La Mort et l'Assomption de la Sainte Vierge: Étude historic-doctrinale*. Città del Vaticano: Biblioteca Apostolica Vaticana, 1944.
Jugie, Martin. "Sur la vie et les procédés littéraires de Syméon Métaphraste. Son récit de la vie de la Sainte Vierge." *Échoes d'Orient* 22 (1923): 5-10.
Kaegi, Walter E. *Heraclius, Emperor of Byzantium*. Cambridge: Cambridge University Press, 2003.
Kaestli, Jean-Daniel. *L'évangile de Barthélomy d'après deus écrits apocryphes*. Belgium: Brepols, 1993.
Kahana, Menahem. "The Halakhic Midrashim." In *The Literature of the Sages*, 2:3-105. 2 volumes. Edited by Shmuel Safrai. Philadelphia, PA: Fortress, 2006.
Kaldellis, Anthony. "'A Union of Opposites': The Moral Logic and Corporeal Presence of the Theotokos on the Field of Battle." In *Pour l'amour de Byzance. Hommage à Paolo Odorico*, 131-44. Edited by Christian Gastgeber, Charis Messis, Dan Ioan Mureşan, and Filippo Ronconi. Eastern and Central European Studies III. Frankfurt am Main: Peter Lang, 2012.
Kalmin, Richard. *Jewish Babylonia between Persia and Roman Palestine*. New York: Oxford University Press, 2006.
Kalmin, Richard. *Migrating Tales: The Talmud's Narratives and Their Historical Context*. Oakland: University of California Press, 2014.
Kane, Michael N. "Empowerment in the Religious Stories and Art of the Virgin Mary." *Social Work & Christianity* 37 (2010): 45-64.
Karras, Valerie A. "Female Deacons in the Byzantine Church." *Church History* 73 (2004): 272-316.
Karras, Valerie A. "The Liturgical Functions of Consecrated Women in the Byzantine Church." *Theological Studies* 66 (2005): 96-116.
Kateusz, Ally. "Ascension of Christ or Ascension of Mary?: Reconsidering a Popular Early Iconography." *JECS* 23 (2015): 273-303.
Kateusz, Ally. "Collyridian Déjà Vu: The Trajectory of Redaction of the Markers of Mary's Liturgical Leadership." *JFSR* 29 (2013): 75-92.
Kateusz, Ally. *Finding Holy Spirit Mother*. Holt, MO: Divine Balance, 2014.
Kateusz, Ally. "'She Sacrificed Herself as the Priest': Early Christian Female and Male Co-Priests." *JFSR* 33 (2017): 45-67.
Kateusz, Ally. *Mary and Early Christian Women: Hidden Leadership*. New York: Palgrave Macmillan, 2019.

Keener, Craig. *Acts: An Exegetical Commentary.* Vol. 1, Introduction and 1:1–2:4. Grand Rapids, MI: Baker, 2012.

Kelhoffer, James A. "The Witness of Eusebius' *ad Marinum* and Other Christian Writings." *ZNW* 92 (2001): 78–112.

King, Karen L. "The Gospel of Mary Magdalene." In *Searching the Scriptures: Volume 2: A Feminist Commentary*, 601–34. Edited by Elisabeth Schüssler Fiorenza. New York: Crossroad, 1994.

King, Karen L. *The Gospel of Mary of Magdala: Jesus and the First Woman Apostle.* Santa Rosa, CA: Polebridge, 2003.

King, Karen L., trans. "The *Gospel of Mary* with the Greek *Gospel of Mary*." In *The Nag Hammadi Scriptures*, 741–7. Edited by Marvin W. Meyer and Wolf-Peter Funk. New York: HarperOne, 2007.

King, Karen L. "Why All the Controversy? Mary in the Gospel of Mary." In *Which Mary?: The Marys of Early Christian Tradition*, 53–74. Edited by F. Stanely Jones. SBLSS 19. Atlanta, GA: Society of Biblical Literature, 2012.

Kirschbaum, Engelbert. *The Tombs of St. Peter and St. Paul.* Translated by John Murray. New York: St. Martin's, 1959.

Klauder, F. "Observations on Father Jelly's Paper." *Marian Studies* 32 (1981): 96–8.

Koester, Helmut. "Apocryphal and Canonical Gospels." *HTR* 73 (1980): 105–30.

Koester, Helmut. *Introduction to the New Testament.* Vol. 2: History and Literature of Early Christianity. Philadelphia, PA: Fortress, 1982.

Konis, P. "The Post-Resurrection Appearances of Christ: The Case of the Chairete or 'All Hail.'" *Rosetta* 1 (2006): 31–40.

Kristeva, Julia. "Stabat Mater." In *The Kristeva Reader*, 160–86. Edited by Toril Moi. New York: Columbia University Press, 1986.

Krüger, Klaus. "Mute Mysteries of the Divine Logos: On the Pictorial Poetics of Incarnation." In *Image and Incarnation: The Early Modern Doctrine of the Pictorial Image*, 76–108. Edited by Walter S. Melion and Lee Palmer Wandel. Leiden: Brill, 2015.

Kugel, James L. *The Idea of Biblical Poetry, Parallelism and Its History.* New Haven, CT: Yale University Press, 1981.

LaRow, Magdalen. "The Iconography of Mary Magdalene: The Evolution of a Western Tradition until 1300." PhD dissertation, New York University, 1982.

LaVerdiere, Eugene. *The Annunciation to Mary: A Story of Faith, Luke 1:26–38.* Chicago, IL: Liturgy Training, 2004.

Le Blant, Edmond. *Les sarcophages chrétiens de la Gaule.* Paris: Imprimerie Nationale, 1886.

Lefort, Louis-Theodore. "Saint Athanase: sur la virginité." *Le Museon* 42 (1929): 197–275.

Leclercq, Henri. "Pola." In *Dictionnaire d'archéologie chrétienne et de liturgie*, vol. 14, part 1, cols. 1342–46. Edited by Fernand Cabrol and Henri Leclercq. Paris: Letouzey et Ané, 1939.

Levine, A. J. Review of Jane Schaberg with Melanie Johnson-Debaufre, *Mary Magdalene Understood*. In *Bible History Daily*, http://www.biblicalarchaeology.org/reviews/mary-magdalene–understood/ (2011).

Levine, A. J. "Gender and Faith." In School of Theology and Ministry, Great Theologians Lecture Series, Seattle University, 2008.

Lévi, Israël. "Le péché originel dans les anciennes sources juives." *Annuaires de l'École pratique des hautes études* 20 (1906): 1–28.

Lidov, Alexi. "The Priesthood of the Virgin Mary as an Image–Paradigm of Christian Visual Culture." *IKON* 10 (2017): 9–26.

Lieu, Judith M. "The Mother of the Son in the Fourth Gospel." *JBL* 117 (1998): 61–77.
Lincoln, Andrew T. *Born of a Virgin? Reconceiving Jesus in the Bible, Tradition, and Theology*. Grand Rapids, MI: Eerdmans, 2013.
Lincoln, Henry, Michael Baigent, and Richard Leigh. *Holy Blood, Holy Grail*. New York: Dell, 1983.
Llywelyn, Dorian, SJ. "The Life of Mary and the Festal Icons of the Eastern Church." *Marian Studies* 40 (2009): 231–52.
Loisy, Alfred. *Le Quatrième Évangile*. Paris: Alphonse Picard, 1903.
Longhi, Davide. *La capsella eburnea di Samagher: iconografia e committenza*. Ravenna: Girasole, 2006.
López Murto, Antonio. *La luz saludable de la América*. México, D.F.: La imprenta madrileña de Don Felipe de Zúñiga y Ontiveros, 1792.
Lowe, Malcolm. "ΙΟΥΔΑΙΟΙ of the Apocrypha: A Fresh Approach to the Gospels of James, Pseudo-Thomas, Peter and Nicodemus." *NovT* 23 (1981): 56–90.
Lucchesi, Enzo. "Évangile selon Marie ou Évangile selon Marie-Madeleine?." *AnBoll* 103 (1985): 366–92.
Lybarger, Loren D. "Gender and Prophetic Authority in the Qur'anic Story of Maryam: A Literary Approach." *JR* 80 (2000): 240–70.
Madigan, Kevin, and Carolyn Osiek, trans. *Ordained Women in the Early Church: A Documentary History*. Baltimore, MD: John Hopkins, 2011.
Maile, John F. "The Ascension in Luke-Acts." *TynBul* 37 (1986): 29–59.
Manns, Frédéric. "La mort de Marie dans le texte de la Dormition de Marie." *Aug* 19 (1979): 507–15.
Marcovich, Miroslav, ed. *Hippolytus: Refutatio omnium haeresium*. PTS 25. Berlin: de Gruyter, 1986.
Marcus, Joel. *Mark 1–8: A New Translation with Introduction and Commentary*. AB. New York: Doubleday, 2000.
Marguerat, Daniel. *The First Christian Historian: Writing the 'Acts of the Apostles'*. SNTSMS. Cambridge: Cambridge University Press, 2002.
Marjanen, Antti. "The Mother of Jesus or the Magdalene? The Identity of Mary in the So-Called Gnostic Christian Texts." In *Which Mary? The Marys of Early Christian Tradition*, 31–42. Edited by F. Stanley Jones. SBLSS 19. Atlanta, GA: Society of Biblical Literature, 2002.
Marjanen, Antti. *The Woman Jesus Loved: Mary Magdalene in the Nag Hammadi Library and Related Documents*. Leiden: E.J. Brill, 1996.
Marker, Gary. "Narrating Mary's Miracles and the Politics of Location in Late 17th-Century East Slavic Orthodoxy." *Kritika: Explorations in Russian and Eurasian History* 15 (2014): 695–727.
Martimort, Aimé Georges. *Deaconesses: An Historical Study*. Translated by K. D. Whitehead. San Francisco, CA: Ignatius, 1986.
Mary, Francis, ed. *St. Thérèse: Doctor of the Little Way*. New Bedford, MA: Franciscan Friars of the Immaculate, 1997.
Matera, Frank J. "Jesus' Journey to Jerusalem (Luke 9:51–19:46): A Conflict with Israel." *JSNT* 51 (1993): 57–77.
McAuliffe, Jane D. "Chosen of All Women: Mary and Fatima in Qur'ānic Exegesis." *Islamochristiana* 7 (1981): 19–28.
McCarthy, Carmel, trans. *Saint Ephrem's Commentary on Tatian's Diatessaron: An English Translation of Chester Beatty Syriac MS 709 with Introduction and Notes*. JSS Supplement 2. Oxford: Oxford University Press, 1993.

McCarthy, R. J. "Mary in Islam." In *Mary's Place in Christian Dialogue*, 205–98. Edited by Alberic Stacpoole. Wilton, CT: Morehouse-Barlow, 1982.

McCarthy, Rebecca Lea. *Origins of the Magdalene Laundries: An Analytical History*. Jefferson, NC: McFarland, 2010.

McEnerney, John I. *St. Cyril of Alexandria: Letters 1–50*. Washington, DC: Catholic University of America, 1987.

Mengestu, Abera Mitiku. *God as Father in Paul: Kinship Language and Identity Formation in Early Christianity*. Eugene, OR: Pickwick, 2013.

Mercenier, F. "L'antienne mariale grecque la plus ancienne." *Le Muséon* 52 (1939): 229–33.

Merenlahti, Petri. *Poetics for the Gospels? Rethinking Narrative Criticism*. Studies of the New Testament and Its World. London: T&T Clark, 2002.

Metzger, Bruce. *The Early Versions of the New Testament: Their Origin, Transmission, and Limitations*. Oxford: Clarendon, 1977.

Metzger, Bruce. *The Text of the New Testament: Its Transmission, Corruption, and Restoration*. New York: Oxford University Press, 1968.

Meyer, Marvin, trans. "The Gospel of Philip." In *The Nag Hammadi Scriptures: The International Edition*, 161–86. Edited by Marvin Meyer. New York: HarperCollins, 2007.

Meyer, Marvin. *Judas: The Definitive Collection of Gospels and Legends about the Infamous Apostle of Jesus*. New York: HarperOne, 2007.

Meyer, Marvin. "Making Mary Male: The Categories 'Male' and 'Female' in the Gospel of Thomas." *NTS* 31 (1985): 554–70.

Meyer, Marvin, with Esther A. De Boer. *The Gospels of Mary: The Secret Tradition of Mary Magdalene, the Companion of Jesus*. San Francisco, CA: HarperSanFrancisco, 2003.

Mimouni, Simon Claude. *Dormition et Assomption de Marie: Histoire des traditions anciennes*. ThH 98. Paris: Beauchesne, 1995.

Mimouni, Simon Claude. *Les Traditions anciennes sur la Dormition et l'Assomption de Marie: Études littéraires, historiques et doctrinales*. Leiden: Brill, 2011.

Mimouni, Simon Claude. "Les *Vies de la Vierge*: État de la question." *Apocrypha* 5 (1994): 211–48.

Murcia, Thierry. *Marie appelée la Magdaléenne: Entre traditions et histoire (Ier-VIIIe siècle)*. Aix-en-Provence: Presses Universitaires de Provence, 2017.

Murcia, Thierry. "Marie de Magdala et la mère de Jésus." *Revue des Études Tardo-Antiques* RET Supp 6 (2018–19): 47–69.

Murray, Robert. *Symbols of Church and Kingdom: A Study in Early Syriac Tradition*. 1975; repr. Cambridge: Cambridge University Press, 1977.

Myslivec, J. "Tod Mariens." In *Lexikon der christlichen Ikonographie IV*, cols. 333–8. Edited by Engelbert Kirschbaum, Günter Bandmann, Wolfgang Braunfels, Johannes Kollwitz, Wilhelm Mrazek, Alfred A. Schmid, and Hugo Schnell. Rome: Herder, 1972.

Nagel, Peter. "Mariammê—Netzwerferin und Geist der Weisheit." In *Divitiae Aegypti: Koptologische und verwandte Studien zu Ehren Martin Krause*, 223–8. Edited by G. Fluck, Lucia Langener, and Siegfried Richter. Wiesbaden: L. Reichert, 1995.

Nau, François, trans. *Histoire de Nestorius d'après la lettre à Cosme et l'Hymne de Sliba de Mansourya sur les docteurs grecs*. Patrologia Orientalis 13. Paris: Firmin-Didot, 1916.

Neumann, Charles William. *The Virgin Mary in the Works of Saint Ambrose*. Fribourg: University of Fribourg, 1962.

Neundorfer, Bruno. *Der Dom zu Bamberg: Mutterkirche des Erzbistums*. Bamberg: St. Otto-Verlag, 1987.

Noga-Banai, Galit. *Sacred Stimulus: Jerusalem in the Visual Christianization of Rome*. Oxford: Oxford University Press, 2018.

Norelli, Enrico. "La letteratura apocrifa sul transito di Maria e il problema delle sue origini." In *Il dogma dell'assunzione di Maria: problemi attuali e tentativi di ricomprensione*, 121-65. Edited by Ermanno M. Toniolo. Rome: Edizioni Marianum, 2010.

Northcote, J. Spencer, and W. R. Brownlow. *Roma Sotterranea: An Account of the Roman Catacombs, Especially of the Cemetery of St. Callixtus*. Volume 2. London: Longmans, Green, 1897.

O'Neill, Maggie. *Prostitution and Feminism: Towards a Politics of Feeling*. Cambridge: Polity, 2001.

Ostriker, Alicia. "Miriam's Songs." In *All the Women Followed Her*, 13-15. Edited by Rebecca Schwartz. Santa Clara County, CA: Rikudei Miriam, 2001.

Pagels, Elaine. *The Gnostic Gospels*. New York: Random House, 1979.

Parsons, Mikeal C. *The Departure of Jesus in Luke-Acts: The Ascension Narratives in Context*. JSNTSS 21. Sheffield: Sheffield Academic, 1987.

Parsons, Mikeal C. "Exegesis 'By the Numbers': Numerology and the New Testament." *PRSt* 35 (2008): 25-43.Parsons, Mikeal C. "The Place of Jerusalem on the Lukan Landscape: An Exercise in Symbolic Cartography." In *Literary Studies in Luke-Acts: Essays in Honor of Joseph B. Tyson*, 155-71. Edited by Richard P. Thompson and Thomas E. Phillips. Macon, GA: Mercer University Press, 1998.

Pearse, Roger. *Eusebius of Caesarea, Gospel Problems and Solutions; Quaestiones ad Stephanum et Marinum*. Translated by David J. D. Miller, Adam C. McCollum, Carol Downer et al. Ancient Texts in Translation 1. Ipswich: Chieftain, 2010.

Pelikan, Jaroslav Jan, David Flusser, and Justin Lang. *Mary: Images of the Mother of Jesus in Jewish and Christian Perspective*. Minneapolis, MN: Fortress, 2005.

Pelikan, Jaroslav. *Mary through the Centuries: Her Place in the History of Culture*. New Haven, CT: Yale University Press, 1996.

Peltomaa, Leena Mari, Andreas Külzer, and Pauline Allen. *Presbeia Theotokou: The Intercessory Role of Mary across Times and Places in Byzantium (4th—9th Century)*. Veröffentlichungen zur Byzanzforschung 39. Denkschriften der philosophisch-historischen Klasse 481. Vienna: Verlag der Österreichischen Akademie der Wissenschaften, 2015.

Peltomaa, Leena Mari. "'Cease your lamentations, I shall become an advocate for you.' Mary as Intercessor in Romanos' Hymnography." In *Presbeia Theotokou: The Intercessory Role of Mary across Times and Places in Byzantium (4th—9th Century)*, 131-7. Edited by Leena Mari Peltomaa, Andreas Külzer, and Pauline Allen. Veröffentlichungen zur Byzanzforschung 39. Denkschriften der philosophisch-historischen Klasse 481. Vienna: Verlag der Österreichischen Akademie der Wissenschaften, 2015.

Peltomaa, Leena Mari. "Roles and Functions of Mary in the Hymnography of Romanos Melodos." *StPatr* 44 (2010): 487-98.

Peltomaa, Leena Mari. "Romanos the Melodist and the Intercessory Role of Mary." In *Byzantina Mediterranea. Festschrift für Johannes Koder zum 65. Geburtstag*, 495-502. Edited by Klaus Belke, Ewald Kislinger, Andreas Külzer, and Maria A. Stassinopoulou. Vienna: Böhlau, 2007.

Pentcheva, Bissera. "The Supernatural Protector of Constantinople: The Virgin and Her Icons in the Tradition of the Avar Siege." *Byzantine and Modern Greek Studies* 26 (2002): 2-41.

Perret, Louis. *Catacombes de Rome*. 5 volumes. Paris: Gide et J. Baudry, 1851.

Pervo, Richard I. *Acts: A Commentary*. Edited by Harold W. Attridge. Hermeneia. Minneapolis, MN: Fortress, 2009.
Peters, Diane E. *The Many Faces of Martha of Bethany*. Ottawa: St. Paul University, 2008.
Petersen, William L. *Tatian's Diatessaron: Its Creation, Dissemination, Significance, and History in Scholarship*. VC Supplements 25. Leiden: Brill, 1994.
Petersen, Zina. "'Twisted Paths of Civilization: Saint Sara and the Romani." *JRPC* 26 (2014): 310–22.
Pfann, S., R. Voss, and Y. Rapuano. "Surveys and Excavations at the Nazareth Village Farm (1997–2002): Final Report." *BAIAS* 25 (2007): 19–79.
Picknett, Lynn. *Mary Magdalene: Christianity's Hidden Goddess*. New York: Carroll & Graf, 2003.
Picknett, Lynn, and Clive Prince. *The Templar Revelation: Secret Guardians of the True Identity of Christ*. London: Bantam, 1999.
Pilch, John J. "The Ascension of Jesus: A Social Scientific Perspective." In *Kontexte Der Schrift: Wolfgang Stegemann Zum 60*, 75-82. Edited by Christian Strecker. Stuttgart: W. Kohlhammer, 2005.
Pinder, Wilhelm. *Der Bamberger Dom und seine Bildwerke*. Berlin: Deutscher Kunstverlag.
Pitts, Andrew. "The Genre of the Third Gospel and Greco-Roman Historiography: A Reconsideration." Paul J. Achtemeier Award, SBL Annual Meeting, Atlanta, GA, November 21-24, 2015.
Pons, Guillermo, ed. and trans. *Vida de Maria by Epiphanius the Monk*. Madrid: Ciudad Nueva, 1990.
Pope Paul VI. "Apostolic Exhortation for the Right Ordering and Development of Devotion to the Blessed Virgin Mary '*Marialis Cultus*' (February 2, 1974)." *AAS* 66 (1974): 113–68.
Pope Pius XI. "Encyclical on Reparation to the Sacred Heart '*Miserentissimus Redemptor*' (May 8, 1928)." *AAS* 20 (1928): 165–79.
Priests for Equality (Organization). *The Inclusive Bible: The First Egalitarian Translation*. Lanham, MD: Rowman & Littlefield, 2009.
Provera, Mario E. *Il Vangelo arabo dell'infanzia secondo il Ms. Laurenziano orientale (n. 387)*. Jerusalem: Franciscan Printing Press, 1973.
Quesnell, Quentin. "The Women at Luke's Supper." In *Political Issues in Luke-Acts*, 57-79. Edited by R. J. Cassidy and P. J. Scharpen. Maryknoll, NY: Orbis, 1983.
Rahmani, L. Y. "Eulogia Tokens from Byzantine Bet She'an." *Atiqot* 22 (1993): 109–19.
Randall, Richard H. Jr. *The Golden Age of Ivory*. New York: Hudson Hill, 1993.
Reid, Barbara. "An Overture to the Gospel of Luke." *CurTM* 39 (2012): 428–34.
Reinhartz, Adele. "From Narrative to History: The Resurrection of Mary and Martha." In *"Women Like This": New Perspectives on Jewish Women in the Greco-Roman World*, 161-84. Edited by Amy-Jill Levine. Atlanta, GA: Scholars, 1991.
Ricoeur, Paul. "*Interpretative Narrative*." Translated by David Pellauer. In *The Book and the Text: The Bible and Literary Theory*, 237-57. Edited by Regina Schwartz. Cambridge, MA: Basil Blackwell, 1990.
Rigney, Daniel. *The Matthew Effect: How Advantage Begets Further Advantage*. New York: Columbia University Press, 2010.
Rivera, Mayra. *Poetics of the Flesh*. Durham: Duke University Press, 2015.
Robbins, Vernon K., and Jonathan M. Potter, eds. *Jesus and Mary Reimagined in Early Christian Literature*. WGRWSup 6. Atlanta, GA: Society of Biblical Literature, 2015.

Roberts, Alexander, and James Donaldson. *The Ante-Nicene Fathers: Translations of the Writings of the Fathers Down to A.D. 325.* 10 volumes. 1885–7. Repr. Grand Rapids, MI: Eerdmans, 1989.

Roberts, C. H., ed. *Catalogue of the Greek and Latin Papyri in the John Rylands Library Manchester. Volume III. Theological and Literary Texts (Nos. 457–551).* Manchester: University Press, 1938.

Robinson, Forbes, trans. *Coptic Apocryphal Gospels.* Cambridge: Cambridge University Press, 1896.

Robinson, James M. et al., eds. *The Facsimile Edition of the Nag Hammadi Codices.* Leiden: E. J. Brill, 1972–84.

Robinson, James M., ed. *The Nag Hammadi Library in English.* 4th rev. ed. Leiden: Brill, 1996.

Rodríguez, Jeanette. *Our Lady of Guadalupe. Faith and Empowerment among Mexican-American Women.* Austin: University of Texas, 1994.

Roger, Eugene. *La Terre Sainte.* Paris: Antoine Bertier, 1664.

Rosen-Zvi, Ishay. *Demonic Desires: "Yetzer Hara" and the Problem of Evil in Late Antiquity.* Philadelphia: University of Pennsylvania, 2011.

Rossier, François, and Thomas A. Thompson. "Biblical Perspectives on Maria Mediation: Lessons from a Failure of Mediation." *Marian Studies* 52 (2001): 53–77.

Royalty, Robert M. *The Origin of Heresy: A History of Discourse in Second Temple Judaism and Early Christianity.* New York: Routledge, 2013.

Rubenstein, Jeffrey. "Hero, Saint, and Sage: The Life of R. Elazar b. R. Shimon in Pesiqta de Rab Kahana 11." In *The Faces of Torah: Studies in the Texts and Contexts of Ancient Judaism in Honor of Steven Fraade*, 509–28. Edited by Michael Bar-Asher Siegal, Tzvi Novick, and Christine Hayes. Göttingen: Vandenhoeck & Ruprecht, 2017.

Rubenstein, Jeffrey. "A Rabbinic Translation of Relics." In *Crossing Boundaries in Early Judaism and Christianity: Ambiguities, Complexities, and Half-Forgotten Adversaries: Essays in Honor of Alan F. Segal*, 314–32. Edited by Kimberly B. Stratton and Andrea Lieber. Leiden: Brill, 2016.

Rubery, Eileen. "From Catacomb to Sanctuary: The Orant figure and the Cults of the Mother of God and S. Agnes in Early Christian Rome, with Special Reference to Gold Glass." *StPatr* 73 (2014): 129–74.

Rubin, Miri. *Mother of God: A History of the Virgin Mary.* New Haven, CT: Yale University Press, 2009.

Ruether, Rosemary Radford. *Sexism and God-Talk: Toward a Feminist Theology.* Boston, MA: Beacon, 1983, 1993.

Sanders, E. P. *Paul and Palestinian Judaism: A Comparison of Patterns of Religion.* Philadelphia, PA: Fortress, 1977.

Santoro, Nicholas J. *Mary in Our Life: Atlas of the Names and Titles of Mary, the Mother of Jesus, and Their Place in Marian Devotion.* Bloomington, IN: iUniverse, 2011.

Saxon, Deborah Niederer. *The Care of the Self in Early Christian Texts.* The Bible and Cultural Studies. New York: Palgrave Macmillan, 2017.

Schaberg, Jane D. "How Mary Magdalene Became a Whore." *BRev* 8.5 (1992): 30–7, 50–2.

Schaberg, Jane D. *The Resurrection of Mary Magdalene: Legends, Apocrypha, and the Christian Testament.* New York: Continuum, 2002.

Schäfer, Peter. *Mirror of His Beauty: Feminine Images of God from the Bible to the Early Kabbalah.* Princeton, NJ: Princeton University Press, 2002.

Schiller, Gertrud. *Iconography of Christian Art*, vol. 1. Translated by Janet Seligman. Greenwich, CT: New York Graphics Society, 1971.

Schliefer, Aliah. *Mary: The Blessed Virgin of Islam*. Louisville, KY: Fons Vitae, 1997.
Schlootkötter, Egbert. *Maria, Corredemptrix und Mediatrix: Miterlöserin und Mittlerin aller Gnaden*. Aachen: Shaker, 2013.
Schmidt, Carl, and Violet MacDermot. *Pistis Sophia*. NHS 9. Leiden: Brill, 1978.
Schmidt, Carl. *Gnostische Schriften in koptischer Sprache aus dem Codex Brucianus*. TU 8/1. Leipzig: Hinrichs, 1892.
Schneemelcher, Wilhelm, ed. *New Testament Apocrypha, Volume One: Gospels and Related Writings*. Translated by R. McL. Wilson. Rev. ed. Louisville, KY: Westminster/John Knox, 1990.
Schrader, Elizabeth. "Was Martha of Bethany added to the Fourth Gospel in the Second Century?" *HTR* 110 (2017): 360–92.
Schröter, Jens. "Zur Menschensohnvorstellung im Evangelium nach Maria." In *Ägypten und Nubien in spätantiker und christlicher Zeit. Band 2: Schrifttum, Sprache und Gedankenwelt*, 178–88. Edited by Stephen Emmel. Sprachen und Kulturen des christlichen Orients 6, 2. Wiesbaden: Reichert, 1999.
Schulte, Francisco Raymond. *Mexican Spirituality: Its Sources and Missions in the Earliest Guadalupan Sermons*. Lanham, MD: Rowman & Littlefield, 2002.
Schüssler Fiorenza, Elisabeth. *In Memory of Her: A Feminist Theological Reconstruction of Christian Origins*. 10th anniversary edition. New York: Crossroad, 1983.
Schüssler Fiorenza, Elisabeth. *Jesus: Miriam's Child, Sophia's Prophet: Critical Issues in Feminist Christology*. New York: Continuum: 1994.
Schüssler Fiorenza, Elisabeth. "Mary Magdalene, Apostle to the Apostles." *Union Theological Seminary Journal* (April 1975): 22–4.
Scopello, Madeleine. "The Dialogue of the Savior." In *The Nag Hammadi Scriptures*, 297–300. Edited by Marvin W. Meyer. New York: HarperOne, 2007.
Sells, Michael. "Sound, Spirit, and Gender in the Qur'án." In *Approaching the Qur'án: The Early Revelations*, 199–223. Edited by Michael Sells. Ashland, OR: White Cloud, 2007.
Shaked, Shaul. "Iranian Influence on Judaism: First Century B.C.E. to Second Century C.E." In *Introduction: the Persian Period*, 308–25. Edited by W. D. Davies and Louis Finkelstein. CHJ 1. Cambridge: Cambridge University Press, 1984.
Sherman, Miriam. "A Well in Search of an Owner: Using Novel Assertions to Assess Miriam's Disproportionate Elaboration among Women in the Midrashim of Late Antiquity." PhD dissertation, University of California, San Diego, 2006.
Shiels, James. "A Rylands Reminiscence." *BJRL* 76 (1994): 181–6.
Shoemaker, Stephen J. *Ancient Traditions of the Virgin Mary's Dormition and Assumption*. Oxford: Oxford University Press, 2002.
Shoemaker, Stephen J. "A Case of Mistaken Identity? Naming the Gnostic Mary." In *Which Mary? The Marys of Early Christian Tradition*, 5–30. Edited by F. Stanley Jones. SBLSS 19. Atlanta, GA: Society of Biblical Literature, 2002.
Shoemaker, Stephen J., trans. "The Ethiopic *Liber Requiei*." In *Ancient Traditions of the Virgin Mary's Dormition and Assumption*, 290–350. OECS. Oxford: Oxford University Press, 2002.
Shoemaker, Stephen J. "The Ethiopic Six Books." In *Ancient Traditions of the Virgin Mary's Dormition and Assumption*, 375–96. OECS. Oxford: Oxford University Press, 2002.
Shoemaker, Stephen J. "Gender at the Virgin's Funeral: Men and Women as Witnesses to the Dormition." *StPatr* 34 (2001): 552–8.
Shoemaker, Stephen J. "Jesus' Gnostic Mom: Mary of Nazareth and the Gnostic Mary Traditions." In *Mariam, the Magdalen, and the Mother*, 153–82. Edited by Deirdre Good. Bloomington: Indiana University Press, 2005.

Shoemaker, Stephen J. *The Life of the Virgin: Maximus the Confessor*. New Haven, CT: Yale University Press, 2012.
Shoemaker, Stephen J. *Mary in Early Christian Faith and Devotion*. New Haven, CT: Yale University Press, 2016.
Shoemaker, Stephen J. "Mary at the Cross, East and West: Maternal Compassion and Affective Piety in the Earliest Life of the Virgin and the High Middle Ages." *JTS*, NS 62, pt. 2 (October 2011): 570–606.
Shoemaker, Stephen J. "Mary the Apostle: A New Dormition Fragment in Coptic and Its Place in the History of Marian Literature." In *Bibel, Byzanz und Christlicher Orient: Festschrift für Stephen Gerö*, 203–29. Edited by Dmitrij F. Bumazhnov, Emmanouela Grypeou, Timothy B. Sailors, and Alexander Toepel. Leuven: Peeters, 2011.
Shoemaker, Stephen J. "A Mother's Passion: Mary at the Crucifixion and Resurrection in the Earliest Life of the Virgin and its Influence on George of Nicomedeia's Passion Homilies." In *The Cult of the Mother of God in Byzantium: Texts and Images*, 53–67. Edited by Leslie Brubaker and Mary B. Cunningham. Burlington, VT: Ashgate, 2011.
Shoemaker, Stephen J. "New Syriac Dormition Fragments from Palimpsests in the Schøyen Collection and the British Library." *Le Muséon* 124.3–4 (2011): 259–78.
Shoemaker, Stephen J. "The (Re?)Discovery of the Kathisma Church and the Cult of the Virgin in Late Ancient Palestine." *Maria: A Journal of Marian Studies* 2 (2001): 21–72.
Shoemaker, Stephen J. "Rethinking the 'Gnostic Mary': Mary of Nazareth and Mary of Magdala in Early Christian Tradition." *JECS* 9 (2001): 555–95.
Shoemaker, Stephen J. "The (Pseudo)? Maximus *Life of the Virgin* and the Byzantine Marian Tradition." *JTS*, NS 67, pt. 1 (April 2016): 115–42.
Shoemaker, Stephen J. "The Sahidic Coptic Homily on the Dormition of the Virgin Attributed to Evodius of Rome: An Edition from Morgan MSS 596 & 598 with Translation." *AnBoll* 117 (1999): 241–83.
Shoemaker, Stephen J. "The Virgin Mary's Hidden Past: From Ancient Marian Apocrypha to the Medieval *Vitae Virginis*." Marian Studies 40 (2009): 1–30.
Shoemaker, Stephen J. "The Virgin Mary in the Ministry of Jesus and the Early Church According to the Earliest Life of the Virgin." *HTR* 98 (2005): 441–67.
Shoham-Steiner, Ephraim. "The Virgin Mary, Miriam, and Jewish Reactions to Marian Devotion in the High Middle Ages." *AJS Review* 37 (2013): 75–91.
Siano, Paolo M. "*Mary 'Mediatrix of All Graces' in the Papal Magisterium up to the Pontificate of Paul VI*." In *Mary at the Foot of the Cross VII: Coredemptrix, Therefore Mediatrix of All Graces: Acts of the Seventh International Symposium on Marian Coredemption*, 65–124. Edited by Peter Damian Fehlner. New Medford, MA: Academy of the Immaculate, 2008.
Sike, Henry. *Evangelium Infantiae; vel, Liber Apocryphus de Infantia Salvatoris; ex manuscripto editit, ac Latina versione et notis illustravit Henricus Sike*. Utrecht: Halman, 1697.
Simson, Otto G. von. *Sacred Fortress: Byzantine Art and Statecraft in Ravenna*. Princeton, NJ: Princeton University Press, 1987.
Slater, Richard N. "An Inquiry into the Relationship between Community and Text: The Apocryphal *Acts of Philip* 1 and the Encratites of Asia Minor." In *The Apocryphal Acts of the Apostles*, 281–306. Edited by François Bovon, Ann Graham Brock, and Christopher R. Matthews. Cambridge: Harvard University Press, 1999.
Sleeman, Matthew. *Geography and the Ascension Narrative in Acts*. SNTSMS. Cambridge: Cambridge University Press, 2009.

Smith Lewis, Agnes, ed. and trans. *Apocrypha Syriaca: The Protevangelium Jacobi and Transitus Mariae with Texts from the Septuagint, the Corân, the Peshiṭta, and from a Syriac Hymn in a Syro-Arabic Palimpsest of the Fifth and Other Centuries, with an Appendix of Palestinian Syriac Texts from the Taylor-Schechter Collection*. StSin 11. London: C. J. Clay, 1902.

Smith Lewis, Agnes, ed. and trans. "Transitus Mariae." In *Apocrypha Syriaca: The Protevangelium Jacobi and Transitus Mariae*, 12–69 (English). StSin 11. London: C. J. Clay, 1902.

SmithLewis, Agnes, trans. *A Translation of the Four Gospels from the Syriac of the Sinaitic Palimpsest*. C. J. Clay, 1896.

Smith, Jane I., and Yvonne Y. Haddad, "The Virgin Mary in Islamic Tradition and Commentary." *MW* 79 (1989): 161–87.

Smith, Yancy Warren. "Hippolytus' Commentary on the Song of Songs in Social and Critical Context." PhD dissertation, Brite Divinity School, 2009.

Smith, Yancy. *The Mystery of Anointing: Hippolytus' Commentary on the Song of Songs in Social and Critical Contexts: Texts, Translations, and Comprehensive Study*. Piscataway, NJ: Gorgias, 2015.

Snow, Clare Marie. "Maria Mediatrix: Mediating the Divine in the Devotional Literature of Late Medieval England." PhD dissertation, Centre for Medieval Studies. University of Toronto, 2012.

Soards, Marion L. *The Speeches in Acts, Their Content, Context, and Concerns*. Louisville, KY: Westminster/John Knox, 1994.

Soper, Alexander Coburn. "The Italo-Gallic School of Early Christian Art." *Art Bulletin* 20 (1938): 145–92.

Sousa, Lisa, Stafford Poole, and James Lockhard, eds. *The Story of Guadalupe. Luis Las, o de las Vega's Huei tlamahuçolica of 1649*. Stanford, CA: Stanford University Press, 1998.

Speck, Paul. "The Virgin's help for Constantinople." *Byzantine and Modern Greek Studies* 27.1 (2003): 266–71.

Sporbeck, Gudrun. "Deux anges provenant d'un Couronnement de la Vierge. Paris, troisième quart du XIIIe siècle." In *Un trésor gothique la châsse de Nivelles*, 354–5. Edited by Anne de Margerie. Paris: Réunion des musées nationaux, 1996.

St. Clair, Archer. "The Visit to the Tomb: Narrative and Liturgy on Three Early Christian Pyxides." *Gesta* 18 (1979): 127–35.

Starbird, Margaret. *The Goddess in the Gospels: Sacred Union in Christianity*. Santa Fe, NM: Bear, 1998.

Starbird, Margaret. *Magdalene's Lost Legacy: Symbolic Numbers and the Sacred Union in Christianity*. Rochester, VT: Bear, 2003.

Starbird, Margaret. *Mary Magdalene: Bride in Exile*. Rochester, VT: Bear, 2005.

Starbird, Margaret. *The Woman with the Alabaster Jar: Mary Magdalene and the Holy Grail*. Santa Fe, NM: Bear, 1993.

Stegmüller, Otto. "*Sub tuum praesidium*. Bemerkungen zur ältesten Überlieferung." *ZKT* 74.1 (1952): 76–82.

Steinmetz, Devora. "A Portrait of Miriam in Rabbinic Midrash." *Prooftexts* 8 (1998): 35–65.

Sternbach, Leo, ed. *Analecta Avarica*. Cracow: Bibliopolam Societatis Librariae Polonicae, 1900.

Stewart, Alistair C., ed. and trans. *The Gnomai of the Council of Nicaea*. Piscataway, NJ: Gorgias, 2015.

Stewart-Sykes, Alistair, trans. *The Apostolic Church Order: The Greek Text with Introduction, Translation, and Annotation*. Strathfield, NSW: St. Paul's, 2006.

Stewart-Sykes, Alistair, trans. *The Didascalia apostolorum: An English Version with Introduction and Annotation*. Studia Traditionis Theologiae, Explorations in Early and Medieval Theology 1. Turnhout: Brepols, 2009.

Stockhausen, Carol. "Luke's Stories of the Ascension: The Background and Function of a Dual Narrative." *Proceedings—Eastern Great Lakes and Midwest Biblical Societies* 10 (1990): 251–63.

Stöckl Ben Ezra, Daniel. *The Impact of Yom Kippur on Early Christianity: The Day of Atonement from Second Temple Judaism to the Fifth Century*. Tübingen: Mohr Siebeck, 2003.

Stowasser, Barbara Freyer. *Women in the Qur'an, Traditions, and Interpretation*. New York: Oxford University Press, 1994.

Strack, H. L. and Günter Stemberger. *Introduction to the Talmud and Midrash*. Translated and edited by Markus Bockmuehl. Minneapolis, MN: Fortress, 1992.

Strycker, Émile de, trans. *La forme la plus ancienne du Protévangile de Jacques: Recherches sur le papyrus Bodmer 5*. Brussels: Société des Bollandistes, 1961.

Stuckenbruck, Loren T. "The Human Being and Demonic Invasion: Therapeutic Models in Ancient Jewish and Christian Texts." In *Spirituality, Theology, and Mental Health: Multidisciplinary Perspectives*, 94–123. Edited by Christopher Cook. London: SCM, 2013.

Reuben Swanson, ed. *New Testament Greek Manuscripts: Mark*. Sheffield: Sheffield Academic, 1995.

Reuben Swanson, ed. *New Testament Greek Manuscripts: Matthew*. Sheffield: Sheffield Academic, 1995.

Takacs, Axel. "Mary and Muhammad: Bearers of the Word—Their Roles in Divine Revelation." *JES* 48 (2013): 220–43.

Taussig, Hal. *A New New Testament: A Bible for the 21st Century Combining Traditional and Newly Discovered Texts*. Boston, MA: Houghton Mifflin Harcourt, 2013.

Taylor, Joan. "Missing Magdala and the Name of Mary 'Magdalene.'" *PEQ* 146 (2014): 205–23.

Terian, Abraham. *The Armenian Gospel of the Infancy: With Three Early Versions of the Protevangelium of James*. Oxford: Oxford University Press, 2008.

Thunø, Erik. *Image and Relic: Mediating the Sacred in Early Medieval Rome*. Roma: «L'Erma» di Brettschneider, 2002.

Tisdale, William. *The Original Sources of the Qur'an*. Repr. London: Society for Promoting Christian Knowledge, 1911.

Toesca, Pietro. *Storia dell'arte italiana I*. Turin: Unione, 1927.

Tuckett, Christopher. *The Gospel of Mary*. Oxford Early Christian Gospel Texts. Oxford: Oxford University Press, 2007.

Urbach, Ephraim E. *Hazal: pirqe emunot vede'ot*. Jerusalem: Magnes, 1969=Urbach. *The Sages: Their Concepts and Beliefs*. 2 volumes. Translated by Israel Abrahams. Jerusalem: Magnes, 1975.

Vachek, Joseph. *The Linguistic School of Prague*. Bloomington: Indiana University Press, 1966.

Van Esbroeck, [Jean-] Michel. "Généalogie de la Vierge en géorgien." *AnBoll* 91 (1973): 347–56.

Van Esbroeck, [Jean-] Michel, trans. *Maxime le Confesseur: Vie de la Vierge*. 2 volumes. SCSO 478 and 479. Scriptores Iberici 21, 22. Louvain: E. Peeters, 1986.

Van Esbroeck, [Jean-] Michel. "Some Earlier Features in the *Life of the Virgin*." *Marianum Ephemerides Mariologiae* 63 (2001): 297–308.
Van Esbroeck, [Jean-] Michel. "Les textes littéraires sur l'Assomption avant le Xe siècle." In *Les actes apocryphes des apôtres*, 265–85. Edited by François Bovon. Publications de la faculté de théologie de l'Université de Genève 4. Geneva: Labor et Fides, 1981.
Vannucci, Giovanni. "La piu antica preghiera alla Madre di Dio." *Marianum* 3 (1941) : 97–101.
Vidal de Figueroa, José. *Teórica de la prodigiosa imagen de la Virgen de Santa María de Guadalupe de México*. México, D.F.: Juan Ruyz, 1661.
Vikan, Gary. *Early Byzantine Pilgrimage Art*. Dumbarton Oaks Byzantine Collection Publications 5. Rev. ed. Washington, DC: Dumbarton Oaks Research Library and Collection, 2010.
Vinken, Barbara. "Das Konzept Madonna." In *Madonna: Frau–Mutter–Kultfigure*, 12–34. Edited by Katja Lembke. Dresden: Sandstein, 2015.
Volgers, Annelie. "Preface." In *Erotapokriseis: Early Christian Question-and-Answer Literature in Context*, 3–4. Edited by Annelie Volgers and Claudio Zamagni. CBET 37. Dudley, MA: Peeters, 2004.
Volgers, Annelie, and Claudio Zamagni, eds. *Erotapokriseis: Early Christian Question-and-Answer Literature in Context*. CBET 37. Dudley, MA: Peeters, 2004.
Vööbus, Arthur. *The Didascalia apostolorum in Syriac (Versio)*. CSCO 402/408. Leuven: Peeters, 1979.
Vööbus, Arthur. *Early Versions of the New Testament, Manuscript Studies*. Stockholm: Estonian Theological Society in Exile, 1954.
Warner, Marina. *Alone of All Her Sex: The Myth and the Cult of the Virgin Mary*. New York: Alfred K. Knopf, 1976.
Weber, Max. *The Theory of Social and Economic Organization*. Translated by A. M. Henderson and Talcott Parsons. Glencoe, IL: Free Press, 1947.
Weitzmann, Kurt. *Age of Spirituality: Late Antique and Early Christian Art, Third to Seventh Century: Catalogue of the Exhibition at the Metropolitan Museum of Art, November 19, 1977, through February 12, 1978*. New York: Metropolitan Museum of Art, 1979.
Weitzmann, Kurt. "The Ivories of the Grado Chair." *Dumbarton Oaks* 26 (1972): 43–91.
Wenger, Antoine. *L'Assomption de la T.S. Vierge dans la tradition byzantine du VIe au Xe siècles. Études et documents*. Paris: Institut Français d'Études Byzantines, 1955.
Whitby, Mary, and Michael Whitby, trans. *Chronicon Paschale 284–628 AD*. Translated Texts for Historians 7. Liverpool: Liverpool University Press, 1989.
Williams, Frank. *The Panarion of Epiphanius of Salamis*, 2 volumes. Nag Hammadi and Manichaean Studies 35 and 36. Leiden: Brill, 1994/1997.
Williams, Ritva H. "The Mother of Jesus at Cana. A Social-Science Interpretation of John 2:1–12." *CBQ* 59 (1997): 679–92.
Williamson, Paul. "Symbiosis across Scale: Gothic Ivories and Sculpture in Stone and Wood in the Thirteenth Century." In *Images in Ivory: Precious Objects of the Gothic Age*, 38–45. Edited by Peter Barnet. Detroit, MI: The Detroit Institute of Arts, 1997.
Wilpert, Giuseppe. "Le due più antiche rappresentazioni della Adoratio Crucis." *Atti della Pontificia Accademia romana di archeologia*, series 3, memorie 2 (1928): 135–55.
Wilson, R. McL., trans. *The Gospel of Philip*. New York: Harper and Row, 1962.
Wright, Deil S. *Understanding Intergovernmental Relations*. 3rd ed. Pacific Grove, CA: Brooks-Cole, 1988.

Wright, William, trans. *Contributions to the Apocryphal Literature of the New Testament: Collected and Edited from Syriac Manuscripts in the British Museum*. London: Williams and Norgate, 1865.

Wright, William, trans. "The Departure of My Lady Mary from This World." *Journal of Sacred Literature and Biblical Record* 7 (1865): 129-60.

Wright, William. "*The Obsequies of the Holy Virgin.*" In *Contributions to the Apocryphal Literature of the New Testament: Collected and Edited from Syriac Manuscripts in the British Museum*, 42-51. Translated by William Wright. London: Williams and Norgate, 1865.

Wilkinson, John. trans. *Egeria's Travels*. 3rd ed. Oxford: Oxbow Books, 1999.

William Wright, trans. *Contributions to the Apocryphal Literature of the New Testament: Collected and Edited from Syriac Manuscripts in the British Museum*. London: Williams and Norgate, 1865.

Wurst, Gregor. "Weitere neue Fragmente aus Codex Tchacos. Zum 'Buch des Allogenes' und zu *Corpus Hermenticum* XIII." In *Judasevangelium und Codex Tchacos*, 1-12. Edited by Enno Edzard Popkes and Gregor Wurst, WUNT 297. Tübingen: Mohr Siebeck, 2012.

Yamaguchi, Satoko. *Mary & Martha: Women in the World of Jesus*. Maryknoll, NY: Orbis, 2002.

Zamagni, Claudio. *Eusèbe de Césarée, Questions Évangéliques: Introduction, texte critique, traduction et notes*. SC 523. Paris: Cerf, 2008.

Zwiep, A. W. "The Text of the Ascension Narratives (Luke 24.50-3; Acts 1.1-2, 9-11)." *NTS* 42 (1996): 219-44.

Contributors

Jo-Ann Badley is Dean of Theology and Associate Professor of New Testament, Ambrose University, Calgary, AB Canada.

Mary Ann Beavis is Professor in the Department of Religion and Culture, St. Thomas More College, University of Saskatchewan, Saskatoon, SK Canada.

Anna Cwikla is a PhD candidate at the Department for the Study of Religion, University of Toronto.

Judith M. Davis is Emerita Professor of French and Humanities, Goshen College, Goshen, IN.

Erez DeGolan is a PhD student at Columbia University's Department of Religion.

Richard Freund is Chair of the Judaic Studies Department, University of Hartford.

Mark Goodacre is Professor in the Department of Religion, Duke University.

Jin H. Han is Professor of Biblical Studies, New York Theological Seminary.

Judith Hartenstein is Professor of Protestant Theology with a focus on New Testament and Religious Education, University of Koblenz–Landau, Campus Landau.

Cornelia Horn teaches in the Theological Faculty of Humboldt University, Berlin.

Ally Kateusz is Research Associate, Wijngaards Institute of Catholic Research.

Kara L. Lyons-Pardue is Associate Professor of New Testament, Point Loma Nazarene University.

J. L. (Juana Laura) Manzo is Assistant Professor of Scripture, St Mary's Seminary, Houston, TX.

Michael Rosenberg is Assistant Professor of Rabbinics, Rabbinical School of Hebrew College.

Deborah Niederer Saxon teaches Religion at Butler University, Franklin, IN.

Miriam-Simma Walfish is a PhD student at Harvard University.

Index

Acts of Philip 14, 16, 23, 28, 88–9
Annunciation to Mary 139, 216–18, 223
  at the well 159, 162, 168
  Church of the Annunciation, Nazareth 154, 161
  Dormition narratives 188, 191
  in the Temple 132, 133-4
  Qur'an 203, 205,
Apocryphon of John 41
Apocryphon of James 41
apostle to the apostles 2, 7, 22, 23, 26–30, 34, 36, 81, 82, 233, 235

Beavis, Mary Ann 2, 4, 60, 76, 89, 95, 235, 236, 237
Brock, Ann Graham 8, 26, 80, 89

censers (for incense) 82, 85, 91, 105, 185–202
censorship 3, 4, 113–30, 131–44, 86–92, 190–5, 202, 236
composite Mary *see* Mary, composite

DeBoer, Esther 8, 9, 18, 26
Dialogue of the Savior 2, 59–67, 84, 236
Diatessaron 79–81, 92–95
Didascalia apostolorum 198
Dormition narratives
  Mary, mother of Jesus 3, 82, 84–6, 88, 89–92, 138, 140, 173, 182, 185–202
  Miriam, sister of Moses 3, 173–83

Egeria, the pilgrim 196–202
Eusebius of Caesaria 69–78, 80, 167, 196

First Apocalypse of James 23, 41, 42
First Book of Jeû 42

Golden Legend 113, 116–17, 120–1
Goodacre, Mark 1, 95, 236–7

Gospel of Bartholomew or *Questions of Bartholomew* 82, 133
Gospel of the Hebrews 95
Gospel of Mary 2, 8–11, 13, 16–20, 21, 39–46, 61, 84, 210, 213, 232, 236, 237
Gospel of Nicodemus 28
Gospel of Peter 41
Gospel of Philip 2, 8, 10, 17–19, 21, 50, 133, 206
Gospel of Ps-Matthew 158, 208
Gospel of Thomas 10, 40, 42
Gregory the Great, Pope 1, 2, 20-1, 27–8, 113, 121, 124–5, 127–9, 235

Hippolytus 27–8, 30

Jerome 28, 92, 231

Kateusz, Ally 2, 3, 131, 210, 235, 236, 237
King, Karen 8, 9, 26, 113

Lazarus 29–31, 33, 36, 60, 232-3

Magdala 15, 18, 75–7, 94, 230
Magdalene *see* Mary called the Magdalene
Magdalene, meaning 15, 94, 230-3
Manichaean Psalms 28
Mariamne 14, 26, 28, 88, 89, 237
  liturgical authority 89
  replaced by Peter 89
Martha 9, 12–15, 18, 19, 20, 23, 25, 26–30, 31, 34, 36, 37, 60–1, 62, 64, 89, 232, 235, 236
Mary, mother of Jesus 47–57, 59–67, 69–78, 79–96, 155–71, 185–202, 215–26
  Annunciation *see* Annunciation
  apostle to the Americas 145–51
  at the altar 133, 135, 139, 141, 204, 218, 226
  Dormition narrative *see* Dormition narrative

Gospel of Mary 15–16
Islam 203–14
leader 99–112, 113–30, 132–44, 203
Magdalene 2, 15–16, 79–96
prophet 211–13
priest or minister 89–91, 131–44, 191–3
Protevangelium see *Protevangelium of James*
Virgin of Guadalupe 145–51
Mary called the Magdalene 7–24, 59–67, 69–78, 79–96, 113–30, 227–34
  Acts of Philip 17–18
  Gospel of Mary 18–20, 39–46
  Leader 8, 22–3
  Magdalene, meaning of 15, 94, 230–3
  Mary of Bethany 10–23, 25–38
  Mary of Magdala 9–10, 15, 18, 75–7, 94, 230
  sinful woman 20–1, 121, 124, 127–9
Mary, composite 7–24, 25, 29, 60–1, 236
Mary of Bethany 7–24, 25–38, 59–67
  Liturgical authority 28
Mary of James 30, 62, 63, 75, 93–4
Mary of Magdala *see* Mary called the Magdalene
Mary of Manichaeism 25
Mary of Nazareth *see* Mary, mother of Jesus
Maryam, mother of Jesus in Islam 1, 203–14, 235, 237
  Prophet 203, 211–13
midwife 115, 117
Miriam, sister of Moses 1, 3, 113–30, 173–83, 235, 236, 237
  Dormition 173–83
  Mary Magdalene 113–30
  Mary the mother 173–83
  prophet 114, 119–20

sinful woman 121–9
Moses 51, 115–16, 118–19, 122, 123, 126, 173–8
Muhammed 1, 210, 211

Peter 18, 19, 29, 30, 39–41, 46, 48–9, 53–4, 60, 61, 82, 94, 120, 124, 150, 188, 231–2, 235
  rivalry with Mary 18–19, 39, 41, 46, 61
  substitution of Peter for a Mary 89–92
Pistis Sophia 8, 10, 11–12, 14, 16–20, 25, 28, 42, 59
Pola ivory reliquary box 199
Protevangelium of James 3, 84, 89, 94, 131, 136, 158–9, 204–5

Shoemaker, Stephen J. 1, 2, 15–16, 60, 61, 64, 66, 80, 86, 88, 137, 141–3, 187–90, 191, 202, 208, 236
Starbird, Margaret 4, 227–34

Tertullian 195, 202

Van Esbroeck, Michel 138, 141–3, 189, 190
Virgin of Guadalupe 145–51

women
  apostles 2, 7, 22, 23, 24, 26–30, 34, 36, 81, 82, 233, 235
  at the altar 133, 135, 139, 141, 195–202, 204
  deacons 28, 198
  leaders 8, 22–3, 79–96, 99–112, 113–30, 121, 132–44, 203
  prophets 114, 119–20, 203, 211–13
  with censers 183–7, 189–202

Index of Biblical References

Genesis
15:1	217
16:7-19	209
21:17	217
24:1	173
26:24	217
27:33	173
33:11	173

Exodus
1:15-17	115
1:22	118
2:1-8	115
2:4	115, 119
2:7	115
15:20	119
15:20-21	115

Leviticus
21:17	123

Numbers
12:1-2	122
12:6-7	122
12:9	123
20:1	173
17:13	179
19:1-22	180
20:1	180

Deuteronomy
10:2	180
10:6	180
24:9	122, 125
32:50	178
33:12	174
34:5	174, 178

Judges
8:17	230
6:23	217
7:25	231
8:17	230
9:46	230
9:49	230
15:8, 11	231
20:45, 47	231

Nehemiah
3:1, 11	230
12:38, 39	230

4 Maccabees
6:28-29	180
17:20-22	180

Job
22:28	118

Psalms
16:9	174, 175

Song of Songs
1:12	233
3:1	27
4:4	230
7:4	230

Isaiah
20:6	231
49:6	149, 150

Jeremiah
31:8	230

Ezekiel
8:14	233

Daniel
8:15-26	217
9:21-27	217

Index of Biblical References

Micah		16:1	21, 63, 94
4:8-11	233		
		Luke	
Zephaniah		1:1-2	48
3:14	217	1:11–13, 19	217
		1:21-22	48
Zechariah		1:1-4	40
9:9a		1:26-28	159, 203
		1:26-38	205, 216
Matthew		1:28, 42, 45, 48	16
1:18-25	203	1:34	53, 205
2:13	216	1:35	54
2:46-50	81	1:42	54
10:2-4	82	1:45	48
13:12	23	1:46-55	49, 53, 94, 212
13:55	63, 197	1:49-50	54
14:27	217	2:6-7	203
15:39	94, 230	2:34-38	212
16:18	231	2:43-45	212
21:8-10	10	4:18-19	49
25:29	23	4:22	50
26:6	13	6:14-16	83
26:6-13	19, 21	7:28	53
26:12	30	7:36-50	13, 19, 21, 22
27:55-56	29	7:38, 44–46	13
27:56	13, 94, 229	7:44-48	128
27:57-59	216	8:1-3	127
27:61	13	8:1-13	15
28:1-10	64	7:38, 44	21
28:1	12, 63, 72, 78	7:38, 44-46	21
28:7	30	7:44-48	128
28:9	12, 18, 34, 77	7:47	21
		8:1-3	29, 114, 127
Mark		8:2	21, 63, 76
1:9	114	8:2-3	82
3:21	49	8:18	23
3:21, 31-15	81	8:19-21	49
3:16-19	82	9:51	48
3:22	49	10:36-50	20, 38
3:35	49	10:38–42	13, 14, 28, 36
6:3	63, 80	10:39	12, 16, 36, 63
8:10	94	10:40-42	28
14:1	21	10:41-42	63
14:3	13	10:42	28, 63
14:3-9	21, 22	11:27-28	49
14:8	30	13:4	230
15:21	230	14:26	49
15:40	63, 94	16:4	47
15:47	63, 94	16:16	53
16:1-8	64	17:21	45

17:23-24	45	12:3	13, 36, 63
18:28-30	49	12:7	29, 30
19:26	23	12:7-8	28, 63
23:56–24:1	21	12:8	30
24:1-11	10	13:23-25	13
24:1-12	51	19:25	18, 29, 63, 82,
24:6-7	51		93, 96, 216
24:8	30	19:25-26	64
24:10	30, 51, 63, 64	19:25-27	81
24:26-27	51	19:40-42	216
24:38	217	20:1	29
24:33	52	20:1-2	29
24:36-39	51	20:1-18	10, 18, 29
24:44-46	51	20:2-18	63
24:39	52	20:11-15	77
24:50-51	52	20:11-18	36, 64, 65
		20:17	36, 76
John		20:17-18	30, 36
1:9	149	20:11	15, 63, 65
2:1-11	81	20:11-18	11, 64
2:1-12	99	20:11, 13, 15	30
2:3	99	20:13	21
2:5	99	20:15	21
2:12	81, 82	20:16, 18	29, 77, 229
9:2	76	20:17-18	29
11:1	30	20:18	11
11:1-3, 28-37	236		
11:33-35	65	Acts	
11:2	13	1:2	48
11:5	13, 19, 28,	1:8	54
	29, 30, 63	1:11	48
11:18	30	1:12-14	51
11:23-33	29	1:13-14	66
11:25	29, 30	1:13	47
11:31, 33	30	1:14	47, 49, 66, 210
11:32	12	1:21-22	22
11:33	11, 21	1:22	48
11:35	11	1:49-50	54
11:38-44	29	2:36	53
11:45	29	2:41	53
11:28-33	28	2:41-47	54
11:32	36	2:43-45	49
11:33	63	4:32-35	49
11:45	28	10:37-41	53
12:1-7	233		
12:1-8	236	1 Timothy	
12:1-11	21	2:8	91
12:1-18	28	2:11-12	91
12:2	14		

www.ingramcontent.com/pod-product-compliance
Lightning Source LLC
Chambersburg PA
CBHW070022010526
44117CB00011B/1675